Inga

INGA

Kennedy's Great Love, Hitler's Perfect Beauty,
and J. Edgar Hoover's Prime Suspect

SCOTT FARRIS

Guilford, Connecticut

An imprint of Rowman & Littlefield

Distributed by NATIONAL BOOK NETWORK

Copyright © 2016 by Scott Farris

British Library Cataloguing in Publication Information Available

Library of Congress Cataloging-in-Publication Data Available

ISBN 978-1-4930-1755-3 (hardcover)
ISBN 978-1-4930-1756-0 (e-book)

∞ ™ The paper used in this publication meets the minimum requirements of American National Standard for Information Sciences—Permanence of Paper for Printed Library Materials, ANSI/ NISO Z39.48–1992.

For Patti, my coauthor in all things

CONTENTS

PREFACE

IN FEBRUARY 1941, MONTHS BEFORE BEGINNING A TORRID ROMANCE
with John F. Kennedy that would draw the attention of the FBI, Inga
Arvad was the subject of a fulsome profile by the *New York World-
Telegram*. The cause of this media attention was an adventure fit for a
Saturday matinee serial; Inga's current (and second) husband, the brilliant
Hungarian filmmaker-turned-anthropologist Paul Fejos (fay-hoash), had
just announced his discovery of two lost Incan cities in the jungles of
Peru. To anyone else, the *World-Telegram* observed, such an achievement
by a spouse would be the "climax to a lifetime." But it was routine to Inga;
"she took it as something to be expected."

Inga, who was twenty-seven but told the newspaper she was twenty-
three, was considered newsworthy not only because of her husband but
also because she had had her own "incredible career," the newspaper
noted, as a film actress in her native Denmark and as a foreign correspondent in Nazi Germany. She had won exclusive interviews and been honored by a private luncheon with Adolf Hitler, who notoriously proclaimed
her the "perfect Nordic beauty." Inga did not confide to the *World-
Telegram* that the Nazis had also asked her to be a spy.

To avoid a confrontation with the Gestapo, she had fled Germany
and joined Fejos in the Far East, where they lived with a tribe of headhunters and allegedly saved the life of the world's richest man, Swedish
industrialist Axel Wenner-Gren (venner-gren), who had become fabulously wealthy by popularizing the home vacuum cleaner before becoming
an international arms dealer. Inga told the newspaper Fejos had first killed
a poisonous snake that landed on Wenner-Gren's neck, then shot a panther as it lunged in attack. "Stories flow from Mrs. Fejos as from a book

of adventures," the *World-Telegram* writer sighed in admiration. "Some people live those lives."

Inga's life was so extraordinary, a friend of Kennedy's once said, that she seemed "a fictional character almost," except most novelists would not have the audacity to make up such a character. "Inga Arvad's life . . . was the sort of true-life tale that Hemingway and his ilk could never get away with putting in their made-up stories," author Dan Simmons said. Simmons, therefore, simply made the real Inga a character (as he did the real Hemingway) in his 1999 thriller *The Crook Factory*, a tale of espionage in the Caribbean that also featured Wenner-Gren, whom the U.S. government had, in fact, put on a blacklist as a suspected Nazi agent. The narrator in Simmons's novel surveys Inga's voluminous FBI file and muses, "It bordered on the unbelievable . . . [she] didn't seem old enough to have done all that was attributed to her here." And yet it was all true—most of it, anyway.

Near the end of her life, which came too young from cancer at the age of sixty, Inga acknowledged that friends and family had been begging her for twenty years to write her life's story. But she never did. "I have always had the capacity that when I'm finished with something, I'm finished," she said. "I sort of close the door behind me."

But that wasn't entirely true. She had never completely closed the door on her relationship with Kennedy, and that was the real reason she never wrote an autobiography. She could not write about her life without writing about him, and their relationship had meant too much and its end had hurt too deeply for her to share the details with the world, even years after Kennedy's assassination.

Their romance had also meant a great deal to Kennedy. Perhaps because Jack gave her the playful nickname "Inga Binga," many Kennedy biographies treat Inga as just another of his innumerable sexual conquests, a casual fling. She was anything but. Those who knew Kennedy well have said that Inga was *"the* love of John F. Kennedy's life." Pulitzer Prize–winning *New York Times* columnist Arthur Krock, a Kennedy family consigliere, sent Inga a letter of condolence after Kennedy's 1963 assassination to assure her that Kennedy had never forgotten her. "I think I told you before that every time I saw President Kennedy he would say to me with a twinkle in his eye, 'How's Inger?'" Krock wrote, mimicking Kennedy's famous Boston accent.

Kennedy should have often thought of Inga while he was in the White House since she had helped put him there. Their romance came at a pivotal time in young Kennedy's life. It began in the weeks before the Japanese attack on Pearl Harbor, when Jack was still finding himself in the world and feeling overshadowed by his older brother. Joseph P. Kennedy Jr., not Jack, was the son the Kennedy family had already declared would become president one day.

As we picture the handsome and urbane President Kennedy, it is difficult to imagine this time in his life, not quite twenty years before he took office, when he appeared disheveled, uncertain, and insecure. It was to Inga that Jack first confided his desire to go into politics and seek the presidency; his family had no clue—they didn't believe Jack had any political ambitions or skills.

But Inga looked upon the vital, appealing man four years her junior and saw that he had the kind of charm "that makes birds come out of their trees." She had no doubt that he had all the tools necessary, far more than his older brother, to achieve the goal of the presidency. "Put a match to the smoldering ambition, and you will go like wild fire," she said, telling Jack with absolute conviction that he was destined to travel "the unequalled highway to the White House."

Inga longed to accompany Jack on that journey, but it was not to be. Talented and accomplished in her own right, Inga's lifelong quest was nevertheless to find a man with whom she could be a full and equal partner. Taught to be self-sufficient since childhood, her longing was to be part of a team of two. "Love?" Inga once said. "Oh, it's wonderful. I'm a firm believer in the power of the woman behind the man."

Inga was a woman in love with love, which she told Jack was "the freest most exhilarating of all feelings." Yet she was constantly confounded by her desire to meld love and career in a single relationship. The men she loved kept leaving her behind while they pursued the adventures she yearned to join. "It's been the bane of my existence," she once told her eldest son, "ALWAYS [her emphasis] to be attached to some male."

Jack might have been different. Those who knew them as a couple noted how remarkably well matched Inga and Jack were. Jack cared deeply about appearance and the ability to charm. He called it "the BP—Big Personality," and was exhilarated that Inga was his equal in charisma. With most women, Jack was a chauvinist, but he admired Inga's intelligence as much as he thrilled to her beauty and treated her as his intellectual equal. She had seen even more of the world than he had, had met more statesmen, and spoke four languages fluently. Under different circumstances, Inga, "laughing, blonde, vivacious," would have made a remarkable first lady, but . . .

In October 1941, when Inga met Jack and they began their romance, not only was she divorced from one man, an Egyptian aristocrat and diplomat, she was still married to another—Fejos—although she planned to divorce him, too. For Jack, a member of America's most prominent Catholic family, marriage to a twice-divorced Protestant would have meant an irrevocable break with his family and no political career.

Jack consulted the Catholic Church about having Inga's marriages annulled so that she could convert to Catholicism. If that failed, he and Inga fantasized about a different kind of life together, perhaps on a ranch out West with Jack teaching history at a small nearby college. But ultimately, Jack could not defy his father or his own ambition. His inner fire for political glory overrode his feelings for Inga, which were greater than he felt for any other woman, including his future wife.

It was a wrenching decision. Kennedy biographer Nigel Hamilton said Inga "tormented Jack with a depth of maternal, womanly affection he would never experience again in his starlet-studded life—an appreciative, forgiving, understanding, tantalizing, humorous, intuitive, feminine love that made every other relationship seem small and artificial." Yet with great difficulty, he cast that aside and said twenty years later, "No man would ever love love more than he loves politics." The loss of Inga changed him, as did the war that made him a hero. And Inga had a hand in the latter, too.

If being divorced, still married, and a Protestant weren't enough obstacles to Inga and Jack's love, there was also the matter of Inga being a suspected Nazi spy. Under the personal direction and orders of President Franklin Roosevelt and FBI director J. Edgar Hoover, while she dated

Jack and for months afterward, Inga was placed under twenty-four-hour surveillance, her phone tapped, and her apartment bugged, so that every conversation and sexual liaison was recorded and put away in Hoover's secret file on Inga, which eventually overflowed to more than 1,200 pages.

When gossip columnist Walter Winchell revealed that Jack was having an affair with a suspected Nazi spy while he was an officer in, of all things, the Office of Naval Intelligence, Jack was nearly court-martialed. Instead, to keep him away from Inga, he was transferred out of Washington, which began a sequence of events that would take him to combat in the South Pacific.

There, the boat under his command, the *PT-109*, was sunk. Though Kennedy managed to save most of his crew, he considered the incident a disaster that had damaged his career prospects. When he returned to the United States, however, Inga was the first reporter to interview him, and her account of how he saved nearly all his men lauded him as a war hero and appeared on the front pages of newspapers across the country.

This tale of heroism and grace under pressure became the basis of Kennedy's campaign biography for the rest of his life. The disaster had become a triumph. Reflecting on the odd set of circumstances that made him a hero, which were triggered by his affair with Inga, Kennedy said, "It was such an accident that it rather makes me wonder if most success is merely a great deal of fortuitous accidents."

Hoover kept his file on Jack and Inga close at hand, particularly as he watched Jack's political career blossom. Aware of how badly Kennedy wanted his affair with Inga kept private, Hoover took steps to ensure that the newly elected president would reappoint him director of the FBI. He quietly reminded Jack that the file on his affair with the suspected Nazi spy was still being "safeguarded" by the FBI.

Jack never forgot Inga, and Inga could not forget Jack, even after she married a third time to movie cowboy Tim McCoy. She ultimately got what she wanted most in life, which was a home and children, just not with the man she loved the most. Her past had collided with Jack's future. Inga had to come to terms with the truth that a life is the sum of the choices a person makes, with some choices precluding others. "At last I realize it is true," Inga ruefully told Jack as they separated in early 1942. "We pay for everything in life."

Prologue, September 26, 1943

Robert F. Kennedy once said of his brother, Jack, "At least one half of the days that he spent on this earth were days of intense physical pain." But in September 1943, while a navy lieutenant assigned to combat duty in the South Pacific, stuck on the tiny, rain-soaked island of Tulagi ten thousand miles from home, Jack was suffering perhaps the greatest agony of his life—and that agony was more mental and spiritual than physical.

Sickly since childhood, with a bad back and an as-yet-undiagnosed Addison's disease that colored his skin yellow, Jack was now also malnourished and recuperating from "fatigue and many deep abrasions and lacerations of the entire body." Always slender, the six-foot-tall Kennedy was now "*really* skinny," weighing barely 145 pounds and walking with a pronounced limp.

But the injuries to his flesh were nothing compared to the damage to his psyche as he replayed in his head the ordeal that had left him in such sorry shape. On the night of August 1, a Japanese destroyer had rammed and sunk the boat under his command, the *PT-109*, killing two of Jack's crewmen and badly injuring two others.

It was the only time during World War II when a normally quick and agile PT boat had been sunk because of a collision with an enemy vessel. Jack won praise for leading the ten other survivors to safety and eventual rescue a week later, but he was stung by criticism, including from his peers, his older brother, and his own conscience, that the tragedy may have been due to his faulty seamanship. "What I really want to know, is where the hell were you when the destroyer hove into sight, and exactly what were your moves, and where the hell was your radar?" scolded Joseph P. Kennedy Jr.

Guilt-ridden, Jack would tear up when discussing the two dead men, one of whom left behind a wife and three children, while the other, as the twenty-six-year-old Kennedy described him, "was only a kid" of nineteen. He was also bitter, "very bitter," according to his squadron commander, Al Cluster, because other PT boats on the mission had seen the fireball when the Japanese destroyer struck Kennedy's boat but they had fled the area, convinced no one on the *109* could have survived such a blast. "I'll never forget this picture," Cluster said. "He and I were sitting on a cot outside and the tears were streaming down his face and he said, 'If only they'd come over to help me, maybe I might have been able to save those other two.'"

Profoundly changed by the experience, his emotions churning, Jack was having trouble finding someone to whom he could articulate his feelings. Writing his parents, he engaged primarily in chitchat, asking for updates on family and friends and reporting that he had been treated to his first fresh egg since his arrival in the South Pacific.

Even in a letter to his best friend, Lem Billings, to whom he usually confided the most intimate details of his life, he summarized the *PT-109* tragedy in a grand total of two sentences: "We have been having a difficult time for the last two months—lost our boat about a month ago when a Jap can cut us in two + lost some of our boys. We had a bad time for a week on a Jap island—but finally got picked up—and have got another boat."

That was it. The rest of Jack's letter to Billings was devoted to gossip and his lack of romantic prospects back in the States now that many of the girls he had known from his school days had married. He acknowledged to Billings that he occasionally corresponded with some showgirls and cocktail waitresses he knew, but they "merely filled the gap" since his relationship with Inga Arvad had ended—or as Jack oddly phrased it to Billings, "when Inga walked out of my life."

Inga, as Billings knew, had not walked out of Jack's life. It was Jack, under heavy pressure from his father and wary of the FBI's near-constant surveillance, who had broken off their romance in March 1942. Even so, their mutual affection was such that they continued to write to each other for several months until Jack heard rumors that Inga had married an old friend from Denmark named Nils Blok. Inga and Jack still spoke occasionally by telephone, but she had passed on word through Jack's sister, Kathleen, with whom she had developed a close friendship, that letters from Jack made life with the jealous Blok difficult.

Jack had obliged Inga's request for several months, but when he reported for duty in the Solomon Islands two thousand miles northeast of Australia in April 1943 he was feeling very lonely and seeking a confidante. So he reached out to Inga, writing her a lengthy letter full of complaints, about the war, about the world, about where he was.

While he had known the Solomons would be no tropical paradise, they were worse than he had imagined. Tulagi received four or five hours of "solid rain" every day, Jack told Inga, which left the air so thick that it was a struggle to catch a breath. There were few diversions beyond drinking homemade hooch distilled by sailors in torpedo tubes, which meant little to Jack, as he wasn't much of a drinker. He could not even enjoy a swim because the local waters contained "a fungus that grows in your ears."

But what particularly irked Jack was the disconnect between what he read in the American newspapers (when back issues finally arrived at the front) and what he was seeing on the ground. Jack did not believe the American people understood how badly the war was going, and how much of that was due to bungling by the American military. "I understand we are winning [the war]," Jack told Inga, "which is cheering, albeit hard to see, but I guess the view improves with distance. I know mine would."

His wartime experience had already badly damaged Jack's faith in America's political and military leadership. Unsurprisingly, he began to focus on those personal relationships that genuinely meant something to him. "A number of my illusions have been shattered," Jack wrote Inga, "but you're one I still have."

This acknowledgment of lingering feelings for Inga brought Jack to the real point of his letter. "What exactly is your situation? Are you settling down permanently to a life of domesticity?" Jack asked, concerned he had lost her forever to Blok. "Or do you remember," he continued, "a certain remark about dinner and breakfast when I got back? Just give me the straight dope on that will you, so I'll know if this whole thing is worth fighting for. You don't need to get too nervous. . . . It will be a few months but I'll be there with blood in my eye."

Despite what was, for the usually reserved Jack, a lavish compliment and a candid expression of affection, months passed and Jack received no reply. What he did not know was that Inga would not receive his letter for four months.

Jack himself caused the delay. To ensure that only Inga and not Blok, her presumed husband, would see his letter, Jack gave it to a fellow officer and friend named Henry James. James was supposed to mail the letter immediately upon returning to the States on leave so that it would arrive in an envelope that did not arouse Blok's suspicion. But Jack had made Inga sound so intriguing that James was determined to deliver the letter in person so that he could see this wonder woman for himself. He did not get around to doing that until August.

Of Inga, James said Jack told him, "I'm afraid she's dangerous. She certainly has connections with the Fascists in Europe, Germany especially. But as to being a spy, it's hard to believe she's doing that, because she's not only beautiful, but she's warm, she's affectionate, she's wonderful in bed. But you know, godammit, Henry, I found out that son-of-a-bitch [FBI director J. Edgar] Hoover had put a microphone under the mattress!"

By September, unaware James had delayed delivering his letter, Jack swallowed his pride and wrote Inga once more. He needed her. As he said many times, there was no one who understood him so well.

Feigning anger, or genuinely hurt at the thought that Inga was ignoring him, Jack demanded to know why he had received no response to his April letter: "What the hell is the story? . . . What's the idea—Has your 'husband' come between us?" To show all could be easily forgiven, Jack begged Inga for a new photograph as the one he had of her, "which was really good," had met a "watery grave" in the sinking of the *PT-109*. He again made no secret of his intentions, telling Inga that when he came home, they could discuss things "over the break-fast table."

But just days after Jack mailed this admonition to Inga, he finally received a letter from her. James, who admitted that meeting Inga had left him completely smitten, had finally delivered Jack's letter from April, and Inga had replied as soon as she had received it in late August.

Whatever irritation Jack felt melted away as he read the momentous news: Inga had never married Blok. In fact, they had broken up entirely and she was leaving New York for Los Angeles where she would take over Sheilah Graham's syndicated Hollywood gossip column. Inga was about to become one of the most powerful people in Hollywood, and be conveniently located on the West Coast when Jack returned from the South Pacific.

Inga expressed amazement at the story of Jack's ordeal aboard the *PT-109*, short summaries of which had made the American newspapers. Jack's spirits rose when he learned from Inga that the sinking of the *PT-109* was not a publicly ridiculed fiasco but was being portrayed as an example of individual heroism. Perhaps the incident had not ruined his future public career after all. War heroes are always welcome in politics.

When Billings later teased Jack about his good fortune in becoming a hero by losing his boat, Kennedy replied, "I imagine I would agree with you that it was lucky the whole thing happened—if the two fellows had not been killed which rather spoils the whole thing for me."

But the beginning of a political career was down the road. Jack first had to recover from his injuries and survive the rest of the war. And in the short term, he was exultant to hear that Inga might once again be available. He wrote her back immediately, asking her to disregard the peckish tone of the note he had mailed just a few days before.

"Dearest Inga Binga," Jack wrote, "You still have the knack of making me feel one hundred per cent better after talking with you or hearing from you." What followed was, as Jack himself acknowledged, "a hell of a letter," a lengthy exposition of Jack's feelings about the war, the fragility of life, and coming to terms with his own mortality. "If anything happens to me I have this knowledge that if I had lived to be a hundred, I could only have improved on the quantity of my life, not the quality," Jack told Inga. "This sounds gloomy as hell . . . I'll cut it. . . . You are the only person I'd say it to anyway. As a matter of fact knowing you has been the brightest point in an extremely bright twenty-six years."

And so Jack returned to the war in command of a new boat, but wreaking revenge upon the Japanese for the fate of *PT-109* was not the only thing he had on his mind. Now he wanted to finish his tour, get back to the States, and back to Inga. Despite all that had happened between them, perhaps he and Inga could start anew from where they had left off more than a year before.

PART I
1941: Inga and Jack Meet

Chapter 1

"Luscious"

In photographs, Inga Arvad is undeniably attractive—a blue-eyed, silky-haired honey blonde with high cheekbones, full lips, a classic profile, a warm smile, and a flawless apricot complexion. The only imperfection is a slight gap between her two front teeth, which has the odd effect of making her even more attractive as it confirms she is a real, flesh-and-blood woman, and not a statue. In full figure, she is tall (five-foot-eight) and athletic, with the trim figure of the ballerina she once hoped to be. Yet lovely as she appears in these images, Inga's one-time boss, *Washington Times-Herald* editor Frank Waldrop, said, "No photograph then, before, or after, ever did her justice." You had to be in Inga's presence, Waldrop said, to fully appreciate her impact upon people.

A reporter named Muriel Lewis, who interviewed a then twenty-four-year-old Inga in Hong Kong, wrote that any words used to describe Inga "would ring flat as the laudations of a cinema star in a movie magazine. . . . Yet there are no new words to take their place." Lewis, writing for a local British newsletter, described Inga's distinctive loveliness—"so fair, so young, blue eyes so candid and interested, so questioning, with a twinkle lurking in the corners. Her skin is clear and fair, glowing with youth and health, perfectly cut mouth to show perfect teeth, her figure is slim, her movements free and assured, graceful as those of a dancer."

Men who knew Inga struggled to find the right superlatives to describe her. "She was as beautiful as a Greek goddess, if you can even use that expression about a Scandinavian blonde," said Pat Holt, a classmate of Inga at the Graduate School of Journalism at Columbia University. Descriptors such as *beautiful* or even *gorgeous* fell short of the mark. "Luscious," John White, one of Inga's reporting colleagues at the *Times-Herald*, called her. "Luscious is the word. Like a lot of icing on the cake." John Gunther, one of the most successful authors of the twentieth century and who pined to marry Inga, agreed; he described her as "the most beautiful & luscious blonde ever known."

As stunning as she was—and some of Hollywood's leading men said she was more beautiful than any of their costars—she captivated men and women with more than her appearance. People, but especially men, simply felt better being in her presence. She "glowed with health and joy," Waldrop said. Inga had trained at the Danish Royal Ballet and moved with grace, poise, and, especially, confidence, the latter being one of her sexiest attributes. Always impeccably dressed, her appearance suggested "State Balls and Court Affairs in general," Muriel Lewis said, yet those who knew her best, such as her third husband, the movie and real-life cowboy Tim McCoy, said Inga was "down to earth and utterly devoid of vanity."

"She had plenty of personality," said Page Huidekoper, another of Inga's colleagues at the *Times-Herald* and (perhaps) once a rival for Jack Kennedy's affections. "She had a lovely, warm laugh, she was vivid, lively, quick." She laughed often, was witty, and possessed an absurdist sense of humor that seemed very Danish. Her humor was never mean-spirited, but she was always candid; coming as she did from the land of Hans Christian Andersen, she was unafraid to point out emperors who had no clothes.

Friends remarked that her liveliness was never contrived or affected. "She was one of those people with a gift for happiness, an internal gift for happiness," Huidekoper said. A free spirit always open to new adventures, she loved to flirt and fell in love too easily. Because of that, she was disappointed many times, but she never became sour. Inga had a remarkable capacity to put disappointment behind her and move forward in the conviction that greater happiness lay ahead. Inga, as she later told one of her sons, believed "that living is a great and glorious experience."

Acquaintances marveled that "she'd *done* so much, been *involved* in so much." She had many stories to tell and told them in a soothing voice of medium timbre, like a cello that could play in four languages. Inga's voice was similar to fellow Scandinavian Ingrid Bergman, but with a much lighter accent. A born linguist, Inga had quickly adopted American pronunciations and slang, a facility that would arouse the suspicion of FBI director J. Edgar Hoover, who could not believe a woman in the country less than two years could speak perfect "Americanized" English.

Born a Dane, Inga spent extensive time as a child in France and Germany, learning to speak those nation's languages like a native, and she later married an Egyptian and a Hungarian. But her mother had been raised in England, and Inga had received part of her education there. English was the lingua franca of all her relationships, except when speaking with her mother or a Danish lover, and when she was trying to conceal her conversation from prying ears—like Hoover's.

If Hoover had listened more carefully, he might have picked up the very slight Scandinavian accent when Inga spoke English. She might make a "w" sound for a "v"—"Wiking" instead of "Viking," for example. But otherwise, except for inserting the occasional odd Danish saying in her conversation, she sounded like a third-generation American, though a highly educated, well-traveled, theatrical, third-generation American. A reporter in California who met Inga late in her life noted that as she told her many fascinating stories, she was "enunciating words as only countesses in Oscar Wilde's plays do."

But Inga was especially fluent in listening. She intuitively understood that being interesting is one thing, but conveying to other people that *they* are interesting makes an even stronger impression. She had that rare talent labeled by social scientists as "synchrony," the ability to respond, as an actor or politician might do with a crowd, to the mood and rhythms of her conversation partner so that they became engaged in a verbal dance, two individuals entwined in one conversation. Inga had a simpler explanation for her listening skills: "I'm very fond of human beings."

She was especially good at reassuring men that they were indeed as special as they hoped they were, so that simply "being in her presence increased their own worth." Demonstrating qualities that might have made her one of the world's great foreign correspondents, Inga peppered those she met with questions and then gazed intently when they responded, as if her partner was full of fascinating tales and insights. "She was brilliant. . . . A genius at getting to know people and getting them to talk," said her son, Ronald McCoy. "She was curious, very empathetic. She could understand different points of view."

Of course, by being the questioner, Inga not only flattered her subjects, she also could control the conversation and deflect inquiries about her own complicated backstory. She had not been in America long before she learned the pitfalls of sharing too much information about her earlier life.

CHAPTER 2

"He likes exploring, and so do I"

INGA ARRIVED IN AMERICA ALONE, WITHOUT HER MOTHER, OLGA
Arvad, or her husband, Paul Fejos, on February 29, 1940, aboard the
Italian liner S.D. *Conte di Savoia*, which had left Genoa nine days earlier.
The ship manifest listed Inga's occupation as "housewife," and Inga
advised immigration authorities that she intended to become a permanent
resident of the United States, as her husband was a naturalized American
citizen.

The voyage was remarkably uneventful, given that the world was in
theory at war. Yet except for the Soviet Union's attack on Finland in
November, there had been no other hostilities on land in Europe since
Germany conquered Poland in September. German submarines prowled
the oceans and there were several naval engagements, but the relative lack
of activity led the British press to declare that, so far, World War II was
a "Phoney War." Most Americans joined most Europeans in hoping it
would stay that way, though large numbers of Americans were determined to keep the United States out of war even if the shooting started
up again.

Fejos had arrived in New York three months before Inga but had left
for Peru on December 31, 1939, with a fully equipped anthropological
and archaeological expedition sponsored by The Viking Fund, an entity
established by Swedish industrialist Axel Wenner-Gren, perhaps the richest man in the world at the time (and whom some believed was a Nazi
sympathizer). Fejos intended to study natives of the upper Amazon and
to seek some "lost" cities of the Incas.

In the library of a Franciscan monastery in Lima, Fejos stumbled upon a lay friar's century-old diary that confirmed native reports of the existence of several great Incan cities long ago consumed by the Amazon jungle. Fejos intended to find them. Inga did not join the first part of the expedition because it was considered too dangerous, but she intended to join her husband in Peru very soon. "He likes exploring," she told a reporter, "and so do I."

When she arrived, Inga knew only one person in New York, a German Jew named Lothar Wolff, who was a senior editor for the *March of Time* newsreel company. In Denmark before the war, Wolff had worked as film editor on Fejos's *Millions in Flight*, which had starred Inga. Although Wolff had considered her a prima donna as an actress, Inga won him over as a friend by repeatedly visiting Wolff's mother in Berlin while working as a reporter there, keeping Wolff informed of his mother's situation until Wolff was able to get his mother safely out of Germany.* When Wolff's mother arrived in America, Inga went out to dinner with her and Wolff, but discerned from the disapproving looks of fellow diners, "It is very evident that it is not popular to speak German in public."

Inga had been in New York barely long enough to secure a room at The Barbizon, a twenty-three-story residential hotel on East 63rd Street that catered exclusively to young professional women, when she received an irresistible invitation from Wenner-Gren's wife, Marguerite. Aware that Inga was lonely without Fejos, Marguerite invited Inga to come relax at the Wenner-Grens' extraordinary Bahamian estate that they had named Shangri-La.

Another guest at the Hog Island retreat was the beautiful and notorious New York debutante Brenda Frazier. With her jet-black hair and bright red lips, Frazier, famous only for being famous, was dubbed America's "No. 1 Glamour Girl," by the nation's frenzied media, who made her the subject of more news stories—five thousand over a six-month period in 1938—than any other American except President Roosevelt. With the

---

*Wolff would later become a noted Hollywood movie producer of such pictures as *The Roman Spring of Mrs. Stone.*

estate's extraordinary privacy, Marguerite was delighted to report that her beautiful young friends were able to "walk around naked in the sunshine!"

The Wenner-Grens had no children of their own, so Marguerite, an eccentric one-time opera singer from Kansas City, enjoyed taking young women under her wing. She took it upon herself to write a friend, cosmetics maven Elizabeth Arden, in hope of helping Inga land a job. In a letter of introduction, Marguerite begged Arden to meet Inga. If she did, she would quickly discover that Inga "can sell herself." Exaggerating only a little, Marguerite wrote, "She is lovely to look at, very cultivated, speaks English, Danish, Swedish, French, German and Italian. She's only 25 [*sic*], blonde with exquisite skin color and hair and very pretty. Especially in an evening dress . . . she has bewitching evening clothes."

While Inga, a lover of fashion, was intrigued, she did not push the idea. Arden, citing her busy schedule, kept postponing the interview, and when they finally met Inga found Arden "violent, mood-swinging, and unsympathetic, but [a] talented business woman."

Arden, meanwhile, later claimed that she found Inga suspicious and sympathetic to the Nazi cause—though how she deduced this from a short job interview is unknown. Yet Arden did not immediately contact the FBI about her suspicions; only a year and a half later would she offer to become an informant against Inga for the Bureau.

Inga was unaware of Arden's suspicions, but it was not only Arden's sour disposition that made Inga ambivalent about pursuing a job with her. At the time, she was distracted by the need to get her mother out of Denmark, which the Nazis, ending the "Phoney War," had invaded and occupied on April 9, 1940, while Inga was still at Shangri-La.

Inga returned to New York and began the process of obtaining all the necessary permissions for Olga to immigrate to the United States. What role Inga's past associations in Nazi Germany played in successfully getting her mother out of Denmark is unknown, but they certainly could not have hurt.

By late May, having disposed of most of her possessions, Olga secured a ticket on the S.S. *Manhattan*, which was making its last voyage from Genoa to New York before Italy officially joined the war as Germany's Axis ally. Olga had a companion on the voyage: a young Danish writer and friend of Inga named Niels Christian Bloch, who had married (and divorced) one of Inga's childhood friends. Arriving in America, Bloch simplified his name to "Nils Blok." He was delighted to see Inga again.

When Olga arrived in New York, she and Inga rented an apartment on Manhattan's Upper West Side at 440 Riverside Drive, just one block from Columbia University. Inga intended to enroll in Columbia's Graduate School of Journalism in the fall, but first she and Olga took a trip to Maryland in the summer of 1940 to visit a wealthy American family, the Sangers, whom they had met a dozen years before in Denmark. A Sanger son, Hamilton, and his friend Talbot "Tot" Walker, had been exchange students in Denmark and had tutored Inga in English and filled her head with dreams of moving to the States.

The Sangers impressed Olga. She described them in a letter to relatives back home as a "cultured old American family" whose home boasted mahogany furniture and "five Negro servants." Inga was impressed primarily by Hamilton Sanger, who was four years her senior and with whom she had previously maintained a flirtatious correspondence when Sanger attended Princeton.

In one playful exchange, Sanger accused Inga of being "fond of flattery, not the flatterer," and offered the perceptive observation that Inga did not "use flattery for its own sake, but as a method of expression." In another letter, Sanger told Inga, "Your frankness, which some people might hold against you, I take as one of your most charming attributes, especially when it is prompted by your capricious fancy to display itself in the form of sauciness."

By 1940, Sanger was well on his way to a successful career in banking and real estate development. That promising future, coupled with their agreeable past relationship, led Inga to stun Lothar Wolff that summer with the announcement that she had fallen in love with Sanger and that she had written Fejos, asking for a divorce. Wolff said it upset him to picture "Fejos in the middle of the jungle receiving such news."

As Wolff predicted, Fejos wrote a series of pleading letters to Inga, assuring her she would soon be able to join the expedition in Peru—so soon, he pledged, that he begged her to begin taking Spanish lessons at once. Inga relented and broke off her romance with Sanger. Months passed, and there was still no word from Fejos, asking Inga to join him in Peru.

Inga did not pursue a divorce from Fejos (for now), but she did begin taking the necessary steps and submitting the necessary paperwork to become a naturalized citizen. She wanted to stay permanently in the United States, and she did not want to depend on being Fejos's wife to ensure it.

CHAPTER 3

"A mysterious veiled quality"

LONELINESS FIRST BROUGHT INGA TO THE ATTENTION OF THE FBI.

By the fall of 1940, Inga and Fejos had been married for four and a half years, but they had been apart for more than half that time. She went to The Viking Fund office in New York in tears, begging that they charter a plane so that she could fly to Peru and be with her husband. Fund officials declined her request. Realizing that she might never be going to Peru, Inga applied and was admitted into Columbia University's prestigious Graduate School of Journalism.

Inga was part of a class of seventy-one students who were from twenty-one states and six foreign countries, yet she stood out in several ways. She was one of only four students who lacked a bachelor's degree. In fact, despite being admitted into graduate school, Inga had never attended college at all. In the school directory, she listed her previous education at Wimbledon, a prestigious London college preparatory school for girls, which she attended briefly at age sixteen.

Inga was in heady company at Columbia. Lecturers included CBS News correspondent Eric Sevareid and the historian and journalist Douglas S. Freeman. Among Inga's classmates were Leonard Sussman, who would go on to serve as the long-time director of Freedom House, a watchdog for freedom of the press around the world, and Daniel Edelman, who would later found the world's largest public relations agency.

Despite such talent, it was Inga, one of about twenty women in the class, who attracted most of the attention of her classmates and who generated the most gossip.

One topic of interest was how Inga had been admitted into Columbia's graduate program in the first place. Not only did she lack an undergraduate degree, but also she was admitted well after the application deadline, as was Nils Blok.

Inga had received a letter of recommendation from Lothar Wolff, who advised Columbia that Inga came from "one of the best families in Copenhagen." A more influential recommendation, however, came from Axel Wenner-Gren, who had strongly encouraged Inga to enroll (perhaps at the behest of Viking Fund employees who wanted no more tearful visits from Inga). Columbia officials no doubt hoped, and perhaps expected, that with Inga's admission the mysterious and controversial international industrialist could be induced to make a substantial donation to the college.

Some of Inga's classmates suspected that the program's male administrators were simply bowled over by Inga's beauty. "She was a sensation," said classmate Everett Bauman. "She made quite an appearance." Another classmate, Pat Holt, related a conversation he overheard between two male professors who were discussing Inga's talents as a journalist. "One said, 'It is too bad she can't write.' To which his colleague answered, 'She doesn't need to.'"

Inga, however, put a great deal of effort into her studies. Olga told friends in Denmark that Inga was often studying "from morning to midnight" and was putting "all [her] energy and will power" into her schoolwork. Nor was Inga without qualifications. During the admissions process, she brought a scrapbook full of clippings from her work as a foreign correspondent for Danish publications in Nazi Germany, most notably articles she had written based upon two exclusive interviews she had with Adolf Hitler, and another exclusive regarding Hermann Göring's wedding, where she had been a specially invited guest. To emphasize the strong impression she had made on Hitler, Inga noted that he had given her an inscribed photo set in an expensive silver frame.

Whatever misgivings school officials may have had about Inga's friendliness with the leaders of Nazi Germany were apparently not enough to dissuade them from admitting her, although their hope of a major endowment from Wenner-Gren never materialized. But Inga's connections with leading Nazis, and most especially her lack of shame about it, troubled a number of her fellow students, particularly those who were Jewish.

Perhaps aware that her classmates did not believe she belonged, Inga foolishly tried to enhance her status by emphasizing her friendship with Wenner-Gren and the positive impression she had made upon Hitler. Older and more sophisticated than her classmates, Inga seemed to want to be known as a *femme fatale*. "She was usually dressed in a long, black dress and smoked cigarettes out of a cigarette holder," Sussman said. The effect meant "Inga exuded not just sexuality, but there was also a mysterious veiled quality to her, bordering on espionage. We had heard that Inga had interviewed top Nazis, and that added further to her secretive reputation, and maybe we fantasized our way to the rest."

This fantasy, which was soon entertained by several of her classmates, was that Inga was a Nazi spy. Classmate and future White House correspondent L. Patrick Monroe alleged that Inga was "outspokenly anti-Semitic" and that her sentiments were "obviously pro-Nazi." This did not stop Monroe, however, from asking Inga on a date, though not a particularly romantic one. Monroe had two tickets to attend a campaign speech by Franklin Roosevelt at Madison Square Garden and invited Inga to join him. Later, as Monroe walked Inga back to her apartment, "she unequivocally gave me the brush off," he acknowledged. Inga may have been unhappily married with an absent husband, but a college student without income was not particularly tempting.

Inga always enjoyed entertaining. Aware of her classmates' suspicions and lonely while living in a city where she knew so few people, Inga decided to win over her fellow students by hosting a series of small dinner parties. Unfortunately, the affairs only served to increase suspicions about her intentions and her purpose in being at Columbia.

Conversation at these dinner parties often revolved around whether the United States should become involved in the now raging war in Europe. This debate was heated everywhere, but, as would be true during the Vietnam War era, nowhere was the debate over war more intense than on college campuses. There was a large and strong isolationist contingent among both faculty and students, but feelings were just as high among those who favored American intervention, and the interventionists were shocked that Inga, despite the Nazi occupation of her native Denmark, was an isolationist. Her position made several of them very suspicious.

On November 16, 1940, following one of Inga's dinner parties, a classmate named Helen Woolsey, wrote to the FBI's main office in Washington, D.C.:

> I would like to call your attention to a Danish fellow-student . . . Mrs. Inga Fejos . . . a very beautiful blonde who claims to have been a well-known feature-article writer in Denmark. She speaks very convincingly of her intimacy with Goering, Goebbels, Himmler and Hess, of the delightful impression she made on Hitler in her two interviews with him. She confesses that she used to be sympathetic to the Nazi regime, but has now seen the light. However, she feels no bitterness about the seizure of Denmark.

Inga also made the impolitic observation that there seemed to be a large number of Jews in the class, and worried that the debate over the United States' participation in the war was so intense that it might lead to civil war. Inga had tried too hard to impress her guests with her savvy and sophistication. "We left very late," Woolsey told the FBI, "dazed by her charms, but with the uncomfortable feeling that we had been somehow threatened."

Woolsey acknowledged she had no "factual basis" to suspect Inga of anything, but said she still had the sense that Inga was somehow working for the German government. "What could be a more perfect blind for a spy" than being a journalist, she asked. Inga, maintaining the fiction that she was four years younger than she was, had been caught telling some small fibs, and she deflected questions about why she had not joined Fejos in Peru. This was all "extremely slight evidence," Woolsey admitted, but it gave the impression that Inga, who was "no fool," was being purposefully insincere. Woolsey concluded, "I can only say that I am one of four who have seen something of her, and who are frightened and suspicious of her though without reasonable evidence."

Inga later brushed off these suspicions, claiming that her Jewish classmates were simply offended that she refused to demonize Hitler. Given the lengths Hitler had gone to charm her, Inga said, "I could not very well say that he had been mean to me; he hadn't. And if they would say to me, 'What was he like,' well, I would have to tell them. I think if I put myself in their position I would have resented that."

Despite the thin evidence suggesting that Inga was doing anything more than trying to dazzle her classmates with her worldliness, FBI director J. Edgar Hoover wrote a note of thanks to Woolsey for bringing Inga to the Bureau's attention and directed the FBI's New York field office to investigate. Agents, however, discovered that Inga's charm had begun to win over Woolsey and Inga's other classmates.

When agents interviewed Woolsey, she said that Inga had "modified" her attitude and no longer seemed sympathetic to the Nazi cause. Dean Carl Ackerman, who had Inga in several of his classes, acknowledged that Inga's "speech and actions at first gave rise to suspicion," but he had since concluded these suspicions were "unfounded," adding he had never heard Inga "express any pro-Nazi sympathies." One of Inga's neighbors told the FBI that while Inga and Olga had initially boasted of knowing Hitler and Göring, implying that "they favored Nazi policies," they no longer "said much on the subject."

Given that no one was still actively accusing Inga of pro-Nazi sympathies, that she had no criminal record, and that it appeared she intended to leave the United States in the spring to join Fejos in Peru, the FBI's New York office cut the investigation short.

Inga did plan to head south once the school term ended, but only as far as Washington, D.C., not to Peru. She was not trying to escape the FBI's scrutiny, only her mother and her new lover, Nils Blok. She had no clue what she might do in Washington, but, fortunately, Inga had spent time in New York actively courting mentors who were anxious to help her.

CHAPTER 4

"Everybody's favorite Jew"

As Inga conceded, she had trouble being without a man. Whether it was the need for love, sex, protection, companionship, or a combination of all the above, she hated being without a partner. When the *New York World-Telegram* profiled Inga in February 1941, after Fejos announced his discovery of several lost Incan cities, she told the paper that despite being so distant from her husband she still felt "terribly married." But she and Fejos had now been apart for nearly a year and a half, and so Inga began an affair with Nils Blok, much to her mother's chagrin.

Blok was tall, well dressed, and unfailingly polite, but he had not struck anyone at Columbia as being particularly exceptional. "Nils was an odd fellow, a little pale and colorless," classmate Everett Bauman recalled. Fellow students could not figure out Inga and Blok's relationship. Because he hovered near Inga everywhere she went, Bauman said he almost seemed to be an "attendant escort." A few students speculated that Blok and Inga lived together, but others found the idea ludicrous because they were such a "mismatched pair." Blok also drank a great deal, but he adored Inga, and he was in New York, not up the Amazon.

Olga was upset that Inga and Nils were often out together late at night. Initially, she was concerned that Nils was simply preventing Inga from getting a good night's sleep and pursuing her studies. "It isn't necessary to squeeze the lemon to the last drop," Olga said. But slowly it dawned on Olga what Inga and Nils might be doing while they were alone, and she told Inga it was indecent to carry on with one man while married to another.

Olga said she finally "lost control of myself" when she caught Blok "making love to Inga." Olga adored Fejos and thought Blok was beneath Inga's attention. "I can't understand why she permits herself to be fooled by a wreck of a person like Nils Bloch [*sic*]," Olga wrote in her diary. "She must have a blind spot where men are concerned."

Two weeks later, on May 30, 1941, Olga and Inga had a terrible fight over Blok, with Inga advising Olga that she was an adult who would do as she pleased. "Inga called me the worst names she could think of," Olga recorded in her diary. "It will take a long, long time to erase them. Our good relations are past. I can't accept a new man until the cards are laid on the table before Paul." Olga continued to brood. "This is what I must reap after trying all my life to give her the best I had," she wrote. "It is a sorrowful reward."

Olga no doubt hoped that Inga would see the error of her ways, but instead Inga announced on June 2 that she was leaving for Washington, D.C., that very night. She told Olga that one of her favorite professors at Columbia, Walter Pitkin, the author of the hugely successful *Life Begins at Forty* and *A Short Introduction to the History of Human Stupidity*, had encouraged her to find work in the nation's capital. Olga admitted Inga's sudden decision had left her "stunned with grief and sorrow."

Inga's decision raises questions about the depth of her feelings for Blok. Had she loved Blok, she would have stayed in New York. But instead, Inga decided she needed to get away from both her mother and her lover, and she sought help in order to do so.

Pitkin was one mentor she turned to, and his affection for Inga seemed to be that of a father for a daughter. Another mentor with less platonic intentions was Wall Street financier Bernard Baruch, who had served as an advisor to every president since Woodrow Wilson.

Baruch was, one biographer said, "everybody's favorite Jew," who was trotted out as proof that America was indeed a land of opportunity for all, and whose friendship was flaunted as proof that the befriended was no bigot. Anti-Semitism, mild or virulent, was simply a given in America at the time. Even a renowned liberal such as Eleanor Roosevelt once attended a gala on Baruch's behalf and reported, "The Jew party [was] appalling. I never wish to hear money, jewels . . . and sables mentioned again."

When he met Inga, Baruch was seventy and had been widowed since 1938. Even while married, he was known as a philanderer who had many high-profile affairs with beautiful, intelligent women, including Clare Boothe Brokaw. This was before Brokaw married Henry Luce and before she had an affair with Joseph P. Kennedy. Baruch's love life fascinated Franklin Roosevelt, especially after he found out that Baruch had given Brokaw a yacht as a gift. FDR's love of such gossip would later impact Inga.

Despite his age, Baruch "was as vigorously flirtatious as a man half his age." Standing six-foot-four with a leonine head covered with thick white hair, Baruch's attraction for even far younger women was obvious. One of his lovers, Helen Lawrenson, who became editor at *Vanity Fair*, described him as "tall, distinguished, loquacious, courtly, masculine, a bon vivant. Women were forever finagling introductions to him."

One of those women was Inga, though she left no record of how she became introduced to Baruch. As Inga herself noted in one of her future newspaper columns, Baruch was considered "one of the greatest brains in America," and was "so handsome that we could wish to see his profile on a silver dollar." Baruch was enamored with Inga, and Inga admitted that if Baruch were younger, "I would probably fall for him." Baruch, meanwhile, assured Inga that she had the talent to "really be somebody."

Inga deftly managed to fend off Baruch's advances without destroying their friendship, though such a balancing act proved difficult. "My old admirer—Baruch—has run completely amok," Inga told Olga in a letter written shortly after she moved to Washington. "He is so silly about me that he calls up every single morning at 7:30 just to ask about something or other, i.e., when am I coming back from this week-end. And he calls just to hear my wonderful voice. . . . He can help me a lot, but by . . . it won't do any good for him to be so much in love."

While Baruch would, as Inga had predicted, later provide her with considerable peace of mind while she was under investigation by the FBI, the mentor who actually helped her obtain employment in Washington was the Pulitzer Prize–winning columnist for the *New York Times* Arthur

Krock. Krock was also said to be a notorious womanizer, but Inga also fended off his advances—if he made any, for it is not clear Krock ever made a play for Inga. He did, however, clearly recall their first meeting even three decades later:

> One day, after a meeting of the Pulitzer board in New York, at which we made the awards, I was standing on Broadway looking for a taxi and an extremely, beautiful, beautiful, beautiful blonde came up to me and said, "You're Mr. Krock?" She said her name was Inga Arvad and she was a student at the school of journalism (Columbia, also home to the Pulitzer committee) and that she would like to work on a newspaper in Washington. If she came, would I help her? I was so stupefied by the beauty of this creature that I said I would.

With no real prospects other than Krock's pledge of assistance, Inga left for Washington. When she arrived, Krock invited her to his Virginia estate and pledged to introduce her to influential people in Washington. At the top of the list was the publisher of the *Washington Times-Herald*, Eleanor Josephine Medill Patterson, the first woman to run a major American newspaper.

CHAPTER 5

"The most hated woman in America"

ELEANOR JOSEPHINE MEDILL PATTERSON, WHOM EVERYONE KNEW AS "Cissy," was a tall, striking woman with flame-colored hair, whose most notable physical quality may have been what her biographer, Amanda Smith (President Kennedy's niece), termed "her unforgettable panther-like grace." *Collier's Weekly* declared Patterson "probably the most powerful woman in America," ahead of even Eleanor Roosevelt. But because of her combative and antagonistic views, especially in regard to keeping America out of the war in Europe, *Collier's* added she was "the most hated" woman in America, too.

Patterson was born to journalism. She was the granddaughter of the founder of the *Chicago Tribune*, which was now being run by her cousin, "Colonel" Robert McCormick, while her older brother, Joseph Medill Patterson, founded the *New York Daily News*. All three shared strong isolationist views regarding the war.

Patterson had worked as editor on two newspapers owned by William Randolph Hearst, the morning *Washington Herald* and the evening *Washington Times*. After years of cajoling, Patterson finally persuaded a cash-strapped Hearst to sell her both papers in 1939. She merged the two to create the *Times-Herald*.

Befitting its owner, it was a quirky newspaper. Unknowingly foretelling the future of online journalism, one *Times-Herald* motto was "Around the Clock," as it published ten editions and more per day. Under Patterson's pugnacious leadership, the *Times-Herald* quickly became the largest circulation newspaper in Washington with the highest advertising revenue. It also led its rivals in both the number of libel suits filed and the size of the libel judgments made against it.

One of its star writers, John White, who knew Inga well, said working at the *Times-Herald* was "like something out of *The Front Page*.* . . . We really picked up the Hearst trick of picking up the picture off the mantelpiece while you were talking to the survivors."

Arthur Krock correctly surmised that the *Times-Herald* was just the kind of paper that might make room for a rare bird like Inga. Based on Krock's recommendation, and with no objection from *Times-Herald* editor Frank Waldrop, Patterson hired Inga personally. From the start, Patterson felt a kinship because Inga's life story was one of the few as exotic as her own.

As a young woman, Patterson had been in an abusive marriage with a Polish count who kidnapped their daughter and held her for ransom when Patterson threatened divorce. Patterson was unable to retrieve her child for eighteen months, and then only because of the personal intervention of President William Howard Taft and Russian czar Nicholas II. Later, Patterson became notorious for her ongoing feud with her once-friend, now nemesis, Alice Roosevelt Longworth, as they competed for the affections of multiple Washington politicians. Patterson skewered Washington society in a novel, *Glass House*, which included this wisdom: "Washington is only a little village and everyone knows everyone else's business."

Inga was regularly to attend the many social events Patterson hosted at her gargantuan, Stanford White–designed white marble mansion located at 15 Dupont Circle. Patterson knew that attractive women helped draw powerful men to her soirées, which would allow Inga to expand her circle of contacts and sources.

But Inga brought a circle of contacts of her own to the job, and it was Inga's promise of a scoop that ultimately convinced Patterson to hire her.

---

*The 1928 Ben Hecht–Charles MacArthur play, later made into at least three movies, about unscrupulous newspapermen working in Chicago during the wild days of Prohibition.

Inga guaranteed Patterson that she could provide the *Times-Herald* with an exclusive interview with one of the most enigmatic and mysterious men in the world, Axel Wenner-Gren, whose net worth was estimated at $1 billion in the late 1930s. The U.S. government also suspected him of being a Nazi agent.

CHAPTER 6

"The sphinx of Sweden"

BETWEEN HER OWN CHARM, ARTHUR KROCK'S INTRODUCTION, CISSY Patterson's amity, and her relationship with Axel Wenner-Gren, it had taken Inga less than ten days to find work in Washington. She officially began at the *Times-Herald* on June 12, 1941, and two days later she had her first front-page byline under the headline WENNER-GREN DENIES PEACE PARLEYS HERE.

Largely forgotten today, Wenner-Gren was one of a new breed of businessman that fascinated people in the years between the two world wars. He was not merely an industrialist, but an *international* industrialist, like other such shadowy figures as Alfred Loewenstein, the Belgian utility financier who died falling out of an airplane, or Ivar Kreuger, the Swedish "Match King" whose assets were eventually purchased by Wenner-Gren. These tycoons with holdings all around the world appeared to have no clear national allegiance, yet they seemed always to be behind a curtain, secretly influencing the course of world events.

The unlikely product that made Wenner-Gren internationally famous and fabulously rich was the home vacuum cleaner. Wenner-Gren was neither an inventor nor an engineer, but like Steve Jobs much later in the twentieth century, Wenner-Gren was a sales genius with an intuitive understanding of consumer desires and a steady stream of ideas on how to either improve existing products or create new ones that no one else had ever thought about.*

---

*Wenner-Gren, for example, later created the company that developed the ALWEG monorail transportation systems still in use at Disneyland and in downtown Seattle, ALWEG being an acronym for Axel Lennart Wenner-Gren.

Wenner-Gren was working as a machine separator salesman in 1908 when he noted a strange-looking contraption in a Vienna shop window that was an early American-made prototype of an electric home vacuum cleaner. At a time when the average housewife devoted seven hours a day, every day, to housework, Wenner-Gren intuitively realized that this was a gadget that every homemaker would want. He purchased a share of the distribution rights to the machine on the spot.

By the end of World War I, Wenner-Gren had purchased and consolidated several companies into the corporation still known as Electrolux, whose success allowed him to expand and diversify his assets dramatically, most notably in airplane manufacturing and armaments. He took control of Svenska Aeroplan AB (Saab), which was a major aerospace and defense company years before it began making quirky automobiles, and he was also a major shareholder in the legendary Krupp operation in Germany, which manufactured steel, armaments, and munitions. Wenner-Gren thereby was a major supplier of war materials for Nazi Germany.

Yet Wenner-Gren wished to be known as a peacemaker. In 1937, he authored and published a slim book titled *Call to Reason* in which he chided both fascism and communism for thwarting free enterprise and individual initiative. He advocated the Swedish "middle way" in which enlightened oligarchs (such as himself) engaged in "industrial self-control" that alleviated the need for government interference. Wars occurred when one nation or people believed they could address a material want at the expense of another, but technology, with its capacity to provide "the means of satisfying the essential needs of mankind," had now made this rationale for war obsolete, Wenner-Gren said, if only there was greater international cooperation.

Much as Henry Ford tried to act as a mediator during World War I, Wenner-Gren thought his negotiating skills in business were transferable to the realm of international diplomacy. In 1939, as war seemed imminent, he tried to freelance a peace agreement between Germany and Britain, acting on his own initiative as an emissary between his friend Field Marshal Herman Göring and Prime Minister Neville Chamberlain.

He failed, of course, but the following year Göring invited Wenner-Gren to help broker peace between Finland and the Soviet Union because Germans feared the war would jeopardize their access to Swedish steel that was vital to the German war effort. Before engaging in this diplomatic mission, Wenner-Gren flew to Washington to confer with President Roosevelt, whom Wenner-Gren had met multiple times during the 1930s and whom Roosevelt had welcomed as a champion and advocate of New Deal programs.

Wenner-Gren was nicknamed "the Sphinx of Sweden," which was an odd moniker given that he had written a book, freely gave interviews, and was often in the news. When a Nazi submarine sank the British ocean liner S.S. *Athenia* northwest of Ireland on September 3, 1939, Wenner-Gren, who was sailing in the area on his way to the Bahamas, used his enormous three-hundred-foot-long private yacht, the *Southern Cross*, to help pick up survivors. (One of those dispatched by the American embassy in London to interview some of those survivors was the U.S. ambassador's son, Jack Kennedy.) Rather than accolades, Wenner-Gren's coincidental proximity to the tragedy led to suspicions that his yacht was being used to fuel Nazi subs.

As the world caught fire, Wenner-Gren removed himself from international politics, retiring to his fabulous Bahamian estate. But even this aroused suspicions, as one of his neighbors and closest friends was the Duke of Windsor, the former King Edward VIII, who was also considered a Nazi sympathizer. Such was the mystery surrounding Wenner-Gren that imaginative writers have tried to tie Wenner-Gren and the Duke of Windsor to the 1943 murder of multimillionaire Sir Harry Oakes, a Canadian and fellow Bahamian resident, who was allegedly prepared to expose both men as Nazi agents. No official inquiry ever implicated either man in the crime.

Now in June 1941, Wenner-Gren was back in Washington, but for what purpose? That Inga, a cub reporter who had never worked for an American newspaper before, was assigned to find out was unusual enough, but what particularly raised eyebrows among some of her new colleagues at the *Times-Herald* was that Inga had apparently secured the interview thanks to some unspecified personal relationship with the tall, suave, silver-haired, sixty-year-old Wenner-Gren.

CHAPTER 7

"Did You Happen to See?"

WHILE IT WAS COMMON SPECULATION THAT INGA WAS AXEL WENNER-Gren's mistress, there is no evidence they were ever lovers. Wenner-Gren and his wife had both simply taken a liking to Inga and felt partly responsible for her well-being, given it was their money keeping her husband far away in Peru.

Just as he had helped Inga get into Columbia University, Wenner-Gren now boosted Inga's journalism career by granting her an exclusive interview that any journalist in the city would have desired. He also wanted to update her on how Fejos was doing in Peru. So, while in Washington, Wenner-Gren took Inga to lunch and dinner twice and to a movie once. They also spoke several times on the phone. We know all this because the FBI had Wenner-Gren under constant surveillance and had bugged his hotel room and tapped his hotel phone.

Nothing in the tapings suggests any inappropriate romantic relationship between Inga and Wenner-Gren. The tapes do, however, expose an inappropriate *professional* relationship between a journalist and an interview subject. The FBI overheard Inga, not remotely a disinterested reporter, allowing Wenner-Gren to shape her story as he wished it. "Shall I say that you spent much of your time trying to keep peace in the world before this war started?" the FBI heard Inga ask Wenner-Gren. "Shall I say in a joking way that no man who spends his time swimming in the beautiful waters around Nassau can be troubled with the world conflict?"

Given this cozy relationship between reporter and source, it is not surprising that Inga's article on Wenner-Gren was a fluff piece, where she described him as "Sweden's great industrialist and philanthropist." Wenner-Gren denied any plans to meet with Roosevelt or any high-ranking U.S. officials, though Inga enjoyed including an inside joke where Wenner-Gren admits that his favorite engagement in Washington had been "lunch at the Carlton today with a very charming young lady." He admitted to being a close friend of his neighbors, the Duke and Duchess of Windsor, but he denied there was anything nefarious in that. "I am much taken with both of them as anyone is who has the good fortune of meeting them," he said. He also insisted he had no political ambitions or plans to negotiate any peace.

Inga's story on Wenner-Gren was prominently placed on the front page above the fold, while the articles surrounding that story were testament to how uncertain the future appeared in the summer of 1941. To the left of Inga's piece was an article headlined ARMY URGES AUTO OUTPUT BE HALVED: MEN AND MATERIALS NEEDED FOR DEFENSE, while to the right was the headline NAZIS DEMAND REDS DISARM IN EUROPE; the surprise Nazi assault on the Soviet Union would begin in less than ten days. And just to the right of that was the most ominous story of the day, even though it played below the fold: FRANCE PLACES CURBS ON JEWS: 13,000 ARRESTED, "PLOT" CHARGED.

Despite all this menacing news, there were many, including the publisher and much of the staff of the *Times-Herald*, who hoped all the nastiness could remain confined to Europe and not involve the United States—unless, in their minds, American Jews and Anglophiles succeeded in provoking American involvement.

Lost in the subsequent mythology of "the Greatest Generation" is how bitterly divided Americans were about U.S. involvement in the war in Europe up to the day Hitler settled the question by declaring war on the United States. Historian Arthur Schlesinger Jr., who became an advisor to President Kennedy and who lived through McCarthyism and the turmoil of the 1960s, still insisted that the question of isolation or intervention was "the most savage political debate in my lifetime . . . none so tore apart families and friendships as this fight."

Charges and countercharges flew throughout the summer of 1941. As reported in the *Times-Herald*, North Dakota senator Gerald Nye, an ardent isolationist, led a congressional investigation into whether the Roosevelt administration had enlisted the help of the "foreign-bred" (by which he meant Jews, foreign born or not) heads of movie studios to turn Hollywood into a pro-war propaganda tool.

Famed aviator Charles Lindbergh, who had emerged as a leading spokesman for the nation's leading isolationist organization, the America First Committee, charged that only Roosevelt, Jews, and the British wanted America to enter the war, and that Roosevelt intended to cancel elections in 1942 and become a dictator if he had not successfully pulled the country into war by then. This led America's greatest hero of World War I, Sergeant Alvin York, to suggest that people like Nye and Lindbergh should be "shut up by throwing them into jail—today, not tomorrow. We can't risk our whole freedom, our country, listening to them." A film based on York's exploits starring Gary Cooper had been released in July and was one of the films Nye and the Senate planned to investigate as pro-war propaganda.

Boding ill for Inga, given that her husband was in South America under the sponsorship of a suspected Nazi agent, there were also a variety of stories suggesting that war was already encroaching on the Western Hemisphere. The *Times-Herald* ran a fatuous story in early September about a government investigation in Argentina, which concluded that a half-million Nazi troops were already stationed at secret bases located all across South America. A week later, Roosevelt lent credence to concerns about Nazi infiltration in the Western Hemisphere when he announced that a secret airfield had been discovered in Colombia within bombing range of the Panama Canal. Neither of these stories proved to be true, but that was unknown at the time.

Though no doubt following these stories with interest, Inga's personal concern, which was still unanswered by the *Times-Herald* editors, was what would she do on a daily basis at the paper?

Inga wrote a short recollection of her meeting Brenda Frazier, who was back in the news because the club-hopping debutante planned to marry professional football player John "Shipwreck" Kelly, and she also interviewed the parents of a murdered fifteen-year-old girl. But "hard news" was not Inga's forte. Journalism's attraction for her was not as a calling in the search for truth but as a means to understand people.

Her disarming knack for getting people to open up and talk about themselves led Patterson to assign Inga to write a new column added to the paper. Called "Did You Happen to See?" its purpose was to introduce *Times-Herald* readers to a few of the thousands of new people flooding into Washington to fill, or in most cases create, critical jobs as the nation prepared for war.

Washington in 1941 was a boomtown. The influx of people who arrived in the capital to work on the New Deal had changed Washington, but the vastly larger numbers arriving to work on the war effort transformed the city. With more than five thousand new workers arriving in Washington every month, the number of federal employees had doubled since the beginning of 1940. Washington would never again have the feel of a sleepy southern village.

Housing was in great demand, but workers even more so. Competent secretaries were so prized that if an applicant had a high school diploma and could type she was hired on the spot, usually before she had even found a place to spend her first night in the city. These women typically received a starting salary of $1,440 per year, but their bosses often received much less. Many of these newcomers had been prominent in their hometowns and industries and simply wanted a chance to serve, but since federal law prohibited anyone from working for the government for free, they often agreed to take a symbolic salary of one dollar per year, mirroring a practice that had also occurred during World War I and during the early years of the New Deal.

There was curiosity about who these new leaders of the war effort were, but the initial columns had been a little flat. "Did You Happen to See?" had been initially assigned to Leon Pearson, a *Times-Herald* writer who was columnist Drew Pearson's younger brother, but Pearson's style did not attract many readers. His profiles were dry recitations of resumes, appropriate to introduce a guest at a Rotary Club luncheon but not particularly engaging or revealing.

Patterson thought Inga might bring pizzazz to the column, and to the surprise of most of her colleagues, who thought the column was a dog,

Inga brought genuine enthusiasm to the work. That enthusiasm became a basis for suspicion. Just as at Columbia, where her fellow students deduced that journalism was the perfect cover for espionage, so now in Washington would the wary conclude that a column designed to meet leaders in the war effort would be the perfect venue to collect intelligence for a foreign foe.

CHAPTER 8

"The sweetheart of the FBI"

WITHIN WEEKS THE *TIMES-HERALD* "DID YOU HAPPEN TO SEE?" column was Inga's alone as Leon Pearson moved on to become the *Times-Herald's* Latin American beat reporter. It was a heavy workload for Inga, as the column appeared every day but Sunday and always at the top of page 2. Its prominent placement reflected its popularity with readers, which baffled Inga's colleagues. Like Inga's classmates at Columbia, they were befuddled by Inga's unique writing style.

Times-Herald editor Frank Waldrop, however, thought Inga and the column were a perfect fit. The *Times-Herald* prided itself on its stable of "young off-beat writers" who added "a little humanness" at a time when the paper was filled with a steady diet of "oppressive" world news. "You wanted a rather artless, open way of looking at these people, which is what Inga had," Waldrop said. He was amused that Inga could become genuinely excited "to meet some clunk from Dubuque who was in the rubber business, who had been brought in here as a dollar a year man to see what he could do [for] the country. She had just the right tone."

More than that, Waldrop said, Inga intuitively understood people and "she could capture in 300 words or so insights into character and personality as good as those Sally Quinn* today spreads over half a page of newsprint. If you think 'interviewing,' as it used to be called, is not one of

---

* Waldrop wrote these words in an article for *Washingtonian* magazine in 1975 when Sally Quinn was a glamorous and award-winning writer for the *Washington Post*. Like Inga, Quinn was also an attractive woman with little experience when she was hired to work at the *Post* in 1969. She later married *Post* editor and Kennedy friend Ben Bradlee.

journalism's very hardest skills you might try it sometime. Inga earned her pay every day."

One reason for the popularity of Inga's column was that it featured women in equal measure with men. "Rosie the Riveter" was still a year or two away from becoming an icon of the new roles played by women during the war, but in mid-1941 government was one of the few professions where women could achieve a considerable level of management responsibility.

Inga's first column, which appeared July 2, 1941, profiled Ruth B. Shipley, who ran the State Department's Passport Division and managed its 125 employees "like a hen mother guarding her chicks." Her second column featured Patricia O'Malley, chief of the editorial section of the Civil Aeronautics Authority, whom Inga said "looks like some rare flower," and who had already begun a second successful career with her novels about the adventures of Carol Rogers, a pretty, globe-trotting "air-hostess."

Another early column featured Lovice Craig, a happily single attorney at the Reconstruction Finance Corporation. Inga asked Craig the question every single woman still receives, to which Craig replied, "Yes, I suppose I shall marry someday. A home is, after all, a woman's logical place." Such an assurance that professional women could still be ladylike and domestic may induce cringes today, but it was the norm for the time and fit into Inga's own worldview, which was that professional achievements were empty if a romantic life was absent.

Inga also did not confine her assessments of appearance to women, which may also have been part of her columns' appeal. The columns were, after all, less about the subjects themselves than of Inga's *impressions* of her subjects.

"Handsome, clean-cut polo-playing" Army captain Joseph P. Haskell may have been an aide de camp to two generals, but to Inga he looked "like a little boy trying to be awfully good." The burly cellist and conductor Hans Kindler, who founded the National Symphony Orchestra, was "genuinely handsome in a teddy bear fashion, or like a Great Dane puppy."

When it came to the attractiveness of men, Inga occasionally dropped hints to ensure her readers knew that she had the proper cosmopolitan background to judge such things. Young War Department official Captain Juan A. A. Sedillo was born in Sante Fe, New Mexico, but to Inga "his immaculate moustache, his dark, brown eyes, right down to the way he shakes your hand—it is so—oh, so Spanish."

Clearly, Inga enjoyed winking at her audience, including them in her private jokes. She often broke the fourth wall with her readers, writing as if she were chatting across the kitchen table. Using the same charm she would have put to use in person, she wanted to know what *they* thought.

Writing of a woman whose job was to coordinate the sale of war bonds, Inga described her as "a little cheerful girl with beaming eyes," but then asked her readers, "Or is that too flippant?" Flippancy was part of the point. She did not take herself, her job, or, for that matter, the world too seriously. It was one of the traits that would make her so attractive to and so well matched with a young naval ensign named John Kennedy, who seldom took the world too seriously either.

With her eye for talent, particularly of the male variety, many of Inga's profiles were of men who would go on to great prominence after the war, including some who would become Kennedy's political rivals. Estes Kefauver, who would edge out Kennedy as Adlai Stevenson's running mate in 1956, was profiled by Inga while he was still a fledgling congressman who still looked like "the handsome athlete who was the best tackle" in the history of the University of Tennessee.

Stevenson, meanwhile, who was only beginning to get national attention as a special assistant to Secretary of the Navy Frank Knox, was impressive to Inga in the forcefulness of his foreign policy views. "No tender sissie [*sic*] he," Inga wrote. "No man who paddles around in a pot of honey." Kennedy would later vigorously disagree with Inga's assessment, chiding Stevenson for being "soft" and delighting in a compliment from columnist Joseph Alsop, who referred to Kennedy (privately) as "a Stevenson with balls."

Inga would not have used such language (in print), but she did use an odd mixture of English and Scandinavian colloquialisms, such as *paddling around in a pot of honey*, that were dubbed "Inga-isms" by her amused colleagues. Her Danish heritage was evident when she wrote of a CBS journalist having eyes "clear as forest lakes," or of a populist politician who "walks into the hearts of people with wooden shoes on."

Amusing in print, men melted when she used English creatively in private conversation. "Her English wasn't perfect," said her colleague John White. "It was better than perfect. 'I have gooey eyes for you' she'd say. . . . She was adorable, just adorable."

Adorable—and persistent. Inga's columns also became noteworthy because she was able to coax interviews out of people who were notoriously shy of publicity, or who simply despised the *Times-Herald*. Few were more publicity shy than Clyde Tolson, who had been associate director of the FBI since 1930. Hoover's most trusted intimate, perhaps physically (according to some rumors) but certainly emotionally, Tolson had gone on the record with a reporter only once the previous decade. Yet he finally succumbed to Inga's entreaties and agreed to an interview, and had to admit later in a thank-you note to Inga that "your article was perfectly fine."

Tolson could hardly have hoped for a less critical portrait, for Inga wrote, "He has what it takes: The keenest, most intelligent eyes, a splendid physique, excellent memory, plenty of hunches, is an expert on human beings, knows the ins and outs of law, is energetic, and has many other qualities which make him a fine aide to his famous boss, J. Edgar Hoover."

Inga also profiled the only other person at the Bureau who was personally close to Hoover, the director's personal assistant, Helen Gandy. Inga's profile of Gandy was mostly a collection of trifles, such as noting Gandy's love of gardening and floral arrangement. But she disturbed some at the FBI when she noted in the column that as she ended the interview with Gandy and walked out of Hoover's office an agent called out, "You better not write anything nasty about the sweetheart of the FBI, because every man here would go out and fight for her."

Inga had probably thought the remark gallant and charming, but the FBI under Hoover had an exaggerated sense of its own dignity; hence, one agent's belief that Inga had placed Gandy, and by extension the Bureau, "in an improper light."

That Inga's columns were intended to be complimentary was underscored by the paper's decision to laminate and mount each one on a lacquered wooden plaque, which was then presented to the interview subject compliments of the *Times-Herald*.

Yet the very banality of the columns was soon cast in a sinister light. Inga might mix up her columns to include the dean of Washington's premier cooking school or the coach of the Washington Redskins (who would boast that his team for the coming season was unusually large, averaging six feet in height and 206 pounds in weight), but soon federal agents would see these as mere diversions intended to throw America's counterespionage agents off the scent.

The columns were so quirky they almost did not seem like journalism. Perhaps they *were* a front. A few of Inga's colleagues began to think so.

Having learned the dangers of sharing too much information while attending Columbia, Inga now shared little of her earlier life with her coworkers. They were aware that she was married and that her husband was off in the jungles in South America searching for lost Incan cities. They also knew she had once worked in Germany as a reporter, but Inga no longer boasted of her interviews with Hitler. At Columbia, her outspokenness had aroused suspicions; now, at the *Times-Herald*, it was what she declined to share that raised questions.

On November 14, 1941, two weeks after Inga's column on Tolson was published, a woman employed at the *Times-Herald* contacted FBI Special Agent L. B. Nichols to ask if the FBI was keeping track of who in Washington might be a Nazi spy. Nichols assured the woman that the FBI "had a fairly good idea" of who was involved in espionage in the capital. The woman asked Nichols if the Bureau was aware that Inga had known Hitler well and was the Nazi's designated publicity agent in Denmark.

Inga must be a spy, the informant explained, because she "could not write," yet she was not only employed authoring a prominently placed column, she also seemed to have "a lot of pull at the *Times-Herald*." Describing Inga as "high-handed . . . very smart and ingratiating," the informant could only speculate how Inga had been hired in the first place. Either she had fooled Patterson and Waldrop, or else they, too, were "were working under orders." The informant was not only a colleague of Inga, she had once been her roommate. Such was the climate of paranoia in Washington as war neared.

CHAPTER 9

"Kick"

THE *TIMES-HERALD* COLLEAGUE AND ONE-TIME ROOMMATE WHO contacted the FBI with her suspicions about Inga was Page Huidekoper. Hailing from a prominent Maryland family, the cultivated Huidekoper used her family's friendship and shared Dutch heritage with Franklin Roosevelt to land a job as an assistant in the press office of Ambassador Joseph P. Kennedy at the American embassy in London. There, she met the entire Kennedy clan and became especially good friends with the Kennedy's second-eldest daughter, Kathleen, whom everyone called "Kick."

After the German occupation of France, and with an attack on Great Britain considered imminent, Ambassador Kennedy sent Huidekoper back to the United States along with his own children. When Huidekoper returned home, she called Arthur Krock, whom she had met during one of his several visits to London, and asked for help finding a job in Washington. Krock was apparently always delighted to help an attractive young woman in need. Frank Waldrop, the editor of the *Times-Herald*, was always equally delighted to hire an attractive young woman in need, once teasing Krock, "What are you, our staff procurer?"

So, when Krock similarly intervened on behalf of Inga, he had no problem asking Huidekoper for a favor, which was to give Inga a place to stay until she could find her own apartment. The housing shortage in Washington during the war was so legendary that film director George Stevens made a successful and delightful screwball comedy about it called *The More the Merrier*, whose plot, in a case of art anticipating life, has the two romantic leads, played by Joel McCrae and Jean Arthur, wrongfully accused of espionage.

Inga spent only a few weeks in Huidekoper's Dupont Circle apartment before she secured her own flat on the fifth floor of a charming art deco building at 1600 16th Street NW. With her husband three thousand miles away in Peru, and her mother and Blok back in New York, Inga enjoyed both a freedom and camaraderie with peers that she had seldom, if ever, experienced. Waldrop said Inga, Huidekoper, and a host of other younger staffers at the *Times-Herald* spent their off hours "whooping it up" in a city getting less elderly and less staid by the day.

"Everything was done in groups," Huidekoper said. "Whole households of boys would take out whole households of girls. . . . And there were so many parties to go to that everyone just traveled in groups. Indeed, you were almost looked at askance if you tried to get someone off by yourself."

Running in packs, however, ran counter to the prevailing mood, for this was a particularly romantic time in American history. The desire of the young to make merry and love is common in any period, but the pace was accelerated in 1941. The specter of war made these last few moments of peace seem even more precious. Now was the time to grab life's pleasures while you could, for tomorrow you, and many whom you knew, may well indeed die.

Such excitement led to impulsive behavior. Belying the common belief that America before the 1960s was sexually repressed, a *Washington Daily News* headline in early 1942 proclaimed: ENOUGH VD CASES IN D.C. TO OVERFLOW THE STADIUM. The *Daily News* was corrected by the district public health officer in charge of overseeing venereal disease: Griffith Stadium, home of the Washington Senators, held only thirty thousand spectators, and there were fifteen thousand more VD cases in the district than that.

One young newcomer to Washington was in no danger of catching a sexually transmitted disease because she intended to remain a virgin until marriage. She was so chaste she reportedly would not say the word *sex* out loud. This was Kick Kennedy, the second daughter and fourth oldest of the nine children of the man who, by 1941, was the *former* U.S. ambassador to Great Britain, Joseph P. Kennedy Sr.

Because her older sister, Rosemary, was developmentally disabled, for all intents and purposes Kick was considered Kennedy's oldest daughter and, by many accounts, including that of her mother, Rose Kennedy, she was her father's favorite child. Perhaps he admired her independent spirit. Kick would be the only Kennedy daughter to marry before turning thirty years old, and then did so against her parents' wishes. Like Inga, she was smart, witty, and exuberant, which may be why they became close friends. But unlike Inga, Kick's sophistication was mixed with a healthy dose of the naïve.

Because of her father's wealth and position, Kick was well traveled and well educated, yet also extraordinarily sheltered. She was not classically pretty, as she had a short neck and stocky legs, but she was dainty, had lustrous auburn hair and laughing blue-gray eyes, and the force of her bubbly, unpretentious personality meant that boys liked her immensely. Worried that Kick was too popular with the opposite sex, Rose Kennedy, who had been educated the same way as a girl and who reportedly held a dim view of sex even *within* marriage, enrolled Kick in all-girl convent schools, first in Connecticut and later in France, that were operated by the Order of the Sacred Heart.

The regimen at these schools was austere to the point of severity. Girls were often forbidden to converse during meals, and mail was censored, even letters from home. They were allowed to bathe only twice a week; the rest of the time they cleaned up using cold water from a basin, which in winter months often had a layer of ice on top in the morning. Dating was strictly taboo (boys could come to tea only on Sunday and only if accompanied by a mother), and out of fear of any potential lesbian relationships forming, the convent sisters prohibited two girls from ever being alone together.

But the strictness of her upbringing did not diminish Kick's gaiety or her later success as a socialite. When her mother became ill with appendicitis, Kick filled in as her father's official hostess at the American embassy in London to great acclaim. *Queen* magazine proclaimed Kick "America's Most Important Debutante" in its May 12, 1938, issue.

Young English gentlemen were mad for her American informality and irreverence, laughing uproariously when she referred to the Duke of Marlborough as "Dukie Wookie." And despite her chaste nature, Kick delighted in telling mildly off-color jokes—when she could get to the punch line before dissolving into laughter. A typical Kick joke, told with her version of a proper British accent, was of an American who told a stuffy Englishman that his favorite breakfast was "a roll in bed with Honey." The Englishman went to his club to tell this "frightfully funny story" to friends. "I asked him, 'What's your favorite breakfast?' And do you know what he said to me? 'A roll in bed with strawberry jaaahm.'" Kick could barely finish she was laughing so hard.

At eighteen, Kick was engaged to twenty-three-year-old shipping heir Peter Grace, but not long after arriving in England Kick broke the engagement because she had become infatuated with Billy Cavendish, the Marquess of Hartington. Cavendish was in line to become the Duke of Devonshire, which would make him one of the richest men in Britain. Unlike many women who hoped to snag Cavendish, wealth was not key to his appeal for Kick, who was, after all, the daughter of one of America's richest men. She liked Cavendish because he was sweet and gentle, while he adored Kick because her exuberance brought him out of his shell.

But there was a serious obstacle to the match. The Cavendishes were one of England's most prominent Protestant families. Kick was devoutly and unabashedly Catholic, known to drop to her knees and pray in front of her friends if she suddenly realized she had forgotten to say her daily rosary. To avoid committing a mortal sin, Kick would have had to insist that any children from their union be raised Catholic. Given that the Duke of Devonshire was obliged to appoint Church of England priests in various parishes among the family's extensive land holdings, Cavendish wondered how his heir, if raised Catholic, could possibly fulfill such a duty.

Resolution of this dilemma was delayed when Kick was sent back to the United States as war began. Kick bounced among colleges, killing time, before she called Page Huidekoper in the summer of 1941 and asked for help in landing a job. Huidekoper, who was being promoted to the city desk, convinced Waldrop to make Kick his new secretary/research assistant.

Keen to fit in, Kick tried to hide the fact that she was the daughter of the enormously wealthy former ambassador. When she had a social engagement after work, she brought her mink coat "carefully wrapped up inside a paper sack." When a coworker peeked into the bag, this led to the preposterous speculation that chaste Kick was the mistress of a sugar daddy.

Given their compatible personalities, the proximity of their desks in the *Times-Herald* newsroom, and that they lived only a few blocks from each other, Inga and Kick soon became good friends. Kick poured out her troubles regarding Cavendish and sought romantic guidance from Inga, particularly once she began dating another writer on the paper named John White, a self-styled eccentric who was also the best feature writer on the paper. As always, Inga proved to be a good listener. She occasionally offered Kick advice, but Inga did not confide a great deal about her own past, though Kick could not have been in doubt about Inga's cosmopolitan past.

She was particularly impressed by Inga's fluency in so many tongues, for Kick had no gift for languages. Friends reported that when Kick traveled to France she would attempt to communicate with Parisians by speaking English with a French accent. She did the same in Italy. Once, when pinched by an Italian man while taking public transit, Kick began screaming to the driver, "Stoppa the bus! Stoppa the bus!"

While Kick did not deprecate her own virtues, she knew Inga was, in terms of sophistication, of a different caste. Kick could think of only one person who was Inga's equal in looks, brains, worldly knowledge, and charm, and that was her beloved older brother, Jack, who, beginning in October 1941, was to be assigned by the navy to work in Washington. Kick could hardly have been more thrilled.

"The charm that makes birds come out of the trees"

JACK AND KICK KENNEDY ADORED EACH OTHER. THEY WERE CLOSER TO each other than to any of their other seven siblings. They were kindred spirits, lively and rebellious (at least as much as their father would allow). Until he met Inga, Kick was really the only woman—and the only member of his family—to whom Jack genuinely confided because "I always knew she loved me." One family friend said Jack and Kick were "so close at times I thought of them as twins."

During his senior year at Choate, Jack's father wrote to tell him how much he meant to his sister. "She has a love and devotion to you that you should be very proud to have deserved," Joseph Kennedy said. "She thinks you are quite the grandest fellow that ever lived and your letters furnish most of her laughs in the Convent."

While the rest of the Kennedy clan believed the eldest brother, Joe Junior, was destined for greatness, Kick was the family iconoclast who judged Jack the superior Kennedy. She marveled at all Jack had already done and all the places he had been—even to the Soviet Union. Only twenty-four when he arrived in Washington, Jack had already written a best-selling book, published the year before, titled *Why England Slept*, which sought to explain why Great Britain had been so slow to rearm to counter the growing Nazi threat.

Shortly after arriving in Washington, Jack had been a guest at one of Cissy Patterson's dinner parties where he debated world politics with such luminaries as Montana senator Burton Wheeler, Undersecretary of the

Navy James Forrestal, the journalist Herbert B. Swope, and Inga's great admirer, Bernard Baruch. Kick had no doubt that Inga would be impressed with Jack and that Jack would be impressed with Inga; Kick's enthusiasm was key to Jack's immediate infatuation.

Knowing that Kick wished him only happiness, and trusting her judgment, Jack consulted and listened to Kick's advice in matters of love. He stressed to the women he dated how important it was that they make "a good impression on Kick." Inga had certainly done that, and now Kick was excited at the prospect of bringing Inga and her brother together, even though she knew Inga was married. As Inga recalled:

> [Kick] was curled up like a kitten, her long tawny hair fell over her face as she read a letter, then she jumped up . . . her Irish-blue eyes flashed with excitement as she leaped onto the floor and began a whirling dance like some delightful dervish. "He's coming to Washington, I'm going to give a party at the F Street Club, you will just love him! . . ."
>
> "Who?" said I, being a few years older and not knowing what sort of a creature could make Kick so happy. Was it one of her many admirers. "WHO?"
>
> "Jack. He's in the Navy and is going to be stationed in Washington. Super, super."

Inga was intrigued but skeptical. Yet when she met Jack he made as great an impression as Kick had hoped. As Inga recalled, "He came. She hadn't exaggerated. He had the charm that makes the birds come out of the trees. He looked like her twin, the same thick mop of hair, the same blue eyes, natural, engaging, ambitious, warm, and when he walked into a room you knew he was there, not pushing, not domineering but exuding animal magnetism."

It was a testament to Jack's charisma that he exuded "animal magnetism," for in many ways he was a physical wreck. For many years, he had severe stomach problems that required him to stick to a bland diet and that kept him perpetually skinny. He had colitis, and the adrenal extracts and hormone treatments used to treat that may also have contributed to severe back problems that began in 1940. And while it had not yet been properly diagnosed, Jack also suffered from Addison's disease, a rare disorder that prevents the adrenal glands from producing hormones, thereby damaging the body's immune system.

Jack had been drafted by the military in the fall of 1940, but since he was enrolled at Stanford to pursue graduate studies, he was not called up until the following year. He failed the army entrance physical, tried to get into one of the navy's officer candidate schools, and failed their entrance physical, too. Jack wanted to serve, telling his friend Lem Billings, "If I don't, it will look quite bad."

Jack was determined to enlist in some branch of the service because he did not want people beyond his family and closest friends to know of his medical problems. His only alternative at the time seemed to be law school, which bored him. His brother, Joe Junior, had enlisted in the navy with plans to be an aviator, and Jack did not want his brother to continue to outshine him. He also knew military service would be important to his professional/political advancement after the war, and he believed failing to enlist would add to the criticism being leveled at his father, who had been called a coward because he remained opposed to American involvement in the war.

Joseph Kennedy did not want to send any American boys to war, most especially his own, but he agreed to pull some strings and get Jack into the navy. Joseph Kennedy contacted Captain Alan Kirk, who had been the naval attaché at the American embassy in London when Kennedy was ambassador and who was now the head of the Office of Naval Intelligence (ONI). The two agreed to fix a medical exam to ensure Jack could enter the navy, which he did in October 1941 as an ensign assigned to the Foreign Intelligence Branch of ONI in Washington. Jack's primary job was to read, analyze, and distill information received from a variety of foreign sources, from secret cables to newspapers.

Perhaps Joseph Kennedy, despite his forebodings about the war, agreed to help Jack get into ONI because he believed that a desk job in intelligence in the capital would not expose Jack to great physical danger or physical exertion. If so, the opposite occurred. Because Jack worked in intelligence, his relationship with Inga, a suspected Nazi spy, would soon become a matter of intense interest to the government, and would set in motion a series of events that would send Jack into combat, where he came very close to being killed.

CHAPTER 11

"Totally woman"

EXACTLY HOW QUICKLY INGA AND JACK BECAME LOVERS IS UNKNOWN, though it appears it was within a day or two of them meeting—perhaps the very day. Jack "was infatuated quite quickly," according to Kick's boyfriend, John White, who understood exactly what enchanted Jack. "Oh, sex," White said. "[Inga] looked adorable and was. She was totally woman."

White had a rare front-row seat to the whole affair. To avoid scandal, as Inga was a married woman, White and Kick routinely acted as a cover for Jack and Inga's illicit activities. The two couples would pretend to double date, beginning an evening together. Then White and Kick would leave Jack and Inga alone for a period of time before rejoining them at the end of the evening.

White outlined the routine in his diary, such as this notation for November 24, 1941: "Supper at Inga's. K and J Kennedy, Inga and I . . . leave them together. Join at end." To any casual observer, it appeared the four had been together the whole time with nothing amiss. Soon, there would be more interested observers who kept close tabs on the comings and goings of Inga and her young navy companion.

White said they engaged in this ruse because Jack particularly wanted to avoid his father's many informants, but initially Joseph Kennedy, assuming the possibility of Jack wanting to marry Inga was nil, had no objection to what he supposed would be a short-lived dalliance. "He thought it was fine," said White, "because she [Inga] could properly initiate him into the mysterious ways of sex, in the fashion of some older, marvelous practitioner."

45

Jack hardly needed initiation into the "mysterious ways of sex." Already by age twenty-four he had had innumerable sexual encounters, but all that practice apparently did not equate to a great deal of skill. Inga, who was seldom shy about discussing such matters, confided to White that Jack had a rather single-minded view of sex, focusing on his own quick climax with little regard to whether the woman was receiving any pleasure or not. "So, he's got a lot to learn and I'll be happy to teach him," she said.

White had no doubt that Jack had found the right instructor. "She was an enthusiastic teacher and practitioner of the art of love," White said of Inga. "She liked to play about, and she played extremely well. It's like the old European tradition of the old mistress for the young boy."

White's emphasis on the sexual aspect of Jack and Inga's relationship, with Inga playing the role of courtesan or something even coarser, skews the nature of the relationship and unfairly places Inga in an unflattering light.

While Inga had a very healthy view of sex as something completely natural between a man and a woman in love, she was not, in fact (unlike Kennedy), terribly promiscuous. Late in life, as she always spoke freely about such things, she made the offhand comment to one of her sons that you could count all the men she had been with on two hands, with fingers left over.

As already noted, rumors that she had had affairs with Arthur Krock, Bernard Baruch, and Axel Wenner-Gren were almost certainly untrue. It is possible that Inga may have had more lovers than she acknowledged, but there is no evidence she did. It is clear that while Inga had a very healthy and uninhibited attitude toward sex, she generally engaged in intimate relations within the context of a long-term romantic relationship. Inga enjoyed sex, but she wanted (and needed) love.

While White was unsurprised about Joseph Kennedy's reaction, he was taken aback by Kick's enthusiasm for the romance, given her own strict views on sex outside marriage—views that kept White a frustrated suitor. But Kick, much like her mother, believed there were different rules for men and women. Once, at a party in England, when guests began criticizing a man who was having an extramarital affair, Kick cut them off. Perhaps thinking about both her father and her brother, Kick said, "That's what all men do. You know that women can never trust them."

For now, Kick was supportive of the match between Jack and Inga. It involved two of her favorite people, and they were well matched. Until Inga, Kick had never known a woman she thought could match her brother in personality, intellect, and looks. It also speaks to Kick's admiration for Inga that she granted her the same uncritical moral latitude she gave her brother, for she did not criticize Inga for being unfaithful to her husband.

Tempering any qualms she may have had was the belief Kick shared with her father that Jack had no notion of marrying Inga. How could he? The Kennedys were America's most famous Roman Catholic family. The idea that her brother would risk scandal and break with the church to marry a once divorced and still-married non-Catholic seemed unfathomable. Kick, after all, had given up her relationship with Billy Cavendish because she was not yet strong enough to go against her family or her faith. When push came to shove, she expected Jack would have to make the same painful decision.

The idea that this was to be a short-term fling was initially fine with Inga as well. She did, after all, still have a husband whom she as yet had no intention of divorcing. There was also Nils Blok, still back in New York, anxious to fill any romantic void in Inga's life. It was her current complicated situation that made Jack so attractive. She told White, "Jack's an interesting man because he's so single-minded and simple to deal with. He knows what he wants. He's not confused about motives and those things. I find that refreshing. I like it—and furthermore I like him. But I wouldn't trust him as a long-term companion, obviously."

But that was her initial judgment. Against the backdrop of looming war, timeframes accelerated and senses were heightened. Inga had previously preferred older, more sophisticated men. Jack was "a wild new experience for her," White said. "She had never dealt with a naïve, spirited person like this." Inga recognized Jack as a man of limitless potential, but one who might need a helper to realize that potential.

So when Cissy Patterson, who had been charmed by Jack when he attended one of her dinner parties, told Inga, "Get an interview for your column with young Kennedy," Inga enthusiastically followed orders. Her profile of Jack ran in the *Times-Herald* on November 27, 1941:

> An old Scandinavian proverb says the apple doesn't fall far from the tree. No better American proof can be found than John F. Kennedy.
>
> If former Ambassador Joe Kennedy has a brilliant mind (not even his political enemies will deny the fact), charm galore, and a certain way of walking into the hearts of people with wooden shoes on,* then son No. 2 has inherited more than his due. The 24 years of Jack's existence on our planet have proved that here is really a boy with a future.
>
> Young Kennedy—don't call him that, he will resent it greatly—did more than boot the football about at Harvard. He was extremely popular. Graduated cum laude, was a class officer, sailed on the intercollegiate sailing team during his sophomore year, and most important, wrote a thesis.
>
> Arthur Krock from the *New York Times* read it and suggested it be put in a book. Henry Luce of *Time, Fortune* and *Life*, must have thought the same because he wrote the foreword, and by putting in 12 hours a day, cooled off with as many showers, Jack polished it off during the summer and the much praised book *Why England Slept* was the result. It sold like wildfire.
>
> "Yes, I certainly still have the same opinions as in the summer of 1940," says Jack Kennedy.
>
> "You must understand that the reason I did not editorialize was because nobody is going to listen to a boy of 23. Besides it was not the idea to say I, I, I. The book is based on facts, and I did a lot of studying in order to be able to write it. I couldn't say if I am going to write another book. Right now, I am in the Navy, that is the most important, but I have many plans for the future. Some day, when I have time, I am going to study law."
>
> Jack hates only one subject—himself. He is the best listener I have come across between Haparanda and Yokohama. Elder men like to hear his views, which are sound and astonishingly objective for so young a man.

---

*In saying that Joseph Kennedy wears wooden shoes, when clogs were the cheap footware of farmers and the working class, Inga means he has the common touch.

It was part of her genius in understanding people that Inga grasped the essential elements of Jack's character so quickly—his ambition, his identity being so entwined with his father's, his desire (like Inga) to hear other's views—even his fanaticism about cleanliness. Within just a few weeks, Inga understood Jack, as Jack himself would later note, better than most of his family members and long-time friends—perhaps even better than he knew himself.

She had learned a great deal about him, but Jack still knew little about Inga. Beyond knowing that she was married—a fact that did not diminish his ardor in the least—he was caught up in the moment. But soon, Inga's past would catch up with them both.

PART II
Inga before Jack

CHAPTER 12

"She had great ambitions for me"

"I WAS PUSHED INTO ADVENTURE BECAUSE MY MOTHER LOVES IT," INGA said in a 1937 interview she gave in Hong Kong while on what was supposed to be a two-year expedition in the Far East with her husband, Paul Fejos. Inga had only been in Asia a few months, but in that time she had toured Japan and Japanese-occupied China, lived among a tribe of headhunters, and now, while she rested in Hong Kong, Fejos was out capturing Komodo dragons for Scandinavian zoos.

But while Fejos had brought Inga to Asia, Inga acknowledged to the reporter that it was Olga Arvad who had driven her to such an exotic locale. Her mother, Inga said, was "restless, full of ideas . . . she had great ambitions for me—always wanted me to 'be' something." But if Olga was a stage mother where the stage was the world, the British reporter talking to Inga in Hong Kong concluded that Olga had done a splendid job. "There is so much to this girl," she wrote, "that one might almost regard that as an *embarrass de richesse*."

Inga claimed no resentment or regret about how Olga had sought to mold her into someone special. "I never look back," she said. For the first half of Inga's life, she and Olga were more than mother and daughter; they were best friends and co-conspirators. In letters, Olga addressed Inga as "my dearest little sausage" or "my little chickadee," while Inga cherished any word from her "Mumse-Wumse."

But Olga's devotion could also be suffocating. In that Hong Kong interview, Inga noted that it was her mother's idea, more than hers, that she seriously study dance and then piano. Such was Olga's influence that men pursuing Inga learned it was smart to spend as much time courting the mother as they did the daughter.

Olga had lost her first child and her husband to early deaths; now, Olga's life was all about Inga, and Inga, as much as she adored her mother, would eventually come to believe her life was too much about Olga. Olga had made so many decisions about her life that Inga once confided to Jack Kennedy, "I have never known what I really want. The other day somebody asked me and I was taken aback."

Inga was not ungrateful for all that Olga had done, acknowledging that she had been "spoilt" as a child, but quick to clarify that she was "never pampered"—an odd distinction. What Inga seems to have meant is that Olga constantly provided her with the opportunity for experiences denied most children, but these opportunities also required a great deal of rigor and discipline.

Inga had few playmates aside from her mother and little time to play for the sake of playing. Every activity had a purpose. Having learned to survive without a husband, Olga believed that Inga needed to learn how to be self-reliant; it was a goal that left Inga conflicted. She admired how her mother had managed as a widow, but Inga viewed life without a male provider as a greater hardship than her mother did. "But I don't want to be independent!" Inga said in that Hong Kong interview. "I want someone who can buy my train tickets and get me the corner seat."

It would be psychology on the cheap to conclude that Inga's lifelong attraction to (and for) talented and powerful men was rooted in the loss of a father she barely knew. But there is no doubt that the death of her father, Anton Margretus Petersen, when she was only four years old left a void that she repeatedly sought to fill. She missed not having a father, and more importantly understood how deeply her mother missed her husband. In fact, Inga believed she owed her existence to Olga's love for her father.

While pregnant with Inga, Olga was pressured by doctors to have an abortion because she was having a difficult pregnancy. "When I think of all the trouble mother had when she was carrying me and how she fought because the doctors wanted to get rid of me, I wonder why she didn't concent [*sic*]?" Inga once told Jack in a letter detailing her childhood. "I guess it was because she was so in love with Dad."

Petersen was the son of a lawyer and, according to Inga, her grandfather's favorite child, "extremely handsome with dark hair and very blue eyes," but also "a difficult boy . . . full of wit and brains." When Petersen's father died, Anton inherited an estate in the north of Denmark that had been in his family for generations and where he grew up "in the happy life of the moors of Denmark."

The Danish word for such a life is *hyggelige*, which can mean either "cozy" or "comfortable"; it happily contrasts the warm comforts of an upper-class home against the often cool and rainy Danish weather and the long nights and short days of wintertime. The pastimes of the Danish aristocracy were similar to those of the upper class in other countries: card games and horse races, sleighing parties, and bird shoots; costume balls and dancing to the latest music played on gramophones; and a good deal of sex with other people's partners to ward off the ennui of being upper class.

Many found it a pleasant life, but for others, which included Anton and Olga, it was pedestrian and suffocating. "The Danish character is like dough without leavening," complained the Danish writer Isak Dinesen, who came from the same social caste as Inga's parents. "All the ingredients which supply the taste and nourishment are there, but the element which makes the dough able to change, to rise, has been left out."

At twenty-one, Petersen was out walking when he spotted a "sparkling" redheaded girl of nineteen who was walking with her father, "a mysterious, but very rich man" named Sophus Houmann, who had left Denmark and made a fortune in England by patenting a new method of producing yeast in packets and distilling whiskey. Ever the romantic, Inga told Jack that Olga and Anton's meeting "was what is commonly known as love at first sight."

Olga was born in Denmark in 1878 and was still a toddler when the family moved to England, making English as much her native tongue as Danish. The Houmanns, who anglicized the spelling of their last name to Howmann, lived in Derby, but Olga regularly visited relatives in her birthplace and felt more Danish than English. Petersen, entranced by the girl with the "green eyes, which laughed all the time, mostly to the world, but now and then at it," as Inga described her, asked Howmann for permission to marry Olga the first summer they met, but Howmann had other ambitions for Olga and refused.

For the next four years, Anton and Olga corresponded while Anton managed his family's farm and studied to become an architect. Olga, meanwhile, studied medicine in England in order, allegedly, to become a doctor—a remarkable aspiration for a woman in the late nineteenth century and a testament to just how unconventional and strong-willed Olga was, although she did not complete her studies.

Then, as now, Scandinavia led the world in expanding the frontiers of sexual freedom and the place of women in society. An example of how Scandinavians were being challenged to see gender roles differently is the then-scandalous Björnstjerne Björnson play *A Gauntlet*, popular when Olga was young. In the play, a young woman refuses to marry her fiancé after learning he is not a virgin. Some misinterpreted Björnson as urging men to "save themselves" for marriage, but others understood his more subversive message that the burden of moral responsibility be equally shared by men and women.

It was in this spirit of a more equitable relationship between husband and wife that Olga and Anton began their life together, and it was this aspiration of equality in a male-female relationship that was absorbed by Inga.

Petersen and Olga were rejoined when Anton spent Christmas 1902 in England with friends. This time, with Anton now twenty-seven and Olga twenty-five, they asked no one's permission to marry and eloped on January 24, 1903. They honeymooned in South Africa with the intention of remaining there indefinitely, predating by a decade Dinesen's own escape from the *hyggelige* life to "a farm in Africa." Olga's brother, Albert, had immigrated to South Africa two years before but died there of complications from malaria. Olga was determined to find her brother's grave. It was a grim task for a honeymoon.

Shortly after arriving in Cape Town, Olga and Anton took a thousand-mile trip by ox cart to what is now Zimbabwe, but they never found Albert's grave. They remained in South Africa where Anton established a successful home construction business until he, too, contracted malaria. The couple returned to Anton's Denmark estate where he could receive treatment and recover. Shortly afterward, in 1906, Olga gave birth to their first child, a daughter given the hopeful name of Vita. But when Vita was only thirteen months old she died from blood poisoning, perhaps the result of being stuck with a dirty diaper pin.

The grief worsened Anton's condition, but even so, or perhaps *because* Olga realized she might not have Anton much longer, the couple decided to have another child. While on an extended trip to Rome, Olga became pregnant, and the couple returned to Copenhagen. Olga was thirty-five, but it may have been more the prospect of Anton soon leaving her a widow than a difficult pregnancy that led doctors to advise an abortion. Olga was determined to have a child with Anton, however, and Inga Marie Arvad Petersen was born on October 6, 1913. Arvad was a Petersen family name.

Inga was a fair-haired and happy child who liked to smile, but her mother found her "terribly stubborn." Inga recalled that her first spanking was "because I deliberately threw mother's new fountain pen on the floor." Inga had only vague memories of her father. Not only did Anton die when Inga was four, but while he was alive he was often gone for extended periods as he sought respite in hospitals and sanitariums. Even when he was at home he often seemed melancholy and lost in thought.

Still, Inga recalled being "very close" to her father, and that he was "sweet and utterly devoted to that little blonde imp of his." One night, when Olga had gone to the opera while Anton stayed in bed, Inga recalled being frightened by the dark and crawling into her father's bed where they cuddled until her mother came home. As Inga later acknowledged, these handful of memories were "not much, but it's something."

Far more vivid was the memory of the day her father died in 1917. At the funeral, Inga had the distinct impression of seeing her father hiding behind a curtain. Olga did not take Inga to the gravesite, but left her home with a nurse. Inga remembered her mother coming back home alone, dressed "all in black," and crying. "I told her, 'Don't cry, you have got me.'"

CHAPTER 13

"An odd bird"

SHORTLY AFTER ANTON PETERSEN'S DEATH IN 1917, OLGA VOWED IN her diary that she would raise Inga to be someone special and to help her marry well. This would be her primary mission in life. A widow now nearly forty, Olga had no intention of remarrying. Inga would be Olga's only child and the focus of all her hopes and dreams.

Just as she and Anton had done to deal with his illness, Olga now traveled with Inga in tow to deal with her grief, as if loneliness was something that could be outrun. Extensive travel also fit in with Olga's plans for molding Inga into an exceptional woman.

It may seem odd that Olga would travel with a young girl while much of Europe was convulsed by war, but an absurdity of the Great War was that while millions of men were dying in the trenches, life went on more or less normally just a few miles from the front. A sign above a British newsstand captured this bizarre duality in March 1917:

BATTLE RAGING AT YPRES
GATWICK RACING—LATE WIRE

Denmark was officially neutral during the war, but its proximity to Germany meant that Danes went out of their way to avoid antagonizing their powerful neighbor. Danes tolerated Germany mining their waters to protect against a British amphibious attack, and Denmark provided resources to take care of prisoners of war held in Germany (and elsewhere) to relieve the bankrupted combatants of the expense and to ensure decent treatment of the captured soldiers.

It is possible that the chaos and misery Inga saw in Germany near the end of the war and in the bitter peace that followed at least partially explains her later initial positive assessment of the Nazis, who superficially seemed to bring order and plenty to Germany.

For four years after Anton's death, Inga and her mother traveled relentlessly through England, France, Germany, Italy, and Switzerland. They climbed the Alps, rode donkeys in the south of France, and enjoyed high teas at a series of fine hotels. Olga dragged little Inga from one museum or castle to another, expounding on local history and culture.

Inga already spoke English and Danish; she now learned German and French. But the more important lesson for Inga was how to be comfortable being in motion, adapting to different places and different cultures, and living with a certain amount of chaos. The constant travel also seemed to have impressed upon Inga how desirable it would be to someday have a stable home.

Inga especially enjoyed her time in Paris, where she made one of her few childhood friends, a young Danish girl aptly named France Ellegaard, who was in the city to study piano. When Inga heard France play at a recital (Ellegaard would go on to have a distinguished career as a concert pianist), Inga vowed to also learn to play.* She envied that little France had two parents and that she went home to the same place every night. Inga was exhausted by all the travel, and so in 1921, just before her eighth birthday, Inga and Olga returned to Denmark where Inga began to attend school. Travel, however, was a feature of every ensuing summer vacation.

At first, Olga and Inga settled in the small town of Fyn, located just outside Denmark's third-largest city, Odense, where Olga had family. For

---

*Like Inga, France Ellegaard's reputation was sullied during the war. Ellegaard was a renowned concert pianist while still in her teens, performing across Europe and noted for her interpretations of Chopin and Rimsky-Korsakov. When Nazi Germany occupied Denmark, Ellegaard was compelled to perform in Berlin as Danish artists were forced to collaborate with German cultural activities. In 1943, Ellegaard was allowed to travel to neutral Sweden, where she remained for the duration of the war. When she attempted to return to Denmark after the war, she found she stood accused of being a Nazi collaborator and was unwelcome. She married a Finnish artist and taught at the Sibelius Academy. She died in Finland in 1999.

five years, Inga attended the Elizabeth Detlefsen Girls School, but at thirteen Olga and Inga moved to Copenhagen where Inga was enrolled in a prestigious Danish school for girls, Ingrid Jespersen School, which featured such unconventional areas of study (at least for girls) as wood-working, which was taught by a woman.

Somewhat like Olga, Jespersen was an early feminist who believed women should be on equal footing with men in the workforce, and her goal was to produce graduates who were independent and who did not need to rely on men to thrive.

While nowhere near as austere as the convent schools attended by Kathleen Kennedy, Jespersen stressed discipline and hard work. Chemistry and physics were part of the curriculum, and were taught with the same rigor as they would have been at a boys' school. Inga's favorite subject, taught by Jespersen herself, was writing. Inga was a good student, but her classmates said the decision to have Inga skip a grade was made by Olga, not the faculty.

Already more mature than most of her classmates from her incessant travels, the change in grade made it even more difficult for Inga to make any close friends within the school. "She was an odd bird," one of her classmates recalled. "It was her mother who was ambitious on her behalf, at least that's how the talk went."

Inga completed all the coursework at Jespersen but skipped taking the graduate examination and so did not officially earn her diploma. Later in America, when she was asked about her academic background, rather than list Jespersen School, which she probably assumed no one in the United States had heard of, she listed her alma mater as Wimbledon High School in London, another all-girls school where she had studied only briefly but which she thought sounded more prestigious to Anglophilic American ears.

Since everything in Inga's life was in flux, it is not shocking that Olga decided that the pair should even legally change their surname. She and Inga filed the required court papers, and on March 22, 1928, they were granted their request to drop Anton's last name, Petersen, and legally change their last name to Arvad.

Why they took this step is not clear, particularly since it severed a tie to Olga's beloved late husband. Nor did Inga ever say whether she approved of the change or not. Given just how close Olga desired to be with Inga, perhaps it seemed one more way for mother to bond with daughter by creating their own distinct family, separated from an unhappy past. Perhaps it was the strongest symbol they could produce to demonstrate that by choosing what they would be called they would be masters of their fate and creators of their own identity.

Perhaps they also found the meaning of the name appealing. Arvad is a Hebrew word, not Danish. It appears in Ezekiel 27:8, and it can mean either "in exile" or "wanderer," the latter a particularly apt designation for the nomadic Inga and Olga. Of course, it was also short, sounded good with "Inga," and was less common than Petersen.

Olga's relationship with Inga has parallels with Joseph Kennedy's relationship with his children, including Jack, which may have been one more factor why Inga and Jack were so attracted to each other. Just as Kennedy did with his children, Olga pushed Inga to try new things and to excel at those she tried. Beginning at age eleven, Inga studied dance at the Royal Theater in Copenhagen. Inga said her instructors told her that she had the potential to be the "next Pavlova," the legendary Russian ballerina.

Inga was good at ballet, but apparently did not have the drive to be the best, so she abandoned dance as a possible career and, inspired by France Ellegaard, instead studied piano under the renowned Danish pianist Max Rytter, a regular soloist at the Royal Chapel and a recording artist who especially enjoyed promoting the works of young Danish composers.

Inga showed considerable promise as a pianist. With Rytter's recommendation, her intention was to continue her music studies in Paris, having been accepted at the Paris Conservatoire to study under France Ellegaard's teacher, Santiago Riéra, one of the world's leading experts on Chopin. Inga even thought she had found a way to pay for her and her mother's travel expenses to Paris by entering a beauty contest. That decision, however, radically changed the trajectory of her life.

CHAPTER 14

"The family would have a fit"

CONSIDERED SEXIST BY MANY TODAY, BEAUTY PAGEANTS IN 1931 WERE rather a sign that women were not bound by old conventions. The modern beauty pageant began after the Great War, coincidental with a time when women were winning new rights and freedoms. The first Miss America pageant, for example, was held in 1921—the year after American women had won the right to vote. Danish women had won that right six years before.

Beauty pageants were a new and even radical expression of female sexuality. The female figure was no longer to be hidden under layers and layers of clothing as in Victorian times, but to be celebrated along with the notion of a woman as a sensual being who did not simply endure sexual intimacy but enjoyed it. This new attitude was mirrored in films, where vamps such as Theda Bara proved at least as popular as innocents played by Mary Pickford.

Denmark's largest daily newspaper, Copenhagen's *Berlingske Tidende*, had sponsored beauty pageants since 1920. In January 1931, when Inga was seventeen, she read that the newspaper was seeking contestants for that year's Miss Denmark contest, with the winner to compete in the Miss Europe pageant the following month in Paris. As a cousin noted, Inga was already planning a trip to Paris to pursue her piano studies: Why not enter the competition, win, and have her trip paid for by the newspaper?

Inga hesitated, aware of how daring the older generation considered beauty pageants. "The family would have a fit," she said, but added that her mother would approve "because she's such an adventurer and finds fun in anything, but the rest, they will just lie down and die of shame."

The competition was open to "any unmarried, Danish-born woman of impeccable reputation" between the ages of sixteen and twenty-five. Entry was simple. For the first round, contestants only had to submit a photograph. No contestant was required to list her measurements or provide other personal information. Where many of the submitted photographs show the contestant peeking shyly at the camera, Inga posed differently. She was in profile with a "serious, slightly dreamy gaze" as she glances over her shoulder. Only seventeen, she cast an air of sophistication. She was among nearly one hundred entrants chosen to compete in the pageant.

Unlike modern pageants, there was little to the Miss Denmark competition. The contestants all wore evening gowns (Inga was in pink chiffon), and they simply paraded before the judges multiple times. "All that was asked [was] that the girls assembled, about thirty or more, marched over a stage several times, turned around, and came back to the point of departure," Inga recalled. Inga did not get to display what might have been some of her stronger assets in a more modern-style competition, for there were no questions about world events and no talent or swimsuit competitions.

The goal, as Inga noted, was only to appear "lovely." The judges, a group of well-known Danish artists, sculptors, and dance masters, made it sound somewhat more exacting; they were seeking, they said, the young woman who best embodied the notion of classical beauty. They chose Inga.

While, as Inga expected, her mother was pleased by her surprise win, Inga's aunts and other relatives were dismayed. Interviewed by *Berlingske Tidende*, Inga said her aspiration was to study piano in Paris, but that could wait while she competed in the third annual Miss Europe competition. She and her mother left for Paris on January 30, 1931. It was probably not apparent at the time, but this journey represented a sharp reversal in roles between mother and daughter. Olga had once taken Inga all over the world; from now on, it would be Inga who would lead Olga on new adventures.

Inga and the other sixteen contestants for Miss Europe were treated as celebrities in Paris. Inga and her mother, as well as a traveling correspondent for *Berlingske Tidende*, were housed with the other contestants in the renowned Hotel Claridge on the Champs-Élysées. Before the pageant, Inga and the other contestants were honored guests at Paris's most elegant annual charity ball, the *Bal des Petits Lits Blanc* ("the small white beds ball") for local children's hospitals, which was held at the Palais Garnier, the famous Paris opera house.

The president of France attended, but the real stars of the event were the notorious bisexual author Colette, dressed in slacks, who served as master of ceremonies, and the scandalous, nearly nude performance by the African American dancer and cultural sensation Josephine Baker. Women were asserting themselves more forcefully in many fields, but sexuality was still the clearest path to notoriety.

Inga had no desire to be sexually notorious, but she hoped the pageant would open the door to opportunities that otherwise might have remained a daydream. The *Berlingske Tidende* reporter asked Inga what she would do if she were to win the Miss Europe pageant. "It has . . . always been my hope to be in the movies," Inga replied, "and even if I don't win in Paris I hope that my 'Beauty Queen' title will be a jumping off point into the promised riches of filmdom."

Fonnesbech, at the time Copenhagen's leading dress salon, provided Inga with an evening gown she found "fit for a queen." It was made of a fabric the reporter for *Berlingske Tidende* described as "phosphorous crepe . . . a new material, that is shiny and soft like satin crepe, but with an even warmer cut." The dress was low-cut with small bows on the shoulders and had a twenty-foot train. The effect, the newspaper said, was "bewitching and fine."

While her fellow contestants did not intimidate her, she knew winning the competition would be difficult. She was particularly impressed by Miss Russia, a stunning near-albino with "huge" gray eyes who was the daughter of the famous Russian opera singer Feodor Chaliapin. Mildly scandalous in Denmark, Inga seemed demure in Paris. While other contestants wore dresses short enough to show some leg, Inga's dress was floor length. Despite her many travels, one of those who saw her compete said she conveyed more the healthy look of a farm girl than of a worldly sophisticate.

Inga did not win. That honor went to local favorite Miss France, Jeanne Juilla, a statuesque brunette from Gascony. But Inga was also a local favorite. With her flawless French, she was often selected among the several contestants to be interviewed on French radio. She was also offered money to appear in a French commercial for skin cream and to "perform"—actually, just walking across stage looking pretty and displaying her 35–18–34 figure in evening dress, Inga said—at the famous Parisian cabaret Follies Bergère—opportunities she declined.

Her popularity was such that, even though she was not one of the runners-up in the competition, she accepted an offer to join Miss Europe and three other contestants on a tour of southern France, Algeria, and Morocco. For the tour, Inga adopted a more sophisticated and mature look, less farm and more femme. Her dresses were shorter, and they were form fitting to accentuate her lithe figure. At each stop, the beauty queens were feted with extravagant dinners, received expensive gifts, and were introduced to the rich and famous of Europe, who were wintering on the sunny Riviera. Inga was thrilled to be presented while in Cannes to Denmark's King Christian X and Queen Alexandrine.

Yet overall, she later insisted, she found "all this luxury and constant festivity . . . boring." Perhaps it was because her mind was preoccupied with bigger decisions than whether to wear diamonds or pearls; she was considering a proposal of marriage she had received while in Paris from an Egyptian nobleman.

CHAPTER 15

"He was jealous, I was jealous, but life was gay"

DURING ONE OF THE MANY RECEPTIONS SURROUNDING THE MISS Europe competition, a strikingly handsome, dark-haired, and almond-complexioned man approached Inga, bowed, took her hand, and kissed it with the query, "Miss Denmark, will you accept homage from an Egyptian?" His name was Kamal Abdel Nabi. At twenty-two, he was five years older than Inga and a student of political science at the École Libre des Sciences Politiques with plans for a diplomatic career. He and Inga waltzed at the reception under Olga's watchful eye.

Nabi was the heir of an Egyptian bey and claimed he could trace his ancestry back to the Prophet Mohammed. His father owned large tracts of land along the Nile River and was a prominent figure within Egypt's nationalist Wafd Party. Inga was intrigued.

Pageant rules forbade the contestants from going on private dates during the competition, but Inga said she found Nabi's "natural elegance masculine and dazzling" and ignored the rule. She accepted Nabi's invitation to have a picnic the next day, with Olga as chaperone, at the Bois de Boulogne, where they took a horseback ride through the massive park and botanic gardens located on the western edge of Paris. At the end of the ride, Nabi proposed. Inga blushed and put him off. She had received other proposals of marriage, from a schoolboy back in Denmark who sent her a postcard of the country church where he hoped they would marry, and another as recently as the week before from an enamored cadet at the

Saint-Cyr military academy. But those proposals were from boys and hardly seemed serious; Nabi, however, was.

There were now unchaperoned dates, more horseback riding, boating, and dinner at Maxim's. "Fontainebleau [forest] looked more enchanting with him, the Left Bank more bohemian," Inga recalled.

While in the south of France with the other Miss Europe contestants, Inga had time to think, and all she could think about was Nabi—even though, by many measures, the match made no sense. She was only seventeen (her mother had been twenty-five when she married). Further, she had the remarkable opportunity to study music under one of the great piano teachers of the time. And then there were the religious and cultural differences. Inga was nominally Christian, though she seldom attended church, and while Nabi lived a very secularized life at the time, his family was devoutly Muslim.

Remarkably, despite these impediments, Olga did not oppose the marriage; in fact, she became quite enthusiastic about the match. Nabi, whose surname* in Arabic means "prophet," saw the intensity of the mother-daughter relationship, and so he courted Olga as assiduously as he courted Inga. He regularly invited Olga to join him and Inga for concerts and trips to the theater, and then flattered her for her own charms and for those she had instilled in her daughter.

Olga began to believe that being the wife of a diplomat was exactly the wonderful and useful life she had planned for Inga. With her mother as a guide, Inga had seen most of Europe and understood the various cultures and histories. Given that she already spoke four languages fluently, it was easy for both mother and daughter to imagine Inga hobnobbing with world leaders and hosting diplomatic receptions, using her charm to help her husband shape global affairs.

Perhaps most important, Nabi *seemed* wealthy, an important factor because Olga's inheritance, assets, and income had taken a hit with the onset of the Great Depression. The goal of making Inga independent took a backseat to making a match that ensured financial stability for both

---

* His given name, *Kamal*, means "perfection."

women. Sadly, they would soon discover Nabi's wealth was a mirage in the Sahara.

But there was no time for background checks. Whatever misgivings Inga had, she found Nabi irresistibly beautiful and the prospect of a cosmopolitan existence delightful. Nabi was no love-struck Danish schoolboy but a man of the world, and he adored Inga. On April 16, 1931, barely two months after they met, Inga married Nabi in a ceremony at the Egyptian Embassy in Paris.

They spent their wedding night at the Hotel George V in Paris, and whatever urbane front Inga displayed to the world melted away with the anxiety typical of any teen bride crossing that sexual Rubicon for the first time. Nabi was "gentle and sweet" and "obviously terribly in love" with his wife, Inga recalled, and the champagne and lamb chops they had for dinner were delicious. "All the time my barely 17 years made me feel that I was doing something 'wrong,'" Inga later recalled. "There was no chaperone, and I was ill at ease."

After this first tremulous night together, Inga and Nabi honeymooned in the south of France, visiting many of Inga's favorite places. Inga was denied entry to the casino at Monte Carlo because those in charge did not believe she, a young Danish teenager, was married to the suave Egyptian; Olga had to send their marriage license by express post as proof. The honeymoon ended with Inga contracting the measles on their way back to Paris, and so, Inga said, "We somehow came down to earth and married life started."

To their dismay, Inga and Olga quickly discovered that Nabi's family's wealth was in land, not cash. Nabi worked hard both at his studies and at his job at the embassy, but the pay was low and the couple were not used to economizing. They constantly fended off creditors, with Nabi dashing out of their apartment's back door while Inga delayed the collectors at the front door. Olga ended up largely supporting her daughter and new son-in-law. "Mother paid the bills," Inga said. "I hated it."

Inga complained that Nabi, being handsome, brilliant, and of high birth, was "spoilt by women," and not just by her mother. She recalled an incident when "[a] woman artist looked at him and said, 'May I paint you?' and I answered quickly, 'Well, we can always put it in the bathroom.'"

Inga also had her own admirers, which displeased Nabi. "He was jealous, I was jealous," Inga recalled, "but life was gay. There always seemed to be some elegant party going on. We were favorite guests [one] so dark, so handsome, [the other] so blonde, so fragile, like extra flowers in a vase we moved from one extravaganza to the other."

Inga's healthy attitude toward sex may be partially credited to Nabi, whom Inga described as a "tender, experienced, wonderful lover." This pleasure, however, was "somewhat ruined" by her mother, who, in one of her most bizarre intrusions into Inga's life, kept track of how often Inga and Nabi made love. Perhaps Olga was anxious for grandchildren or worried about Inga's relative youth and inexperience, but Inga said Olga would make note each morning of whether it appeared Inga or Nabi had gotten up to enjoy a postcoital snack in the kitchen. For perhaps the first time in her life, Inga began to imagine life without Olga constantly by her side.

Inga's interest in Nabi and Nabi's in Inga was not all sensual, however. There was also a strong intellectual component. Inga labored to help Nabi complete the examinations necessary to obtain his diplomatic credentials, which in turn led to intense discussions on world affairs. Presaging her relationship with Kennedy, Inga said she often got up early and stayed up late to listen to Nabi "extolling on the economics of the world—we hadn't gone off the gold standard yet."

After his graduation from the École Libre des Sciences Politiques, Nabi worked for the Egyptian Foreign Service, first in Brussels and then in London. But after a year, he decided he wanted to go home to Egypt, deferring Inga's dreams of hosting important diplomatic receptions. With Olga in tow, Inga finally met her father-in-law, Mahmud Bey Abdel Nabi, the title "bey" indicating that he was an important local magistrate. Her father-in-law was, Inga recalled many years later, "the most imposing man I have ever laid eyes on," a remarkable assessment given the powerful men she would know. Nabi's father spoke neither English nor French, but Inga was grateful to see approval in his eyes. At their meeting, she had worn a demure full-length gray dress with a high collar and long sleeves to signal her intent to respect the more conservative customs of her new home. Yet while initially fascinated with Egyptian history and culture, and just how new and exotic the experience seemed, Inga could not accommodate herself to this new world. "It was too different, too foreign," she said.

It was a different life, certainly, but far from deprived. Inga was allowed to choose the couple's home and selected "a beautiful place right on the edge of the desert" in the affluent Cairo suburb of Maadi that was popular with many European expatriates. Her father-in-law put a Mercedes-Benz and driver at her disposal, and she had a half-dozen servants to keep house. People were cheap in 1930s Egypt, but other things were not. "We lived like millionaires," Inga recalled, "but hadn't got the cash to pay for the resoling of a pair of shoes." Just as in Paris, creditors lined up outside the front door, and Inga grew tired of telling lies to send them away.

CHAPTER 16

"East is East and West is West"

THE PROVERBIAL STRANGER IN A STRANGE LAND, INGA REALIZED ONCE she was in Egypt that she should have listened to her inner doubts when weighing whether to marry Nabi. Despite her father-in-law's graciousness, Inga said she never felt fully accepted. In an interview she gave a few years after she left Nabi, she told the Danish magazine *Vore Damer* ("Our Ladies") that she knew many of Nabi's family members considered it "a great and indelible shame" that Nabi had chosen to marry a European Christian instead of a nice Muslim girl. Inga believed even her father-in-law, despite his superficial kindness, "almost couldn't recover from the wound his son gave him by committing such a blunder."

Most of the Egyptian women Inga knew were wives of the aristocracy and lived a life of luxury similar to her own, but "all lit up . . . by diamonds." Inga complained that while running a large household was "fun in the beginning," she soon found a life of luxury to be "an empty life [that] simply isn't bearable." She was heartened to learn that some of the Egyptian women felt the same.

Many upper-class Egyptian women had been educated in Europe, Inga discovered, and Nabi himself had a female cousin who ran a school in India. These women had been active in the struggle for Egyptian independence from Great Britain that had been granted in 1922, barely a decade before.

Inga became fascinated with the growing women's movement in Egypt, which was aimed not only at improving the lot of women but also the poor, for as Inga noted, there was no middle class in Egypt in the

1930s, only the few rich and the many poor. And although the status of women in Egypt bothered Inga, the status of the lower "fellah" peasant class disturbed her more.

Inga noted most fellahs "can't even afford to eat to fullness," and were treated no better and often worse than animals. A writer from the United States could think of only one comparison that might resonate with American readers: "The Egyptian peasant lives very much after the manner of the old-fashioned Southern Negro of our cotton plantations."

One day, Inga recalled for *Vore Damer*, she and Nabi were driving through the countryside when they came upon a peasant and his animals blocking the road. Nabi's chauffer jumped out of the car and began to beat the peasant with a cane. Nabi was amused when an enraged Inga jumped out of the car, knocked the cane from the chauffer's hand, then picked it up and began to beat the chauffer. Her husband's bemused attitude unsettled Inga. "I had missed the truth of Kipling's words," she later said. "East is East—and West is West."

Probably through a combination of idealism and boredom, Inga, now nineteen, decided to join the struggle and try her hand at journalism. Nabi, still very secular in his outlook and proud of his wife's intellect, encouraged her writing. "There is one thing I ask of you and it is most essential," Nabi told her. "In writing about foreign countries and especially oriental nations, European writers in their zeal to amuse, to thrill, or amaze their [readers] have such a disrespect for truth. They seek in their own imagination things that never existed and they are usually under the impression that a book written about these far countries should contain funny and unusual things. They forget that if they write the exact truth they will obtain a far better result."

Nabi offered several story ideas, such as translating traditional Egyptian fables that would make "awfully nice" short stories, or perhaps an essay on the lives of Egyptian villagers. He warned Inga about tackling anything "very serious—I mean [that] would have a regular criticism of the social order in Egypt." Inga ignored that warning and authored an article on the fledgling women's movement in Egypt. As Nabi no doubt predicted, she was unable to find a publisher for the piece in Egypt—or abroad.

Inga then tried selling a personality profile she wrote on German film comedian Willy Fritsch, who was in Egypt to make the movie *Season in Cairo*. She found no publisher for that, either, though Fritsch, taken with Inga's beauty and personality, suggested she consider a career in film if she were ever to return to Europe. The idea of returning to Europe—and finally trying her hand at films, a dream she had expressed while competing in the Miss Denmark contest—grew on Inga.

It was not an easy decision. Egypt was a fascinating place, and she still admired Nabi and did not want to humiliate him with a divorce. A Christmas card Inga had written to her old school principal, Ingrid Jespersen, demonstrated her ambiguity. In her greeting, Inga raved to Jespersen about the "wonderland" where she now lived—but then she never mailed the card.

Discouraged, bored, claustrophobic, and now aware that her husband's "ethics were different from mine," Inga schemed with her mother and an uncle, who was an attorney in Denmark, to get out of Egypt. Under Egyptian law with its limited rights for women, Inga could not leave the country without her husband's permission, and Nabi had no desire to grant a divorce. When Inga came down with pneumonia (so she said), her uncle and some sympathetic doctors advised Nabi that Inga could only receive the treatment she needed in Davos, Switzerland.

Inga had promised Nabi she would return, but she never did. Nabi was anguished. In words that Inga would use a few years later regarding her relationship with Jack Kennedy, Nabi told Inga, "I am perfectly dead inside I feel it so." He begged her to consider returning to him. "Don't take . . . that hope from me," he wrote. "It is my only reason to live for now. . . . If God will allow it I might yet try and make [you] happy had I to give up everything."

Even when it was clear Inga was not coming back, Nabi refused to finalize the divorce in his own mind by uttering, as required under Islamic law, "I divorce thee" three times. When Inga's and Nabi's paths crossed again, decades later, Nabi insisted they were still married, even though Nabi, by this time having served as one of Egypt's most important and influential ambassadors, had another wife.

After a brief stopover in Switzerland to maintain the ruse, Inga returned to Denmark, where she reclaimed her Danish citizenship and officially obtained a divorce, at least under Danish law, in January 1933, less than two years after she had wed Nabi. She and Olga again settled in Copenhagen. When a local journalist asked Inga if she felt Danish again, Inga said yes but with this qualifier: "All my life . . . I've spent a lot of time abroad, and therefore I almost feel cosmopolitan, feel like I'm everything and nothing. I am quite adaptable and will be capable of fitting in everywhere." Over the next decade, Inga would repeatedly demonstrate the truth of that self-assessment.

CHAPTER 17

"You are either crazy or you're a genius!"

AT HER AND OLGA'S APARTMENT ON COPENHAGEN'S FASHIONABLE Store Kongensgade thoroughfare, Inga decorated their dwelling with Oriental carpets and other Egyptian curios, but otherwise left her life with Nabi behind. The question now was: What to do next, and what would it pay?

There had been no divorce settlement from Nabi. Because of the market crash, Olga had only a small income from her inheritance. Inga stood to inherit a trust account of roughly $5,000, but even during the Depression that would only go so far.

Remarriage, perhaps this time to a wealthy Dane, was apparently not discussed as an option. Olga continued her push to make Inga independent, and Inga's romantic nature would not have allowed her to marry for money anyway. And so far, she had not met anyone with whom she had fallen in love. Inga needed to find a job and an income.

While none of her work was published in Egypt, Inga felt drawn to journalism. It matched her curious nature, and she enjoyed writing. She also still had dreams of breaking into films. While she had never acted, she had performed, first as a budding ballerina and later as a nascent concert pianist. She recalled the encouragement she received in Cairo from Willy Fritsch, who as the veteran of nearly fifty films must have had some sense of potential talent.* Fortunately for Inga, the Danish film

---

*Unlike his most frequent costar, Lillian Harvey, Fritsch never went to Hollywood. However, he has his share of American fans. The 2009 Quentin Tarantino film *Inglourious Basterds* features a recording of Fritsch and Harvey performing the musical number *Ich wollt'*

industry was seeking to revitalize itself by luring proven international talent to work in Denmark.

Without the barrier of language, silent films made in many different countries found a global audience. Denmark's Nordisk Film, established in 1906 and still the oldest continually operating film studio in the world, had produced a large number of silent films that proved popular around the globe, including in the United States through its U.S. distribution company, The Great Northern Film Company.

But the advent of sound, coupled with the effects of the Great Depression, had caused the studio's fortunes to decline. Danish financier Carl Bauder took over the studio in 1929, injected some needed cash into the enterprise, and decreed Nordisk would again be an international player by bringing in established foreign talent to especially make comedies, which Bauder believed would be easier to market globally.

On the recommendation of a Swedish film producer, one of the directors Bauder recruited to Denmark was a Hungarian American director named Paul Fejos, whom no less an authority than Charlie Chaplin had declared a "genius."

Fejos was one of many artists who left Central Europe before and after the Great War to reinvent themselves and their pasts in other countries. Like the director and actor Erich von Stroheim, who was the son of a Viennese hat maker but added the "von" to his name on the pretense he was an Austrian count, Fejos, too, exhibited "a stubborn refusal to be contained by anything so prosaic as facts."

Born in Budapest in 1897, making him sixteen years older than Inga, Fejos said that his father was an official in the Imperial Court; his father was, in fact, a pharmacist. Fejos also claimed that during the war he had been an officer in the famed Hussars cavalry unit and a pioneering fighter pilot, assertions that one biographer noted, "all seem to be more interesting than accurate." Fejos, who had briefly studied medicine, was a medical orderly on the Italian front, where, reflecting his true interests, he organized a theater company to entertain the troops.

---

ich wär' ein Huhn ("I Wish I Was a Chicken") from the 1936 film *Glückskinder*, which was a German musical comedy remake of the American film *It Happened One Night*.

Fejos's great love was theater and films. He never seems to have become, despite his later claims, a doctor, and instead abandoned his medical studies after the war to become a set painter, first for the Budapest Opera and then for a small local Hungarian film company that also gave him the opportunity to direct some shorts. Hungary was at the time a major center of international film, producing such noted directors as Alexander Korda and Michael Curtiz.

In 1923, already once married and divorced (his first wife accused him of "irrational jealousy"), Fejos left Budapest for Vienna, where he worked under Max Reinhardt, the Austrian stage director known for his innovative productions of Shakespeare. Then, in rapid succession, Fejos moved to Berlin, where he worked as an extra in some Fritz Lang films, and then to Paris, where he staged an avant-garde play that flopped. By late 1923, he decided to try his luck in America, arriving in New York in October of that year.

Penniless, he held a variety of odd jobs, including in a funeral parlor and a piano factory, before falling back on his medical training to gain work as a laboratory technician for the Rockefeller Institute where, allegedly, exposure to radium left him sterile. He married a coworker named Mimosa Pfalz, but the marriage reportedly lasted only thirty days, another victim of Fejos's temper. He also volunteered at the Theater Guild, where he advised how to evoke Budapest in a production of Molnar's play *The Glass Slipper*.

But Fejos was just killing time in New York while he improved his English and saved enough money to travel to Hollywood. Spending his entire savings—$45—on an ancient Buick, Fejos drove cross-country and arrived in California once again penniless. He lived as a vagabond, sometimes surviving only by hitchhiking to Pasadena to steal oranges from groves there. By remarkable chance, one person who gave Fejos a lift was Edward Spitz, a wealthy young New Yorker who had come to Hollywood with $10,000 from his father and dreams of becoming a film producer.

Spitz was overwhelmed by Fejos's patter and vision for what film could do, and by Fejos's pledge that he could make a great film with a miniscule amount of money. Fejos lectured Spitz that most filmmakers did not understand that film was far more about creating arresting images than telling a story, that cinema was "closer to painting than the theater." Nor, Fejos argued, did most directors understand that one of the great assets of film is that the filmmaker can play with time. "I told [Spitz] that I would like to make a story which had happened during an impossibly short time," Fejos recalled. "He said, 'How short?' I said, 'A second, a fraction of a second.' He looked at me and said, 'You are either crazy or you're a genius!'"

Spitz gave the suave and persuasive hitchhiker $5,000 to make his first Hollywood film—an amount equal to about 1 percent of the budget for a typical major motion picture of the day. Twenty-eight days later, in October 1927, having used existing sets, rented studio space not by the day but by the minute, and getting friends and complete strangers to act for free, Fejos completed *The Last Moment*, the story of a suicide victim who sees his life in a series of flashbacks as he drowns. In a coup, Fejos used the charm that made so many women become his wife to convince one of Charlie Chaplin's favorite actresses, Georgia Hale, star of *The Gold Rush*, to appear in his film without payment. Hale's usual salary was $5,000 per week.

No surviving copy of *The Last Moment* has been found, but those who saw it declared it visually stunning. Lauded by Chaplin and many others, Fejos was compared to German expressionist filmmaker F. W. Murnau, when he was not being compared with Ernst Lubitsch. Following a bidding war for his services, Fejos signed a contract with Universal because the studio agreed to give him complete control over his next picture.

His first movie for Universal, 1928's *Lonesome*, is considered his best, one of the genuine classics of the late silent film period.* A tender love story, *Lonesome* follows a young couple who live in the same apartment building but don't know each other until they meet by chance during a Sunday trip to Coney Island and fall in love. Separated in the bustle of the crowd, they are devastated to have lost this chance at love until they are reunited in the final scene, having finally realized they are next-door

---

* *Lonesome*'s reputation has continued to grow over the years. The Criterion Collection released *Lonesome* and two other Fejos films (*The Last Performance* and *Broadway*) on DVD in 2012.

neighbors. One of the title cards captures the film's theme: "In the whirl-pool of modern life—the most difficult thing is to live alone."

Lonesome was Fejos's Hollywood peak. He made several other films, silent and sound, and most were well received. He became angry, however, when he lost his bid to direct *All Quiet on the Western Front*, and instead was tasked, now by MGM, with directing French- and German-language versions of that year's popular prison drama *The Big House*—versions some said were superior to George Hill's original.*

Fejos had soured on Hollywood. There, he complained, films were an industry, not an art form. "I found Hollywood phony," Fejos ironically recalled many years later. He had particularly harsh words for studio writers, whom he denigrated as "utterly uneducated, stupid hacks." But perhaps his most telling comment, which revealed much about his personality, had Fejos explaining, "I had fallen out of love with Hollywood."

He had also fallen out of love with actress Barbara Kent, the petite star of *Lonesome* who began dating her director when he was thirty and she was seventeen. As his most sympathetic biographer noted, Fejos "had a habit" of falling in love with his leading ladies, and that "his favorite girls were always young." When an affair ended, the restless Fejos was ready to move on.

In 1931, Fejos returned to Hungary, where he made two films with the beautiful, dark-eyed French actress who used only the single stage name Annabella. Annabella was a twenty-five-year-old widow at the time, and Fejos, true to form, fell madly in love with her. When filming wrapped and Annabella was on her way home to France, Fejos piloted a plane over her train and "showered it with roses." Despite this gesture, Annabella married a French actor named Jean Murat in 1934, and Fejos was again ready to move on, this time to accept Nordisk's offer to make films in Denmark.†

---

*Fejo's French version of *The Big House* costarred Charles Boyer in his first role in Hollywood.

†In 1937, single once again, Annabella went to Hollywood, made several well-regarded films, and married Tyrone Power.

CHAPTER 18

"Almost a fiasco"

FEJOS, THE DIRECTOR WHO BELIEVED FILM WAS ALL ABOUT IMAGE, NOT words, authored the screenplay for his first Nordisk film, titled *Flugten Fra Millionerne* ("Millions in Flight"). It was a screwball comedy in which two young socialites must pretend to be in love and marry in order to secure a large inheritance.* But on the day filming was scheduled to begin, Danish newspapers reported that Fejos was still without an actress to play the leading role of Lillian. Fejos told the press he had even taken to walking the streets of Copenhagen in hopes he might stumble across the perfect candidate for the role.

Inga read of Fejos's dilemma and realized this was her chance to break into film. When it came to pursuing happiness, "I had always acted quickly," Inga said. "Just a few minutes later I had put myself in touch with Dr. Fejos [*sic*], who auditioned me that same day."

Fejos was overwhelmed by Inga's beauty, but he was even more excited to learn that she spoke English, French, and German, for Fejos planned to dub the film for foreign markets and having the same actress involved in all the versions would simplify the process. After a short screen test, he hired Inga on the spot. Cast as the male lead was the handsome Danish actor Erling Schroeder, but the sparks on the set were not between Inga and Schroeder but between Inga and Fejos.

In the early days of film, with the star system in full force, actors and

---

* The plot from *Flugten Fra Millionerne* was borrowed for the 2008 film *What Happens in Vegas* that starred Ashton Kutcher and Cameron Diaz. The remake was poorly received, too.

directors seemed to believe their own lives needed to be as large as those they projected on thirty-foot-high screens. As he had with Annabella, when he aerially dropped roses upon her departing train, Fejos sought to win over Inga with extravagant gestures.

Fejos shot a good deal of the movie aboard the Danish ocean liner *Stavangerfjord*. One day, during a break between scenes, Inga casually expressed admiration for Fejos's expensive watch, "a complicated mechanism with dates and stop-mechanism and phases of the moon as well as the time of day." Fejos removed the watch from his wrist and insisted Inga take it as a gift. Inga said she couldn't possibly accept such a lavish present. Saying that if she would not have it then no one would, Fejos threw the watch, which had cost hundreds of dollars (this in 1934), overboard into the Baltic Sea.

Fejos later insisted that initially he had no romantic interest in Inga "inasmuch as she was very young, immature, and too frivolous." This is malarkey, as we know Fejos *preferred* younger women, but the relationship ended up exhausting both Inga and Fejos. Inga recalled that she and Fejos "quarreled all the time and we tore out each other's hair" during filming. Yet the production's film editor, Lothar Wolff, claimed, "It was rather obvious that Inga had fallen in love with Paul," while Fejos "spent a great deal of his time in the Arvad home."

It is remarkable that any romance blossomed on the set, for it was a very tense and troubled production. Inga was understandably nervous about her acting debut, confiding to a Danish newspaper, "The only comedy I've played is the one I've played in my private life." She also recognized her responsibility as the film's female lead. "If it goes well, then it is to Dr. Fejos's credit," Inga said. "If, on the other hand, it is a flop . . . then I have to take the responsibility for that. I don't have any past experience, after all. [I] have never before stood before a camera. Everything in my acting is natural. But the artist does also come from nature."

Fejos was a temperamental director, and Inga's lack of experience was evident to everyone on the set. Fejos demanded take after take, once requiring Inga to redo a scene fifty times. Feeling the pressure, Inga began lashing out herself, to the degree that Wolff considered Inga a "headstrong" prima donna.

While Inga gamely took a great deal of the blame for the film's failings, the truth is that Fejos's script was flat. A key problem was that he did not speak Danish. He wrote the screenplay in English, and it lost something in translation. But the fact is he was simply a better silent than sound film director, and large portions of the film ultimately had little to no dialogue, which makes judging Inga's capabilities as an actress difficult.

After the film's release, a Danish journalist described Inga as "fresh and sweet and not even a little affected," but little of her natural charm came through in the film. As production continued, it was evident to all involved that the film was not working. The chemistry between Inga and Schroeder was so weak that Fejos reworked the film to instead focus on the slapstick antics of two minor (and not particularly amusing) characters. It was difficult to imagine that the same man responsible for the light and lyrical *Lonesome* directed such a leaden farce.

Fejos knew it would be a flop. When *Millions in Flight* premiered at Copenhagen's Palace Theater shortly before Christmas 1934, Fejos declined to attend. Inga was one of the courageous few among the cast and crew who did attend the premier and received a bouquet of flowers when she came onstage after the curtain came down. It was her only reward of the evening.

Her reviews were not good. One critic panned her performance as "strained," and said she seemed no more than a "debutante . . . under heavy coaching." Another critic quipped that "Garbo won't have her Christmas ruined" by Inga's emergence as a rival. No one in the cast received positive reviews, and the entire film was "almost a fiasco," according to one critic.

Even though Fejos did not stand by her at the premier, and despite the difficulties during filming and the negative reviews, Inga seemed, as Wolff observed, to have developed a crush on Fejos. She favored older men of accomplishment and, in an interview during filming, gushed that Fejos "can do everything." She and Fejos now regretted their behavior on the set. Without the daily conflict between director and star, they began to focus on each other's attractive qualities.

Fejos remained a regular visitor to Inga and Olga's home for tea, but Fejos was now busy romancing the female lead of his next Danish film.

This was another poorly received comedy, *Prisoner Number One*, a farce set in a world where there are no prisons or policemen. The lead actress was another beautiful young blonde, Tove Wallenstrøm, who had just turned twenty. Fejos sent her flowers every day of shooting, but Wallenstrøm was engaged to another man and, as she recalled seventy-five years later, she rebuffed his advances and declined his offer to travel to Paris to make films.

If Fejos hoped to have Inga to fall back on, he was disappointed, for Inga had moved on. Inga did not let the negative reviews of her performance get her down, but tellingly, in a repeat of her approach to ballet, neither did she commit to the effort to become a better actress. Rather, she abandoned acting for the time being and decided to pursue yet another career, the one she had toyed with in Egypt: journalism. But being Inga, she did not set her sights low. Rather, she wanted to go where the biggest story in the world was, and in 1935 that story was in Nazi Germany.

PART III
Jack before Inga

CHAPTER 19

"Smitten beyond the ordinary"

WHAT ALL INGA LATER REVEALED TO JACK KENNEDY ABOUT HER EXPE-
riences in Nazi Germany is unknown. They enjoyed talking a great deal,
often about important topics such as world events, but as Inga noted (and
FBI records confirm), the talk tended to revolve more around Jack and
his views and plans rather than hers. Jack was thunderstruck by Inga's
ability to stimulate his mind as well as his body. Sex with Inga was sub-
lime, certainly, but to those who knew Jack it was clear that their relationship went far beyond physical attraction; his feelings for Inga were unique
from any he had had (or would have) for any woman.

"I always felt [Inga] had an enormous effect on him," said Betty Coxe,
a friend of Kick Kennedy's who later married one of Jack's closest friends,
Chuck Spalding. Coxe acknowledged that she "never knew why or how"
Inga changed Jack "or what went on between them," but Coxe had known
many of the women Jack dated and bedded and there was no doubt that
Inga "was different from the others." Prior to Inga, Jack preferred flashy
women—showgirls, actresses, and cocktail waitresses—who were sex
objects and little else. Inga "was a very different relationship!" Coxe
emphasized. "There was no question but that she had a hold on him."

Chuck Spalding concurred with his wife that Inga held a special spot
in Jack's heart. "Of all the people that I *ever* saw him with I'd say she was
the most compatible," said Spalding. "Her conversation was miles and
miles ahead of anybody. . . . There was something adventurous about her,
which I'm sure appealed to him—she'd *done* so much, been *involved* in so
much. She was almost—you know, she was a fictional character almost,

walking around." Certainly, Inga was beautiful, Spalding said, but that wasn't why men found her so appealing. She was "just sexy because she felt good about herself. She liked being with Jack; he amused her."

Jack and Inga's romance was the subject of a great deal of gossip at the *Washington Times-Herald*. As with the Spaldings, what especially struck those who knew Jack or at least knew his reputation was that Inga seemed to have changed his attitude toward women. "We all knew that he was smitten with her beyond the ordinary," *Times-Herald* editor Frank Waldrop said.

One of Jack's most devoted friends, Harvard classmate Torbert Macdonald, who would put aside his own promising career to play the role of Kennedy acolyte, grasped Jack's special feelings for Inga. To further ingratiate himself with Jack, Macdonald spent a great deal of time trying to win Inga's favor. He flattered her with reports on how deeply Jack cared for her. "I discovered a new Kennedy," Macdonald told Inga in a conversation recorded by the FBI. "Something new has been added. . . . It seems to me that he has a sort of different attitude toward girls now." To which Inga replied, "I love you, Torb. You're just the sweetest thing in the world."

Inga liked Macdonald a great deal, except for his habit of addressing her in letters as "the scandalous Scandinavian," a nickname she despised. Macdonald was also in love with Kick but was unsure of his chances to win her heart. Inga gave him advice born of personal experience: "I don't think you should leave her alone for years," Inga said. "No girl is good left alone. Absence does not make the heart grow fonder."

There is a tone of amazement among those who knew Jack that he had appeared to have genuinely fallen in love. This was not the same Jack Kennedy who, before Inga and afterward, had a lifelong obsession with sexual conquest coupled with a lifelong fear of commitment. For Jack, as was once said of his father, sleeping with attractive women was something a rich man was entitled to, "like caviar"; it was "his idea of manliness."

Entire books have been devoted to explain Jack's compulsive womanizing, with armchair psychologists outlining four basic theories to explain his behavior.

The first is that he was simply following the example of his father,

Joseph P. Kennedy, who was a notorious philanderer. Joseph Kennedy was so blatant about his affairs that he once brought his then-mistress, actress Gloria Swanson, on a family cruise with his wife and children.

Rose Kennedy insisted her whole life that her husband had not had an affair with Swanson, and in her memoirs she even fondly recalls going shopping with Swanson and how "it was fun being with her and sharing in the excitement she generated." A flabbergasted Swanson later wondered whether Rose Kennedy was "a fool . . . or a saint? Or just a better actress than I was?"

Joseph Kennedy attempted to seduce his daughter's friends and his son's girlfriends (he would also make a play for Inga when Jack was not around). Rose Kennedy found this behavior amusing. In a 1949 letter to her daughters, Rose joked about her husband's pledge to bed youngest son Ted's youthful-looking date just as soon as she turned eighteen. "As she is already eighteen, she was really dumbfounded," Rose said. Joe was sixty at the time.

Joe's affairs were so accepted as normal within the family that the Kennedy children, girls as well as boys, helped procure women for their father. Washington socialite Kay Halle recalled how Jack, while a congressman, and his younger brother, Robert, approached her at a restaurant to tell her their father would be in Washington a few days and would be in need of female companionship.* "They wondered whom I could suggest," Halle said, "and they were absolutely serious."

That Jack and his siblings would facilitate their father's betrayal demonstrates a remarkable lack of respect for their mother, which Jack may have translated into a lack of respect for all women—the second theory behind his womanizing. Certainly, Rose Kennedy's meek acquiescence to her husband's boorish behavior would not have engendered much respect. But Jack had other issues with his mother.

---

* The father returned the favors. One weekend during his freshman year at Harvard, when Jack brought some friends home for the weekend, Joseph Kennedy directed his secretary, Edward Moore, to arrange to have four girls available for the boys, and the weekend turned into a "sex party." (Geoffrey Perret, *Jack: A Life Like No Other* [Random House: New York, 2001], p. 50)

One was fear of abandonment. When Jack was three, in her only known protest of her husband's infidelities, Rose left her husband and children for three weeks until her father ordered her to return home. Thereafter, Rose coped with Joe's philandering by regularly taking extended trips away from home. When Rose was preparing for a three-week trip to California without her family, six-year-old Jack protested, "Gee, you're a great mother to go away and leave your children alone."

But even when she was home, Rose was remote from her children. Rose adhered to a childrearing philosophy popular at the time that counseled parents to limit displays of affection to their children. "My mother never hugged me . . . never!" Jack once exclaimed, adding that his mother had also never told him that she loved him. Instead, Rose was a "tough, constant, minute disciplinarian with a fetish for neatness and order and decorum," said Kennedy friend Lem Billings. Chuck Spalding called Rose "cold [and] distant," while Jack, with typical understatement, publicly acknowledged his mother "was a little removed," and blamed her religious piety for being that way.

Jack was left confused by what constituted intimacy; he pursued women in order to commit the most physically intimate of acts, yet the women involved said he seldom bothered to kiss them during the act itself. "Sex was something *to have done, not to be doing*," one woman said. "He wasn't in it for the cuddling."

Jack seemed to discount even the good things Rose represented about women. He credited his mother with helping to instill in him the love of reading, and Rose was proud of her own rigorous convent education. Yet when Jack became president, despite a growing women's movement, he appointed nearly a third *fewer* women to senior government posts than had *either* Truman or Eisenhower. British economist Barbara Ward, one of the few women whose advice Kennedy took seriously, agreed that "President Kennedy . . . had little empathy for the trained intelligent woman."

The third factor cited by biographers in explaining Jack's casual attitude toward women and sex was his premonition that he would die young. From the time he had scarlet fever and nearly died at the age of three until his assassination forty-three years later, Jack suffered from an extraordinary array of illnesses.

Jack received last rites three times before he was elected president. In 1947, when he was thirty, Jack was diagnosed with Addison's disease and was told he would be lucky to live another ten years. When writer Margaret Coit expressed dismay that Jack tried to seduce her on their first date and asked what the hurry was, Jack replied, "But I can't wait, you see. I'm going to grab everything I want. You see, I haven't any time."

As a youth, Jack spent a tremendous amount of time in various clinics, being subjected to a variety of humiliating examinations and treatments as doctors puzzled over what was wrong. Fortunately for Jack, he had made one extraordinary friend to whom he could confide his fears and insecurities behind the mask of adolescent humor. That friend was his Choate classmate and roommate Lem Billings. Few subjects were off limits between the two. Writing from the Mayo Clinic, Jack reported to Billings that he had had eighteen enemas in three days and lost eight pounds as doctors poked and prodded him for clues to his illness. "My poor bedraggled rectum is looking at me very reproachfully these days," seventeen-year-old Jack reported to his roommate.

Billings treasured these letters, not only for their ribald humor but also because he was in love with Jack. Billings had had a crush on Jack for some time but had not had the courage to express his feelings, worried they would not be reciprocated. Once he began receiving these intimate reports from Jack regarding his bodily functions, Billings apparently perceived that their personal intimacy might evolve into physical intimacy.

Following a Choate tradition that was not unusual at an all-boys school, Billings wrote Jack a letter on toilet paper, the preferred medium for signaling sexual interest in another boy, because it could be easily destroyed. Jack wrote back immediately, saying, "Please don't write to me on toilet paper anymore. I'm not that kind of boy."

Remarkably, given the prevailing hostility toward homosexuality in the 1930s, Jack did not end his friendship with Billings. Before Inga, and except for his sister, Kick, Jack received unconditional love from very few people—certainly not from parents who made clear to their children that their love was tied to behavior and achievement. Jack, then, was not going to abandon the rare person in whom he could occasionally confide. Jack pretended Billings's overture had never happened.

Jack's kindness toward Billings is all the more laudable because a sexual proposition from another male may have been particularly stinging to Jack, who considered his constant health problems a mark of effeminacy that he tried to hide with excessive bravado. His illnesses ensured that he remained underweight (at fifteen, he still weighed only 117 pounds) and therefore unable to excel and prove his masculinity on the football field. (A Kennedy aide once said Jack "would rather have been a pro football quarterback than president.") Middling at sports, sex provided Jack with another physical activity to prove his masculinity.

And so the fourth reason cited for Jack's obsession with seduction and sexual conquest was that he was good at it. As a small, sickly, and often lonely child, Jack found that women (other than his own mother) wished to mother him. "Jack is certainly the nicest little boy I have ever seen," said one of the nurses who cared for him during one of his many hospital stays. The nurse so missed Jack when he was discharged that she took the time to write the Kennedys and request a photograph of him.

While a teenager, Jack was surprised (and delighted) to learn how attractive he was to women. "I can't help it," he told Billings. "It can't be my good looks because I'm not much handsomer than anybody else. It must be my personality." When Billings countered that Jack's success was due to his family's wealth, Jack challenged Billings to a double date where they would switch identities; Jack still successfully seduced his date.

Jack lost his virginity at the age of seventeen to a prostitute in New York City (and would continue to use prostitutes throughout his life), but he soon found an amazing array of willing sexual partners. He was especially pleased that he was able to seduce more women than his older brother, who was considered better looking and far more athletic. His earlier winsomeness about his sexual appeal gave way to vulgarity. By the time he was at Harvard, Jack bragged to his valet that if a woman would not sleep with him on a first date, he did not bother to call her again. To Billings he boasted, "I can now get my tail as often and as a free as I want which is a step in the right direction."

While president, Jack confided to British prime minister Harold

Macmillan (who will play a key role in Inga's story), "If I don't have a woman for three days, I get terrible headaches." Headaches, then, were one of the few pains Jack did not suffer on a daily basis, for he seldom went three days without sex. The number of women he slept with ran into the hundreds and hundreds. Some were famous actresses, such as Marilyn Monroe, Gene Tierney, Angie Dickinson, and a by-then sixty-one-year-old Marlene Dietrich, but most were coeds, models, stewardesses, nurses, waitresses, and showgirls—any reasonably attractive woman who had a spare ten or fifteen minutes. The only common denominator among them is that Jack was faithful to none of them—save one.

From all that we know, from the time Jack and Inga began their romance in October 1941 until the summer of 1942, Jack was faithful to Inga. This fidelity is especially remarkable because there were many temptations to stray. As John White noted, with so many available young women flooding into Washington to work, there were "six women to every man! It was a lovely time."

A six-to-eight-month period may not seem a great stretch of faithfulness, but it was (and would be) unprecedented for Jack, and is the clearest demonstration we have that Betty Spalding and the others were correct when they said Jack's relationship with Inga was different from any other that he had with any woman, and that Inga had an impact on Jack unlike any other woman.

CHAPTER 20

"I'm not bright like my brother Joe"

FOR ALL ITS PASSION, JACK AND INGA'S ROMANCE WAS NOT GLAMOROUS. When still a civilian, Jack loved to hobnob with his dates at New York's hottest nightspots, such as the Stork Club or El Morocco. Now that he was in the navy and seeing a married woman, his routine with Inga was considerably more discreet and mundane.

Most nights, whether they ate out or Inga made supper at home, the menu was the same: steak, peas, carrots, mashed potatoes, and ice cream. It was Jack's favorite meal, and he never seemed to tire of it, though bland food was likely a concession to his delicate stomach. Jack could also not tolerate much alcohol and seldom drank; neither did Inga.

When Inga and Jack were not "double dating" with Kick and John White, there were other Kennedy friends around. If Macdonald or Billings were present, there would be touch football, which Inga called "an incomprehensible game to a Dane." If the weather outside was intemperate or the mood struck them, the game was played in either Inga's or Kick's living rooms with little thought to the danger of broken lamps or bones.

But more than anything (except perhaps sex), Jack and Inga's relationship was full of talk—about friends and the war, but mostly about Jack's future. "He was all of 24 and torn between a life of service to his country and teaching at some college," Inga later wrote. "We planned halfheartedly and in some fun that some day he should be President. He laughed and said, 'If I ever decide to run for office, you can be my manager.' "

But Jack's jocular tone belied the seriousness with which he was contemplating a political career. And not just any career; Inga was the first person to whom Jack confided that he was intent on running for president some day. There was, however, one formidable obstacle in the way of his ambition: his older brother, Joseph P. Kennedy Jr.

On the day Joe Junior was born, his proud grandfather, Boston mayor John "Honey Fitz" Fitzgerald, proclaimed to reporters, "Of course he is going to be President of the United States, his mother and father have already decided that he is going to Harvard, where he will play on the football and baseball teams and incidentally take all the scholastic honors." For the Kennedy clan, this was not blarney, but prophecy.

Joe Junior was, in the words of biographer Doris Kearns Goodwin, "a child gifted by the gods . . . strong and glowingly handsome with his dark-blue eyes and his sturdy frame filled with vitality, health, and energy." Joe Junior was so adored by his parents, said Goodwin, "At the sheer sound of his voice calling or talking, the faces of both Rose and Joe Senior would break into radiant smiles."

Jack, on the other hand, was sickly, disorganized, disheveled, and deceptively reserved. The idea that Jack might have political aspirations, let alone be presidential timber, was considered laughable within his family. The assumption within the Kennedy family was that Jack and his siblings would play a supporting role in Joe Junior's quest to become America's first Roman Catholic president.

Kick, who was the only member of the family who thought Jack superior to Joe, said it visibly upset her father if she ever uttered the "heresy" that Jack was better than Joe at anything. When Jack confided to Inga that he hoped, even intended, to play the leading role instead, he was essentially planning a coup d'état within in his own family.

Inga assured Jack that he possessed all the skills and tools necessary to become president, instilling in him the courage and confidence he was denied by his own parents.

Years later, Joseph Kennedy admitted, "All my plans for my own future were all tied up with young Joe." Of course, Joseph Kennedy wanted all his children to be successful, but it is clear that his and Rose's expectations for Jack were lower and secondary to their hopes for Joe

Junior. Joe Senior seemed irritated by Jack's health problems, which he also seemed to see as a mark of effeminacy. Once, when Jack brought a date home to meet his parents, Joe sneered to the girlfriend, "Why don't you get a live one?"

Joe Senior's belief that Jack was inferior was reinforced by observing Jack as a youth repeatedly failing to compete with his older brother, who took advantage of his age and size to torment his little brother, sometimes to the point of deliberately inflicting pain. "He had a pugnacious personality," Jack said of Joe Junior. "Later it smoothed out, but it was a problem in my boyhood." It remained a problem well into adulthood.

A woman who dated Jack in college recalled that he spoke constantly and monotonously about how much better his brother was at virtually everything: Joe was a better athlete, a better dancer, and got better grades. When Jack was at Harvard, the first thing he told his dorm master his sophomore year was, "Dr. Wild, I want you to know I'm not bright like my brother Joe."

When Jack did find a few things that even he knew he was better at than his brother, he pursued them with gusto. One was talking women into bed, and another was writing. Because he spent so much time ill in bed, Jack was an avid reader, not only of histories and tales of great men but also of current events. He was the only boy at Choate who not only subscribed to the *New York Times* but actually read it.

At fifteen, he entertained himself by reading all five volumes of Winston Churchill's history of the Great War. This was the productive side of a rebellious streak that got Jack into trouble fairly regularly at Choate, and which led his mother to observe that Jack "did things his own way, and somehow just didn't fit any pattern," traits that might have been viewed as admirable, but which Rose Kennedy acknowledged "distressed me."

It was only in Jack's junior year at Harvard, with Joe having graduated and moved on, that Jack began to emerge from his brother's shadow. When his father was appointed ambassador to Great Britain, Jack took full advantage of the situation to travel all across Europe. Using author and journalist (and future Inga admirer) John Gunther's *Inside Europe* as a guide, Jack toured France, Italy, and Germany, and sent his father detailed and insightful reports on his impressions of the political situation in all the countries he visited. In contrast, Joseph Kennedy sent Joe Junior to Spain for an assessment of the civil war there, but Joe Junior's pedantic summary provided little that was useful or even very interesting.

Aware that war was imminent and the opportunity for touring near an end, Jack took a second trip in 1939, returning to Nazi Germany, then going on to Poland, the Soviet Union (which he found "crude, backward"), and the Baltic republics, before heading south and traveling through Turkey, Palestine, and Egypt. He arrived back in London in late August—just days before Hitler invaded Poland to begin World War II.

The most important result of all these travels is that it gave Jack the idea to base his senior thesis at Harvard on the question of why Great Britain had been so slow to rearm and prepare for war, even when German aggression seemed a foregone conclusion. Using his father's connections (and a put-upon embassy staff) for assistance, Jack articulated the theory that democracies are at a great disadvantage compared with dictatorships, as political leaders in a democracy must win public approval before pursuing any new course of action.

Kennedy ended up defending Prime Minister Neville Chamberlain's so-called policy of appeasement toward Hitler as the logical result when public opinion, still primarily focused on the Depression and with vivid memories of the horrors of the last war, resisted expenditures for rearmament. Chamberlain was forced to simply barter for time with Hitler until he could move public opinion to prepare for war.

Noted economics professor Harold Laski, a Kennedy family friend, dismissed Jack's thesis as "immature," and added, "In a good university, half a hundred seniors do books like this as part of their normal work in their final year." But those seniors did not have Joseph P. Kennedy as a father who could summon great resources for his children's benefit.

Kennedy called upon another family friend, *New York Times* columnist Arthur Krock (who did favors even if the recipient was not a beautiful young woman), to polish Jack's manuscript and find a publisher for a book that was titled *Why England Slept*. The book was well reviewed and became a best seller, which, thanks in part to bulk purchases made by his father, netted Jack the large sum of $40,000 in royalties.

While Joseph Kennedy was proud of Jack's success, it is telling that he suggested that Jack's next project should be to chronicle his father's record as America's ambassador to Great Britain. Joe Senior did not see *Why England Slept* as reason to reassess Jack's place in the family pecking order, but instead as reaffirming that Jack would be primarily useful as a helpmate, a family scribe, in service to the broader household ambitions in which Jack would play a supporting role.

Uninterested in the mundane assignment suggested by his father, in the months before he entered the navy, Jack instead joined his mother and sister on a tour of South America, where he had a two-week fling with an Argentine named Stella "Baby" Cárcano. Baby adored Jack, and would for the rest of her life, but Jack emphasized to Baby that there was no chance of a long-term relationship, for he did not believe in "fidelity."

But six months later, after a few weeks with Inga, Jack was reconsidering his views on monogamy. Many women, not just Baby Cárcano, thought Jack was terrific fun. But Jack needed no reassurance that he was amusing, witty, or dashing; he knew that. With her remarkable gift of perception, Inga understood that under a bon vivant exterior lay deep insecurities, and so she spent her time with Jack not just making love and laughing at his jokes, but listening to his ambitions in life and assuring him they were within his reach.

"We all built him up," Inga said. "He was devoid of conceit, but maybe a tiny hope was gleaming." There were many who enjoyed the pleasure of Jack's company, but Inga saw in Jack the potential to be the great man that he hoped to become. She measured Jack against the great men she already had known, and saw in Jack the potential that remained hidden from most of his own family. Inga did what few others had yet bothered to do; she took him seriously.

Jack returned the favor. Two of Jack's most overlooked qualities were his ability to listen and his genuine interest in other people's opinions. In some ways, he was as empathetic as Inga, and he understood how hard won her wisdom was. She, too, had been pushed and prodded to be something special, only to be consistently underrated and judged by the superficial when she had great depth. And so he confided in Inga. He trusted her judgment. He saw she was, for him at least, a perfect match, perhaps a perfect mate, a woman worth the price of fidelity.

Inga recalled this time of falling in love, writing about it several years later in the third person. She did that quite often, trying to make sense of events in her own life by writing about them as if they were a story in which she was the narrator, not the protagonist. "The atmosphere is one of understanding and great happiness," Inga wrote of this time. "Their conversation is lively, sprinkled with good-natured gossip."

The happiness was so great that it began to make them giddy and to believe the impossible might be possible. Inga forgot that she had told John White she did not consider Jack a suitable long-term companion. As Jack spoke about a life in politics, Inga could imagine the role she had once envisioned with Nabi, hosting important dinners and charming important men who might help her husband—oblivious to how American public opinion might react to politician with a wife who was twice divorced and foreign born.

The fantasy was too delicious to sour with a dash of reality. Perhaps she might have done so anyway—she later insisted she would have—but now Inga began anew to investigate how and when to divorce Fejos.

Jack, meanwhile, contacted officials within the Catholic Church, asking for information on how Inga's past and current marriages could be annulled. And as he realized how impossible a political career might be with Inga as his wife, he briefly indulged in another fantasy where he might forsake politics altogether so that he and Inga might run away and live together on a ranch in the West.

Jack had spent the summer of 1936 working at the Jay Six Ranch near Benson, Arizona. He had gone there for his health and found it dull, populated mostly by visitors recuperating from tuberculosis in the hot and dry desert climate. To ward off boredom, he had crossed the border and availed himself of the services of a Mexican brothel, where he feared he had contracted a disease. But as he fantasized about a life with Inga, these unpleasant memories were forgotten. Inga and the West represented a new frontier, not the kind he talked about while president of public renewal, but a frontier of personal discovery.

As he noted many times in jocular fashion, he had become tired of being known as Joseph Kennedy's son or Joe Junior's little brother or Kick's big brother. It was time to find out who Jack Kennedy really was. Instilled with a desire for adventure since birth, Inga was exactly the right guide for such an expedition.

John White had heard about Jack requesting paperwork on annulments and marriage from the Catholic Church, but he remained skeptical that marriage was in their future and believed that, for Jack, Inga was still a "flesh thing." Jack was "a typical Don Juan," White said. "You could almost imagine him checking off names in a book."

But others, including Joe Senior and Kick, were less certain. It began to dawn on them that Jack was more serious about Inga than any woman he had known, and that he was serious about marriage, complications be damned. Rumors of matrimony reached the FBI: "Ambassador Kennedy's son . . . is reported to be going to marry a woman who will divorce her present husband."

But as with so many other couples in these days, Jack and Inga's love was at the mercy of global events. America's preparation for war had helped bring them together; now, the onset of war would begin to tear them apart.

The Japanese attacked Pearl Harbor on Sunday, December 7, 1941. Jack and Lem Billings had spent the afternoon on the Washington Mall, playing a game of touch football with other like-minded young men. As they were driving back to Jack's apartment to prepare for dinner with Inga and Kick, they heard news of the attack on the car radio. Driving around Washington they saw thick, black smoke billow from the chimney of the Japanese embassy as diplomats hurriedly burned sensitive papers.

There were no more leisurely workdays at the ONI. The agency had closed each day at 5 p.m. but now implemented a round-the-clock schedule. Jack began working seven days a week, with his shift running from 10 p.m. to 7 a.m. He confessed that he was soon exhausted from lack of sleep as he had trouble getting used to working nights. It also made it difficult to spend as much time with Inga as he would have liked. But bigger problems lay ahead.

PART IV
Love during Wartime

CHAPTER 21

"This young lady says this young lady is a Nazi spy"

DECEMBER 11, 1941, IS NOT A DATE THAT "WILL LIVE IN INFAMY," AS President Franklin Roosevelt declared December 7 would be. But on that date Adolf Hitler created nearly as much surprise as the attack on Pearl Harbor when he inexplicably declared war on the United States. In justifying his declaration, Hitler said, "President Roosevelt's plan to attack Germany and Italy with military forces in Europe by 1943 at the latest was made public in the United States, and the American government made no effort to deny it."

Hitler based this accusation on leaked reports that had been published in the *Washington Times-Herald* (and its sister publication the *Chicago Tribune*) exactly one week before and which had created a political firestorm. In its December 4 editions, the *Times-Herald* published excerpts from secret U.S. war plans allegedly approved by President Franklin Delano Roosevelt under the headline "F.D.'s Secret War Plans Revealed."

Particularly irksome to the U.S. government was that the article laid bare the truth that its military was in such sad shape that the nation would need eighteen months before it could possibly be ready to send a significant expeditionary force to Europe.*

---

*In a memoir written after the war, a member of the German High Command agreed that the leaked war plans had provided invaluable information. The German military had been as surprised by Hitler's declaration of war as Americans were. They had not contemplated war with the United States and so had done little analysis of American capabilities. Now, thanks to the *Times-Herald* and the *Tribune*, they had at least some

Given the intensity surrounding the isolationist versus interventionist debate, many charged the *Times-Herald* with treason. There was talk of prosecuting not only Cissy Patterson and her cousin at the *Tribune* for espionage but also members of the *Times-Herald* and *Tribune* staffs. Curiously, at least to Interior Secretary Harold Ickes, Roosevelt was *not* "particularly interested" in prosecuting anyone for the leak.*

Critics charged that the *Times-Herald* and the *Tribune*, by exposing American military weakness, had emboldened America's enemies with their irresponsible publication of the so-called Rainbow Five plan.† *Times-Herald* editor Frank Waldrop said critics left no doubt that they believed "the dirty fascists at the *Times-Herald* . . . were personally responsible for Pearl Harbor."

Hitler's declaration of war had finally settled the interventionist-isolationist debate in favor of the interventionists, but the interventionists were in no mood to be magnanimous. The "prize" for winning that debate was, after all, war. If anything, the anger at isolationists was stronger than before, as it became apparent just how much the America First crowd had slowed American preparations for war, which would make ultimate triumph that much more difficult.

---

insight into America's current state of readiness, the Roosevelt administration's current strategic vision, and an assessment of what America's eventual military capabilities might be.

*Who leaked the secret plans to Montana senator Burton K. Wheeler who then provided them to *Tribune* reporter Chesly Manly remains a mystery. Among the suspects identified over the years have been an American general of German descent and isolationist views who leaked the plans to embarrass Roosevelt; a separate general who leaked the plans to alert Americans to how woefully unprepared America was for war; British intelligence, which believed analysis contained in the plans might help push America to enter the war; and Roosevelt himself, who authorized the leak for the same purpose of frightening the American people into supporting the war effort. The latter scenario would explain FDR's lack of interest in locating the source of the leak.

†It was called "Rainbow Five" because the plan envisioned five hypothetical war situations, each designated by a separate color. The fifth plan, which envisioned a U.S. alliance with Great Britain and France with offensives against German troops in North Africa and Europe, was, in fact, the basis for America's strategy during the war. (Raymond J. Batvinis, *Hoover's Secret War against Axis Spies: FBI Counterespionage during World War II* [Lawrence: University of Kansas Press, 2014], p. 12)

Waldrop said long-time friends now refused to greet him on the street and would turn their backs on him in elevators. Washington was "not a nice town in those days," Waldrop said, and criticism of the *Times-Herald* only intensified after Hitler's declaration of war. "The United States found itself in war, East and West, and in Washington the knives flashed as never before," Waldrop recalled. Inga would be among the first to suffer a cut.

Times-Herald management and employees were well aware of the recriminations they and their paper faced as they came to work on December 12, the day news of Hitler's declaration appeared in all the papers. The paper was receiving a "barrage of hate mail," and there was still talk of Waldrop and Patterson, among others, facing government prosecution (though no one ever did). "There wasn't any doubt about our 'treasonableness,'" Waldrop said. With the United States now at war, machine guns appeared on the Capitol's roof, and there were flak towers in the trees of Potomac Park.

Everyone was on edge, which explains why an incident at the *Times-Herald* that would normally have been treated as routine office gossip was instead turned over to the FBI for adjudication. No one at the *Times-Herald*, especially Patterson and Waldrop, wanted to provide their enemies with more ammunition.

In early November 1941, Page Huidekoper had gone down to the *Times-Herald* "morgue" (the place where newspapers keep old clippings and photographs for future reference) to retrieve information requested by an editor or reporter. While there, a *Times-Herald* employee casually asked Huidekoper if she had ever seen the photograph in the morgue files of Inga posing with Hitler. Huidekoper said she was "shocked" to learn of the photograph, which purportedly showed Inga posing with Hitler in the Nazi leader's private box during the 1936 Berlin Olympics.

Ruminating on what to do with this information, Huidekoper said her thoughts turned to her time working at the American embassy in London under Joseph Kennedy. In May 1940, just as Huidekoper was preparing to return home to the United States, one of the embassy's code clerks, Tyler Kent, the son of an American diplomat, was arrested (and later convicted) for spying for a British pro-Nazi group, which had then turned over the documents stolen by Kent to senior Nazi officials in Germany.

A rattled Huidekoper decided to pass on what she had heard about Inga to FBI assistant director L. B. Nichols during an interview that she already had scheduled with him on November 14, 1941. As Nichols recalled the encounter, their talk strayed from the subject at hand when Huidekoper asked if the FBI knew "who all the spies were" in Washington. "I told her we had a fairly good idea," Nichols said, and it was then that Huidekoper told Nichols how she had been told that Inga was "Hitler's publicity agent in Denmark." Huidekoper said she had long questioned why Inga "had a lot of pull" with Patterson "because she could not write"; Huidekoper then "stated she thought that Arvad was a spy." But Nichols took no action to have Inga investigated.

Over the following weeks, Huidekoper decided it was her patriotic duty to pursue her hunch, and she sounded out others in the newsroom to determine if they had seen Inga act suspiciously. Eventually, she approached Kathleen Kennedy, "And I said, 'Kick, do you think it is possible Inga could be a spy?'" As Inga related the story a few years later, an astonished and appalled Kick went immediately to Inga and told her that "a girl in the office was telling people that I must be a spy or something or other because in the 'morgue' she had seen a picture taken during the Olympic Games in Berlin and I was with Hitler in his box."

Inga had no recollection of having her picture taken with Hitler at the Olympics or anywhere else. Even if she had, given that all sorts of diplomats and journalists were routinely photographed with Hitler in public situations, such an image could be easily explained and was not particularly incriminating. She initially feigned nonchalance. "I'm not a bit surprised," she said. "I hear this all the time."

But when Hitler declared war on the United States on December 11, Inga became concerned that she could no longer simply ignore the rapidly spreading rumor. Inga was aware there were "a lot of things" that, added together, could justify suspicions: she worked for an isolationist newspaper, her job at the newspaper was to interview prominent officials within the government, her husband was on an expedition financed by Axel Wenner-Gren, who was suspected of Nazi sympathies, the expedition was in South America where there were worries of Nazi infiltration, and she was having an affair with an officer assigned to Naval Intelligence. It was an extraordinary amount of circumstantial evidence.

An increasingly concerned Inga consulted Bernard Baruch, whom she hoped would be her protector, given his considerable political influence. Waldrop recalled, "Once somebody with little enough sense asked [Inga] some impudent questions, and she said, with total poise, that she had no fear as long as Mr. Baruch asked her for dinner."

Baruch offered little comfort when he told Inga the sad story of a former paramour named May Ladenburg who had been falsely accused of espionage during World War I. In a story known to Patterson, who knew Ladenburg well, a jilted lover attached to the British embassy had implicated the beautiful twenty-two-year-old socialite as a German spy after Ladenburg shifted her affections to Baruch, then chairman of the War Industries Board.

Among those recruited to help dig up dirt on Ladenburg were Assistant Secretary of the Navy Franklin Roosevelt and his cousin, Alice Roosevelt Longworth, Patterson's great society rival. Roosevelt and Longworth allegedly went so far as to plant a crude listening device in Ladenburg's parlor so that government agents could eavesdrop on Ladenburg's conversations with Baruch. Ladenburg was innocent and never charged, but her reputation and social standing never fully recovered.*

The story left Inga shaken. "Vexed and mad as a hatter," she sought Patterson's advice. "I can still see Cissy Patterson sitting in her office disgusted with the rumors, wishing very much to help me," Inga later said, but at the same she could also see Patterson's journalistic instincts kicking in and "seeing a wonderful story in the whole thing." As Inga herself noted, "it was a ticklish time as far as politics were concerned," given the hot water that still submerged the paper following the publication of the Rainbow Five war plans. Patterson realized that the issue could not be resolved internally at the *Times-Herald*. The paper could not afford to appear to be anything but patriotic and cooperative.

---

* Alice Roosevelt Longworth had no regrets about her role in the escapade or the damage done to Ladenburg's reputation. She later said of her involvement, "We were doing a most disgraceful thing. It was sheer rapture!" (Amanda Smith, *Newspaper Titan*, p. 237)

Convinced it was best to "face head-on charges that the *Times-Herald* might be harboring a German spy," Patterson directed Waldrop to take both Inga and Huidekoper to the nearest FBI field office and leave the matter in their hands. Inga readily agreed, she said, because she believed once the FBI investigated her she would be "completely cleared and practically receive a bill of health. . . . That's where I made my first mistake." Huidekoper had no choice but to go along at her boss's command, but she was already embarrassed to have become involved in the unfolding drama.

Inga said observers must have been amused to see the trio, determined, unsmiling, and likely not speaking, as they marched the four blocks from the *Times-Herald* office at 1307 H Street N.W. to the FBI field office in the old Panama Railroad Office Building on Lafayette Square. When they arrived, Waldrop's desire to extricate himself as quickly as possible from the situation was evident by his supposed greeting to the agent in charge: "This young lady says that this young lady is a Nazi spy. Good afternoon!" And then, so he said, he turned around and left.

CHAPTER 22

"All of the FBI trailing me"

FRANK WALDROP'S UNUSUAL INTRODUCTION AND ABRUPT EXIT LEFT
Inga and Huidekoper alone in the murky FBI office with Agent C. A.
Hardison, whom Inga said looked more than startled by this unexpected
interruption to his day. As he tried to absorb what he was being told, Inga
said Hardison looked "frightened . . . [like] a little pink mouse caught in
the act of stealing a Gorgonzola cheese."

Before rushing out the door, Waldrop had, despite his more colorful
version of an immediate departure, outlined the basics of the situation,
emphasizing that he and Patterson had "complete faith" that the FBI
would discover the truth of the matter and that the truth was that Inga
was innocent. Hardison invited Inga to take a seat while he interviewed
Huidekoper in another room.

Huidekoper recounted her trip down to the *Times-Herald* morgue
and how a fellow employee had discovered a photograph of Inga and
Hitler together in the Führer's private box at the 1936 Olympics in Berlin
with a caption that stated Inga had been "doing work for the German
propaganda ministry." Huidekoper, however, then admitted that *she had
never actually seen the photograph*! She promised to produce the photograph and turn it over to the FBI.

Beyond the photograph she did not see, Huidekoper admitted that
Inga had done nothing more suspicious than hold "strong isolationist"
views, which also described a good portion of the *Times-Herald* newsroom. The only other incriminating gossip was that Inga's absent husband
was on an archaeological expedition in Peru funded by Axel Wenner-

Gren, whom Huidekoper had heard might be involved in "un-American activity." The name did not ring a bell with Hardison, who wrote it in his report as "Wintergreen."*

When it was Inga's turn to be interviewed, she freely acknowledged that her husband's activities were being funded by Wenner-Gren. In fact, Inga's strategy, such as she had one during the interview, was to ensure the FBI knew that she was close to many prominent people, and not only the richest man in the world.

She told Hardison that Cissy Patterson was "one of her very close friends." She then casually mentioned her friendship with Bernard Baruch by bringing up the May Ladenburg affair, stating that Baruch had "told her of an instance in the last World War in which some young newspaper woman [*sic*] had been falsely accused of being a spy and that the Federal Bureau of Investigation had harassed her until her career was ruined."

Inga may have overplayed her hand, for Hardison recorded that he found Inga to be "a rather haughty person [who] emphasized that she had considerable 'pull' with prominent persons in the United States." Inga had perhaps not considered that her friendships with prominent people might cast further suspicion upon her. Of course, of even more interest to the FBI was her acquaintance with prominent people in Germany.

Inga candidly admitted to Hardison that she had interviewed Hitler—and Göring and Goebbels, too—but that "her interviews with these individuals were not along political lines but were in the nature of human interest stories." To the degree she was friendly to any leading Nazi, it was solely because of her work as a reporter, Inga said, and because it was necessary to be "agreeable" to land the interviews she desired. Inga then less than candidly insisted "she has no close friends in Germany" and "very heatedly stated that she had the utmost contempt for the German people, except that she must admit that they were cunning and clever in many respects."

Having answered what seemed "a million questions" from Hardison,

---

*Perhaps Hardison's mistake was Freudian: "Wintergreen" is the name of the fictional bachelor presidential candidate in the 1931 Gershwin musical *Of Thee I Sing*, in which Wintergreen refuses to marry the beauty queen being foisted upon him by his handlers.

Inga said, "In my innocent belief in justice I asked this man if I could have a certificate from the FBI saying that I was all right provided they found nothing against me, which of course I knew they couldn't dig up even if they tried ever so hard, as there *was nothing but silly rumor* [her emphasis]." But Hardison shook his head and replied, "I'm terribly sorry, we couldn't give you such a diploma because if we did, you might become a spy the next day even if you weren't today. But if . . . you are not arrested that will prove that you are all right."

Inga wasn't arrested, but that was not because the FBI thought she was all right. Inga left the FBI office aware that she had failed to convince Hardison of her innocence. If anything, Inga's attempt to exonerate herself further intrigued the FBI. "I went home feeling as if I had all of the FBI trailing me," Inga said. She was not far from wrong.

Meanwhile, the FBI pressed Huidekoper to produce the incriminating photograph, but Huidekoper admitted to agents that she had made no effort to track down the photograph and said she did not want to be involved any further in the affair because "she had to continue to work in the same office with Miss Arvad." The FBI, however, insisted, and around December 22 Huidekoper provided the photograph "which was probably the one that [her friend in the morgue] had in mind."

But the photograph was not a photo of Inga and Hitler together. Rather, as Hardison described it, it was "a typical studio photograph posed by Miss Arvad. No one else appears in the picture." It was a publicity still from the film *Millions in Flight*, which in March 1936 the International News Service had circulated with this intriguing caption: "Meet Miss Inga Arvad, Danish Beauty, who so captivated Chancellor Adolf Hitler during a visit to Berlin that he made her Chief of Nazi Publicity in Denmark. Miss Arvad had a colorful career as a dancer, Movie Actress and newspaper woman before Herr Hitler honored her for her 'perfect Nordic beauty.'"

Inga was right. There was no photograph of her with Hitler, but in many ways this photograph was far more damning, for the caption stated that Inga had accepted an appointment to serve the Nazis. Inga professed that she had been completely unaware of the photograph's existence, though she did not volunteer to the FBI (or anyone else at the time) that the Nazis had tried to recruit her to become a spy.

PART V
Inga and the Nazis

CHAPTER 23

"People down here care about me"

IN THE SPRING OF 1935, JOURNALISTS, FROM NEOPHYTES SUCH AS INGA to some of the most famous reporters in the world, flocked to Germany to try to explain how that nation had been transformed by one of the most improbable leaders in world history.

Adolf Hitler had been a failure most of his life with no typical qualifications for leadership. He rose no higher than the rank of corporal during the Great War, was physically unimposing with a ridiculous moustache, and had been dismissed for most of his relatively short political career as an anti-Semitic crank. Yet he was able to enthrall tens of thousands of people with his oratory, and after coming to power in January 1933 he brought stability and even prosperity to a nation that had been on its knees since the end of World War I. And he was also still only forty-four years old in the spring of 1935.

Among the foreign journalists who flooded into Germany were a large number of women correspondents. There had been a handful of women involved in journalism since the advent of newspapers in the eighteenth century, but by the 1930s journalism had joined teaching and nursing as a more or less respectable profession for women game enough to give it a try. It also promised more adventure than being a secretary, which is why popular culture embraced the idea of the wise-cracking, glamorous "gal reporter" in films like *His Girl Friday* with Rosalind Russell and in the Dale Messick comic strip *Brenda Starr*, which debuted in 1940.

The real-life models for these characters were not necessarily glamorous, but they were great reporters: Anne O'Hare McCormick of the *New*

York Times; Dorothy Thompson, wife of Sinclair Lewis, who became Berlin bureau chief for the *New York Post*; Sigrid Schultz, who became chief of the *Chicago Tribune's* Central Europe bureau; and Hearst's Lady Hay Drummond-Hay, who became the first woman to circumnavigate the globe by air (aboard a Graf Zeppelin).

Although a novice, Inga had journalistic aspirations as great as these women. In March 1935, she convinced the conservative weekly Danish women's magazine *Vore Damer* ("Our Ladies") to provide her with press credentials that would allow Inga to identify herself as the magazine's Berlin correspondent.

Inga had been the subject of a *Vore Damer* profile herself during the filming of *Millions in Flight*. The magazine's focus was in sync with her own interests, which were on personality profiles, travelogues, and, especially, news from the worlds of theater and film. The failure of *Millions in Flight* had not soured Inga on the movie industry. She still found film enthralling, perhaps because it was the finest means for personal reinvention yet conceived.

Berlin had been one of the world's great cultural capitals, and like many around the world, Inga was a particular fan of German cinema. Because of World War I and the hyperinflation that followed during the 1920s, few American or other foreign films were seen in Germany. As a result, with limited exposure to outside influences, the German film industry developed its own unique style that was in many ways superior to Hollywood in terms of innovation and quality, highlighted by the expressionist films of cinematic geniuses such as Fritz Lang and F. W. Murnau.

The question was whether this cinematic artistry and freedom would continue under Nazi rule. Some of the greatest talents working in German film, such as Billy Wilder and Marlene Dietrich, had already left for America, and many more would follow. But other stars, such as Willy Fritsch and Lillian Harvey, remained, and Inga was thrilled that her editor at *Vore Damer* was also an editor at *Filmjournalen*, Scandinavia's largest and most influential publication on world cinema. Inga hoped to provide stories for both publications.

Inga did not intend to avoid politics altogether. Like Thompson,

Schultz, and McCormick, Inga hoped to interview the top Nazis, but with a different twist. Unlike other correspondents, Inga was less interested in Nazi policies than she was in the Nazis as people. She wanted to do what is commonly called "human interest" stories on people the world would soon judge as inhuman, although with war and genocide still several years away that judgment had not yet been made.

In 1935, the Nazis appeared to have achieved an almost unbelievably positive transformation of Germany. They had brought stability to a nation previously ravaged by warring militias, and Hitler was "arguably the most popular head of state in the world." In 1933, the year Hitler came to power, six million Germans, one-third of the German workforce, were unemployed. Less than three years later, the number of unemployed in Germany was less than one million and the unemployment rate was less than 5 percent. In the United States, by contrast, the Great Depression remained in force and the unemployment rate in 1935 was still nearly 17 percent.

An exclusive interview with Hitler was at the top of Inga's journalistic wish list. But while other journalists were interested in what Hitler wanted and what he intended to do, Inga was more interested in who he was. Inga knew that she would not get such an interview her first week on the job, but it is remarkable how quickly she did secure an audience with arguably the most powerful and insulated leader in the world.

When Inga arrived in Berlin by train in March 1935, the scope of her ambitions can be sensed by her decision to stay at the swank Hotel Adlon, the lodging of choice for visiting movie stars, industrialists, and heads of state, as well as most leading foreign correspondents. Located on the grand Unter den Linden Boulevard, just a block from the Reich Chancellery, the Adlon, decorated in an elaborate Neo-Baroque style, was to Berlin what the Waldorf Astoria was to New York.

Inga's went to work immediately after disembarking from the train. Sending her luggage on to the hotel, she traveled straight to the Danish embassy to introduce herself to the press attaché, Per Faber, and to request his assistance with several story ideas. First on her list was a profile of the daughter of the Danish ambassador to Germany, Britta Zahle. The attractive daughters of foreign diplomats were desired guests at Nazi functions, as the Nazis sought to assure the world of their supposedly honorable intentions. Martha Dodd, daughter of the American ambassador, was particularly popular at such functions. Soon, so was Inga.

With her modest notoriety as a former actress and beauty queen, Inga quickly attracted attention in Berlin and moved easily within Nazi social circles. She even made the local society columns when she was reported seen in the company of the proverbially tall, dark, and handsome Viktor de Kowa, one of the Nazis' favorite film and stage actors, usually as the male romantic lead.* One Berlin newspaper featured a photograph of Inga and the divorced de Kowa attending a film festival together. Inga enjoyed the attention and felt welcome in Nazi Berlin. "It's like people down here care about me, and that is always nice," Inga wrote to Olga.

Having secured her credentials as both a foreign correspondent and a film critic, Inga began producing copy for *Vore Damer*. She landed interviews with Werner Krauss, star of *The Cabinet of Doctor Caligari*, whom Inga considered "the biggest actor in Europe," and the renowned female sculptor Renée Sintenis. It was a nice start to a young career and certainly met *Vore Damer*'s interests and needs, but Inga hungered to make a bigger splash. She had pestered both the Danish embassy and the German ministry of foreign affairs to give her the opportunity to do a personality profile of Hitler's second in command, Reich Marshal Hermann Göring. German authorities told Inga that Göring did not give "the kind of interview" that she wanted to do. They underestimated Inga's resourcefulness.

---

*De Kowa stayed in Germany for the duration of the war and even directed a Nazi propaganda film, which Goebbels thought was badly done. In a testament to his apparent charm, de Kowa continued his film career after the war in West Germany. His appearance with Inga, a beautiful blonde, was apparently for publicity as there is no evidence their acquaintance blossomed into romance.

CHAPTER 24

"The First Lady of the Reich"

On a snowy afternoon in late March 1935, just a week or two after she arrived in Berlin, Inga was invited to a luncheon at Danish ambassador Herluf Zahle's residence. Fresh salmon flown in from Finland was washed down with champagne in Venetian glasses followed by cordials of Akvavit, which helped facilitate a lively discussion. As at most diplomatic luncheons, Inga said, there were only two topics of discussion: "politics or gossip. As quite a few women were present, it naturally turned to the latter."

At first, Inga said, the talk focused on Joseph Goebbels who, despite his diminuitive size and clubfoot, had "innumerable mistresses"—particularly actresses who knew their careers (and perhaps more than that) were at the mercy of the minister of propaganda. A recent favorite was reportedly the young Austrian actress Luise Ullrich, at least until Goebbels' wife, Magda, discovered the affair and threatened divorce.

Gossiping about Hitler was considered in poor taste. Further, there was little to gossip about, Inga said, beyond that he loved Wagner or that he would attend the same play dozens of times and laugh uproariously at each performance.

But then, Inga said, someone at the table mentioned that Hermann Göring intended to finally marry his long-time companion, "that tall, Valkyrian actress Emmy Sonnemann," and the conversation stopped. "Eyes popped, knives and forks were put down, ears stood on edge," Inga recalled.

The reaction was understandable. As Hitler's second in command,

Göring's marriage would generate the same world interest as a sitting American vice president's engagement. More than that, since Hitler had no spouse, Göring's wife would become "the First Lady of the Reich," as Hitler himself noted. Danes were particularly interested in Göring's love life, as his first wife, Carin, had been a Swedish baroness whom Göring continued to adore in death, naming his massive estate after her and plastering its walls with portraits of his beloved departed. Scandinavians hoped this affection might extend to the whole region should Germany once again go to war.

Aware of Inga's stated ambition to secure an interview with Göring, the Danish press attaché, Per Faber, impishly peered at Inga and said in a voice that sounded like a dare, "Now why doesn't somebody go and interview [Sonnemann]? It would make a wonderful story." Feeling put on the spot, Inga accepted Faber's challenge—to his disdain, for he then chided Inga that she was "a mere slip of a girl . . . [who] doesn't even know the ABCs of journalism. It's ridiculous; besides, how would you get hold of her? You have no credentials." Credentials, Inga knew, mean little measured against chutzpah. She told Faber she would simply call Sonnemann on the telephone and excused herself from the table.

To Inga's good fortune, Sonnemann had a listed number. Inga called, said that she was an important newspaperwoman traveling through Berlin, and was told that Sonnemann would be happy to receive her if she could be at her apartment within fifteen minutes. Inga did not even stop to thank Ambassador Zahle for his hospitality.

Aware that Göring's intended had been described as "a big horse," Inga was surprised to find that Sonnemann was not the real-life Brünnhilde she had expected, but a tall, refined blonde with a "bewitching manner." Sonnemann graciously invited Inga into her dressing room, where Inga was taken aback to see not only a cherished photo of Göring but also a prominent photo of Göring's late wife! "She is *the* woman I admire greatly," Sonnemann explained. "I wish that I could be just as wonderful."

Sonnemann was a minor celebrity in Germany, having been a regular player in the Weimar National Theater. A divorcee for the past nine years, she had no interest in politics, and her life had been devoted to the theater until she met Göring at a café where he was lunching with some friends of hers. They took a stroll through a nearby park, where Göring spent most of the time talking about his late wife. Instead of finding the conversation awkward, Sonnemann said Göring spoke of Carin "with so much love and genuine sadness that my esteem for him grew with every word."

When Inga finally broached the question that had brought her, Sonnemann shyly acknowledged that, yes, she and Göring planned to marry the following month, and she further stated that Hitler would act as Göring's best man. Inga asked if she was free to print this exciting news, and Sonnemann granted her permission provided that Inga first clear her story with Goebbels.

Inga, a cub reporter with literally only weeks of experience, now had a news flash of global interest, but as Faber had taunted her, she hardly knew the first thing about journalism, and so she bungled her great scoop.

The work of German journalists was routinely censored, but as a foreign journalist Inga was under no obligation to have her copy cleared by the ministry of propaganda. Either she did not understand that or felt she had made a commitment to Sonnemann, but Inga did not immediately file her story with *Vore Damer* or any other Danish publication. Instead, she provided her copy to the ministry for approval.

A full day passed before Goebbels's office cleared her story. By then, Göring had learned that his betrothed had spilled the beans and issued a formal announcement that the wedding would be held April 10. Still anxious to be one of the first in print, Inga bypassed *Vore Damer* and tried to sell her story to Copenhagen's *Berlingske Tidende*, Denmark's oldest and most respected daily newspaper. Unfortunately for Inga, one of Denmark's princes also just announced his engagement, so Inga's interview with Sonnemann was spiked for several days before finally running in *Berlingske Aftenavis*, the paper's evening edition, and then as a profile of Sonnemann, not breaking news.

Getting a story first and getting it in print first are two different things, of course, but Inga always insisted that she had "scooped the rest of Europe." Her deference to government authority demonstrated that Inga lacked the competitive fire to be a truly great reporter, but Inga did demonstrate enterprise in getting the story first. She was convinced that journalism could and would be her livelihood. "I really want it," she wrote Olga. "I wonder if I now, by detours, have ended up on the right shelf?"

By the "right shelf," she meant journalism, but where the Sonnemann interview really placed Inga was within the highest circle of the Nazi leadership. Inga had fulfilled a promise to Sonnemann and taken the time to translate her article into German and sent it to her. Pleased with the story and apparently in gratitude, Sonnemann personally invited Inga to attend the wedding that, even planned in less than a month, was so lavish it surpassed the pomp of the 1981 union of Prince Charles and Lady Diana.

This time, Inga prearranged to sell her story of the wedding to *Berlingske Aftenavis*, and this time it ran on the front page the day after the wedding with the large byline she coveted. Told in the first person, Inga admitted to her readers that tight security made her late to the first event of the nuptials, a special performance for the bride and groom of the Richard Strauss opera *The Egyptian Helen*. There followed a lavish reception at Göring's estate, where the happy couple displayed the extraordinary wedding gifts sent by industrialists and potentates from around the globe, which, as Inga catalogued, included a sixty-place dining set once owned by Frederick the Great, a cigarette case covered in precious stones from the king of Bulgaria, and a live nightingale inside a cage of gold from the emperor of Japan.

Finally came the wedding itself with not one, but two, ceremonies. The first was a civil ceremony held at the Berlin City Hall where the mayor officiated with Hitler as witness. The second, public ceremony was held at the massive Lutheran Berlin Cathedral where the ceremony was officiated by state-appointed Reichsbishop Ludwig Muller, a devoted Nazi who preached that Jesus Christ was Aryan, not a Jew.*

Inga's report on the ceremony was in the same unaffected prose that would raise eyebrows but also draw readers to her work at the *Washington Times-Herald*. "Never has Emmy Sonnemann looked more enchanting,"

---

* Hitler regretted appointing Muller head of the German Lutheran Church, even though Muller was so zealous a Nazi that he committed suicide when he learned Hitler had done the same.

Inga wrote. "The white dress, that is quite simple with big white sleeves, sits loosely on her figure, the veil is gathered with orange flowers, as a halo that frames her Gretchen-face [sic]."

As Sonnemann and Göring made their way through Berlin in an open car, the bride's arm extended in a Nazi salute, scores of warplanes flew overhead in noisy tribute, while tens of thousands of onlookers, including thirty thousand soldiers and Stormtroopers, lined the streets and were packed so tightly that Inga questioned whether a needle could have found space to squeeze in. Inga was struck by the contrast between the bright colors of the women's dresses and the dull black, green, and gray uniforms of the Nazi officers, "but all this was yet nothing against the spring impressions made by the pink and white hydrangeas and the just barely blossomed birch trees" decorating Berlin's spring.

Even amid all this loveliness, Inga stood out. Many high-ranking Nazis, at least those who had an eye for beautiful women, such as Goebbels and Deputy Reich's fuhrer Rudolph Hess, made a special point to introduce themselves to Inga and to volunteer their assistance should it ever be needed.* Inga would happily take them up on their offer and admitted she was flattered by the attention. As she later told Olga, "They spoil me down here, but flirting is after all an empty dish. I must have real love."

Olga thought Inga's story was so well written that she must have had help from a more experienced journalist. Inga was offended by the suggestion, and protested that no reporters, including *Berlingske Tidende*'s Berlin bureau chief, seemed interested in mentoring her. Perhaps these professionals were wary of Inga's appeal to the Nazi leadership and how these relationships might compromise her—and them. Inga was not sorry to be on her own. She wrote Olga in April, "I stand alone; there is no one

---

* An informant would later tell the FBI that Inga and "the tall, handsome, dark-haired" Hess, as Inga described him, were particularly close, though there is no evidence they were romantically linked. Hess had spent his youth in Egypt, and perhaps he and Inga enjoyed comparing notes on living in that exotic country. Hess shocked the world in 1941 when he flew solo to Great Britain and tried to broker peace. Instead, he was arrested, tried, and convicted of war crimes, committing suicide in prison in 1987. (Inga Arvad memoir, undated, RMP)

to advise me along + I feel myself lucky . . . for the first time I have a chance to be independent both in body and spirit . . . it gives me an inner satisfaction."

And yet, she was considering sacrificing that independence. Back in Copenhagen, Fejos had proclaimed his love, and Inga was thinking of remarrying. While she weighed her options, the editors at *Berlingske Tidende* advised Inga that they would also welcome future copy, particularly, one editor smirked in jest, if she could get "an interview with Adolf Hitler."

CHAPTER 25

"Enthusiastic about the New Germany"

INGA PUT THE CONTACTS SHE MADE AT GÖRING'S WEDDING TO GOOD use. She soon lined up an interview with Goebbels and gushed in her article, "Dr. Goebbels is not only a brilliant speaker and a skilled Propaganda Minister; he is also a big personality."

Inga's admiration for Goebbels shines through even as he argued the superiority of a dictatorship over a democracy—"Look at the results we can display!"—and he did not deny that Germany might one day resort to war—"If a people live too long in peace . . . the men lose their manliness." Goebbels acknowledged that sometimes the Nazis used a "hard hand" to get what they wanted, but argued, "If you absolutely want to find faults, you can find them anywhere." He laughingly dismissed accusation that "I always go armed with a rubber truncheon and . . . every day I kill off a couple of Jews."

Writing in his diary after the interview, Goebbels also gushed about Inga, describing her as "a beautiful Dane . . . enthusiastic about the new Germany." But how enthusiastic was Inga? And how much did she know about what was going on in the "new Germany"? The answer to the first question is difficult to parse, but there is little doubt that she was aware of just how "hard" a hand the Nazis used even in 1935.*

---

* Five years later, Inga amended her profile of Goebbels for a class assignment at Columbia. She still noted his "melodious voice, his brilliant velvety brown eyes, his charming manners, his excellent wit," but now also called him "warped" and bitter because of his "lameness," which led to him to hold "a contempt of humanity." (Inga Arvad, "Goebbels," May 6, 1941, RMP)

Another of Inga's early interviews was with Berlin's elderly chief of police, the former Admiral Magnus von Levetzow, whose father was Danish, which made him feel a kinship with Inga. Inga became close to Levetzow after Levetzow introduced her to his adult daughters, and soon Inga was included at family gatherings.

Levetzow was appointed chief of police in 1933, but he was dismissed in July 1935 for being insufficiently anti-Semitic when he tried to suppress anti-Jewish riots that he believed were damaging Germany's international reputation. Before his dismissal, however, Inga interviewed Levetzow at the Berlin jail that police shared with the Schutzstaffel (the "SS") under the command of Heinrich Himmler.

The subject of Inga's interview with Levetzow was how Germany was pioneering new methods, including the use of pediatric psychiatrists, to interview children who were victims of crime, particularly child molestation. As she exited the interview, Inga ran into Himmler, who provided Inga with a demonstration of the Nazis' more sadistic interrogation methods.

Thirty years later, Inga said she could still "vividly" recall seeing Himmler, who usually delegated violence to subordinates, brutalize a female prisoner. "I can still see the woman, [a] sort of auburn haired woman with long hair—and he grabbed her by the hair and as they went down the steps her head conked—conked—conked against each step and it sounded like a pumpkin, you know."

Perhaps noting Inga's appalled facial expression, Himmler gave her a quick tour of the jail to demonstrate that it was clean, if crowded, emphasizing that the prisoners would soon be transferred to roomier quarters. "Did I see a gas chamber in my mind's eye? Certainly not," Inga said, but there were other signs of Nazi brutishness.

The Nazis established their first concentration camps in 1933. Inga later said neither she nor the average German understood what was going on within the camps. "They knew there was something fishy, there was something going wrong somewhere," Inga said. "But the point was, you didn't ask. Because you knew if you asked you would be gone the next day. You knew because you saw that with your neighbors." Once, Inga recalled many years later, she was on a bus that passed what she later learned was a concentration camp. When she mused aloud, "What is that in there?" other passengers "held their finger to their mouth as if to say, 'don't talk about it.'"

Fear was as omnipresent as the air. "You would hear the sirens coming up in the middle of the night and stopping and you prayed to God it was not outside your door," Inga remembered. "So you didn't ask, 'What happened to my neighbor? He isn't here anymore.'" But that was Inga recalling events thirty years after the fact, when the knowledge of history had shaped her memories. If what she saw bothered her a great deal at the time, there is little record of it.

First, it is doubtful that Inga saw many of her neighbors rounded up in the middle of the night. The Nazis escalated their reign of terror slowly, which was one reason it did not generate a greater public backlash. Those initially rounded up were Hitler's political enemies, not Jews or other ethnic or religious minorities. These enemies of Hitler were usually communists or, as journalist and historian Otto Friedrich noted, "villainous characters" whose deaths or disappearance did "not inspire great sorrow." Hundreds were killed during the 1934 Nazi purge dubbed "Night of the Long Knives," but the popular perception, in Germany and abroad, was that Hitler was cleansing his movement of its worst and most extreme elements, albeit through murder.

While many were certainly horrified that people were being arrested and killed for their political beliefs, and many more lamented the loss of personal freedom enjoyed under the Weimar Republic, one freedom not missed, as the Nazi joke went, was "the freedom to starve." As journalist William Shirer noted, Hitler was not just liquidating his enemies, he was "liquidating the past, with all its frustrations and disappointments."

The Nazis were not ashamed of what they were doing. Unlike the Soviet Union under Stalin, Nazi Germany was a relatively open society. Visitors, including journalists and diplomats, could not visit military facilities or the concentration camps, but otherwise they were free to roam about. There was much to see that was troubling, such as the increasing persecution of Jews, but anti-Semitism was hardly unique to Germany, and no one could yet imagine persecution would evolve into extermination. The separation of races was also hardly unknown elsewhere in the

1930s, including, as the Nazis pointed out, America with its Jim Crow laws, particularly—but not exclusively—in the South.

What made the persecution of Jews startling to foreigners was that many now suddenly excluded from society were some of the most prominent citizens of Germany. Even among the upper class, there was a new norm for social interaction. After the Nuremberg Laws of 1935 were passed and forbade marriage between Jews and non-Jews, Inga interviewed actor Gustav Fröhlich, star of Fritz Lang's *Metropolis*, who was married to the Jewish Hungarian opera singer Gitta Alpar.* Inga said, "I dare an extremely tricky question: Are you still married to Gitta Alpar?" Fröhlich confirmed he was divorcing Alpar but insisted it was not because she was Jewish. "There are other issues than the race question in marriage," he said.

Inga's questions and her subject's answers were far more direct when she interviewed Levetzow's replacement as chief of police, the far more militant Count Wolf-Heinrich von Helldorf, who bragged to Inga that crime had been cut in half since the Nazis took power, in large part because of restrictions on Jews.† "So you're a Jew-hater?" Inga asked, noting that Helldorf replied with "an endearingly boyish smile, 'I've always been anti-Semitic, and it is my fixed meaning that the Jews have been our downfall. . . . I know that foreigners look on us as barbarians, but that is because they haven't suffered under this as we have.'"

It is impossible to extrapolate Inga's views on the "Jewish question" from these two brief mentions in her writings of that time. Later in life, she condemned anti-Semitism in strong terms and developed close

---

*As we grapple with whether Inga was anti-Semitic (as was later alleged by some in America who suspected her of being a spy), it is interesting to note, as documented in Bo Lidegaard's 2013 book *Countrymen*, that Denmark was the one nation occupied by Nazi Germany that flatly refused to cooperate with the deportation of Jews. Denmark had a relatively small Jewish population, but Danish resistance likely saved as many as ten thousand lives.

†Despite his militant anti-Semitism and his past as a Stormtrooper, Helldorf turned on the Nazi regime even as he continued as chief of police and was executed for his role in the failed plot to assassinate Hitler in July 1944, which was dramatized in the 2008 Tom Cruise movie *Valkyrie*.

friendships with several Jews and an intense romance with a Jewish doctor who roused Inga's social conscience. But at the time, in neither her articles nor in her letters to Olga, did Inga ever directly endorse or condemn any aspect of Nazi ideology, though it would have been unwise to put any condemnation in writing. Despite her encounter with Himmler, what she heard, and what she must have occasionally seen with her own eyes, it appears she had no conception of the scope and depth of Nazi brutality.

This is evident from an offhand remark made in a letter to Olga where she noted that the lovely weather in Berlin during Easter 1936 had been a pleasant surprise since the forecast had been for cold and rain. The unexpected fair conditions must have been "especially . . . nice for the many people who otherwise are locked up week out + week in," Inga wrote, as if the concentration camps were common jails where boredom and gloom were the greatest hardships.

Inga was, of course, hardly the only person in Germany blind to the Nazis' intentions and actions. It was especially difficult for those who found the Nazis charming to believe them to be fiends. Even after a year in Nazi Germany, Martha Dodd, the beautiful daughter of the American ambassador, insisted, "The press reports and atrocity stories were isolated examples exaggerated by bitter, close-minded people." When American journalists insisted they had seen cruelties with their own eyes, Dodd did not believe them. Instead, she insisted Germany was enjoying a rebirth, all the more thrilling because it emphasized the vitality and virtues of youth. Dodd would eventually sour on the Nazis, but in a letter to the writer Thornton Wilder six months after arriving in Germany, Dodd raved about the Nazi youth who were so "bright faced and hopeful."

Inga used almost identical language in a story she wrote after visiting a Nazi youth camp where young women were taught skills in line with the Nazi belief that men were superior to women, and that motherhood was a woman's highest calling. Inga reported she found only "happy, fresh girls" whose eyes said "isn't life wonderful!"

Inga, who still hoped to have a new husband and children of her own, saw something affirming in women being part of a great social experiment, rather than consumed by the frivolities of modern consumerism. In an article headlined "The Woman in the Third Reich," which appeared in the *Berlingske Tidende*'s Sunday magazine a few weeks before Christmas 1935, Inga acknowledged that Berlin was not chic like Paris, but said that was a virtue. In Berlin, she saw "intelligent, cheerful women, who set their low-heeled shoes to the ground with purpose and energy. One doesn't miss the outer show—it is as though they have something more necessary to think about than whether the skirt should be three or six thumbs under the knee."

Inga told Olga that when she spoke of landing an interview with Hitler, "everyone thinks I could just as well run around the world on one leg." But glowing observations such as those she made about the role of women in Nazi Germany are what led Goebbels to conclude that Inga's wish for a private interview with the Fuhrer should be granted.

CHAPTER 26

"The Führer says come over at once!"

SECURING AN EXCLUSIVE INTERVIEW WITH HITLER WAS THE GOAL OF every correspondent in Germany—and it was a rare feat. Often, Goebbels, or, in the case of American correspondents, Hitler's Harvard-educated minion Putzi Hanfstaengl, would tell a journalist that Hitler had granted their request for a one-on-one exchange, but when the reporter arrived he or she would discover that Goebbels or Hanfstaengl had made the same guarantee and reserved the same time for multiple journalists.

Further, these were less interviews than privately delivered monologues. As Hearst reporter Karl Wiegand noted of Hitler, "Ask him a question and he makes a speech." Even diplomats, such as U.S. ambassador Frederic Sackett, said that when it was possible to speak with Hitler privately he spoke "as if he were addressing a large audience."

There was little that could be called conversation even when Hitler was with his closest confidantes. Hanfstaengl's wife, Helen, a German American blonde whom Hitler adored, confirmed that Hitler preferred monologues even in the most intimate of settings. "He couldn't stand anyone who wanted to talk," she said.

This trait was no doubt partly due to Hitler's peculiar megalomania, but there was also shrewdness involved. Hitler intuitively understood how to handle the news media, especially when he could not or did not want to answer reporters' questions. And so he numbed them with meandering tirades that might go on for an hour or more.

During his early years in power, most reporters considered Hitler a typical, if eccentric, radical, and gifted, politician. So they asked questions they would have asked any politician: What was National Socialism? What did it stand for? What were his economic policies? They were on a fool's errand, for Hitler had no coherent answers to such questions, at least not within any traditional political framework they would have understood.

Hitler was "wholly ignorant of any formal understanding of the principles of economics," his finest biographer, Ian Kershaw, said. "His crude social-Darwinism dictated his approach to the economy, as it did his entire political 'world-view.'" Hitler cared nothing about budgets, interest rates, regulations, or any other aspect of a modern economy, including public works, such as the famed Autobahn, unless there was a military purpose involved. Hitler had a single plan: Germany would become great through war—"Guns Before Butter" was the Nazi slogan—and would enrich itself through the plundering and enslavement of inferior conquered peoples. That was his politics, almost in its entirety, but it was so bizarre most outsiders could not immediately fathom it.

The key to understanding Hitler, then, was not understanding his politics—that was nigh impossible—but understanding the person. Captain Truman Smith, a military attaché at the U.S. embassy, sent numerous reports on Hitler back to Washington, but later regretted that he "focused so much on the substance of Hitler's political message rather than on more observations about his personality."

A few reporters made a stab at grasping Hitler's person, but they did so primarily in terms of his public image and appearance. Renowned reporter Dorothy Thompson secured a private interview with Hitler shortly before he came to power and formed her opinion of Hitler's essence "in something less than fifty seconds" after they met:

> It took just about that time to measure the startling insignificance of this man who has set the world agog. He is formless, almost faceless, a man whose countenance is a caricature, a man whose framework seems, cartilaginous, without bones. He is inconsequent and voluble, ill-poised, insecure. He is the very prototype of the Little Man. . . . The eyes alone are notable. Dark gray and hyperthyroid—they have the peculiar shine

which often distinguishes geniuses, alcoholics, and hysterics. There is something irritatingly refined about him. I bet he crooks his little finger when he drinks his tea.

Thompson's startling misjudgment of Hitler as a person of no consequence has been forgotten and forgiven, largely because she erred on the side of disdain, which is a response to Hitler that does not draw condemnation. It is not that Thompson was completely wrong in her judgment. Even Kershaw has suggested that there was "emptiness" to Hitler as a person. "He was, as has frequently been said, tantamount to an 'unperson,'" Kershaw said; he had no private life, and whatever he had once been as an individual had become totally subsumed in his public role of "the Führer."

On the other hand, Hitler must have had some personal charm or traits that endeared him to his followers, or he would not have had any—certainly not in the early days as he slowly developed the National Socialism movement. Of course, finding anything redeeming in Hitler seems an obscenity now that we know the horrible destruction wrought by the will of this one man. As Joachim Fest, another biographer of Hitler, noted, "Any consideration of the personality and career of Adolf Hitler will for a long time to come be impossible without a feeling of moral outrage."

But that was not true in 1935 when Inga interviewed Hitler. While the disdain expressed by Thompson was a common reaction, there were many observers who found Hitler fascinating and believed the world might learn something from the Nazi experiment that had lifted up a prostrate Germany.

Inga's purpose was more modest. "I don't want a political interview," she told Goebbels. "I don't know anything about international relations, I just want little things about the Führer." Her goal was personal; she knew that interviewing Hitler would make her career. It would show that she was a serious journalist even if she did not plan a serious interview. In seeking to understand Hitler the person and his well-known quirks, such as his vegetarianism, she was not looking for clues to the origins of a war that had not yet begun or a Holocaust that was still years in the future.

Inga simply saw Hitler as a celebrity, a person of interest to herself and her readers, much like a film star. This type of political journalism is common today but was still new in the 1930s. Inga was not consciously trying to develop a new journalistic form where politicians are treated as another type of celebrity, but her approach did reflect how the relationship between politics and entertainment was changing. With newsreels shown in conjunction with movies, and politicians appearing on radio right before or after popular entertainment shows, the lines were blurring, and the Nazis were helping to blur them.

In a story on Berlin's culture scene, Inga included a plug for Leni Riefenstahl's film *Triumph of the Will*, which had caused "the greatest sensation" when it was released in March 1935, the same month that Inga had arrived in Berlin. Using a variety of innovative techniques, Riefenstahl, under Hitler and Goebbels's sponsorship, had filmed a massive Nazi Party rally in Nuremberg the previous year. Inga joined critics around the world in raving about the film, calling it "indescribable," and stating that it left her "captured, captivated, and . . . convinced" that Germany was undergoing a renaissance. She added, however, "It is a propaganda film and therefore impossible to sell outside the country—unfortunately." While Inga was correct that *Triumph of the Will* was not a box office success outside Germany, it did win several international film festival awards—even in Paris!*

Such innovations stoked Inga's seeming enthusiasm for the "New Germany," and so she kept pestering Goebbels for an interview with Hitler. "I shall arrange that," Goebbels promised, and several weeks later Inga received a telegram while she was in Copenhagen that read, "The thing you want in Berlin can be had." After advising her editor at *Berlingske Tidende* that an exclusive interview with Hitler that he had not believed

---

*The influence of *Triumph of the Will* was immense. American filmmaker Frank Capra said when he saw Reifenstahl's masterpiece he was convinced, "We can't win this war." But then Capra had the idea of using scenes from Nazi propaganda films in his own *Why We Fight* series to demonstrate to American soldiers just what type of fanaticism they were fighting against. (Mark Harris, *Five Came Back: A Story of Hollywood and the Second World War* [New York: Penguin Press, 2014], pp. 141–42)

could happen was happening, Inga flew to Berlin the next morning, October 17.

She called Goebbels's office when she arrived, and was told her interview with Hitler would be within the next few days. So Inga went shopping. When she returned to the Hotel Adlon that evening around 6 p.m., a frantic desk clerk told Inga that Hitler's adjutant had been calling every ten minutes for the past three hours, looking for her. Inga immediately called the Reich Chancellery and was told by the adjutant that she had just missed the opportunity to have a private dinner with the Führer, for he had already eaten. (Hitler both lived and worked at the Reich Chancellery, which also, ominously, had a bunker in the lowest level.) While she had no desire to dine only on carrots and spinach, Inga was crestfallen at this missed opportunity—but only for a moment. She heard a familiar voice in the background. It was Hitler. The adjutant came back on the line. "The Führer says you may come over at once."

On the ride from the hotel (Hitler had sent a Mercedes Benz limousine with an SS escort), Inga tried to organize her thoughts.* Even though she had plotted (and bragged) for six months that she would land such an interview, she was not well prepared, assuming she would have more notice. As she thought during the car ride about what she would ask, her first question was for herself: How do you say hello to Hitler?

---

*Rumors later passed on to the FBI that Inga rode around Berlin in "a huge state car in which the curtains were tightly drawn" sought to imply that Inga was both a Nazi stooge and possibly engaging in illicit behavior in the back of the limousine. (Memo from L. B. Nichols to Mr. Tolson, February 19, 1942, FBI)

CHAPTER 27

"One likes him immediately"

WHEN INGA ARRIVED AT THE REICH CHANCELLERY, SHE FIRST NOTICED that the SS guards standing at the entrance on the Wilhelmstrasse were "the tallest and prettiest [soldiers] to be found in Germany." After checking Inga's papers, the guards opened the massive iron doors and turned Inga over to the guide who would lead her through a maze of long corridors and up marble stairs to Hitler's office. The thick red carpet meant that footsteps made no sound, and Inga found the whole atmosphere "hushed." The furniture and doors were all made of dark "noble" woods, and upon the walls hung portraits of famous German statesmen and landscapes of the German countryside.

As she first waited in an anteroom, Inga noted how this new set of SS guards eyed her with both suspicion and flirtatiousness. Goebbels arrived at some point, and the pair entered Hitler's private office. The dimensions of the room were "impossible" to grasp, Inga recalled, but it appeared to be at least twenty-five yards long. Near the very end was a massive desk. Moments later, Hitler walked in, wearing the brown jacket and black trousers of a Stormtrooper uniform, yet it was not a grand entrance at all, Inga recalled. Her first impression was that the Führer seemed exceedingly shy.

Hitler's expression softened as he seemed to recognize Inga, having met her at Göring's wedding. He and Inga moved toward each other until Inga suddenly stopped and exclaimed, "Heil Hitler!" Hitler seemed startled and confused, particularly when Inga repeated the salute. While a common greeting among Germans, Inga had debated whether it was proper to address Hitler this way personally, but in her excitement she had just blurted it out.

An embarrassed smile crossed Hitler's lips. Hitler could be gallant, even charming, with women, and as he led Inga to a large, overstuffed armchair, he remarked that Inga was "the most perfect example of Nordic beauty" that he had ever seen. It was a compliment that would come to haunt Inga.

As they sat and began to talk, Hitler complimented Inga on her German before suddenly looking about. "What happened to Dr. Goebbels?" Hitler asked. It was unusual for him to be left alone with a journalist with no staff present, but Goebbels had slipped out of the room for another appointment, and now Hitler and Inga were alone for the next hour and a half.

For the first few moments, Inga could hardly think as "a million questions boiled in my head in utter confusion." So Hitler began conducting his own interview. How did Inga like Germany? What had she seen? What impressed her?

"Little by little," Inga recalled, "we warmed up and sat comfortably back in our chairs. He became exceedingly human, very kind, very charming, and as if he had nothing more important in this world than to convince me that in National Socialism lay the salvation of the world." Unlike most journalists, Inga was not on the receiving end of a monologue; she and Hitler were having an actual conversation.

As Inga relaxed, she recalled the focus of her story was to be "a kind of personality sketch in the line of 'little things about a famous man.' Suddenly, I remembered that he was a vegetarian, and I asked him why. I also asked him why he wasn't married."

Hitler was pleased to talk about such things, for his popularity was based on two counter images that together, he believed, made him a German ideal. He was the dashing, charismatic leader who "commanded thousands" and induced awe, but he also promoted himself as the sentimental man of the people "with his dogs and tea." By focusing on his daily habits, which Hitler considered a template for all good Germans, Inga had found a topic on which he was happy to expound.

Inga was thrilled by Hitler's kindness. Her article, headlined "An

Hour with Adolf Hitler," ran in *Berlingske Tidende* on November 1, 1935. "One likes him immediately," Inga told her readers. "He seems lonely. The eyes, which are tender hearted, look directly at you. They radiate power."

She asked about his private life. "Private life is a thing that as far as I'm concerned stopped many years ago," Hitler replied. "From the moment you become a public figure you must give up that side of your life. But I can just as well admit that I sometimes miss it, and also sometimes would like to be an ordinary citizen who could pull on my jacket and go for a walk in the parks or look at store windows, but it can't be done. People would stand still [and] turn around."

Why was he a vegetarian, Inga asked? "It's partly from desire, partly on principle," Hitler replied. "Animals are a strange form of food which I don't even believe humans are supposed to live off of. I look on [meat] as an unhealthy stimulant. . . . Then I also think you live longer this way— are in much better shape and have greater endurance." How did Hitler become such a mesmerizing speaker; "Is it innate or learned?" Inga asked. "Both," Hitler replied. "You don't even know if you are in possession of such a talent; you first discover it when you've spoken for a while. But then the ability must be absolutely developed. It requires great practice and much patience to become a speaker people listen to with pleasure."

Inga was running out of questions and kept trying to end the interview, but Hitler insisted they continue. Goebbels rejoined them, and Inga decided to end with a question about the role of women in the Third Reich. Could a woman, for example, ever be appointed as a government minister? "No," Hitler replied, "our women should be real women and they have it good. We raise healthy, skilled, and athletic men for them. You couldn't possibly ask for more as a woman, could you?"

At that, Inga rose from her chair and offered Hitler her hand. Obviously in a good mood from his modest flirtation, Hitler told Inga, "I find you amusing. Please let me know the next time you come to Berlin." Goebbels observed how much Hitler had enjoyed Inga's company. In his diary that night, Goebbels again noted what "a delightful woman" Inga was. "The Führer was thrilled with her," he added.

How thrilled became a subject of gossip. Inga later insisted "there was nothing to indicate that [Hitler] was even the least bit interested in me as a woman." But others were happy to make insinuations.

If Inga hoped that the achievement of securing an exclusive interview with Hitler would generate respect for her as a journalist, the result in some quarters was just the opposite.

Danish embassy staff were baffled at how Inga was able to secure a private interview with Hitler. Ambassador Zahle, ignoring Inga's scoop regarding Göring's wedding, told the Danish foreign ministry that Inga's previous journalistic experience had been limited to a series of "rather naïve interviews with some of the ministry wives." Zahle passed on gossip he had heard from a German diplomat that Inga was using some "not-so-fine measures" to gain access to senior Nazi officials. Rumors that Inga was Hitler's mistress were so widespread that they would later be noted in Inga's FBI file.

Embassy press attaché Per Faber, who had long dismissed Inga as nothing but a former beauty queen, now sarcastically referred to Inga as "Die Grosse Arvad [the Great Arvad]." Faber's theory was that the editors at *Berlingske Tidende* were using Inga to gain "access to those places where the lady apparently can move about," while the Nazis were using Inga for propaganda purposes.

In letters to her mother, Inga told of enjoying parties and flirtations with Nazi officials, but she made no mention in these letters or anywhere else of any serious or intimate relationships while in Germany. There is absolutely no evidence that Inga and Hitler had a physical relationship.* There is some doubt that Hitler ever had sex with any woman.

---

*The possibility that a lover of John Kennedy's might also have been Hitler's lover is tantalizing to some. In a 2008 collection of short stories that imagine couplings among famous people, Pulitzer Prize–winning author Robert Olen Butler speculates that had Inga and Hitler had sex, Hitler would have thought of himself as a "wolf" devouring "a perfect Aryan mouse," while Butler imagines Inga being seduced by the "unlikely quietness" of Hitler's voice and the "fragile bird's-egg blue" of his eyes. Butler also imagines an encounter between Inga and JFK where Jack is so entranced with Inga during sex that he can imagine giving up all his political ambitions to be with her until his climax, when he suddenly comes to his senses and "then I'll want to be President again." (Robert Olen Butler, *Intercourse: Stories* [San Francisco: Chronicle Books, 2008], pp. 148–53)

Hitler periodically developed crushes on attractive women, usually much younger blondes, and sometimes the wives or relatives of friends, such as Magda Goebbels or Helen Hanfstaengl. He would dote on such women for weeks, sometimes longer, sending them notes, flowers, and occasional gifts, then forgetting about them and moving on to another platonic infatuation. Such relationships were superficial, "a matter of affectation, not emotion," as Ian Kershaw said. The only woman Hitler seemed to have loved in a romantic sense was his niece, Geli Raubal (the daughter of his half-sister), who chafed at her uncle's domination and shot herself to death in 1931 with Hitler's own revolver.

The absence of a normal sex life led to considerable speculation that Hitler was a closeted homosexual, but his close early associate Putzi Hanfstaengl concluded that Hitler was "neither fish . . . nor fowl, neither fully homosexual nor fully heterosexual." Hanfstaengl's wife, Helen, the object of one of Hitler's "theoretical passions," described Hitler as a "neuter" and said Hitler never did more than kiss her hand. (She also considered Hitler "a warm person" who was particularly fond of and good with children.)

Yet despite his own lack of passion, and the fact that he was not physically attractive, "the mystique of power" made Hitler a sex symbol to many women. While Raubal killed herself to get away from Hitler, several women, including Eva Braun, attempted suicide to get his attention, and some were successful in the attempt. The beautiful British fascist, Unity Mitford, part of a remarkable clan of six glamorous sisters, died of complications from a suicide attempt made in 1939 for the dual reasons that Hitler declined her romantic overtures and she could not reconcile her native Great Britain and adopted land of Germany being at war. Despite that tragedy, Unity's sister, Diana, did not regret her family's fascination with Hitler, writing in 2000, "The truth is anyone but a moron would have loved the opportunity to talk in private to Hitler."

All the gossip was a reminder for Inga that while her charm and beauty opened doors, they were also obstacles to being taken seriously. Not that she ever complained. She understood that her assets were assets, and opportunity meant more to her than approbation. Criticized by her classmates in school, rebuked by family members when she entered the

Miss Denmark pageant, blistered by her film notices, she was learning to ignore critics and to focus on what she wanted from life.

She was also learning, she told Olga, how to handle unwanted advances without alienating the spurned suitor, particularly if said suitor might prove helpful to her in some way. In a letter to Olga, Inga noted that she had been flirting with an "older gentleman" from The Netherlands, but admitted "that type just isn't for me." Bored, she then began to flirt with the owner of a major Copenhagen department store, a man named Lau Westerby. "Now, I can see you wrinkling your nose hard now, you dear soul," Inga told Olga, "but . . . it didn't become anything serious."

While keeping an amorous Nazi minister of propaganda at bay would be a different challenge than doing the same with a middle-aged businessman, Inga never ceded control of herself to any man. She had not traded sexual favors for access to Hitler, Goebbels, or any other leading Nazi. She hadn't needed to. Her looks and joie de vivre were enough to make men, even the heads of a dictatorship, desire her presence.

But to those who knew Inga only superficially, it still seemed fishy. Faber, the Danish press attaché, was certain that the Nazis must have "certain hopes with regards to Miss Arvad's usefulness."

Here was a grain of truth. The Nazis were not always pleased with Inga's reporting. They had been particularly annoyed by her interview with Berlin police chief Wolf-Heinrich von Helldorf, in which he happily admitted to being a "Jew hater" when the Nazis were trying to head off an international boycott of the 1936 Berlin Olympics. But they still believed, as Goebbels noted, that Inga was enthusiastic about the new Germany. Most of her articles, including her profile of Hitler, could hardly have been more positive. And if these Nazi leaders had found her charming and granted her access into their inner circles, perhaps men in other countries, including Germany's rivals, might do the same. That, at least, was their hope.

CHAPTER 28

"Chief of Nazi Publicity in Denmark"

BACK IN COPENHAGEN, PAUL FEJOS PINED FOR INGA. HE HAD JUST finished his third film for Nordisk, *The Golden Smile*, which was the best of the three. It told the story of a performer (played by Bodil Ipsen, one of Denmark's greatest film stars) who was so consumed with acting that she was no longer capable of being sincere.

Despite receiving critical acclaim, Fejos was unhappy and feeling as trapped in Copenhagen as he had felt in Hollywood. He was also lonely. Rebuffed by his previous leading lady, Tove Wallenstrøm, there had been no romance with Ipsen either, given that she was eight years his senior and had just married her fourth husband. With rumors circulating that he was using cocaine to enliven his outings at Copenhagen's nightclubs, Fejos began plotting to get out of his contract with Nordisk.

He also spent many evenings with Olga, playing cards. Like Nabi before him, Fejos was shrewd to court Inga's mother with as much fervor as he did the daughter, for she remained a powerful influence in Inga's life. He wrote longing letters to Inga, who reported to Olga that she had received "a glorious letter from Paul—that poor thing is not doing so well." She begged Olga to "console him well."

Still, after their tempestuous relationship during the filming of *Millions in Flight*, Inga was ambivalent about starting anew with Fejos. At first, preoccupied with her own social whirl in Berlin and her flirtations there, she often did not bother to answer his letters. This only seemed to enhance the thrill of the chase for Fejos, and Inga could not help but be flattered by his persistence.

Their regular separations, as Inga commuted between Copenhagen and Berlin, reduced the level of friction that had existed when Inga and Fejos had worked together almost daily during filming. Inga began to forget Fejos's less appealing qualities.

But it was more than growing affection for Fejos that led Inga to contemplate another change in career and location. Inga still felt welcome in Berlin, but under Nazi control it was not the gay metropolis with the vibrant cultural scene that it had been just a few years before under a democracy. The topic Inga most enjoyed writing about was German cinema. So inventive during the freewheeling days of the Weimar Republic, it had lost much of its fascination now that Goebbels insisted that virtually every film be propaganda.

Another problem was that success had come too easily. Her great goal had been to get the interview that no one thought she could get. Now that she had had her exclusive with Hitler, she had nothing left to prove—at least to herself. As for those who ridiculed her as "die Grosse Arvad," she knew she could not win them over. And the joy of working in journalism only went so far with Inga. As with ballet and acting, Inga seemed content to prove she could do something without the desire or commitment to strive for excellence. She had so many options that she could not focus on one thing.

But most importantly, what she craved more than a satisfying profession were new adventures and male companionship. She believed that she had simply been too young and naïve when she married Nabi. Older and wiser, perhaps she was now ready for marriage. Further, she was thrilled to learn that Fejos (by near accident) had stumbled upon an idea for a truly great adventure, and Inga wished to be part of it.

After completing *The Golden Smile*, Fejos asked Nordisk to release him from the two years remaining on his contract. The company refused. Fejos then claimed to be too sick to work. The company did not believe him. Fejos insisted he could no longer remain in Copenhagen. The head of Nordisk told Fejos that he was free to make pictures anywhere he chose, but that he must make them for Nordisk. Where did he wish to go? London? Paris? Fejos wanted a more radical change to refresh his soul. "Tell us where," company executives said. "We'll finance the picture and you'll make it there."

As he later told the story—and we should recall one biographer's warning that Fejos preferred to be "more interesting than accurate"—Fejos looked around the company's boardroom and spotted a world map. His eyes fixed on a large island east of Africa, a place he had heard of but knew nothing about. "The only place I would like to make pictures is Madagascar," Fejos announced. Why? "Because there are native people there and I would like to work with native people," Fejos responded.

To his astonishment, Nordisk agreed and Fejos was now obliged to make the journey and a film. He quickly warmed to the idea, however, and began making preparations for departure, beginning with a trip to the library to learn at least a little something about the place he allegedly had randomly selected on a map.

Fejos also made another major commitment. He asked Inga to marry him, and she accepted his proposal. They wed on January 28, 1936, in a civil ceremony at Copenhagen's city hall. Inga was twenty-two; Fejos had just turned thirty-nine.

While she left behind no written complaint, it seems likely that Inga expected Fejos to take her with him to Madagascar where she might have continued her writing and submitted stories about this exotic locale to Danish magazines and newspapers. If that was her plan, she was disappointed. Fejos, who later described Inga as an "intelligent and independent and sensible" wife, insisted that she remain in Copenhagen with her mother and set up the household where they would live when Fejos returned.

As had been the case with Nabi, Inga was again not being treated as a full partner in her husband's work. Still, wishing to be a dutiful wife, she cut back on her reporting trips to Berlin and focused on her domestic skills so that Fejos would live in a well-ordered household when he returned. Absent from Berlin, Inga was unaware (so she later said emphatically) when she became the subject of a story out of Berlin that would cause her great anguish later in life.

On the afternoon of March 16, 1936, while Inga was in Copenhagen helping Fejos prepare for his April journey to Madagascar, the International News Service (INS)* distributed by wire a headshot of Inga that Nordisk had used to promote *Millions in Flight*. In the photograph, Inga is wearing a sparkling evening gown with narrow straps, so her shoulders are nearly bare. Her head is titled back and looking over her left shoulder as she displays a fetching smile while holding a bouquet of roses. Back-lighting gives the effect of her hair bathed in an aurora of light. It was the type of "cheesecake" photograph newspapers routinely published for decades before it was deemed sexist.

But the caption provided by INS was considerably different than that attached to the typical photo of a beauty queen or bathing beauty. With a dateline of Copenhagen, it read: "Meet Miss Inga Arvad, Danish beauty, who so captivated Chancellor Adolf Hitler during a visit to Berlin that he made her Chief of Nazi Publicity in Denmark. Miss Arvad had a colorful career as a dancer, Movie Actress and newspaper woman before Herr Hitler honored her for her 'perfect Nordic beauty.'"

This was the photograph that would lead Page Huidekoper to specu-late that Inga was a Nazi spy, and the FBI spent considerable time trying to determine its origin. The Bureau discovered that the INS New York office had received the photograph and caption by mail from the Berlin office of the Keystone View Company, a freelance news photography ser-vice that routinely supplied INS and other news organizations with pho-tographs of interest from Europe.

But when the FBI tried to determine how Keystone had obtained the information, they ran into a dead end. The company's Berlin office had closed several years before, and most of the records had been lost. The man who had led Keystone's Berlin office was now living in London, but he could recall nothing about the photo. It had been insignificant to him; it would be of great consequence to Inga.

Keystone had not made the caption out of whole cloth; Hitler did tell Inga that she was the "perfect Nordic beauty." But only two people had heard the remark: Inga and Goebbels. Had Inga boasted about receiving

---

*William Randolph Hearst had formed the INS in 1909 to compete with the United Press Association and the Associated Press. In 1958, INS and United Press merged to form United Press International (UPI).

the compliment so that it gained wide circulation and caught the attention of an editor looking for an excuse to run a photo of a beautiful woman?

Or had the minister of propaganda been involved? Was it a joke, which Goebbels thought might amuse Inga and prove to the world that the Nazis were not beasts if they were appointing beauty queens to key posts? Or did he believe that Inga would genuinely be flattered by such an "honor," and thereby demonstrate a willingness to help the Nazi cause in other ways?

The latter theory is undermined by the fact that the photograph only seems to have been distributed in the United States, where it in ran in dozens of U.S. newspapers with variations of the same caption. If the photo with the incriminating caption did not appear in any European papers (why is unknown), this supports Inga's claim that she could not protest its publication because she was unaware it existed. "I married early in 1936 and was busy being just a wife," she said.

There is also the possibility that Inga was lying, and that she not only knew about the photo but also had made some comment, seriously or in jest, about helping the Nazis in Denmark. Inga, however, adamantly denied that she had ever agreed to be "Chief of Nazi Publicity" in Denmark or anywhere else. Insinuations that she had ever cooperated with the Nazis were "IRRESPONSIBLE LIES," [her emphasis] she later wrote.

Even if no one in Europe was aware of the photograph and Inga's apparent faux appointment, it is remarkable that no Danish diplomats working in the United States, where the photograph was widely published, took notice or made inquiries about this person whom the Nazis had appointed chief of publicity for their nation. Perhaps it was overlooked, or perhaps no one in the Danish embassy took it or Inga seriously; to them, she was still only a former "beauty queen"—"die Grosse Arvad," a big joke.

The Nazis, on the other hand, remained serious in their efforts to woo Inga. She received an invitation to return to Berlin in August as Hitler's special guest at the summer Olympics. He even planned to host a private lunch in her honor. Inga accepted with the proviso that she wished another exclusive interview with the Führer. Her request was granted; though what followed so unnerved her she fled Germany in the middle of the night.

CHAPTER 29

"To Inga Arvad, in friendly memory of Adolf Hitler"

HOSTING A SUCCESSFUL OLYMPICS WAS IMPORTANT TO HITLER. THE International Olympic Committee had awarded the games to Germany in 1931, two years before Hitler came to power, and he was initially unenthusiastic, claiming the Olympics were "an invention of the Jews and Freemasons." But then he saw parallels between the pageantry of the Olympics and the massive Nazi Party rallies and how both could glorify the Nazi cause. (It was no coincidence that Leni Reifenstahl made renowned films about each.)

To stave off talk of a boycott to protest Nazi persecution of Jews, the Nazis made token efforts to appease international opinion. A few Jews were allowed to participate on the German Olympic team, some (but not all) anti-Jewish signs were removed from public view, and there was a brief lull in the recurrent assaults on Jews and the looting of Jewish-owned stores. The Nazis were giddy that the winter games held in February at the Bavarian ski resort of Garmisch-Partenkirchen went off without a hitch.* No nations boycotted the winter games, and there would be no boycott of the summer Olympics in Berlin either.

Hitler deduced, from international acceptance of Germany hosting the Olympics, that the other world powers, especially France and Great

---

*The highlight of the winter games was Norwegian Sonja Henie's victory in women's figure skating. Henie would soon go to Hollywood and become both a film star and one of John Kennedy's lovers.

Britain, desired to avoid a confrontation with Germany. This international imprimatur gave Hitler the confidence to take his first great step in reasserting Germany as a military power by reoccupying the Rhineland with German troops in March, days after the winter Olympics successfully concluded. Hitler was careful not to be seen as an aggressor, and the world shrugged at this violation of the Versailles Treaty.

Given that Inga was now spending less time in Berlin, it is somewhat surprising that she was invited to sit in Hitler's private box in the 120,000-seat Berlin Olympic Stadium on the afternoon of August 9, 1936. Prior to that she was accorded an even greater honor: a private luncheon with Hitler at the Reich Chancellery.

It was not a casual lunch. Hitler had gone to the trouble of directing that all the food prepared be Danish, although Inga later said she could not recall the exact dishes that were served. (Presumably all these delicacies were vegetarian.) "The thing that impressed me the most," Inga recalled, "was the sternness with which Hitler treated the two SS men who waited on us. Hitler had tea. One of the SS guards brought that pot of tea forth and back to the kitchen three times before it had the satisfactory strength."

Between bites, Inga conducted another interview with Hitler, and at the end of the luncheon Hitler presented her with an autographed photo in a heavy silver frame that was inscribed, "To Inga Arvad, in friendly memory of Adolf Hitler." The sentiment is hardly intimate but was typical of the language Hitler used when offering presents to his current infatuations. Inga later displayed the photograph prominently in her and Fejos's Copenhagen apartment, and boasted about it when applying at Columbia University—until she realized that it diminished rather than enhanced her reputation there.

In her later recounting of the event, Inga makes clear that her final encounter with Hitler discomfited her. As she insisted to the FBI in later interviews, she had attended the Olympics as Hitler's guest only in her capacity as a foreign journalist. Yet few journalists were accorded a private luncheon where they were the guest of honor. Nor did most (if any) journalists receive an inscribed photograph in an expensive frame as a personal gift from the Führer.

Further highlighting Inga's discomfort was her later insistence that Fejos had accompanied her to the Olympics. She said it was only because Fejos had gone to Berlin on business that she agreed to accompany him and join Hitler at the Olympics. Fejos, however, was still in Madagascar in August while Inga was in Berlin; Fejos did not return to Europe until four months later.

For obvious reasons, Inga never mentioned her private luncheon with Hitler to the FBI. It would have been difficult to explain. But she freely acknowledged being present in Hitler's box during the Olympics, pointing out that she did not sit directly beside him, and that there were many others in the box as well.

Those present were treated to a historic and exciting day of track and field competition when Jesse Owens unexpectedly won his fourth gold medal of the games by running a blistering opening leg of the winning men's 4 × 100 relay team. The American victory had been expected, but Owens's participation on the team had not. American Olympic officials, led by the pro-German and anti-Semitic Avery Brundage, made a last-minute decision to replace the only two Jewish members of the American track and field team, Marty Glickman and Sam Stoller, with Owens and another brilliant African American sprinter, Ralph Metcalfe. An angry Glickman was certain that Brundage and other American officials were anxious to spare "Hitler embarrassment by having two Jews stand on the winning podium." Presumably, by the time Owens won his fourth gold medal, Hitler was used to seeing African Americans on the victory stand.

In truth, Hitler might not have even noticed, for he was preoccupied with distress at the German women's 4 × 100 relay team's unexpected loss to the Americans when a German runner dropped the relay baton. A disappointed Hitler belied his growing reputation for ruthlessness by sending the unfortunate athlete and the rest of the German team "a car stuffed with flowers" as consolation.

Inga returned to Copenhagen and spent several weeks writing up her interview with Hitler. The resulting article was published first on September 5, 1936, on the front page of *Berlingske Tidende*, but it was also syndicated and "published all over Europe," Inga recalled, earning her "a tidy sum of money, though nothing extraordinary." While Inga acknowledged the interview had produced "nothing particularly sensational," it was hyped by many of the papers that chose to run it.

"Seldom does Herr Hitler, leader of the German nation, reveal his inner thoughts and his dreams to the world so freely as he has done in this remarkable interview," raved London's venerable *Sunday Dispatch*, describing Inga as a "brilliant young Danish journalist and film star." Inga's byline was in enormous type and appeared next to a particularly glamorous headshot showing her wearing a fashionable wide-brimmed hat and gazing upward in a dramatic pose, the very model for Brenda Starr. She had "interviewed most European celebrities for Danish papers," the newspaper said, embellishing Inga's resume, and added that she was also "a great personal friend" of Hermann Göring's wife.

Inga was happy to report that, just as had been true ten months before, Hitler "is the easiest person to interview" (a sentiment shared by few of her fellow reporters). Inga was correct; there was nothing sensational in the article. Hitler expressed pleasure with how well Germany had hosted the Olympics. As a *New York Times* correspondent noted, foreigners attending the games who did not know better came away with the impression that Germany was "a nation happy and prosperous beyond belief; that Hitler is one of the greatest political leaders in the world today; and that Germans themselves are a much maligned, hospitable, wholly peaceful people who deserve the best the world can give them." As German athletes won more medals than those of any other nation, many Olympic officials, including those from America, vowed to imitate the more serious Nazi approach to sports.

Inga again focused on themes that interested her, especially the role of women in Nazi Germany. When Inga said that the Nazi philosophy was that women should only stay home and raise children, Hitler had a different answer than the one he gave her the year before. "How very wrong you are!" he said. "We have a great number of women working in high positions. No! We certainly do not want to keep our women from working, but we want them to be working in such a way that they do not lose their sex characteristics." Of course, Hitler hoped that each woman would have many children, but he saw nothing strange in that. "The greatest happiness in life is surely to be found in a young couple who have settled down to married life and the care of their children."

Childless himself, Hitler nonetheless worshipped youth, noting that "only optimists made history," and the most optimistic of all are the young. They were "always brimming over with ideas," Hitler told Inga. "All my plans were formed when I was young. Even the great motor roads (*auto-stradas*) we are building were in my mind 15 years ago." It was because he had so many plans, Hitler said, that he needed peace in Europe to carry them out. He did note, more presciently than he might have imagined (or hoped), "Most likely I will not live to see all our schemes put into operation, but the next generation will go on with them. I shall do all I can."

Included in the *Berlingske Tidende* article, but edited out of the syndicated version that appeared elsewhere in Europe, was Hitler's immodest acknowledgment that the German people adored him. "I think they love me," he said. "If you just once could be in my shoes, you would understand it. These thousands on the street who wait time after time to greet me, their enthusiasm, their shouts, their expressions. That can't be ordered or commanded. It must be true. It is true!" Given that Hitler enjoyed the adoration of a nation, did he have a secret wish, Inga asked? "Yes, I would like to travel," Hitler said. "Unfortunately, it doesn't look like I'll ever have the time."

And so ended the last story Inga would write as a foreign correspondent in Germany, for travel was in *her* future. Fejos would be home soon, and she intended to join him on his next adventure to the other side of the globe. But first, she had to leave Germany quickly as she faced the choice of becoming a spy or being arrested.

CHAPTER 30

"Spy offer"

FROM DELILAH OF THE BIBLE TO MATA HARI DURING WORLD WAR I, beautiful women have been recruited as spies. Being a beautiful, intelligent, and multilingual woman in time of war is sometimes considered prima facie evidence of being a spy. Jaroslawa Mirowska, a mistress to several SS officers, was thought to be providing intelligence on the Polish underground. SS Judge Konrad Morgen, a perceptive man, met Mirowska and concluded, "[A] woman as beautiful and charming as she is intelligent and unscrupulous, expert in languages, known internationally, a leader in society and fashion—she would be an excellent tool for espionage." Acting on his hunch, Morgen instituted an investigation, and Mirowska was revealed to be a double agent working *for* the Polish underground.

In the United States, Ann "Cynthia" Thorpe, the elegant daughter of a marine colonel, spoke fluent French and seduced a high-ranking Vichy official at the French embassy in Washington into helping her steal the Vichy codebooks. Thorpe and her lover had convinced embassy guards that they needed to use embassy offices for their midnight trysts to avoid detection by the man's wife. A wink, a bribe, and a glass of drugged wine led them past an embassy guard and into the embassy's locked code room. Thorpe wrote in her diary a sentiment that Inga might have shared: "I love to love with all my heart, only I have to appear cool. Life is but a stage on which to play."

The fear of secrets being passed pillow to pillow led British military authorities to widely distribute a poster featuring a gorgeous blonde, a languorous expression on her face, lounging seductively upon a couch while wearing a revealing evening gown, surrounded by lonely military officers, drinks in hand, with the warning: "Keep mum, she's not so dumb! Careless talk costs lives."

Given the trope of the femme fatale, it is not surprising that Inga was later suspected of being a spy, nor is it surprising that the Nazis tried to recruit her as one—at least that is what Inga claimed in a reminiscence she wrote titled "Spy offer."

In September 1936, a few weeks after her second interview with Hitler was published, with Fejos still in Madagascar, Inga returned to Berlin to attend a party at the home of a German prince. Still aglow about her second exclusive interview with Hitler, which had received international attention, Inga was again enjoying Nazi high society.

As those gathered at the prince's home sipped Moët & Chandon champagne and nibbled on fresh peaches, a man whom Inga described as a "top man" in the Nazi Party began "chatting away at me" and complimented her on her interviews with Hitler. What was especially captivating about her articles on Hitler, the man continued, was that they were "so delightfully non-political that they seem to belong to another era, more like a Madam Récamier letter" (the French noblewoman who hosted the leading salon in early nineteenth-century Paris).

Inga was no doubt wondering where this unusual line of flattery was leading when this Nazi "top man" asked her, "How would you like to change [your] venue? How would you like to go to Paris and work?" Inga did not follow. "And what would I be doing there?" she asked innocently, noting that there was no one in Paris she wished to interview, and even if there were, *Berlingske Tidende* already had a skilled correspondent in the French capital who would resent her interloping. "I was listening to the voices in my chicken brain when I heard his voice amble on," Inga said.

"You know everybody, why not go for us?" the Nazi official inquired. "We will pay you, furnish you with a large expense account, and all we would ask is that you to go to all the parties and REPORT TO US, WHAT THE CONVERSATIONS THERE ARE ABOUT." Inga wrote out these words in all capital letters, to emphasize that it had now sunk in what she was being asked to do. "That hit me like a sledgehammer," Inga said. "As innocent and naïve as I was, and maybe unfortunately have remained, even I understood that this wasn't exactly what I would call kosher. I secretly prayed that the expression on my face didn't divulge what was going on in my mind."

As Inga mulled this extraordinary offer to become a Nazi spy, she could only mutter meekly, "Let me think about it." The Nazi wrinkled his brow, surprised that Inga would hesitate to serve the Third Reich. Perhaps she worried about dual loyalties? "You wouldn't be doing anything against your own country," the man assured Inga.

Now in no doubt as to what was being asked, Inga smiled, set down her glass of champagne and a half-eaten peach, and excused herself, thanking her host as she prepared to leave. Suddenly, another party guest, German foreign minister Konstantin von Neurath, appeared at her side and asked if he might escort her home. Even though it was two o'clock in the morning, the sixty-three-year-old von Neurath suggested they walk rather than drive to the Hotel Adlon where Inga was staying.

Von Neurath had observed Inga's recruitment and was concerned. Von Neurath had a soft spot for Inga, not only because she was young and beautiful and a favorite of many high-ranking Nazis but also because she was a Dane. Von Neurath had enjoyed his time as German minister to Denmark immediately after World War I. He had been in the German Foreign Service since 1903, had served under many governments, and was still not a member of the Nazi Party in 1936, though he became one the following year. The Nazis used him because his stature gave the Third Reich an air of legitimacy.*

On this night, he chose to work against the Nazi cause—or at least in favor of Inga. "Inga, you know what you were offered?" von Neurath asked. "I suggest that you refuse. But this man can NOT [Inga's emphasis] be refused without recrimination." If Inga refused to cooperate, von Neurath advised, she would almost certainly be reported to Himmler, and she would soon receive a visit from the Gestapo.

Inga was silent for a moment as they strolled along the Unter den Linden. "What do I do?" she asked plaintively. Von Neurath responded,

---

*At the Nuremberg trials, von Neurath was sentenced to fifteen years in prison.

"I suggest that you take the first plane out of here tomorrow morning and don't return until he has forgotten." Von Neurath then warmly took Inga's hands, but the comfort of the gesture was lost when she noted the troubled look in his eyes.

As Inga walked into her hotel room, the phone rang. It was Olga, who said she had been trying to reach her daughter all evening. "I called, darling, because I have had the most dreadful premonition that you are in great danger," Olga said. "Won't you please come home at once?" Inga calmed her mother, packed her suitcase, immediately left for Berlin's Tempelhof Airport, and took the first available flight to Copenhagen that morning. "And that was my swan song" in Germany, Inga said.

Inga would soon travel as far away from Nazi Germany as was physically possible, to Southeast Asia with her husband, Paul Fejos. But it was in the jungles of Malaysia where she and Fejos met Axel Wenner-Gren and began an association that was every bit as intriguing to the FBI as her time with Hitler.

PART VI

Headhunters and a Billionaire

Chapter 31

"It takes courage"

Shaken by the effort to recruit her as a Nazi spy, Inga was relieved when Fejos finally returned from Madagascar in December 1936. She and her husband had been separated for nine of their first eleven months of marriage. It was the beginning of a pattern.

While in Madagascar, Fejos shot one hundred thousand feet of film (ten times what typically goes into a two-hour movie), but the footage was unsuitable for the feature film he had envisioned. Instead, he refashioned the footage into several short documentaries, the highlight of which was *The Bilo*, which chronicled the funeral of a native chief that included the slaughter of eight hundred of the chief's oxen as both tribute and the victuals for a memorial feast.

His contractual obligation to Nordisk complete, Fejos had planned on moving to New York with Inga, but to his delight his documentaries received great acclaim when shown to the Royal Geographic Society of Denmark. To his surprise, Fejos found that anthropology and ethnography scholars treated him not as a fakir but as a colleague. Fejos's documentaries were not merely exciting, but revolutionary. Unlike previous docudramas of aboriginals that melded fact with fantasy, such as the pioneering *Nanook of the North* (a 1922 silent film subtitled *A Story of Life and Love in the Actual Arctic*), Fejos had not created a fictional storyline around native life. Instead, he portrayed native activities as they occurred without dramatic embellishment.

His films provided a lasting record of ancient societies that would soon irrevocably change as they encountered modern technology. Without any conventional credentials, Fejos had stumbled upon a new career as a pioneering anthropologist, which provided him with the kind of prestige he craved. Thoughts of moving to America were scrapped for the time being as Fejos instead accepted a generous offer from Svensk Filmindustri (Swedish Film Industry) to continue making ethnographic documentaries.

Given his choice of going anywhere in the world, Fejos chose the Dutch East Indies, now the nation of Indonesia, an archipelago of more than seventeen thousand islands populated by hundreds of different ethnic groups. While there, Fejos also intended to collect live Komodo dragons for the Copenhagen and Stockholm zoos; the world's largest lizards had become known to Europeans only a quarter-century before.

There would also be visits to Hong Kong, China, Japan, Korea, the Philippines, Siam (now known as Thailand), and New Guinea—and this time (unlike Madagascar) Inga would accompany him.

While she intended to write and sell articles about her upcoming adventure to various Danish publications, Inga was thrilled that Fejos had also tasked her with two key roles in the expedition. First, she was to be the team's radio operator, and she spent most of February 1937 learning Morse code and how to use the short wave radio transmitter. Fejos was amazed at how quickly and well she learned both. Such talents would be essential should the expedition run into trouble deep in the jungle. The second duty assigned to Inga was that of "script girl."* It was to be her job to keep track and make detailed notes of what was filmed and to ensure everything was properly labeled and organized for later editing.

In Inga's mind, these assignments indicated that Fejos intended to make her a full partner not only on this expedition but also in this new career that promised one exotic adventure after another. Inga and Fejos's relationship, however, was not based on equality. Fejos was sixteen years older than Inga, whom he commonly addressed in their correspondence as "my dear child" or "my darling baby of mine." These come across less

---

*In the early days of film, these duties were considered secretarial and usually given to women, but today the title is "script supervisor."

as terms of endearment than regular reminders of his senior status in the relationship.

Fejos and the rest of what the Danish magazine *Familie Journalen* (Family Journal) billed as the largest ethnographic film expedition ever sponsored by a Scandinavian company left Göteburg, Sweden, on February 24, 1937, aboard the M.S. *Canton*, a six-thousand-ton ship operated by the Swedish East Asia Company.

One member of the expedition, however, was not yet on board. Inga was still busy packing and boarded ship a week later in Hamburg. Despite Konstantin von Neurath's warning that her refusal to become a spy for the Nazis could lead to her arrest, Inga apparently believed the quick border crossing required to reach the German port posed a minimal risk. *Familie Journalen*, of course, had no knowledge of Inga's problems with the Nazis, but noted that "it takes courage" to go away into the jungle for two years.

Inga's closest call, however, came while they were still off the coast of Europe. The North Atlantic in late winter features rough seas, and Inga's seasickness was severe enough, with traces of blood in her vomit, that Fejos worried she was suffering from something far more serious. Even when the seas calmed as the ship entered the Mediterranean, Inga was unable to keep any food down. Down to 110 pounds on her five-foot-eight frame, Fejos intended to put Inga ashore at Port Said at the entrance to the Suez Canal and then have her return to Denmark.

Perhaps in response to the threat of being left behind, Inga's condition dramatically improved. She "eats as a wolf," Fejos happily reported to Olga. Now with the Indian Ocean smooth "like a billard table," Inga was enjoying the voyage, practicing her French every day with "an old Belgian lady, who is travelling to Hong Kong." Fejos also used time onboard to teach Inga how to shoot a small rifle and, as with her mastery of the wireless, he was amazed at how quickly Inga became an "accomplished shot . . . [she] can hit a penny with it like anything."

Fejos's letters to Olga during the voyage expose his unusual relationship with his mother-in-law, whom at times he seemed far closer to than his wife. Fejos, who called Olga "mor" ("mother") and signed his letters to her "your boy Paul," confided in Olga in ways he did not seem to with his wife. Oddly, he made a point of noting in his letters how often he and Inga quarreled, and he seemed to enjoy causing trouble between mother and daughter.

During dinner at the captain's table, Fejos reported to Olga that he had referred to his mother-in-law as "a lady with dignity." For reasons unknown, though perhaps she was just tired of Fejos's constant posturing, this irritated Inga. She told Fejos, according to the account he gave Olga, that he was "an idiot and her mother definitely does not have dignity." "What do you say to that?" Fejos asked Olga incredulously, seeming to delight in sharing this humiliating exchange with his wife's mother.

It seems cruel to have passed on this particular anecdote, even if true, as Fejos would have known how desperately Olga must have missed her daughter, having never been separated from her for this long a time or by such a great distance. To think that her daughter, the sole focus of her life, had disparaged her publicly would have wounded Olga deeply.

It is also odd that even when Inga's health had improved so that she could continue the voyage, Fejos still included with this cheery update his earlier letter in which he detailed just how sick Inga had been, as if to torment Olga with a reminder of just how fragile her daughter's health was—just as Inga was preparing to spend nearly two years in the jungle and presumably far away from adequate medical care. It presaged continued tensions within his and Inga's marriage.

CHAPTER 32

"The white goddess"

TWO MONTHS AFTER LEAVING HAMBURG, INGA AND FEJOS BEGAN THEIR Asian expedition in Manchuria, then under brutal occupation by the empire of Japan. Inga reported that she and Fejos were required to step off the sidewalk to let any Japanese soldier pass, just as the Chinese were forced to do.

Seeking a less tense atmosphere off the streets, Inga and Fejos attended a showing of the new American film, *The Good Earth*, based on the Pearl S. Buck novel, which Inga had read and enjoyed as a schoolgirl. Inga noted that while the story of a struggling peasant family is a drama, the Chinese audience laughed uproariously at seeing Paul Muni and Luise Rainier, both Austrian born, made up to supposedly look Chinese.

Inga admired the Chinese and their culture. "I would love to come back and stay in China some day," she said. "I want to know the people. I believe they're grand. They have a look about them—worthwhile somehow."

Before beginning their search for primitive tribes, Inga and Fejos took a tour of Asia's cultural offerings. In a letter written to Inga after she had returned to Denmark, Fejos recalled their "long auto drives" through the romantic Philippine countryside; how they had enjoyed sitting on the floor, "munching peanuts," at the Ken Geki ("sword play") theaters in Kobe, Japan; and of their "evening escapades" (which he did not detail) in Batavia (now the Indonesian capital of Jakarta).

But Fejos said little, then or later, about the one great adventure of which Inga was a part. In an extensive oral history that Fejos did with

Columbia University some twenty years later, he does not mention even in passing the several months he and Inga lived among primitive tribes on islands west of Sumatra. Yet for Inga, this was the central experience of her time in Asia and one that profoundly moved her.

The East Indies offered the thrill of danger that Inga had hoped to find on this adventure. On the island of Sumbawa, Inga and Fejos went hunting on Mount Tambora, the volcano whose 1815 eruption poured so much ash into the atmosphere that it created a "year without summer" around the globe. While standing in the "velvety jungle blackness," Inga said a wild boar, which "looked as large as an elephant to me," charged the party. Before Inga could react, a gun was fired. "It was Paul's shot," Inga later boasted to a newspaper reporter. "He never misses. He doesn't dare!"

After resting in Batavia, Inga, Fejos, and a camera crew traveled on through the Sunda Strait and up the west coast of Sumatra to the port city of Padang, where they boarded a steamer that took them west to the island of Nias. The several tribes on Nias had actively practiced headhunting until just a few years before Inga and Fejos's arrival.

The fact that the last known incidence of headhunting on Nias occurred at least two years before their arrival did not stop Inga from telling a few tales later in life for effect. She claimed that while dining with a tribal leader she noted a curious object in the back of his hut. Upon inspection, she discovered (so she claimed) that it was a "smoke-darkened, shrunken, but still recognizable head of a red-haired German missionary" who she allegedly had met previously during her travels. Asked why the missionary had met such a fate, the chief allegedly replied, "Bad manners."

The story is certainly apocryphal, intended by Inga to be a macabre joke, but it does capture her mixed feelings about the natives she encountered. At one level, she liked them a great deal. They were generous and kind and projected the innocence of a paradise lost. But Inga was still young and very much a European, and possessed the sense of superiority common to both circumstances.

The fierce reputation of the people of Nias had discouraged visitors through most of history, and so they had developed a unique culture and language.* Inga marveled at how their huts were placed on tall stilts so that they lived high among the trees, making their villages almost invisible from the ground. She noted that the only way to reach each hut was by climbing a long notched board, which none of the Europeans could climb. But the natives with their "prehensile toes," as Inga called them, could shoot up the board with "a swiftness to make an elevator envious!"

The reference to the "prehensile toes" make it appear that Inga considered the natives part beasts, but she was, in fact, often impressed by the sophistication of native customs. She noted, for example, that the people of Nias were naked except for a loincloth made from bark, but at first glance they appeared fully clothed because they were tattooed head to toe "with pinstripe lines so close together a Bond Street tailor might be envious!"

The people of Nias fascinated Inga, but she developed a much more personal and rewarding relationship with the less fierce Mentawai people on the island of Sipura, two hundred miles to the south, where she, Fejos, and their team headed next. While on Sipura, Inga became extraordinarily fond of a four-year-old Mentawai boy named Peipepteoman.

"He had big coal black eyes, soft dark hair, a lovely golden brown body, and a smile that won my heart the minute I set eyes on [him]," Inga wrote a few years after her encounter. Peipepteoman was equally taken with Inga and, bolder than the other children, he slowly approached her to accept the gift of a small, bright green ball on a fuzzy stick. Inga put him on her lap, "and with gestures tried to indicate what the lollipop was meant for." Peipepteoman struggled to get away, but Inga held him tight until he finally took a lick of the candy and smiled.

Inga typically wore an outfit not markedly different from the men in her party: a pair of khaki pants, boots, a short-sleeved blouse, and a broad-brimmed hat that offered protection from the tropical sun. Despite what Inga considered her slightly androgynous appearance, the Mentawai considered her a "white goddess," she said, and made dolls in her image, using straw for her blonde hair.

Inga was amused by how the simplest of modern pleasures were won-

---

*Today, Nias is an international surfing destination.

ders to the Mentawai, but she was self-aware enough that she understood that the Mentawai themselves did not consider her, Fejos, or any of the other Europeans to be their betters. In fact, while Inga's yellow hair fascinated the Mentawai, she understood it was not because they thought it made her more beautiful than they—in fact, just the opposite.

Inga wrote that her fair hair and skin "puzzled and irritated" Peipepteoman. "He glanced from his own [skin] with the rich brown tone to her anemic lightly tanned one with disapproval," Inga later wrote. "The blue of her eyes was decidedly not to his liking, and that her eyelashes and brows existed at all disturbed his sense of beauty. In fact he tolerated her mostly because by this time, he had tasted the sweet on the little stick and liked it."

CHAPTER 33

"A delight to the eye"

INGA AND FEJOS, LIKE MANY WESTERN VISITORS, FOUND THE INHABI-tants of the East Indies to be a remarkably attractive people. W. Douglas Burden, a trustee of the American Museum of Natural History, visited the Indonesian archipelago in 1926, partly for the same purpose as Fejos: to capture a Komodo dragon.* Burden, whose adventures allegedly helped inspire his filmmaker friend Merian Cooper to make *King Kong* (1933), wrote in *National Geographic* that on Bali and other East Indian isles "one never sees the thin, scrawny type of humanity so common to India. There is but slight variation from physical perfection. Everywhere the girls, like plump partridges, adorn the landscape."

Fejos was determined to find the plumpest partridge among the Mentawai to star in his film. While Fejos wanted the natives to act naturally in his documentary, he realized that focusing on a beautiful native acting naturally, particularly given that the Mentawai women wore only a skirt and no top, would enthrall European and American audiences more than a less attractive female (or a male native) acting naturally.

When Fejos told a Mentawai elder that he wanted a special girl for his film, the man asked, "Does that mean that you want a girl who can cook well and bear many children?" No, Fejos answered, he wanted a girl

---

* As a sign of how much the philosophy of conservation has changed in the past century, Burden's expedition captured fourteen Komodo dragons. Twelve were killed and stuffed for exhibit. The two live specimens were taken to the National Zoo, where they quickly died. The Komodo dragon's inability to adapt to captivity simply meant more expeditions to capture new specimens.

who was "a delight to the eye." "You mean," said the tribal elder, "a girl whom all the men in the Kampong (village) desire?" "That is closer to the point," Fejos agreed.

The young woman selected was a sixteen-year-old named Ngenakan whom Inga acknowledged was a stunning beauty and who, in her description, seemed to epitomize the exotic (and erotic) beauty of the South Seas:

> She stood in her fringed banana skirt, barely reaching her knees. Her young, small, firm breasts pointed to the tropical blue sky, while black hair hung straight to her shoulders. The eyes were large and expressive, the mouth deep red and hungry. The nose slightly arched, the ears small and lovely. She wore dark red hibiscus flowers in her hair and adorning her round arms.

Innocence is easily corrupted, however. Once Ngenakan understood her central importance to Fejos's plans, which she did very quickly, she adopted the carriage of a movie star with "more whims, more demands, more caprices than any Hollywood darling," Inga wrote.

As evidence that they had created a diva, Inga reported that Ngenakan's seventeen-year-old husband complained that Ngenakan had ceased to cook or clean their hut since filming began. "I don't think she loves me either," he said. "She refuses to share my mat because she says the constant work in the sun wears her out and she wants to be left in peace." To ensure that neither the husband nor the tribal elders would pull Ngenakan from the shoot, Fejos intervened and told Ngenakan she could not ignore her wifely duties. "The girl promised to improve," Inga said, "She never did"—at least not until the filming was completed and Inga and Fejos left.

Inga emphasized, however, that Ngenakan had a charming side as well. Inga had brought a bottle of her favorite perfume, Chanel No. 5, into the jungle (!) and Ngenakan was enthralled by the scent. Noting the girl's enormous smile at her first whiff of perfume, Inga insisted she keep the bottle as a gift. Afterward during filming, Inga said, if Ngenakan had been scolded or was in a bad mood, she would pull the perfume bottle out and "inhale very slowly. Then she would smile to herself and cheer up considerably."

When their filming was done, as Inga boarded the boat to depart, Ngenakan presented her with a freshly made banana skirt as a parting gift. What brought "a tear to the corner of my eye," Inga said, was that Ngenakan had scented the skirt with some of her newest and most precious possession, the Chanel No. 5.

Inga had an even sadder farewell with Peipepteoman. She and the boy had become very close. "He would sit by her side hour after hour," Inga recalled in an essay she wrote while at Columbia University, "just waiting for her to give him presents, and she showered him with anything she thought might please the beautiful child."

Peipepteoman called Inga "darling," assuming that was her name as that was how Fejos usually addressed her, but they could not converse beyond a few gesticulations. Inga sometimes wondered whether Peipepteoman truly cared for her, for while he brought her gifts of seashells in trade for chocolates, he did not demonstrate any physical affection. This saddened Inga, who would have enjoyed snuggling with the boy.

That did not happen until the day Inga and Fejos left. When the boat arrived to take Inga, Fejos, and crew back to Padang and then Batavia, Peipepteoman realized Inga was leaving for good and threw his arms around her waist and refused to let go even as his father struggled to take him away. "He clung to [me] with all his might," Inga said, "and with tears streaming down his little brown face he murmured, 'Darling.'"

CHAPTER 34

"You will be with me from now on"

DESPITE THE PLUCK SHE HAD SHOWN ON SIPURA AND NIAS AND THE fact she was the team's radio operator, Fejos insisted that Inga remain in Hong Kong to rest while he went on to Komodo to capture specimens of the island's dragons for the Copenhagen and Stockholm zoos.

While relaxing at the Helena May Institute, an elegant "residential club" for unaccompanied, non-Asian professional women located on Hong Kong's famed Garden Road, Inga was interviewed by a British newswoman named Muriel Lewis.* Lewis gushed that no adjective "could be too extravagant" in describing Inga, "but I am checked by the fear of seeming cheaply fulsome."

Lewis expressed surprise to find Inga in Hong Kong while her husband was on his way to Komodo, for she said Inga not only had "the urge to 'do things,' as her mother wishes, but the ability to 'deliver the goods.'" Inga professed, "I'd fly to the moon to be with my husband," but said Fejos had her safety in mind. Komodo dragons can reach ten feet in length and weigh up to two hundred pounds and have been known to break a man's leg with a swish of their tail. Fejos was prescient; the trip was a disaster.

Just the journey to Komodo aboard the S.S. *de Klerk*, a livestock freighter, was unpleasant enough. "The stench and stink of the deck—full of horses, chickens, ducks, and cattle, is unimaginable," Fejos wrote Inga. But the great problem was actually landing on the island. Komodo is

---

* The Helena May did not begin admitting women of all nationalities until the 1980s.

isolated in part because strong ocean currents of up to ten knots surround it. When the freighter dropped the launch that would take Fejos and his team to the island, the ship's captain misjudged the tide, and the launch was thrown against some rocks and sank. Most of the expedition's supplies, including the supply of drinking water, were lost.

Using outdated maps, Fejos and his men could find no source for fresh water on the island and became frightened at the prospect of a slow, unpleasant death from dehydration. But that very night, one of Fejos's companions spotted a pair of lights at sea. Fejos at first refused to believe the lights could be from a ship, as Komodo was far from any shipping lanes, but they built a bonfire anyway. The ship returned the signal, and the next morning it came close to shore and sent lifeboats to pick up Fejos and his men. Remarkably, it was the S.S. *de Klerk*; the ship had gone back around the island to avoid a storm. "It was really a miracle," Fejos said with his usual understatement.

Fejos returned to Komodo a few weeks later, this time with native boats and guides and plenty of water, and captured three live dragons.* Inga had hoped to be part of that expedition, but Fejos again insisted that she rest, this time on a Swedish coffee plantation on Sumbawa. There, Inga enjoyed the routine of a daily walk, a daily drive, a daily bath ("the Dutch way, of course, which means that you pour the water over yourself from a little ladle"), and evenings of badminton and cards with a glass of sherry.

After a month of restful monotony, Inga was ready to rejoin Fejos on the next planned adventure in Siam. Fejos said his near-death on Komodo had cured him of taking risks, and to hold himself to this pledge he told Inga this meant, "You will be with me from now on," adding in all capital letters for emphasis, "INCLUDING NEW GUINEA!" Yet on the *same day* he made that vow to Inga, he pledged in a letter to a worried Olga, "I can definitely promise you that [Inga] will NOT come to New Guinea, as long as I have something to say about it."

---

*The animals did not live long in captivity, Fejos reported. The one at the Copenhagen zoo swallowed a beer bottle cap that a visitor had thrown into its pen, perforating its intestine. (John W. Dodds, *The Several Lives of Paul Fejos*, pp. 60–62)

Fejos then broke his promise to Inga and declined to take her to his next destination—Chiang Mai in the mountains near the Burmese border. While Fejos journeyed north to film wild elephants and to follow the elephant driver who was the focus of the most notable film Fejos made during his Asian trip, Inga was left behind in Bangkok, albeit at another elegant hotel, which may have softened the sting of separation.

Fejos again assured Inga that she was being left behind for her own good. It was mountainous terrain and most of the views were obscured by fog, Fejos told her, clearly grasping at reasons why she should be happy not to be at his side. Besides, he said, "People [here] look just like people in Bangkok."

While Fejos framed his refusal to let Inga go into the field as genuine chivalry, it is more likely that Fejos considered Inga's presence a distraction from his work. He was under considerable pressure as Svensk Filmindustri executives proclaimed themselves dissatisfied with the film footage (and the bills) Fejos had already sent back to Sweden. The company sent him a new cameraman and an assistant director named Gunnar Skoglund, whose job was to get the expensive expedition under control.

While Fejos was alternately disheartened and furious about this interference, the result of his labor was a truly touching sixty-seven-minute docudrama initially titled *A Handful of Rice*, though it was released many years later in the United States by RKO under the title *The Jungle of Chang* (1951).*

The story followed a young Thai couple of the Maio tribe. After their marriage, the man went into the jungle to start a rice field, but drought forced him to find work as an elephant driver on a plantation in northern Siam. When he returned home, the entire crop from the field he and his wife had planted amounted to only a handful of rice. In a departure from documenting only what he observed, Fejos added a coda to the film where a Swedish couple is seen thoughtlessly throwing a handful of rice into the garbage following a dinner party—an amount equal to what the young Maio couple had struggled for a year to produce as their entire livelihood.

---

*Titles of some of the other films Fejos produced on his Asian expedition were *The Tribe Lives On*, *The Age of Bamboo at Mentawai*, *The Chief's Son Is Dead*, *The Dragon of Komodo*, *The Village Near the Pleasant Foundation*, *Tambora*, and *To Sail Is Necessary*.

Such a scene might seem ham-handed, but Fejos's delicate handling of the scene imparts pathos into the documentary that is characteristic of his best commercial films, such as *Lonesome*. Sadly, the RKO theatrical version dropped this scene from the film, a decision that film historian Graham Petrie noted eliminates "the central theme of Fejos's best work; that everyone deserves the opportunity to succeed in life and be happy, and that it is an offense against human dignity to deny or thwart this."

If Fejos emphasized this theme in his work, he missed its importance in marriage. Inga was unhappy being left to lounge in Hong Kong or Bangkok while her husband was off exploring and seeing things almost no Europeans had ever seen and which she very much wished to see. A frustrated Inga prepared to abandon Fejos to his work entirely. Then, by chance, she and Fejos met Axel Wenner-Gren, the richest man in the world, who would change both their lives.

CHAPTER 35

"My husband shot him in mid-air"

YEARS LATER, INGA DESCRIBED BANGKOK IN A LETTER TO JACK Kennedy. "The temples with their many colors, [were] so gorgeous that the town looked like a huge rainbow when the sun glittered on the dragon-like roofs, winding and twisting themselves towards the sky, as if they wanted to pierce it and touch the throne of God." The city seemed to have as many statues of Buddha as people, she said. "Most of them were made of gold, emeralds or other precious metals and stones," she said. "Many had a smile, which was very benevolent, or as if they would say, 'Why do you believe in me?'"

Inga, nominally a Lutheran, was always fascinated by religious faith and seems to have wished that she had more of it. She watched women pray to become married or pregnant and watched the poor, "who looked as if they had never had a meal in their lives," give alms to the Buddhist monks in their saffron-colored robes. "And the monk would take it with a gesture as if he was doing them a great favor, and that, dear, is exactly what they themselves felt, too. That is faith," she said.

Belying the notion that she needed or wanted rest, Inga "stamped all over the town buying beautiful old things. Gold and silver with crafts-manship which had taken patient months to make, and which they sold unwillingly to people who didn't appreciate it. . . . China so thin that an eggshell is fat compared. Gong-gongs with a sound reminding you that there is going to be a doomsday somewhere, sometime."

But shopping and sightseeing, even in a place as fabulous to the senses as Bangkok, soon grew old. To placate an increasingly lonely and irritated

Inga, Fejos took a break from filming in Siam and took Inga on a trip to Malaysia, where he hoped to film a tiger hunt in the jungles of Penang in December 1937.

When they arrived, Fejos's sound engineer, Baron Åke Sixten Leijonhufvud, recognized the enormous three-hundred-foot-long ivory and gold yacht docked in the Penang harbor as the *Southern Cross*, which belonged to Axel Wenner-Gren and his wife, Marguerite. With lavish wood paneling, three master bedrooms, a formal dining room, multiple fireplaces, and crystal chandeliers, the Art Deco steamer was essentially a mini ocean liner, "as long as a destroyer and a lot wider," according to *Time* magazine.

Wenner-Gren had purchased the *Southern Cross* two years before for $2 million from Howard Hughes, who had found the magnificent vessel an extraordinary help in the seduction of starlets in the early 1930s when he was splitting his time between aviation and producing Hollywood films. Wenner-Gren, who as far as is known stayed faithful to Marguerite, used the *Southern Cross* to fulfill his wanderlust and to stay at sea long enough to avoid certain Swedish income taxes.*

Leijonhufvud sent word to the Wenner-Grens that fellow Scandinavians were nearby making documentary films about life in the Orient and, intrigued by the news, Marguerite invited them to dinner, adding, according to Fejos, the notation "black tie." When Fejos advised Marguerite that he had neglected to pack a tuxedo or Inga an evening dress for the jungle, she cheerily replied, "Come as you are!"

It was a lively dinner. Wenner-Gren and Inga no doubt compared notes on their mutual acquaintance, Hermann Göring, though Marguerite held Inga's attention for most of the evening while the men discussed a mutual interest in exploration and primitive cultures. Marguerite, who loved to talk, appreciated that Inga was a good listener. Meanwhile, Fejos, the master raconteur and a man who knew a potential patron when he

---

*The legacies of Howard Hughes and Axel Wenner-Gren are so shrouded in legend that even the exact dimensions of the ship they each once called their own are in dispute. Various sources list the length of the boat anywhere from 286 to 320 feet, while *Time* magazine claimed the ship carried a crew of 315, not thirty. ("Man of Peace," *Time*, June 29, 1942, p. 30)

met one, enthralled Wenner-Gren with stories of his adventures and his passion for anthropology. Wenner-Gren, himself one of the world's greatest salesmen, appreciated Fejos's brilliant pitch, particularly on a subject of personal interest; Wenner-Gren liked to think of himself as "the last Viking" in search of new frontiers and lost civilizations.

At this meeting in Penang and a week later when they all dined again on the *Southern Cross* in Singapore, Wenner-Gren and Fejos began to discuss a potential partnership. Wenner-Gren suggested that they continue their discussion at his castle in Sweden when they all returned to Europe. Fejos said he thought of it as a "one of those casual invitations" that Wenner-Gren would never follow up on. He was wrong.

Part of the reason Wenner-Gren did not forget Fejos is that Fejos claimed to have saved Wenner-Gren's life on January 10, 1938, though the story was substantiated by only one other witness, and that was Inga. Other eyewitnesses debunked the claim.

As Fejos told the tale, he had invited Wenner-Gren to go on a tiger hunt. They flushed a tiger from the bush and Fejos, "always the perfect host," according to his admiring biographer, John W. Dodds, insisted Wenner-Gren make the kill. But Wenner-Gren only wounded the poor animal. Fejos waited for Wenner-Gren to fire again but claimed that the man who coolly made billion-dollar deals and sought to broker world peace was "shaking violently." Fejos, therefore, "moved in and shot the charging tiger about ten feet away, just as it was ready to leap."

Inga told an improved version just a few years after the supposed incident. In her version relayed to a New York newspaper, Inga asserted Fejos saved Wenner-Gren's life not once but twice! Inga said Fejos first knocked off a poisonous snake that had landed on Wenner-Gren's neck. "Then," Inga told a reporter, "we came suddenly on a black panther. My husband shot him in mid-air. I was there and gave him a big hand. The skin is stuffed and in Mr. Wenner-Gren's castle in Sweden."

But Genevieve Gauntier, Wenner-Gren's American-born sister-in-law (who was a pioneering actress and screenwriter in the motion picture industry), was present as an eyewitness and recalled the episode quite differently. Gauntier said that Fejos invited Wenner-Gren to observe the filming of what Fejos hoped would be a tiger fight—not a tiger hunt—

with Fejos staging the entire event. In a scene abhorrent to modern sensibilities, Fejos placed a live deer in a compound with six newly captured tigers in hope that the tigers would fight over the deer. Instead, the deer and tigers laid down together, much to Fejos's chagrin. Fejos then shot the deer, hoping the blood would rouse the tigers, but still there was no fight. By the time the tigers finally ate the poor dead animal, it was dark and Fejos could not film the scene.

During this episode, Gauntier wrote in her diary, Fejos shot a black panther that tried to escape the compound, though it never menaced Wenner-Gren or anyone else. Gauntier said an "ugly snake a yard long" brushed against Wenner-Gren's hand, but Gauntier made no mention of Fejos knocking it off Wenner-Gren's neck. In his own diary, Wenner-Gren made no mention of the snake at all, and said only that "a black panther that was close to escape had to be shot."

Wenner-Gren biographer Ilja Luciak has said that Fejos likely came to believe this "tall tale he created himself," and could no longer accurately recall the event as it truly happened. Fejos hated to be subordinate to anyone, so if he believed that Wenner-Gren owed him his life, then this fanciful incident helped level the relationship between benefactor and beneficiary.

Inga's understanding of her husband's fragile ego may explain why she repeated the myth, and it may also be one reason why she eventually broke with Fejos. Inga's tendency to unnecessarily embellish her adventures in Asia was uncharacteristic. Throughout most of her life, she leaned toward understatement. But under the influence of Fejos, serial fabulist, Inga also tended to inflate events, and she may not have liked how he influenced her personality in this way.

The most remarkable story Inga told to Muriel Lewis was her assertion that Fejos was "the most fascinating personality—complex, of course, erratic, but absolutely honest. He does nothing for effect. He's been too much in the theater for that. Twelve years directing at [sic] Hollywood teaches . . . personal sincerity." It is unlikely that even Fejos could have said this with a straight face.

CHAPTER 36

"The expedition is not bona fide"

FEJOS COULD NOT RETURN TO EUROPE TO CONTINUE HIS DISCUSSIONS with Wenner-Gren until he had completed his work in Asia, which he decided to do without Inga.

Before returning to Chiang Mai to finish *A Handful of Rice*, Fejos put Inga aboard the M.S. *Panama*, which set sail from Bangkok for Rotterdam on February 28, 1938. Instead of the planned two years, Inga had been in Asia barely ten months.

Less than two weeks after Inga departed Bangkok, Germany annexed Austria in the Anschluss, further aggravating tensions in Europe. Fejos and Olga each urged Inga to remain on the *Panama* all the way to Rotterdam in the neutral Netherlands and avoid travel in any part of Europe where war might erupt.* But Inga wanted to be in Copenhagen for Olga's sixtieth birthday on April 16, and so, exhibiting the dogged stubbornness that usually served her well, she left the *Panama* when it docked in Palermo, took a boat to Rome, and then a train to Denmark. Fortunately, war was still more than a year away and the trip was uneventful.

Fejos left Asia three months after Inga, upset that he had lost control of his expedition to the bean counters at Svensk Filmindustri. He never did make it to New Guinea. On his return voyage, Fejos was in no mood to make amends to his wife and, in fact, gave Inga the sour news that her dream of moving to America was, for now, "quite out of the question."

---

* When war did break out, asserting neutrality meant little. The Nazis occupied The Netherlands in May 1940, one month after the German occupation of the similarly neutral Denmark.

Such a move would cost too much, and he had no desire to return to Hollywood, which was the only place he knew how to make good money in the United States. Fejos said he had "a few little ideas in the back of my head" about what he would do next, meaning he wanted to continue his discussions with Wenner-Gren.

Back in Copenhagen, Fejos traveled regularly to Sweden to complete the editing of his films and to continue discussions with Wenner-Gren at the latter's Häringe Castle. By the following year, Wenner-Gren had established The Viking Fund (now called the Wenner-Gren Foundation), which would be headquartered in New York City and which would bankroll Fejos's future anthropological expeditions.* Fejos, thanks to a great deal of chutzpah but no formal training whatsoever, was on track to becoming one of the world's leading anthropological experts.

Fejos hoped to return to Asia and take a crack at finding unknown primitives in New Guinea, but Wenner-Gren insisted that Fejos instead travel to Peru and explore the upper Amazon. While some suggested Wenner-Gren founded The Viking Fund for tax purposes, he was genuinely interested in anthropology, and he wished to be at least tangentially involved in this first expedition. South America was close to Wenner-Gren's Bahamian estate, which would allow him to check in on Fejos from time to time—something far more difficult to do if Fejos was in New Guinea.

Wenner-Gren also had a strong desire to expand his business interests in Latin America. Publicity surrounding Fejos's expedition would open doors and expand opportunities. Wenner-Gren's interests in South America drew the attention of the American government.

Fejos left Copenhagen (and Inga) on November 22, 1939, arrived in New York City on December 1, and was on his way to Peru on New Year's Eve two months before Inga arrived in America. As had been true in Asia, in his letters to Inga (and Olga) Fejos emphasized the hardships he was facing in the jungle and how it was best that Inga was not with him. He came down with various fevers, claimed to have lost thirty-five

---

*The Wenner-Gren Foundation is still headquartered in New York City and remains one of the world's most important sponsors of anthropological research.

pounds, and survived a native tribe's attack on his expedition. "I have lost some of my men—only natives," Fejos wrote Olga, "but still we came back, ragged, terribly worn, but still back to civilization."

Fejos assured Inga he would be back in New York and with her by Christmas 1940. When that did not happen he pledged to be there by Easter. He wasn't. He knew Inga was angry and wrote Olga how much he appreciated that his mother-in-law had tried to "smoothen over things," adding, "Do not tell it to my wife, but I miss her unspeakably."

In between fending off tropical diseases and attacks from native tribes, Fejos was able to complete an extensive study of the Yagua Indians at the headwater of the Amazon in northeastern Peru.* In the process, he eventually discovered a total of eighteen lost cities of the Incas, which Fejos knew would create "a tremendous sensation" and briefly steal a few newspaper headlines away from the war, which it did.

Despite these discoveries, the FBI, which FDR had placed in charge of monitoring Axis activities in Latin America, insisted that Fejos's "archaeological expedition to Peru was not bona fide." The American government was convinced that the expedition was, at best, a cover for Wenner-Gren to pursue steel and electricity business interests in Peru. At worst, they believed Wenner-Gren was helping pave the way for Nazi infiltration of Latin America.

In a 1940 fireside chat, President Roosevelt warned that the Axis powers had designs on the Americas, which he said, "constitute the most tempting loot in all the world." As proof, Roosevelt later displayed a map purportedly taken from a Nazi agent that showed how Germany intended to organize the Western Hemisphere after it was conquered. The map, however, was a phony produced by British intelligence for the purpose of frightening Americans into supporting the Allied cause.

It wasn't only the Roosevelt administration sounding the alarm. In late summer 1941, the government of Argentina announced that a half-

*The Yagua inadvertently gave the Amazon its name. When Spanish conquistadors first encountered the Yagua, the Yagua attacked with their blowguns. Because the Yagua warriors wore palm skirts, the conquistadors initially thought they were women and so named the region after the Greek myth of female warriors called Amazons.

million Nazi troops were *already* in South America and stationed at secret bases in a half-dozen countries. To keep them secret, so an Argentine congressional probe alleged, the Nazis had purposely established them in remote areas, such as the upper Amazon—which was where Fejos's Wenner-Gren–sponsored expedition was operating.

Nelson Rockefeller, coordinator of Latin American Affairs for the U.S. State Department, sent Stanford professor Paul Hanna as an emissary to determine whether the Fejos expedition was part of an attempt by the Nazis to infiltrate South America. Hanna concluded that Fejos was in no way affiliated with the Nazis, but his finding did not end suspicions the U.S. government maintained about Fejos, Wenner-Gren, or Inga.

In truth, there was no Nazi infiltration of South America—no secret Nazi bases, airfields, armies, or even a significant Fifth Column there despite being the home of one million people of German or Japanese descent. After the war, an FBI internal study acknowledged, "There was a complete absence of any accurate data or details concerning the true extent or nature of subversive activities, current or potential, in Latin America."

Wenner-Gren insisted that the American government had never sincerely suspected him of espionage, or even of facilitating the transfer of wealth and needed raw materials from Latin America to Nazi Germany. Rather, he believed American businessmen "resented him as an industrial interloper in Latin America," an assessment that *Time* magazine concluded "was plausible enough as far as it went."

Whether the American government was sincere in its suspicions of Wenner-Gren or not, on January 14, 1942, while the *Southern Cross* was anchored at Vera Cruz, the American and British governments placed Wenner-Gren on their "blacklist." His assets—at least those within the authority of the Allied powers—were frozen, and he was forbidden to do business in the United States or Great Britain.

Wenner-Gren demanded the opportunity to clear his name, but there was no tribunal to hear his plea. He tried suing in federal courts, but the case never went to trial. So, Wenner-Gren stayed in Mexico and became an advisor to that country's president, presenting the *Southern Cross* as a gift to the Mexican navy. He also used the limited funds at his disposal and his business genius, even while on the blacklist, to corner the world's silver market and create the Mexican telecommunications giant TELMEX, which is the foundation of the fortune of one of today's wealthiest men, Carlos Slim.

By then, Inga was sorry she had ever met the Wenner-Grens, especially, she said, after Wenner-Gren offered her $1 million to be the mother of his child.

CHAPTER 37

The $1 million offer

AXEL WENNER-GREN HAD BEEN INSTRUMENTAL IN GETTING INGA admitted into Columbia University. Later, by granting her an exclusive interview, he helped her secure employment at the *Washington Times-Herald*. Marguerite extended a month of hospitality to Inga at Shangri-La and tried diligently to obtain employment for Inga with Elizabeth Arden. Yet Inga came to intensely dislike both Wenner-Grens.

Some of this hostility was due to Inga's belief that it was her association with Wenner-Gren, more so than her time among the Nazis, which was the reason for her continued harassment by the FBI. Severing this relationship was a key reason Inga began to contemplate divorcing Fejos because, as Inga told Jack Kennedy, "the only thing they have on me is that my husband works for Wenner-Gren."

When the War Division within the Department of Justice asked the FBI to interview Inga in February 1945, "the principal reason was to determine whether 'Miss Arvad was employed by Wenner-Gren as a private intelligence agent.'"* Inga insisted, as she always had, that her relationship with Wenner-Gren was "purely social" and said the only money she received from Wenner-Gren was Fejos's "salary," deposited in their joint account, for his leading The Viking Fund expedition to Peru. The total amount, Inga said, was $3,000. She told the FBI she had not seen

---

*This February 1945 interview was the only time, outside of Inga's initial interview with FBI Agent Hardison in December 1941, that the FBI actually spoke directly to Inga during their investigation.

Wenner-Gren since November 1941, when she saw him at a party hosted by Cissy Patterson.*

Inga's distaste for the Wenner-Grens was so great that she did something uncharacteristically mean-spirited. During her short tenure as a screenwriter at MGM in 1945, Inga wrote a treatment based on the Wenner-Grens that, had it ever been made into a movie, would make Orson Welles's controversial *Citizen Kane*, a thinly-veiled biography of William Randolph Hearst, seem the embodiment of subtlety and fair play.

Inga had a particular dislike of Marguerite, who even close friends acknowledged could be difficult. In a eulogy delivered at her 1973 funeral, one of those friends, the Swedish journalist Gunnar Unger, described Marguerite as "bizarre, spoiled, tactless—she could be impossible to stand," although Unger added (no doubt to the relief of discomfited mourners) that Marguerite also possessed "an aura of charm, a special magic around her and it was never boring in her company."

The "special magic" eluded Inga. In handwritten notes she made years later while contemplating writing an autobiography, Inga referred to Marguerite as "rich, demanding, unreasonable," someone who kept Inga "up till all hours, her drinking champagne, my listening." In Inga's spiteful screen treatment, the character based on Marguerite is a frustrated opera singer who nags her Swedish husband into becoming one of the world's wealthiest men who owns the world's largest yacht. If the resemblance to persons living was not clear enough, Inga's screenplay also has the Swedish businessman exiled for the duration of the war to Mexico, "where the rest of the international garbage can be found." The dismal tale ends with the couple's only son killed in the war, and the husband also dying in a plane crash while traveling to Washington to clear his name.

Even if Inga primarily blamed her association with Wenner-Gren for her harassment by the FBI, Inga's animosity was so deeply personal that there must be another reason for it, particularly since she herself was

---

*The FBI report states Inga last saw Wenner-Gren in November 1942, but that is an error as Wenner-Gren did not enter the United States during the war years once he was blacklisted in January 1942.

convinced that Wenner-Gren had been unjustly accused of being a Nazi agent.

One possible explanation is a story that Inga told each of her two sons in which she claimed that Wenner-Gren offered her $1 million to be the surrogate mother of his child, using, it should be emphasized, artificial insemination, which was becoming more common in the 1940s. The story cannot otherwise be substantiated, but it is unclear why Inga would make up such a story years after the fact.

The Wenner-Grens never had children. Marguerite once suggested the couple formally adopt a French-born boy they already treated as a "foster son," but Wenner-Gren rejected the idea. Perhaps Wenner-Gren wanted a biological heir.

Inga and Fejos also had no children, reportedly because Fejos was sterile from working with radium. Wenner-Gren, being the consummate dealmaker, perhaps believed he had found a solution for all concerned. He wished to have a biological child but had a barren wife; Inga could have children but was married to a sterile husband. Wenner-Gren had a great deal of money; Fejos and Inga had very little.

If Wenner-Gren truly made such an offer, he badly misjudged Inga. As she demonstrated in her relationship with Peipepteoman, the young Mentawai boy, Inga had a strong maternal instinct. She would have been repulsed by the idea that she could give birth to a child and then give it up, no matter her financial circumstances and no matter that such a child would have grown up in wealth and privilege.

Despite the winks and nudges that accompany a mention of "Inga Binga" in many Kennedy biographies, she had very conventional views of marriage and family. As she told her son, Ronald, in a letter late in her life, "I am a strong believer in two parents, NOT just one."

By the end of 1941, Inga had concluded that she if she were to become a mother, there was only one man whose children she wished to bear; that was Jack Kennedy, and, as the FBI soon learned, she believed that she was carrying Jack's child.

PART VII
Winchell Tells All

CHAPTER 38

Elizabeth Arden, FBI informant

FOR YEARS, *Washington Times-Herald* editor Frank Waldrop wondered who had alerted Page Huidekoper to the photo with the caption that proclaimed Inga "chief of Nazi publicity in Denmark." Through a Freedom of Information Act request made in the 1970s, Waldrop discovered that the man was Charles Latin, the *Times-Herald*'s purchasing agent, whose job was to figure out how much newsprint cost or "how many sheets of toilet paper [are] on a roll," Waldrop said. What was he doing going through old newspaper clippings and passing on tidbits he had found to reporters and other staff?

Waldrop learned that Latin had been working as an informant for the FBI, along with two other *Times-Herald* employees. "God damn it, see how clever they were!" Waldrop exclaimed. "I give Hoover full credit. They planted this thing—this 'third man,' planted it with Page Huidekoper to start an embarrassment, harassment, what have you."

Then it dawned on Waldrop that Latin and the other informants at the *Times-Herald* were keeping an eye not only on Inga but on him and the rest of the paper's senior management, too. Waldrop was stunned. He knew the *Times-Herald* was under scrutiny because of its isolationist and antiadministration views, but the paper had always been a strong and enthusiastic editorial supporter of the work of the FBI.

Waldrop's outrage at this violation of his civil liberties is amusing because Waldrop was an FBI informant, too. He routinely provided tips to the FBI, usually possible drug violations, racketeering, and other "law and order" issues. But he had also been keeping tabs on Inga for the FBI.

Waldrop would tell an FBI agent in December 1942 that he was "never sure about Inga," and so had been providing "regular notations" about her to FBI deputy director Edward A. Tamm since the incident with Huidekoper. Waldrop justified his cooperation as being equally for Inga's benefit. Waldrop told the FBI that if Inga "were innocent he wanted *her* to have the protection, and if guilty he wanted the *paper* to have the protection of being able to say there was never an occasion when they had information that they did not keep us fully informed."

Inga would have been unsurprised to learn that "Sir Francis," as she called Waldrop, displayed this lack of loyalty. Inga never gave a specific reason why she disliked Waldrop beyond the complaints that an employee typically has of an employer, but perhaps she sensed that he did not trust her. Inga usually kept in touch with old friends and acquaintances, so her lack of fondness for Waldrop is evident by the fact that she never contacted Waldrop again once she left the *Times-Herald*.

But Inga likely would have been surprised to learn that cosmetics mogul Elizabeth Arden had also offered to inform against her to the FBI, particularly given that her and Arden's entire association had consisted of no more than a few exchanged notes and a fifteen-minute interview in the spring of 1940. Yet Arden had not forgotten about Inga, whom she was now convinced "was a Nazi sympathizer."

While Arden had not hit it off with Inga during their brief encounter, the person who seems to have raised suspicions about Inga was J. Edgar Hoover himself. According to Arden, Hoover had once asked her (the circumstances are unknown) whether she knew anything about Inga. Now, on December 17, 1941, Arden placed a call to Hoover, who was out of the office, so Arden left a message that "Axel Wenner-Gren is trying to use pressure to get a certain woman a position; that in this position she would [be] in a good spot to make trouble and to put Miss Arden in 'a beautiful predicament.'" Arden added, "Mr. Hoover would know what she means."

Arden traveled to Washington the next day to provide the Bureau with copies of her correspondence with both Inga and Marguerite Wenner-Gren. Hoover was again unavailable, so Arden met with assistant director Percy Foxworth, who reported back to Hoover that Arden had volunteered to do much more than just inform against Inga. "[Arden], as you know, has a chain of beauty salons, and at any time we are interested in any particular women, she will personally ascertain if they are customers of hers, and if so, will arrange to notify us of any comments made by them while receiving treatment," Foxworth said.

Why Arden suddenly contacted the FBI so long after she and Inga crossed paths is unknown. There is no evidence that she had had any additional contact with Inga since that brief interview in New York. Perhaps Arden had picked up on the growing rumors that Axel Wenner-Gren would soon be put on the government's "blacklist" as a possible Nazi agent and worried that her past friendship with Marguerite might damage her own reputation—and business.

Having beauticians report on overheard conversations at notoriously chatty beauty salons seems unusually seamy, but in the early days of World War II there were many who believed being an informant was being a patriot. People like Arden or Latin who volunteered to inform on their employers, customers, neighbors, or friends were not doing anything contrary to the wishes of President Franklin Roosevelt, who had also taken a personal interest in Inga's case.

CHAPTER 39

J. Edgar and FDR

No GOVERNMENT AGENCY IN AMERICAN HISTORY HAS EVER BEEN SO closely identified with a single person as the FBI was with J. Edgar Hoover. For forty-eight years, from the day in 1924 he was appointed director of the Bureau of Investigation (the forerunner to the FBI) until his death in 1972, America's chief law enforcement agency responded primarily to the caprices of this one man.

Neither Hoover's ostensible bosses, the attorneys general of the United States, nor even *their* bosses in the White House directed the activities of the FBI. Their wishes might occasionally be in sync with Hoover's, or Hoover might choose to humor them in service to his own ends, but it was Hoover who decided where the energies of the FBI would be directed, and who was considered a friend (or at least a temporary ally) and who an enemy. Tom Wicker of the *New York Times* once wrote that Hoover "wielded more power, longer, than any man in American history."

If the FBI was a body, Hoover was its cerebellum. All information collected by the Bureau's agents flowed through him in one form or another, and all of it was filed in a myriad of forms, usually in triplicate. When a case was of a particularly salacious nature or because the FBI had gathered information using sensitive—that is, illegal—means, Hoover placed it among his "Official and Confidential" files. These files were usually maintained in his private office and kept separate from the Bureau's general file, away from the prying eyes of overseers in Congress or the administration. As one historian noted, this system "enabled FBI officials to affirm truthfully in legal proceedings that their 'central records system' contained no record of suspected illegal conduct." This is where Inga's case was kept. Her file would grow to more than 1,200 pages.

Inga had caught Hoover's attention even before he knew about her relationship with Jack Kennedy. First, she had had the audacity to peer into the FBI's inner sanctum when she interviewed Hoover's two closest associates, his deputy, Clyde Tolson, and personal secretary, Helen Gandy. The interviews were complimentary, but Inga's portrait of Gandy, "the sweetheart of the FBI," was cheeky, while her profile of Tolson and his "splendid physique" highlighted one reason why Hoover was not only attracted to but also envious of his second in command. If Inga was a spy, she seemed to be toying with the FBI, and Hoover could not tolerate that.

Second, Inga had powerful friends. She seemed to be a protégé of Cissy Patterson, and she was getting around town and interviewing lots of important people. Posing as a newspaper reporter in order to meet those in charge of America's secrets suggested "a most subtle type of espionage," Hoover told Attorney General Francis Biddle.

Third, Inga's connections with the prominent gave Hoover license to pry into some lives he dearly wanted to pry into. This included Hoover's supposed superior and rival within the intelligence community, Col. William J. "Wild Bill" Donovan, who had been one of Inga's interview subjects.

Hoover acted quickly after receiving Agent Hardison's report of his interview with Inga and Page Huidekoper. Less than two weeks after the interview took place, on Christmas Eve 1941 (since holidays didn't mean much to Hoover when there was work to be done), he directed that an extensive follow-up investigation be made, involving as many field offices as necessary, "to determine the truth of the allegations against Miss Arvad." He expected a full report "in the near future," and he told Sam McKee, the special agent in charge of Inga's investigation, that, because of its "potentialities," Inga's case should receive "continuous attention and your close personal supervision." To underscore his personal interest in Inga's fate, he added that he expected to receive updates on the investigation "not less frequently than weekly." Hoover sent out reprimands if he thought agents assigned to monitor Inga had become lax.

Hoover obtained Biddle's permission to tap Inga's phone, but agents also bugged Inga's apartment and hotel rooms where she stayed, stole her mail, broke into her apartment (and her mother's apartment), catalogued and photographed the contents of both domiciles, and had Inga under physical surveillance twenty-four hours a day.

They convinced Inga's banker to let agents review her financial records and Western Union employees to let them read her telegrams. They interviewed all manner of acquaintances, while Inga's apartment manager in Washington joined Frank Waldrop and Elizabeth Arden in becoming an FBI informant against Inga; the manager of the apartment she had in New York was also happy to cooperate with the FBI.

The FBI did all these things without a warrant, and although Biddle had granted authorization to tap Inga's phone, even this was extralegal. The Communications Act of 1934 prohibited the disclosure of information gathered during wiretapping, and the U.S. Supreme Court in several opinions affirmed that information gathered by wiretapping was inadmissible in court. Hoover and President Roosevelt, however, agreed that there was a large loophole in both the law and the court opinions.

Whatever his many other virtues, Roosevelt was not a great champion of civil liberties. Most infamously, he issued two executive orders in early 1942 that placed 120,000 Japanese Americans—two-thirds of them native-born citizens—in internment camps for the duration of World War II. Even Hoover, perhaps the greatest single violator of civil liberties in American history, was shocked by this "utterly unwarranted action."

Told that those destined for internment were essentially being robbed of their property without any safeguards or just compensation, Roosevelt replied, "I am not concerned about that." Biddle, the fourth Attorney General to serve under FDR, noted, "the Constitution has never greatly bothered any wartime President."

Roosevelt was on war footing well before Pearl Harbor. He and Hoover vividly recalled Germany's efforts at espionage and sabotage during World War I while America was still neutral. In 1916, to prevent a shipment of arms from reaching Britain and France, German saboteurs blew up a munitions depot in New York Harbor, which killed seven and damaged the Statue of Liberty. Then there was the notorious "Zimmerman

Telegram," in which German diplomats promised Mexico it could reclaim sovereignty over Texas, Arizona, and New Mexico if it declared war on the United States.

Warily watching Hitler's remilitarization of Germany, Roosevelt began worrying about Nazi espionage as early as 1934 when he called Hoover to the White House and requested that the FBI investigate the extent and influence of fascism in the United States. Hoover, who considered communism the much greater threat to national security, did little more in regard to homegrown fascism than have his agents scan newspaper clippings and collate files forwarded by local law enforcement agencies.

But Hoover became increasingly interested in foreign intelligence operations, particularly as the Axis powers in Europe began to eclipse homegrown gangsters as more glamorous public enemies for an agency that was always ravenous for good publicity. Hoover went to Roosevelt in August 1936 to request authority to engage in wiretapping, arguing that Congress and the Supreme Court had only declared that information gathered through wiretapping was inadmissible in a court of law. Hoover said this meant that information gathered only for intelligence purposes and not for criminal prosecution was legal. Roosevelt put nothing in writing, but Hoover's notes from the meeting claim that Roosevelt signed off on his interpretation and approved his wiretapping plans.

In the spring of 1940, as the Germans were overrunning France, the Low Countries, Norway, and Inga's native Denmark, Roosevelt warned that all nations now faced "a new method of attack . . . the Trojan horse, the fifth column that betrays a nation unprepared for treachery." If these methods arrived on American shores, Roosevelt promised to "deal vigorously" with all "spies, saboteurs, and traitors." Roosevelt was reluctant to increase immigration quotas before and during the war, even for persecuted Jews, partly because he was afraid Nazi agents would infiltrate the refugee populations to gain entry into the United States.

Roosevelt and Hoover's fear of Nazi collaborators and saboteurs in the United States was confirmed in 1938 when a plot to steal America's coastal defense plans was uncovered. But the agent in charge of the investigation blundered by announcing subpoenas would be issued before the suspects were in custody, and most fled the country before arrest. This fiasco, followed by revelations that a Soviet agent had infiltrated Naval Intelligence, led FDR to express dismay at "how unprepared we are to cope with this business of spying which goes on in our country." British intelligence officials sniffed that this was another example of the FBI being a "smash and grab" operation better at generating headlines than results.

Embarrassed that the FBI looked foolish, Hoover asked Roosevelt to strengthen the FBI's role in intelligence. FDR declined Hoover's request that he be made the nation's intelligence "czar," but he did secretly divert funds to allow the FBI to hire additional agents, made the FBI primarily responsible for counterintelligence activities in the Western Hemisphere, and appointed Hoover to chair a secret new commission that would coordinate intelligence activities.

In 1939, the Supreme Court again ruled that evidence gathered by wiretapping was inadmissible in a court of law. Attorney General Robert Jackson (Biddle's predecessor) ordered Hoover and the FBI to cease wiretapping. Undeterred, Hoover went around Jackson and convinced columnists such as Walter Winchell and Drew Pearson to opine that the wiretap ban was handcuffing the FBI. But what really convinced Roosevelt to ignore the court ruling was evidence supplied by Hoover that the Nazis intended to funnel $500,000 to the Republican presidential campaign in hopes of defeating Roosevelt and ensuring the election of an isolationist candidate in 1940.

FDR sent Jackson a secret note, saying that the court decision on wiretapping could not possibly have been intended "to apply to grave matters involving the defense of the nation." Roosevelt then stretched the definition of national defense to include political dissent. He gave Hoover a stack of telegrams received at the White House from America First supporters and directed him to investigate those who sent the telegrams and to learn the source of America First's funding.

It was another disturbing aspect of Roosevelt's complicated personality that he would countenance the abuse of civil liberties for political reasons. When the Senate Intelligence Committee conducted an investigation in 1976 on U.S. covert activities during the previous half-century, it concluded that "political belief and association" was the primary reason individuals were targeted with wiretaps prior to World War II. Wiretapping was used "not to assist in the enforcement of criminal laws," the committee concluded, but rather "to provide top administration officials with political information," setting a template for abuse by the FBI that lasted until Hoover's death.

Roosevelt, of course, had no insight into whether the case against Inga was compelling or not, but based on Hoover's reports it appeared that Inga's investigation could provide some interesting, even salacious, political information. Another word for that, of course, is gossip, which is as essential and pervasive a feature of politics as campaign donations or bumper stickers. FDR loved gossip, and Hoover loved providing Roosevelt (and every president under whom he served) with as much gossip as they were willing to hear.

FDR was willing to hear a great deal, and Inga's case provided him with inside dope about two public figures he found both fascinating and worrisome: Joseph P. Kennedy and Bernard Baruch. When even Hoover believed the surveillance of Inga had run its course, FDR insisted that it continue. Roosevelt had gleefully helped bug May Ladenburg's home during World War I when he was Assistant Secretary of the Navy; now his attention turned to reviewing reports of private conservations Inga was having with two of his nemeses, and nemeses who were noted philanderers at that.

Of course, Roosevelt would certainly have disputed that obtaining political information, entertaining or not, was his primary purpose in granting Hoover extensive counterintelligence tools. In 1941, Roosevelt could support his case by pointing to the fact that there were real-life Nazi spies running about on the East Coast. Not particularly adept spies, true, but they were present in the United States, and one high-profile case even involved a femme fatale—the very type of spy some believed Inga to be.

CHAPTER 40

"Some fine lemons"

On December 12, 1941, the very day Frank Waldrop marched Inga and Page Huidekoper to the FBI field office in Washington, D.C., a nine-man, three-woman federal court jury in Brooklyn delivered guilty verdicts against fourteen people accused of being part of a major Nazi spy ring in New York. Nineteen others members of the spy ring either already had or soon would plead guilty to various charges of espionage. Collectively, the thirty-three convicted spies were sentenced to a total of more than three hundred years in prison.

One who received prison sentences totaling twelve years was a twenty-four-year-old Vienna-born brunette named Lilly Stein, who was described by an FBI agent as "a well built, good-looking nymphomaniac with a good sense of humor." Stein, who made ends meet as a nude model and a prostitute, pleaded that she had agreed to work for Abwehr, the German military intelligence agency, only to avoid being sent to a concentration camp.

Stein was primarily a mail drop for her compatriots, but she was also tasked with prowling nightclubs in search of men who might spill a defense secret or two during pillow talk. The FBI seemed fascinated by Stein's many lovers, which included boxers, racecar drivers, and a young American diplomat named Ogden Hammond Jr. A chronicler of the whole episode noted that when it came to Stein's role in the spy ring "the FBI seemed to be most occupied with cataloging her love life."

That would soon seem to be the primary task of the FBI agents assigned to Inga's case as well. This lack of professional focus is unsurprising. While popular fiction writers from Ian Fleming to John le Carré portray those involved in espionage as operating at superhuman intellectual and physical levels, the fact is that at the beginning of World War II the intelligence agencies on both sides were heavily populated by ill-trained amateurs.

The group of which Stein had been a part was undone not by brilliant detective work, but by one of its own, a man named William Sebold, who clamed that he, too, had been blackmailed by the Abwehr into committing espionage. Sebold turned himself in and offered to become a double agent, but the FBI did not believe his story until Sebold removed his wristwatch, opened the back, and withdrew five tiny photographs that, read under a microscope, contained his orders for obtaining information on American military secrets.

As the FBI assumed the role of chief American intelligence agency for the Western Hemisphere, Hoover himself fretted that many of his agents, particularly the large number of new hires, were not up to the task of counterintelligence. As war loomed, the number of agents within the Bureau nearly doubled to 1,600. Such rapid growth strained the FBI's ability to properly screen candidates. "We certainly picked some fine lemons," Hoover acknowledged. Nor was their much opportunity to turn them into lemonade. Training in counterintelligence was virtually nonexistent because the FBI had so few personnel with experience in such matters.

This became evident as the FBI began its near round-the-clock surveillance of Inga. Like eyewitnesses to a robbery, agents could not even agree on what Inga looked like. Various reports list her as being as short as five-foot-four or as tall as five-foot-eight. One report described her as stocky; another said she was slender. At least all reports agreed she was blonde and had blue eyes.

When agents began breaking into Inga's apartment, they discovered, as they likely would in anyone's home, a variety of things that made sense only to those who lived there. But as the old saw goes, when you are a hammer, everything looks like a nail. In one of the FBI's first "black bag jobs" in her apartment, agents discovered a telegram sent from Peru by Inga's husband, Paul Fejos, which said only "Asavakit." Hoover and his agents were baffled and sent the telegram to the FBI's Technical Laboratory for analysis by linguistics and code experts.

After weeks of research, the best guess the laboratory analysts could make was that the telegraph operator may have simply misheard the word, which might have been the phrase *aksam vakit*, which in Turkish means "until tonight." However, the FBI report noted, "Inasmuch as there is nothing to reflect that Miss Arvad uses the Turkish language in corresponding to her husband, who is Hungarian, it is believed that this is probably a code word figured out between the two of them." *Asavakkit* (the telegraph operator did misspell the word) is actually from Kalaallisut, the language of Greenland's aboriginals, a people who fascinated Fejos; it means only "I love you." It was an inside joke, not code.

As they rifled through Inga's papers and possessions, FBI agents discovered that Inga had several peculiarities. She was compulsive about keeping meticulous records of her expenditures, and proudly made a note to herself that in the nearly two years she had been in the United States her expenses had averaged a frugal $213 per month. The FBI took photos of her expense book and other writings and had her handwriting analyzed with the conclusion that it was "of continental, if not German, strain."

That the FBI was relying on handwriting samples to determine if Inga was indeed a spy (phrenology was apparently not a viable option) underscores how little they uncovered in their initial investigation that would implicate Inga in espionage. In her apartment they discovered a handful of materials that theoretically had some national defense implications. Inga had made some notes about both commercial air routes and rubber supplies. She had done several articles with officials of the Federal Aviation Administration, which may explain the former, while the latter was compiled at the behest of her admirer Bernard Baruch, who wanted Inga to do a story on the need for rubber rationing.

The FBI pored over Inga's columns in the *Times-Herald*, trying to discern a pattern that would confirm that Inga was diligently infiltrating America's defense establishment. But for every incriminating interview with a U.S. Marine Corps colonel or the wife of Army Chief of Staff general George C. Marshall, there were a half-dozen more seemingly random topics of no national security consequence where Inga profiled the only known female owner of an Arthur Murray Dance Studio, a visiting solo violinist from Guatemala, or the son of Arthur Conan Doyle who was touring the United States as a Christian evangelist. This only led to speculation within the FBI that Inga was simply unusually clever in obfuscating her true intentions.

Even the liveliness of Inga's writing and conversation was viewed with suspicion. Inga may have claimed that she had been in the United States less than two years, but Hoover, for one, did not believe it. Overlooking that she had studied in England and was obviously talented with languages, Hoover said, "Her conversational English . . . certainly is not that of one of such short acquaintanceship with this country's colloquialisms and phraseologies." If this were not damning enough, the War Department passed on word to the FBI that Inga "frequently has been known to utter exclamations in German," which actually would have been a rather odd thing for a Nazi spy to do if they were seeking to avoid exposure.

While speculation within the FBI was often lively, what the agents observed or overheard was remarkably banal. Agents followed Inga's every move and noted every time she went to work, went shopping, or engaged in some occasional sightseeing. The records monotonously record Inga's every call to her mother, to her bank, or to check on a train or plane reservation.

One agent dutifully recorded a less than stimulating conversation Inga had about cheese. She had sent a "lovely note" to a man named Gene Kovacs to thank him for some assistance he had provided, and he in turn had sent her a gift of homemade cheese from his farm. Kovacs called Inga to advise her he was back in town, and the FBI agent on stakeout diligently noted, "She said she is eating some of his cheese, and likes it very much. They thought it a coincidence because he was about to invite her over to have some cheese with him. The next time she comes he hopes to have some country sausage for her." Crackers must not have entered the conversation, or the FBI would certainly have taken note.

Given this attention to detail, it is remarkable that the FBI agents staking out Inga had trouble identifying the man who came in and out of her apartment on a nearly daily basis. As with Inga's initial description, there were again discrepancies in how various agents described this man, so much so that the FBI initially thought Inga was having a romance with *two* naval ensigns. As Hoover explained to Attorney General Frances Biddle, "She is carrying on an affair with one such naval officer . . . and it is reported that another man in a similarly commissioned position has indicated he is engaged to marry her."

Eventually, it became clear that only one ensign was regularly spending the night at Inga's apartment, but his identity still eluded the FBI. For weeks, they repeatedly described him in various reports and memoranda as "the Ensign known only as Jack." The failure of the FBI to clearly identify "Jack" as Jack Kennedy is baffling because the FBI had examined all of Inga's *Times-Herald* "Did You Happen to See?" columns and must have seen her November 27 profile of Jack, which included a photograph of the young ensign.

Of course, Jack might also have been easily identified by America's top law enforcement agency because he was the second son of one of the most famous men in America who headed a family that had regularly been featured in magazines such as *Look* and *Life*. Or they might have identified him because Jack had achieved a modest level of celebrity on his own as a best-selling author.

Even when it was finally discovered that his last name was Kennedy and that he was the son of the former ambassador, Jack just didn't ring a bell. The FBI initially mistook him for his older brother, Joe Junior, and when they later referenced Jack's status as a published author agents mangled the title as "*Why England Slipped* [*sic*]."

As with Lilly Stein's case, it seemed as if the FBI was only cataloguing lovers rather than uncovering genuine evidence of espionage. One weary agent questioned how active a spy Inga could be when "the only people she contacts are those she writes articles about and her friend Kennedy."

Others in the Bureau, however, still had high hopes that Inga's case would soon break wide open. McKee, one of the FBI's star agents as the man who shot the bank robber Pretty Boy Floyd in 1934, was playing a leading role in Inga's investigation, and he was convinced that Inga's case had "more possibilities than anything I have seen in a long time."

CHAPTER 41

Strange bedfellows

INGA INITIALLY ADOPTED A "DEVIL-MAY-CARE ATTITUDE" TOWARD being an accused spy, but that attitude changed to fear after coworkers at the *Times-Herald* advised her that they had heard from sources that the FBI had tapped her phone and bugged her apartment. "After all," Inga later recalled, "I had heard of innocent people spending years in jail, even going as far as the electric chair." She was now alert to the danger she faced. "Every time I heard the phone click, I was sure that it was the FBI," Inga said, "and every man who looked at me twice or followed me for a block, I was convinced must be an FBI agent."

Inga spoke to Cissy Patterson about whether she should quit her job and move away from Washington, but Patterson convinced her to stay. Patterson told her that to leave now would be "an admission of guilt," and how, she asked Inga, would she be able to land a job in another city if it was learned that she was under investigation by the FBI?

The situation became more complicated when Paul Fejos finally returned to New York from the jungles of Peru in December 1941, just a few days before Inga was trotted down to the FBI's Washington office. Inga thought she had made up her mind to divorce Fejos, whether her relationship with Jack worked out or not, but when she came face to face with her husband of nearly six years she became uncertain what to do.

Inga traveled to New York to meet with Fejos shortly before Christmas. Their reunion was unpleasant. Inga told him she wanted a divorce. Fejos knew Inga had been seeing other men. Inga herself had told him about Hamilton Sanger the previous year. Olga likely spilled the beans about Nils Blok. And somehow Fejos had also learned about John Kennedy, and it was Inga's relationship with Jack more than any of the others that made Fejos "insanely jealous," Inga said. To know that Inga was involved with a rich young man twenty years his junior must have been a significant blow to Fejos's ego. Fejos did not directly accuse Inga of adultery—that would have been "the surest way" of losing her, she said—but when talking about Jack, Fejos was "unable to keep a sneer from his tone of voice." Fejos asked whether Inga was in love with Jack, and Inga, "being truthful," said she was.

Fejos tried to win back his wife and to overcome the effects of having been separated from her for more than two years. While his behavior in their six years of marriage would not have necessarily substantiated his claim, Fejos told Inga that no one could love her more than he did. He pledged to Inga he would stay in New York and go on no further expeditions. He promised to buy her a lovely new home, and he took Inga on long walks along 57th and 59th streets so that she could browse the antique stores and imagine how they might furnish this new home.

When bribery did not work, Fejos tried to frighten Inga with the idea that she might "ruin John's future" by involving him in a divorce scandal. Inga, aware of her husband's tempestuous nature, understood the implied threat immediately. "Through John he can hurt her," Inga said, "and maybe bully her into returning to him." Yet when their weekend together ended, Inga insisted she had made up her mind: as she and Fejos parted, Inga said she wanted a divorce.

Three hours later, however—the time it took Inga to travel back to Washington by train—she called Fejos to tell him that she had changed her mind and concluded, "My place is [at] the side of you." But as Fejos reported to Olga in a letter the next day, "my happiness did not last long. This morning [Inga] called again and said to me that she has changed her mind—and now it [their marriage] is off again."

Inga admitted feeling desperately confused. She loved Jack, but Fejos still had a strong hold on her. Several years later, as she reflected back on her feelings at that time (and writing in the third person), Inga said, "She is undecided, she hates to hurt him, and feels a strong loyalty towards a man to whom she has been married for six years. The fascination which always overcame her when he was present still works magic, but she knows that she doesn't love him. It isn't only because she loves John, it is because she married him when she was nearly a child, a child full of admiration for a brilliant and famous man, who completely enveloped her in his adoration."

This fascination Fejos had for Inga bordered on sorcery. Theirs had not been a happy marriage. He had been apart from her for more than two years—they had been apart for the majority of their marriage. And when they were together, they quarreled constantly. On some matters, Fejos had a very low opinion of his wife. When the FBI later questioned Fejos about whether Inga could have been a Nazi, "he refused to concede that Inga could ever intelligently be interested in political matters." Fejos's attraction for Inga at this stage was that he represented a haven away from the turmoil of being the target of an FBI investigation and the uncertainty surrounding her relationship with Jack.

Fejos believed he had made his case for why they should stay together. "I am completely at a loss just how I could do more than I did in the last two weeks," Fejos wrote Olga at Christmas. "I see it now, that it is just no use trying any further. Evidently, Inga wants her freedom and wants it badly enough to have no regard [for] making people's life a sorry mess. I am not saying this with anger . . . I have loved, and love her way too much for that."

With this false tone of resignation, Fejos hoped to hide the fact that he remained very angry, understandably so, given that someone young enough to be his son was cuckolding him. More out of pride than love, he was not ending his quest to keep Inga as his wife. Love, like politics, can make for strange bedfellows, and in his fight to keep Inga, Fejos chose a remarkably strange bedfellow: Joseph P. Kennedy, the father of his romantic rival.

Fejos arranged to meet Kennedy in New York around the New Year. We do not know what exactly was said, but the meeting certainly made Kennedy keenly aware that Jack's romance with Inga was no longer a harmless romp and a giddy opportunity to develop sexual technique under the tutelage of an older woman. Fejos was clearly an emotional and a worryingly unpredictable man, who no doubt made the same, vague threats regarding Jack's future to Kennedy that he had previously made to Inga.

What Kennedy said in return is unknown. He was not impulsive like Fejos. He also valued his close relationship with his children. He knew Jack was strongly attached to Inga. Whatever he might do would be subtle. He would leave no fingerprints behind. He wished to maintain his otherwise warm relationship with Jack. But based on what Fejos told Olga and what Olga passed on to Inga, Kennedy apparently told Fejos that he would join him in doing what he could to break up the romance.

Olga wrote Inga with the news that Fejos and Joseph Kennedy were now working in tandem, for Fejos had said "that in two months you would be out of your job and the old Kennedy would not be sorry for you because he doesn't want his son to have anything to do with you." Olga added the further troubling development that Fejos had hired a private detective to follow Inga, and that Fejos now knew "when Jack comes in your apartment and where he goes; he knows how many lights are burning and when the lights are turned off."

This development also troubled the FBI. They became worried that so many men were now keeping an eye on Inga that they would begin to bump into one another. An observant private detective might easily discover the FBI's presence. FBI agents assigned to watch Inga and her apartment were warned to use discretion and break off surveillance if necessary to avoid any shamus found on the premises.

In addition to enlisting Joseph Kennedy, Fejos hoped to keep Olga in his corner. He continued to woo Olga, apparently unaware how much Olga's influence over her daughter had waned over the past two years. Olga reported to Inga that Fejos had invited her over to his apartment and suggested that she think about moving in, but Olga was less moved by his generosity than the suspicion that Fejos was looking for a free housekeeper. Olga also declined Fejos's invitations to dinner and the theater.

She noted to Inga that when she visited Fejos she noticed that he kept several framed photographs of a beautiful young Austrian-born singer named Marianne Arden, who had become a popular entertainer in New York's cabarets. Olga could only shake her head upon discovering that Fejos was taking his marriage vows with no greater seriousness than her daughter was. "I find it strange," Olga told Inga, "that he has so quickly soothed his feelings with a neat young singer of 24 years of age who likes him insanely, without Paul's yet returning it."

With as many lovers and detectives present as might be found in a French farce, Olga was worried that Inga would soon be caught up in something truly tawdry. "As your mother, I only beg you, little Inga, to live your life in accord with the finest and the best in yourself; do not lose your self-respect," Olga wrote Inga. "You will never in life regret that rule. I feel that you have only a little respect for my ideas, but a mother never gives up hope for the best for her children."

But Inga still was baffled as to what "the best" was. Into early January she was still agonizing over whether to divorce Fejos or not. On January 11, 1942, Fejos wrote Inga, "I am a bit puzzled by your intentions as to the future. You, dearest, can be more cryptic than the prophets of the Old Testament. You write that if you would be eighteen, you would probably marry Jack. . . . Then you follow up with, 'But I would, might probably, choose you instead.' Now, my inconsistent child, what is all this about? Has anything gone wrong with yours or Jack's love?"

But Fejos also left no doubt that his playing the role of sympathetic "ex" was only a pose. "There is one thing I want to tell you in connection with your Jack," he continued. "Before you let yourself go into this thing any deeper, lock, stock and barrel, have you thought that maybe the boy's father or family might not like the idea?"

That thought had almost certainly crossed Inga's mind, but so far, at least, no clear objection had been expressed. That would change the very next day, and millions of people would read about it.

CHAPTER 42

Winchell knows all

GOSSIP COLUMNIST WALTER WINCHELL'S MOTTO WAS, ACCORDING TO biographer Neal Gabler, "HE SEES ALL . . . HE KNOWS ALL." To the degree he is remembered at all, Winchell is recalled primarily for being the inspiration for the vicious gossip columnist J. J. Hunsecker in the 1957 film *Sweet Smell of Success*, but at the peak of his power he may have had "the largest continuous audience ever possessed by a man who was neither politician nor divine." Fifty million Americans, a remarkable two-thirds of the entire adult population of the United States, either listened to his weekly radio show or read his daily column, which appeared in more than two thousand newspapers nationwide.

One of those newspapers was the *Washington Times-Herald*, whose readers—and certainly its employees—were abuzz about an item contained in Winchell's column for January 12, 1942. Inga recalled her shock when she strolled into the office that morning (a Monday) and one of her friends, probably Kick, asked, "Did you read the item about yourself in Walter Winchell's column?" Inga had not, but quickly grabbed a newspaper and rapidly began scanning Winchell's work under the headline "On Broadway." She did not have to read far.

Midway in the first paragraph, sandwiched between a report of a nasty catfight between two Broadway actresses and a report that jazz greats Louis Armstrong and Gene Krupa had been seen about town, was this blind item written in Winchell's typical rat-a-tat-tat style: "One of Ex-Ambassador Kennedy's eligible sons is the target of a Washington gal columnist's affections. So much so—she's consulted her barrister about divorcing her explorer-groom . . . Pa Kennedy no like."

Inga was dumbstruck. "My name wasn't mentioned," she recalled a few years later, "or I don't believe it was, but at the time I was the only blond [*sic*] columnist in Washington with an explorer husband, and Washington is a very small rat hole when it comes to gossip."

Inga knew Winchell, for she had featured him in a "Did You Happen to See?" column exactly two months before, interviewing the wisecracking columnist while he had his hair cut. As the interview began, Winchell told Inga, "Now do me a favor. Distort all that I have said, or what I am going to say, because nothing sounds so silly as a person who is being interviewed." As Winchell departed the barbershop through a revolving door, Inga noted that he was "out hunting again—but what?" Now, she was the prey.

The *Times-Herald* office was in turmoil. "All manner to do," John White wrote in his diary. "No sooner in office than became embroiled in the great case of the Ambassador's Son and the Beautiful Blonde Spy." Jack shortly appeared at the *Times-Herald* office and huddled with Frank Waldrop and Cissy Patterson to discuss options. He didn't have many.

Waldrop was furious, White said, certain that Winchell's source had been the FBI. Without noting that he himself had begun feeding information about Inga to the Bureau, Waldrop explained to Jack that Winchell had a vendetta against Patterson and was determined to wreck the paper. That actually wasn't true. Winchell and Patterson had been on friendly terms—until this perceived assault on Inga.

Patterson ordered the offending paragraph of Winchell's column removed in subsequent editions of the *Times-Herald* and thereafter began regularly spiking Winchell's column, riding out complaints from the large number of *Times-Herald* Winchell fans who wanted to know all. On January 17, Patterson penned an editorial that appeared on the front page of the *Times-Herald*. It did not mention Inga or her case directly, but instead attacked Winchell and J. Edgar Hoover in a roundabout way by revisiting the unfounded suspicions that had dogged May Ladenburg during World War I because of her romance with Bernard Baruch:

What story? Intrigue? Incriminating documents? International spy business? Oh, no. No. Not a shred of evidence did he or his assistants discover. Not by conscious or unconscious act could this girl be accused of disloyalty to her country. But the gossips were almost as well pleased as if a first-class international melodrama had come to light. For he dug up a fascinating romance between this woman and one of the most celebrated men of the day.

Most readers must have been baffled why an incident from a quarter century ago merited such a prominent place in the paper. It was Patterson's way of placing Winchell and Hoover on notice—using the prerogative of a powerful but eccentric publisher to send a personal note to two men on the front page of a newspaper that had a quarter-million loyal subscribers. The message was received and understood. FBI special agent Sam McKee said Patterson's association of Inga with Ladenburg was clearly a signal that "the *Times-Herald* would be quick to expose any investigation of the FBI." The FBI would need to maintain the utmost discretion in Inga's case.

Winchell said that when he later ran into Patterson at a dinner party honoring the British ambassador to the United States, Patterson screamed at him, "Why the hell don't you quit looking under the bed for Nazis?" Winchell claimed surprise at Patterson's vehemence until Hoover later explained to him in a letter, "She apparently has a very strong feeling for this Arvad woman."

All the excitement was not limited to Washington. Winchell's column appeared in newspapers coast to coast, including several in New York City. One interested New Yorker was Paul Fejos, who immediately sent a sarcastic telegram to his wife much different in tone from the understanding letter he had sent Inga the day before. "Well here it is," an angry Fejos wrote, "your first break in the greatest institution of newspaper writing in the US. You made Winchell's column."

Fejos followed up the telegram with a self-pitying letter in which he played the greater victim. Fejos saw himself as "the clown of the act, and all the laughs are on me. I have had enough in these last weeks." Fejos felt particularly humiliated by how Winchell had made it appear that Inga was pursuing Jack, rather than the other way around. "If it would have been *you* who was the target of the affections of the gentleman, it would be better. But that HE should be the target—that is to say that you are the one who does the running after—that is pretty sour. That my proud, always dignified, ramrod wife gets this fifth rate slap across the face, that hurts. I feel like hell about it."

White admired how well Inga seemed to be handling the fuss. Inga later admitted she felt both humiliated—and worried. While she appreciated Patterson coming to her defense, by calling out Winchell and Hoover by name Inga worried she had now made two very powerful enemies. But she would not let the worry show. "Must say Inga looking her very best," White noted, despite her being caught in such a tempest.

White was surprised that Kick was also reacting to the Winchell bombshell with great equanimity. According to White, the day after Winchell's item about Jack and Inga appeared, Kick literally shrugged off the brouhaha and reported that her father was not the least upset, despite Winchell's assertion that he "no like." Kick said her father had just happened to pass through Washington the day before, and she reported to White that he found the whole Inga scandal "very funny." He even told Jack to "do just as he wished."

Here, then, is a significant clue as to who the source of the item in Winchell's column really was, and despite what Waldrop insisted, it was probably not the FBI.

For one thing, the FBI had not yet learned all the information contained in Winchell's thirty-word tittle-tattle. In early January, the FBI still was unsure of the identity of the naval ensign spending nights at Inga's apartment. Nor did they know that Inga had contacted an attorney about getting a divorce, nor would the FBI have known for a fact that Joseph Kennedy was unhappy about the affair as Kennedy was masking that fact even from his children. Only a handful of people knew all the elements contained in the item in Winchell's column, and only one had a motive to see the item published: Joseph P. Kennedy.

Having met with the mercurial Fejos and taken his measure, Kennedy would not have found the situation between Jack and Inga "very funny," despite what he may have told Kick. Kennedy had expended a great deal of energy and money throughout his adult life crafting an image of the Kennedys as the exemplar of the perfect American (and Catholic) family.

Having his second son embroiled in what might become a particularly messy divorce would have tarnished that image to the detriment of all Kennedy's plans for himself and for his sons, particularly Joe Junior's political career.

Winchell said he received the item on Jack and Inga from fellow columnist Drew Pearson, who wrote Winchell on January 6 that Inga was "casting eyes in the direction of ex-ambassador Joseph P. Kennedy's offspring [and that] Old Joe is reported to be very hot and bothered about it." Pearson mailed this letter to Winchell just a few days after Kennedy had met with Fejos in New York.

Neither Winchell nor Pearson ever explained why Pearson did not use the item in his own column, "Washington Merry-Go-Round," and instead passed it on to Winchell, but there are several plausible explanations. Pearson was Cissy Patterson's former son-in-law and Pearson's brother, Leon, still worked at the *Times-Herald*. Patterson still had fond feelings for Pearson, even after he divorced her daughter, but the relationship soured in the wake of Pearl Harbor as Pearson had been an interventionist and Patterson could not let go of her isolationism. Knowing, as he probably did, not only Patterson's affection for Inga but also his former mother-in-law's temper, Pearson probably wanted to avoid the fireworks that Patterson tossed Winchell's way.*

But it may not be that Pearson gave Winchell the item of his own volition. Kennedy never liked his children to know just how much he interfered in their lives. Each of his children knew their father was always (quietly or not) pulling strings, but for a host of reasons—love, fear, money—they never confronted their father about his manipulations.

For example, White was flabbergasted when Kick explained that her father always hired detectives to do background checks on anyone his

---

* Pearson failed to prevent a complete break with Patterson. She had already relegated his column to the comic pages when Pearson made disparaging remarks about one of Patterson's heroes, General Douglas MacArthur. She spiked the column entirely, which infuriated Pearson. He and Patterson never agreed on whether he had quit or she had fired him, but his column moved to the *Washington Post*. Patterson then fired Pearson's brother out of spite. (Ralph G. Martin, *Cissy: The Extraordinary Life of Eleanor Medill Patterson* [New York: Simon and Schuster, 1979], pp. 424–27)

children dated. "They are very efficient people," Kick told White, "so the reports are very complete." Since White considered himself a bit of a rake, he asked how Kick's father could have approved of her seeing him? "Oh, he considers you frivolous, but harmless," she replied.

But as his children grew older, Kennedy grew subtler. "Old Joe had learned by then to mask what he was doing," said Waldrop. "He was smart enough to know he didn't want to make a big thing about it in front of the children for fear his disapproval would backfire, but he certainly was not going to just sit back and let Jack's reputation be hurt by a misguided relationship with a woman."

It seems very probable that Kennedy approached Pearson with his concerns about Jack and Inga's relationship, but then asked him to pass the item to Winchell to create another layer of deniability should Jack get the idea that it was his father who had planted the news. Joseph Kennedy was friendly with Winchell, who was an occasional guest at Kennedy's Palm Beach estate, but Pearson was a close friend. Jack knew that his father was a regular source for Pearson's column, while Pearson often used his column to Kennedy's benefit, such as when he floated a trial balloon in late 1939 to ascertain public reaction to the idea of Kennedy being a candidate for president in 1940 if FDR did not plan on seeking a third term.

Kennedy would have trusted Pearson to handle the situation with discretion, which he did as the initial assumption of most of those involved (except for Inga) had been that the FBI leaked the item to Winchell. Inga, intimate with one Kennedy child and best friends with another, understood the reach of Joseph Kennedy.

Those who have suspected Hoover leaked to Winchell have erroneously assumed Hoover would have enjoyed embarrassing Joseph Kennedy. In fact, Kennedy was "an old friend of the director's." Beginning in the 1930s and continuing until Jack was elected president, Kennedy maintained a long-running correspondence with Hoover consisting "almost entirely of flattering letters to the director." The apex was in 1955 when Kennedy told Hoover it would be "the most wonderful thing for the United States" if Hoover ran for president and promised, whether

Hoover ran as a Democrat or Republican, "the largest contribution you would get from anybody."

Far from seeking to embarrass Joseph Kennedy, Hoover wished to help, both because he appreciated Kennedy's flattery and because Hoover would have considered Jack's tryst with Inga extremely immoral and he would have been pleased to help end it. Following the Winchell column, and almost certainly at Hoover's direction, Joseph Kennedy was regularly apprised of the status of the FBI's investigation of Inga—though not all of it. It seems Kennedy was unaware the FBI was recording even some of his conversations when Jack phoned from Inga's apartment.

Though nothing can be proven through documentation, even if Joseph Kennedy was not the source of the item that appeared in Winchell's column, it served his purpose. It set in motion a chain of events that would eventually separate Jack and Inga, though it also would nearly get Jack killed.

CHAPTER 43

"They shagged my ass down to South Carolina"

ON JANUARY 13, 1942, THE DAY AFTER WALTER WINCHELL'S COLUMN
ran in the *Washington Times-Herald* and two thousand other newspapers,
Jack received word by telephone that he was being shipped out of Washington to another desk job at a navy yard in Charleston. As Jack later
confided (off the record) to a reporter, "They shagged my ass down to
South Carolina because I was going around with a Scandinavian blonde,
and they thought she was a spy!"

ONI had been aware for several weeks that Jack was "playing
around" with Inga, and had already been contemplating transferring
Jack out of Washington to avoid a scandal. The sense of urgency to
make that transfer increased in late December when ONI commanders
were made aware that the FBI was now investigating Inga. ONI provided the photographs that led the FBI to finally confirm that Jack was
indeed the naval ensign spending the night at Inga's, and from there
on the two agencies began sharing information and even, occasionally,
surveillance duties.

On January 9, 1942, a request to transfer "Joseph F. Kennedy" (the
FBI was not the only agency having trouble with names) was finally submitted by the chief of Naval Operations to the Bureau of Navigation, but
the Bureau saw no reason to rush the request with other more pressing
tasks at hand as America entered its second month of war.

With the publication of Winchell's column, however, there was suddenly a "really frantic" atmosphere among the ONI brass, according to

Jack's boss at ONI, Captain Samuel Hunter. ONI had been one of several entities harshly criticized for the intelligence failures that led to the disastrous losses at Pearl Harbor, and its leaders did not want that criticism compounded by the public thinking ONI now had allowed a Mata Hari in its midst. Some, including ONI assistant director Howard Kingman, wanted to cashier Jack out of the navy entirely, a black mark on Jack's record that, as Hunter later noted, would have made it "rather doubtful" that Jack would ever have been elected president.

Given Jack's status as former ambassador Joseph Kennedy's son and the attention a court martial would attract, cooler heads prevailed, and it was decided that the best thing to do was just get Jack quickly out of Washington and to keep him away from Inga, if possible. To that end, Jack was advised that he would be restricted to travel within a seventy-mile radius of the Charleston Naval Yard, meaning no trips to Washington without special permission, although ONI could not, of course, prevent Inga from traveling to Charleston.

Joseph Kennedy, meanwhile, called Jack to discuss Winchell's column, Jack's impending transfer, and how both might impact his relationship with Inga.

As we deduce just how serious Jack and Inga's romance was, we must take into account how the war and its stresses heightened emotions and compressed time for the millions whose lives were turned upside down by the conflict. Carpe diem was a rallying cry, and a regular feature of popular culture in these days was just how quickly initial passion could blossom into a genuine romance. In the movies, the conceit was that it could happen in less than a day, as it did in *The Clock* (1945) with Judy Garland and Robert Walker. Inga and Jack had had the luxury of two months to deepen their relationship.

Perhaps, as John White believed, when Jack and Inga began their affair two months earlier neither saw the relationship lasting for long. It was not simply that they became increasingly cognizant of their remarkable compatibility, which would have deepened the relationship regardless of other forces, but the whole world had changed in the two months since they had met. More than that, because of the FBI investigation and the Winchell column, they had already been through the type of stress that knits a stronger relationship when the strain does not instead tear a couple apart.

Friends and family were aware of how intense the relationship had become. Just as Torbert Macdonald had assured Inga how much she meant to Jack and how her love had fundamentally changed him, he now advised Jack of how devoted Inga had become to him. Macdonald wrote Jack that he had recently seen Inga while in Washington and that he had "a long chat with her—on our only subject—and controlled my nausea long enough to do a journeyman's job—She is either crazy about you or is fooling a lot of people. 'How was *he*—what did *he* say etc. etc.'" Kick, meanwhile, told Inga "she would go insane if she didn't quit talking to her about Jack."

As they faced a jealous husband, a disapproving family, an FBI investigation, and now a forced separation, it is likely that more than once it occurred to Inga and Jack that they, like Romeo and Juliet, were star-crossed lovers, so that their love achieved a depth and passion that might not have occurred in a different time in their lives—and which did *not* reoccur for either of them later in life. So as we judge just how serious Jack and Inga were about being together for a lifetime, the best measure is just how worried Jack's father was about the possibility.

Inga was in the room when Jack spoke to his father, and she recalled the scene several years later: "From years of habit, which John hasn't outgrown, he is scared of his father. 'Of course,' the old man says, 'you are not going to marry her, are you?' John wants to explain, but feels that it can't be done on the phone. He replies meekly, 'Honestly, Dad, I don't know, she is a great girl.'"

Inga later insisted that Jack had definitely asked her to divorce Fejos and marry him. Jack had even consulted a priest to determine how Inga might have her two marriages annulled so that she and Jack could get married in the Catholic Church. The FBI, too, heard from sources at the time that Inga had "stated she is engaged to marry" Jack. With his many spies, Joseph Kennedy had undoubtedly heard the same reports.

Kennedy, however, also decided not to force a confrontation with his son over the phone. As Inga said, he knew better than to run her down when emotions were high and also when she was right there in the room with Jack to blunt whatever argument Joe Senior might make.

Instead, Kennedy suggested to Jack that he fly down to Palm Beach to relax and "talk the whole matter over." Jack replied that he did not know if he could get any leave before he had to report to his new assignment. His father replied, "I guess I can pull a few strings for you." At that, Inga said, a light bulb went on in Jack's head, and he began to truly wonder just how much his father had to do with the events that led to this sudden transfer. Jack was granted several days leave before he had to report for duty in Charleston and visited his father in Florida.

In his diary entry for January 17, John White recorded that both Inga and Jack seemed very sad about their impending separation, and had tried to squeeze as much time together as they could before Jack left. As the FBI dutifully noted, Jack spent the nights of January 16, 17, and 18 in Inga's apartment, and Inga joined Jack at Mass on Sunday, the 18th. Inga and Kick helped Jack pack that afternoon, and then he departed for Palm Beach by plane on January 19.

Jack had been gone only a few hours when Inga wrote him a letter. "Is the sun shining, the pool tempting and your family spoiling you?" she asked. "I do hope so dearest Jack that you are having all the fun in the world. You should. Why? I don't know, except that you seem to be one of the very rare people born to sunshine and happiness."

Inga then spoke of mothers, hers and his. Inga was amused that in a recent letter from her mother, Olga's only comment about Winchell was, " 'How sad about the item in W.W.'s column.' That is all [she said]. I like a woman who has self control." Inga then told Jack that she had taken the liberty of sending his mother a telegram. "I said you were looking forward to seeing her," Inga said.

Rose Kennedy did not acknowledge the telegram, nor did she acknowledge Jack's relationship with Inga in any way. It was one thing for her boys to sleep around with available women, but a serious relationship with a married woman when there was talk of divorce and a marriage that would bring scandal to the family was too much for Rose Kennedy to consider. She therefore kept her distance from Inga, whom she likely considered a trollop unworthy of notice. This meant that Rose never got to know one of the few intimates of Jack who claimed that he definitely loved his mother. "I am happy you love yours so much, and I understand why she is so fond of you," Inga wrote.

Then again, perhaps Jack never declared his love for his mother in Inga's presence, and Inga included these lines only because she assumed Jack's family would open his mail and she hoped to make a good impression as they snooped, for she also included praise for Kick and even Papa Joe. She noted that she was finally reading *Why England Slept* and pledged to follow his direction and read more American history. "So much has gone wrong here, but I only love America more and more," she said. She seemed intent on proving to Jack and the whole Kennedy family that she was worthy of him and being part of their clan. But the decision to exclude her had already been made.

CHAPTER 44

"Realizing what makes Inga tick"

IT IS A TESTAMENT TO JUST HOW MUCH TIME INGA AND JACK SPENT together that by just the first full day of Jack's absence, January 20, Inga was extraordinarily and uncharacteristically gloomy. Jack's departure and Inga's fear of the pressure that was even then being brought to bear on him by his family to end their romance sapped Inga of any interest in her normal routine. As she stared at that day's edition of the *Times-Herald*, Inga wrote Jack another letter and told him that her work now seemed unendurably trivial. She said she thought to herself, "'Inga, you will have to do something else, something constructive, because it actually doesn't matter if you are dead or alive.' What a feeling. . . . Cheerful, isn't it, young Kennedy?"

Inga was feeling deeply sentimental. It was in this letter that she told Jack about her parents and her childhood, including the first time anyone told her she was pretty ("I was four"); the first time another girl told her she was ugly ("but one consolation was that she admitted liking my blonde hair"); and the time when Olga became very sick and she thought her mother might die. "That was the first time I saw the world crumbling."

Now, with the thought that she might soon lose Jack, Inga saw her world falling apart again. She imagined the case Pa Kennedy was making to convince Jack to end the romance. How she wished she could be by Jack's side at the pool in Palm Beach, where she knew the right smile or a gentle touch would easily rebut all of his father's objections. Instead, she would have to rely on words for her own defense, hoping that she might immunize Jack from his father's argument by evoking memories of their time together. She recalled meeting Jack, "a boy who was supposedly brilliant, who laughed the whole time", at a Washington cocktail party, which was followed by "dozens of dinners with the following menu—Soup, Steak [*sic*], mashed potatoes, green peas, carrots—and ice cream."

Inga desperately hoped that Jack felt some of the emptiness she now felt at their separation, "the first time I missed anybody and felt lonely and as though I was the only inhabitant of Washington," but also some of the fullness, "loving—knowing it, being helpless about it, and yet not feeling anything but complete happiness. At last realizing what makes Inga tick."

But what made Jack tick? As Inga wondered what "Big Joe," as Inga often referred to him, was telling Jack about her, the more intriguing question was what was Jack telling his father about himself?

There is evidence to suggest that Jack, having been "built up" and given a great boost of confidence by Inga, finally confided to his father his hopes to pursue his own political career. Inga, who had the gift for making men feel as special as they hoped they were, had given Jack the courage to reveal his dreams to his father.

Jack's older brother, Joe Junior, had always—always—been the focus of the Kennedy family's political aspirations. Later, when Jack began his political career, he and his father developed the fiction that such a career for Jack had never crossed either's mind until Joe Junior was killed in August 1944. "But I didn't even start to think about a political profession for more than a year later," Jack said in 1960 when he was a candidate for president. Based on Inga's letters and her and others' recollections, we know that was untrue.

But Jack's father (and mother) had believed that Jack lacked political skills and, so far as they knew, any political ambitions. After Jack graduated from Harvard, Joseph Kennedy said he and Rose could not have imagined Jack as a politician because he was "rather shy, withdrawn and quiet. . . . We were sure he'd be a teacher or a writer." It was an opinion Joseph Kennedy had long held. While still ambassador in London, he introduced his three eldest sons to a British guest by pointing to them one by one and saying, "There's young Joe—he's going to be President of the United

States; and there's Jack—he's going to be a University President; and there's Bobby—he's the lawyer."

Almost immediately after his meeting with Jack in Palm Beach, there was a clear shift in how Joseph Kennedy viewed his second son. Within days, he began taking concrete steps to advance the political careers of both Joe Junior *and* Jack. Joseph Kennedy had gone to considerable trouble to shift his entire family's legal residence to Florida, but now, shortly after meeting with Jack, he arranged for *both* of his eldest sons to become residents of Massachusetts on the well-founded belief, given the family history, that this would be where both boys would pursue their political careers.

Then, on February 2, 1942—less than two weeks after his and Jack's tête-à-tête—Joseph Kennedy wrote David Sarnoff, the head of both RCA and NBC, to inquire about purchasing radio stations in Massachusetts. "Since my *two* [emphasis added] boys are eventually going to make their homes in Massachusetts, if they get through this war successfully, I would be interested in purchasing any radio stations that you might have for sale in Boston or Massachusetts," Kennedy said. "My energy from now on will be tied up in their careers rather than my own."

That Kennedy now spoke of the ambitions of Joe Junior and Jack in the same breath represents a remarkable evolution in the family dynamic. Jack had been unable to tell his father what was in his heart before. The great change that allowed Jack to finally be candid with his father was his relationship with Inga. Without her influence, he may have remained a callow youth doomed to play second fiddle to his golden brother.

Joseph Kennedy may have been too quick to place each of his children in a box of his own design ("he's the lawyer"), but he loved his children too much not to help them achieve whatever laudable goal they might set for themselves. If Jack wished to try politics, surprising as it must have seemed at the time, then Joe was certainly going to provide Jack with all the help he could to give it a go.

After Jack returned from the Pacific, Joseph Kennedy asked Joe Kane, a cousin and a veteran Boston political operative, to meet with Jack and assess whether he had the goods to be a successful politician. Kane's verdict, similar to that delivered years earlier by Inga, was very positive. He told Joe, "There is something original about your young daredevil," adding that Jack had made a most positive impression while making some brief remarks at a dinner honoring his grandfather, John "Honey Fitz" Fitzgerald.

Unfortunately for Inga, Jack's revelation that he wished to get into politics gave Joe Senior the most effective ammunition he could have had to convince Jack that marriage to Inga was impossible. As a student of history, it certainly occurred to Jack that only one first lady in history had been a divorcee, and that was Florence Harding.* Of course, as Jack's father pointed out, Inga was not yet even a divorcee. She was still married—and to a man working with Joseph Kennedy to keep his wife.

---

*There has been only one more in the ensuing seventy-five years, and that was Betty Ford.

Part VIII

The Break Up

CHAPTER 45

"We pay for everything in life"

INGA, CURIOUS AND MORE THAN LITTLE WORRIED ABOUT WHAT JOSEPH Kennedy had told his son during their visit in Palm Beach, hurried to meet Jack when he arrived in Charleston to report for duty on January 24, 1942. The FBI had lost track of Inga, aware only that she was no longer in Washington. Only later, while listening in on her phone calls, did they learn that she had been visiting Jack in Charleston.

Therefore, we have no FBI report of Inga's weekend with Jack, but Inga recalled the highlights in a letter she wrote to Jack immediately after she returned to Washington. They had taken a lovely walk through the famed Middleton Place gardens—the oldest landscaped gardens in the United States—and she teased Jack about his miserliness. Despite being a multimillionaire, Kennedy was notoriously cheap, and Inga teased, acted as if he "would rather have chewed one of his fingers off than pay [the] $2 admission."

But the very romance of historic Charleston, with its moss-covered oaks, stately homes, and formal gardens behind ornate iron gates made Inga melancholy and reminded her of "the ugly status of a woman without anything that a woman should have."

What Inga wanted was Jack. She had warned Torbert Macdonald that absence does not make the heart grow fonder, and her separation from Jack, even if only for a week, had made Inga more desperate. She had won Jack over so easily when they first met. Then, she had been the one wary of a lasting relationship and Jack was the one talking about marriage. The tables were now turned. She told Jack that she loved him "more than anything else or anybody in the world," but now Jack was the wary one.

Inga blamed herself for her predicament. "In reality, we are so well matched," Inga wrote Jack. "Only because I have done some foolish things must I say to myself 'NO!' At last I realize that it is true: 'We pay for everything in life.'"

Inga yearned for a simpler time, by which she meant all of four weeks before. She recalled picking up Jack at Washington's Union Station on New Year's Day after their only previous and brief separation when Jack had gone to visit his parents. On that day, Inga said, she and Jack had both been "happy as a bird, without a care, a fear or trouble in the world—just in love—remember?"

Then, there had seemed plenty of time to work out the difficulties that stood in the way of a lifetime together. But that was before Winchell's column, before Jack's transfer, before Wenner-Gren was placed on the blacklist, and before Fejos joined forces with Joseph Kennedy to tear their romance apart. Much had happened quickly.

The problem was not only Inga's past; it was also Jack's future—and his father's newfound plans for Jack's future. Inga knew that Jack's "big white teeth are ready to bite off a huge hunk of life. There is determination in his green Irish eyes." But she told Jack that his handsome physique had an anatomical abnormality: "He has two backbones: His own and his father's." Was one stronger than the other, or would they fuse into a single purpose?

During that long walk through Middleton Place gardens, Inga began to feel Jack pull away emotionally even as they held hands. There had been no definitive break. Jack did not even hint he was contemplating a break. He was still mulling things over, and Inga remained hopeful that their love was just as before when they had talked about moving to a ranch out West.

Their weekend together over, as Inga's train pulled out of the Charleston station she looked back longingly to see Jack waving good-bye and said, "There was the good old feeling of stinging eyes and a nasty pull at the heartstrings, which always show up when too great a distance is put between us."

Kick, unaware what had happened between Jack and their father in Palm Beach, playfully asked Inga when she returned, "Have you started making the baby yet?" But the next day, Kick received a letter from Jack. He confided to his sister that their father now advised him to end the affair—but he was worried about repercussions. Kick shared this information with Inga. Why is unknown. Perhaps she believed she owed Inga the truth, or perhaps Kick believed that she was helping her brother make the break easier by preparing Inga for the inevitable.

Inga was crestfallen—and angry. She dashed off a letter to Jack, saying she now understood why he had not been writing her any letters; he was afraid of putting anything in writing. "Distrust is a funny thing, isn't it?" she wrote Jack. "There was a peculiar feeling at the realization that the person I love most in the world is afraid of me. Not of me directly, but of the actions I might take someday."

Inga told Jack she knew it had been his father who had convinced him to "disbelieve in me." That made her angry, but she told Jack—and perhaps it was a taunt—that she would do nothing to counter his father's arguments, implying that Jack still lacked the courage to defy his father and live his own life. "It would be without result anyway," Inga said, "because Big Joe has a stronger hand than I. Probably the above is a thing which will put a wrinkle of bitterness to my mouth, but why worry, why actually care?"

Of course, as Inga noted in the next paragraph, the problem was "I care too much." But she could not think what to do. "The problems are unsolvable to me," she said. Jack wished to pursue a career in politics, but he could not do that and marry Inga. No politician in America in the 1940s could be successful if he was considered a home wrecker, and certainly no member of America's most famous Catholic family could marry a twice-divorced Protestant and hope to have a successful political career.*

"I have made up my mind that nothing can be done, I can kick and scream and it will not bring me any further," Inga told Jack. "A very passive part in a tragic-comic play. That is the one I have." Inga pledged

---

*This would remain basically true well into the 1960s when New York governor Nelson Rockefeller's presidential prospects fell apart when he not only divorced his own wife but also stood accused of breaking up a friend's marriage in order to marry his second wife, the former Margaretta "Happy" Murphy.

not to write again until her spirits improved, which given her resilience was the very next day. She told Jack again how much she had enjoyed their weekend together in Charleston. "Take all the love you want," Inga told him, "there is plenty more for you where it comes from—afraid I shall never run out of it."*

Despite these new, reassuring words, Inga's previous letter rattled Jack. He wrote back immediately to discuss "Exhibit 3c in the case of Inga Binga vs. JPK Sr." Jack's father had made a powerful case for why the relationship needed to end soon, but Jack was lonely in Charleston and still in love with Inga. Still unsure of what he planned to do about their relationship, Jack tried to assuage Inga with humor. "What do you write that kind of stuff for, that I am afraid of 'your future actions' (very diplomatically put)," he wrote. Jack told Inga he had not written because he had already given her plenty to read, meaning a copy of *Why England Slept*, "and by God you won't read it."

Jack then changed the subject by telling Inga how much he, too, had enjoyed their weekend together. Addressing his parsimony in balking at the $2 admission fee, Jack said the walk through Middleton Place gardens "was easily worth $400, but [the weekend] would have been just as pleasant even if we hadn't gone into the gardens."

Jack also said that he had discovered his transfer orders had been dated January 7 (five days before the Winchell column). Perhaps, he thought, his abrupt transfer had had nothing to do with Inga but was the result of his father pulling strings to get Jack sea duty. ONI, of course, had already planned on transferring Jack out of Washington, not because

---

*Inga was always remarkably generous. Even though the FBI was tormenting her and Jack seemed to be on the verge of abandoning her, she was helping Jack's good friend Torbert Macdonald to try to get a job—at the FBI. Macdonald, who had been captain of the Harvard football team and was an all-round golden boy on campus, was exploring options to avoid military service. Inga asked a former FBI lawyer, Lyle O'Rourke, whom she had once profiled in her column and who was now her personal lawyer, to meet with Macdonald to give him tips on how to secure employment at the Bureau. Macdonald ultimately did not apply and entered the navy instead, later serving seven terms in Congress as a representative from Massachusetts.

his father intervened, but because of his relationship with Inga; the Winchell column simply made action on the transfer urgent.

Jack, still not fully cognizant of just how much the FBI was interested in Inga, then joked about her alleged espionage activities. "I've returned from an interesting trip, about which I won't bore you with the details," he said, "as if you are a spy I shouldn't tell you and if your [*sic*] not you won't be interested. But I miss you."

Still worried that an angry Inga might do something rash, Jack also called her late Friday night, January 30, to smooth things over, but the first thing he noticed and asked about were the strange sounds on the telephone: "What are all these clickings going on?" he asked. The FBI was listening in, but Inga left Jack's question unanswered. She had more pressing matters to discuss.

Inga told Jack she would be traveling to New York City the next day and casually mentioned that she planned to have dinner with Nils Blok, but she assured Jack she would be staying at the Barbizon Hotel for Women. "I am glad to hear that," Jack said, though he hastened to add he was not worried about her seeing other men. Inga said she was not trying to make Jack jealous, which was exactly "why I am staying there." She then sought to reassure Jack that "everything is fine." Relieved, Jack then began to banter with Inga about her supposedly telling Torbert Macdonald that he was a better dresser than Jack, to which Inga replied that Jack had no reason to worry about his clothing because, "Darling, you look best without anything." This kind of titillation made Jack reluctant to end the affair.

They ended the call with Jack pledging to try to come to Washington the following weekend, but if he could not get permission to travel he hoped Inga would come to Charleston. She said she would. A few days later, Inga told a friend who inquired about her love life that "everything was lovely" with her relationship with Jack. But that was not true. The unraveling would continue in New York, where Inga would learn something shocking from her spiteful husband.

CHAPTER 46

"Something I picked up on the road"

INGA WAS BUOYED BY HER JANUARY 30 TELEPHONE CONVERSATION WITH Jack. Even though talking on the telephone was "uncozy," she said, hearing from Jack while he was in such a jocular mood reassured Inga that he still loved her, and it reminded her of why she loved him. The night before she was to leave for New York, she wrote him a letter, filling him in on the details of her daily routine when he was not in Washington.

Still in a frisky mood, she referred to herself, as Winchell had, as a "gal columnist." Inga told Jack that earlier in the day she had interviewed the man in charge of designing camouflage for the U.S. Army. An army intelligence officer was present during the interview and, curious about Inga's unusual accent and national origin, asked her if she spoke German. "Sure and Japanese, too," Inga replied, noting the officer "nearly fainted"—and that she never did answer his question of where she was from.

Getting friskier, Inga complained that her finances were in bad shape, and so "I have made up my mind to turn out a few stories—and when I get time a few babies—hope illegitimacy becomes a fad after the war as I only know one man worth reproducing a perfect copy of." It was an interesting way to flirt and stroke Jack's ego while simultaneously acknowledging that marriage to Jack was unlikely.

The good cheer generated by Jack's phone call, however, dissipated the next day when she traveled to New York. Fejos met Inga at the Barbizon to discuss how they would go about getting a divorce. It turned into an ugly scene.

The cuckolded Fejos said some "very terrible things" to her, Inga said. He told her he was "ashamed of the way she is acting with Jack." While he finally agreed to give her a divorce, Fejos warned Inga that she would be the one left alone, not him. Fejos boasted that he had already found a new intimate companion and, in an ungallant remark, pledged he would learn to love his new girlfriend, the chanteuse Marianne Arden, even "if he had to croak doing it."

Fejos told Inga once more that the Kennedys would never allow Jack to marry her. Adding a particularly vicious twist to the knife, Fejos added that he had heard on good authority that Jack himself had privately disparaged Inga. A furious Inga responded in kind, though she did not detail what she had said to try to hurt Fejos. She would, however, confront Jack with what she had heard.

A shaken Inga spent much of the rest of her time in New York with Nils Blok. The couple went sightseeing and had dinner together. Despite their previous intimacy, on this occasion Blok played the role of sympathetic friend as Inga relayed her troubles, but he was elated that Inga might soon be free of both Fejos *and* Jack. Blok prayed that an emotionally vulnerable Inga might be ready to fall into the familiar arms of an old lover, a man who did not offer the promise of excitement or prestige, but who was comforting and comfortable, available, and devoted to the point of subservience.

When Inga returned to Washington on Monday, February 2, she called Jack but was initially reluctant to discuss her trip to New York until Jack unwisely decided to tease her about her implied promise of fidelity when she had told him that she had planned to stay at the Barbizon Hotel for Women.

"I heard you had a big orgy up in New York," Jack said. Inga pretended to be amused, though her voice must have curdled when she replied, "I'll tell you about it. I'll tell you about it for a whole weekend if you'd like to hear about it. My husband has his little spies out all over the place."

Jack's ears perked up. What, he asked, had Inga heard? Inga, flushed with hurt and anger, said that Fejos "told me all sorts of things about you, none of which were flattering. He knew every word you said to your father about me. It made me look like—[the FBI transcriptionist could not bear to type out the word *shit*]. It amused me very much."

Clearly, Inga was *not* amused, and reading the FBI transcript you can feel a lump rise in Jack's throat as he asked, "What does he mean by 'every word I said to my father about you'?" Inga gave a roundabout explanation that Fejos claimed to know someone who knew the Kennedys well (although Fejos almost certainly got the information directly from Joe Senior). Jack was probably unaware that Fejos and his father were working in tandem, but he was less interested in *how* Fejos knew what he knew than *what* he knew.

Inga told him, "He said, 'Jack Kennedy shrugged his shoulders and said I wouldn't dream of marrying her; in fact, I don't care two bits about her. She's just something I picked up on the road.'" Inga then disingenuously pretended that what she had just relayed had not ripped her heart in two but rather had not bothered her in the least, "It's very amusing, darling. Tell me, when you are you going away?"

This time, Jack was not ready to change the subject. He needed to know what else Inga had heard, and not only how angry she was and what she might do but also how angry Fejos was and what *he* might do. "I'm not leaving for a while yet," Jack said. "What all did your husband say?"

Inga, despite the grievous wound to her heart and pride, did not lash out, but reassured Jack. "Why, he said I could do what I wanted. He said he was sad to see me doing things like this . . . [but] I swear that he is not bothering us and that you need not be afraid of him. He is not going to sue you though he is aware what he could do by suing you."

Jack never denied that he said what Fejos claimed he had said, nor did he apologize for saying such hurtful things about the woman whom he had not picked up along the road but with whom he had discussed marriage. Instead, Jack thought about Jack and expressed relief that he would be spared involvement in a messy divorce scandal. "He would be a big guy if he doesn't sue me," Jack said, adding almost as an afterthought, "I didn't intend to make you mad."

Inga insisted that she was "not mad," and instead asked if Jack would like her to come to Charleston the coming weekend, to which Jack replied, "I would like for you to." Inga said she would think it over and let him know.

It is, of course, difficult to discern solely from a written transcript the tone in Inga's and Jack's voices, and so it is not clear why Inga chose to treat Jack so gingerly despite the pain and humiliation she must have felt. Kennedy biographer Nigel Hamilton interpreted the exchange as Inga "playing the young ensign expertly. She had indicated she knew exactly how duplicitous he was in what he said to others—he didn't deny it, either—but also that she would overlook it. Maybe."

There are other possibilities. As Inga noted, she found the telephone an "uncozy" way to communicate. She would be better served if she were physically present with Jack to have such an important conversation about what he now intended, where her gaze and her touch would give her a considerable advantage in resolving any discussion in her favor. There is also the very real possibility that Inga, on the precipice of securing a divorce that would leave her alone in the world, was so desperate to keep Jack that she was willing to overlook this faithlessness rather than force a confrontation and risk losing him permanently.

Inga had acknowledged the week before that she knew she was play-ing a weak hand compared to Jack's father, and she knew that Jack, despite his steps toward being independent of his father and family, still was not strong enough to risk a complete break with them. Only Kick would prove to be a strong enough Kennedy to do that.

The aspirations that the Kennedy family had of its members may seem stifling, but viewed from another angle there was also something oddly liberating about those expectations.

Arthur Krock once tried to explain the hold Joseph Kennedy had over his children. Certainly, he was a powerful personality and, given Rose Kennedy's emotional distance, was the prime parental provider of love for his children. But Krock ultimately concluded that the Kennedy children's obsessive desire to please their father, however much he might interfere in their lives, was because his wealth offered them a type of freedom unavailable to most people. "These boys were born to wealth because of their father," Krock noted. "They knew they owed their financial independence to him. . . . They were grateful for it, enabling them to go out and pursue careers they had mutually decided on, and be able to afford it."

When Jack first met Inga, he had felt confined by his family's expectations, not because the expectations were so high, but because they were so low. Jack had chafed at being harnessed behind the lead dog in a family team that *always* placed Joe Junior alone in the first position. In that construct, Inga had once offered liberation, the chance to be unshackled so that Jack might run free and as far as his talents and ambition could take him without deference to his older brother. But in fomenting in Jack a spirit of revolt, Inga undercut her own cause.

She had built Jack up just enough so that Jack could confront his father without having to break with him. When he finally had the courage to confide in his father that he had political ambitions as great as those held by (and for) his older brother, Joe Senior surprised Jack (and perhaps Inga) by acceding to Jack's desire to at least have the same chance as his golden older brother to try for the White House. In a family with a fetish for competition, Joe Senior probably concluded that having two of his sons competing for the same prize would do them both good, though at this stage there is no doubt that Joe Senior still expected Joe Junior to be the first Catholic president, not Jack.

In their conversation in Palm Beach just two weeks before, Jack's father had promised to commit the resources to give Jack that chance to compete. That kind of freedom, if we accept Krock's definition, to embark on a political career and make a legitimate run at the presidency was much different than the freedom of the heart that Inga offered. Inga still hoped her way offered its own pleasures and fulfillment, and so she was not ready to surrender to Jack's ambition or his father just yet, and Jack was not quite ready to give her up either.

CHAPTER 47

"Sexual intercourse on numerous occasions"

ALTHOUGH JACK NEITHER DENIED DISPARAGING HER NOR APOLOGIZED for doing so, Inga found their talk cathartic. She wrote Jack a cheerful letter the next day, February 3, talking about how the weather was so sunny and unseasonably delightful that she and Kick walked to work. Inga did not revisit the previous night's conversation, nor did she mention that she had called Nils Blok immediately after hanging up from her call with Jack.

She was trying to renew her enthusiasm for her work at the *Times-Herald* and told Jack she especially enjoyed finding people at the Navy Department to interview. "It has sort of become my hang-out, if you know what I mean," Inga said. "That is the place where I go down and get a bit of a heart beat, when I see an ensign."

Inga assured Jack of two things: She was finally reading *Why England Slept*, and she would come down to Charleston for the weekend. She promised to tell him more about her trip to New York and her conversation with Fejos. Better to do so in person, Inga said, because "I think it will be more amusing when told and not written. I can use gestures and my subtle charm to illustrate."

Inga was in such a fine mood that she also wrote an apology to Fejos for her role in their quarrel. Fejos quickly replied that she had nothing to apologize for. "I myself always had such a beastly temper during the [past] six years that I wouldn't have any right to notice such a thing," he said. Their nasty confrontation in New York seemed to have chastened Fejos. He now encouraged Inga to make arrangements to travel to Reno to secure the divorce and asked only that she give him at least a week's notice before she left so that he would have time to raise the money that she would need for travel, an attorney, and the various filing fees.

But as some of the complications in Inga's life were being sorted out, others were arising—and without her knowledge.

On February 4, Edward J. Ennis, director of the Alien Enemy Control Unit within the Department of Justice, wrote J. Edgar Hoover, demanding a report on all the information the FBI had compiled on Inga to date. Ennis said he wanted this information "in considering whether a Presidential Warrant of Apprehension should be issued." Hoover, however, did not appreciate Ennis butting in on the FBI's business.

Hoover was hardly collegial to anyone within the Department of Justice, including the attorney general. Ennis, only thirty-three, was a meddlesome whippersnapper as far as Hoover was concerned. Hoover did not bother to respond for more than two weeks and then sent Ennis a desultory two-page response. It contained only basic biographical facts of Inga's life and nothing that would have encouraged Ennis to issue a warrant for Inga's arrest. Anyone who read Hoover's memorandum to Ennis would have concluded that Inga posed no threat to national security, and so Ennis let the matter drop.

Ennis, however, was not the only high-ranking government official who had heard rumblings that the FBI was hot on Inga's trail—and that Inga's trail was leading to some interesting places. Yet even more so than with Ennis, Hoover was dismissive when his rival (and supposed superior) within the American intelligence community, Coordinator of Information William J. "Wild Bill" Donovan, also inquired about "the rumor around town" that Inga was "a German spy."

Hoover provided Donovan with even less information than he had provided Ennis. Hoover did not even directly acknowledge that the FBI was investigating Inga. In a three-paragraph note, Hoover told Donovan nothing Donovan did not already know and instead asked Donovan to pass on any information that he came across "which you feel lends credence to the rumor you mention."

Despite, or perhaps because of, the belief by some of his underlings that Inga's case had "more possibilities" than any other ongoing espionage investigation, Hoover had no interest in having Inga arrested. She had done nothing to warrant arrest, and her case had led nowhere so far. If it *was* to lead anywhere, Inga needed to remain free and under FBI surveillance. If she were a spy, eventually she would stumble and be caught. On the other hand, if Inga was arrested and proved innocent, Hoover was afraid of the angry crusade Cissy Patterson and the *Times-Herald* would launch against the FBI.

This attention from others within the American intelligence community, however, did convince Hoover that the FBI needed to expand its investigation of Inga. Knowing that Inga had caught the FBI unaware when she went to Charleston the previous weekend, and knowing that she intended to visit Jack again the coming weekend (this time using the alias Barbara White and staying at the Fort Sumter Hotel), Hoover directed the FBI's Savannah field office to work with the hotel to ensure Inga's room was bugged.

When Inga arrived in Charleston by train on the morning of February 6, a Friday, Jack met her at the station and took her to the hotel before he had to report for duty. Inga browsed a variety of Charleston's antique stores until Jack got off work and picked her up for dinner. Jack and Inga dined at the hotel and then took a romantic walk along the harbor before returning to the hotel for the night.

Saturday, Jack worked a half-day before coming back to the hotel shortly after lunch. This time, he and Inga stayed in Room 132 until after 10 p.m., when they went out to dine at a famous local fish house called Henry's on Market Street. Following a short walk around White Point Garden, Inga and Jack returned to the hotel, arising the next morning to attend Mass at the Cathedral of St. John the Baptist. Afterward, they took a drive north of Charleston on U.S. Highway 52, returned to the hotel at 7 p.m., staying in their room until they left for the train station after midnight so that Inga could take the train at 1:09 a.m. back to Washington, sleeping in an upper berth along the way. We know all this thanks to the FBI's commitment to record even the mundane.

But not everything was mundane. As the FBI noted, Jack and Inga spent a great deal of time in the hotel room, where the FBI recorded that they "engaged in sexual intercourse on numerous occasions." The FBI reports do not go into detail as to what was overheard (and taped) during these passionate interludes.

Beyond that, which also had very little to do with espionage, the agents listening in on Jack and Inga's most private moments reported they heard very little pertaining to the possible case of the United States vs. Inga Arvad. Jack and Inga gossiped briefly about the poor health of presidential aide Harry Hopkins, and Jack noted he would be going to Norfolk to study fire control. Otherwise, Inga "did not press him further as to his future plans," and advised Jack only that she was now considering traveling to Reno to divorce Fejos. Jack and Inga seemed intent on keeping the weekend pleasurable and not rehashing the unpleasantness of the previous week.

That there once existed tape recordings of the future thirty-fifth president of the United States having sex with Inga has led to considerable prurient speculation as to what became of the tapes.

Within the FBI's old Washington headquarters, in the basement of the Department of Justice, next to a small theater where Hoover and other select FBI officials allegedly watched "surveillance films and pornographic movies," was an "ultra-secure" room where photographs, films, and sound recordings were stored that Hoover had "deemed worth preserving." "Presumably," one Hoover biographer noted, "the Inga Arvad sex tapes which John F. Kennedy so feared were among the items stored here."

Yet it is not clear the sex tapes were ever in Hoover's possession. There is no record of Hoover acknowledging the existence of the tapes if, in fact, the tapes had been preserved. Typically, the original recordings, which were on acetate discs, not tape, were held for no more than thirty days until they could be transcribed, and then they were destroyed—unless they contained valuable information worth preserving.

At least one of the recorded discs made by the FBI of Jack and Inga in Charleston was preserved and sent back to the Washington office for review, presumably by Hoover and other FBI officials. But this disc was of interest not because it was pornographic, but because it involved a telephone call between Jack and his father in which Joseph Kennedy told

Jack that he had offered his services to President Roosevelt but complained that FDR was snubbing him.*

This was the type of political intelligence that Hoover could (and usually did) put to good use. He knew FDR would enjoy hearing that his former ambassador to Great Britain, who had fallen far out of Roosevelt's favor, was still anguished by the lack of presidential attention. But what political value would a recording of Jack and Inga engaging in sexual intercourse have held for Hoover in 1942?

It is certainly possible that one of the recordings of Jack and Inga engaging in sexual intercourse was forwarded to Hoover and that he got his jollies listening to it, but that seems unlikely. First, given Hoover's reputation as a prude, true or not, it would have taken a bold agent to forward such an otherwise frivolous recording to Hoover with the recommendation that he listen to something that might have offended the director and ended the agent's career.

But what makes it most unlikely that Hoover ordered Jack and Inga's "sex tapes" preserved is that Jack Kennedy meant nothing to Hoover in 1942. At that time, the only thing of genuine interest about Jack was that he was a son—and not the most promising son at that—of a famous public figure. This son was foolishly engaged, in Hoover's view, in an immoral affair with a woman who was under investigation as a potential spy, but unless Jack was passing on sensitive information to this possible spy, his sexual activities were of minor interest to the FBI.

Had Hoover had the prescience to guess that Jack might become president in less than twenty years, he *certainly would* have preserved the tapes, but such a prediction for Jack Kennedy in early 1942 would have been beyond the powers of Nostradamus. Except for authoring a mildly successful book, Jack had done little to suggest that he was a budding public figure in his own right. It was simply not something Hoover would have contemplated at this time.

---

* FDR, who well knew Joseph Kennedy's capabilities but otherwise considered him a nuisance or worse, eventually offered Kennedy a minor position with limited authority under the Maritime Commission. An offended Kennedy turned it down.

Therefore, it seems likely that most if not all of the recorded discs that captured Jack and Inga in the act of love were, following Bureau policy, erased after they were transcribed, their future value unappreciated.

It is not known whether Hoover later hinted to Jack that the tapes *might* exist. We do know that once Jack was nominated for president Hoover went out of his way to let Jack know that the file on him and Inga remained in the FBI's possession and within Hoover's ready access. Not coincidentally, Jack reappointed Hoover as director of the FBI immediately after his election to the presidency in 1960.

And if, by unlikely chance, Hoover had kept these sex tapes, they were certainly destroyed after his death in 1972. Hoover's devoted assistant, Helen Gandy, whom Inga had described as "the sweetheart of the FBI," testified before Congress that she destroyed in total what she described as her boss's "Personal File." Gandy did not specify exactly what was in those files or even how large these files were, but insisted that she had reviewed the files page by page and concluded they contained nothing of "an official nature." Of course, tapes of Jack and Inga having sex were hardly of an official nature.

Even if the tapes no longer existed, Jack was reminded that they once had. One of the young agents charged with transcribing the Charleston tapes and who listened in on Jack and Inga's lovemaking was Frederick Ayer Jr., a former Harvard classmate of Jack's. In 1963, when Jack was Grand Marshall at Harvard's commencement, Ayer was in the crowd and delighted in leaning over and loudly whispering as Jack walked by, "How's Inga?" Jack whirled around and hissed, "You son of a bitch!"

CHAPTER 48

"I don't want to sleep with a dozen men at one time"

SHORTLY AFTER INGA RETURNED FROM CHARLESTON, KICK KENNEDY and her beau John White had a row that left Kick in tears, and it led Kick to express admiration that Jack and Inga "never quarrel, do you?" Inga admitted that they didn't, to which White astutely observed, "No wonder: Inga lets him walk all over [her] like linoleum." Inga told Jack that White's observation was "not exactly flattering, but I think it was meant as a joke. I took it as such."

Inga had had no desire for a quarrel with Jack in Charleston, but that also meant that she and Jack had not had an honest discussion about their feelings or their future. When they were together, they focused on the present. Avoiding the issues, however, meant that there was unresolved tension between them.

When Inga returned to Washington, she telephoned an irritated Jack. Jack relayed that when he had tried to quietly sneak out of the hotel the morning after Inga left, the hotel clerk, whom Jack suspected was a navy informant, loudly harangued him about Inga's unpaid bill, causing other patrons to stare. "My name is mud down here," Jack complained. When Inga wondered whether the incident might get Jack kicked out of the navy, he replied, "There is more truth than poetry to that."

Inga invited Jack to come to Washington the next weekend. Cissy Patterson had invited her to a party in honor of Count Oleg Cassini and his new wife, the gorgeous movie actress Gene Tierney, and Patterson urged Inga to bring her "beau."* Cissy's enthusiasm for including Jack in the invitation, coupled with Clare Boothe Luce's obvious fondness for Jack, led Inga to tease that Jack was "the young Darling of the American women intelligentsia."

But what Jack was focused on, as evidenced by his unhappiness with being recognized at the Fort Sumter Hotel, was whether his and Inga's relationship would be attracting any more publicity. He had heard a rumor that *Life* magazine might run an item based on Winchell's column and asked Inga if she had heard any more about it. Inga said she had asked Frank Waldrop if he would check on whether *Life* was planning such an article, but Waldrop cut her short and told her "not to get mixed up in it at all." *Life* never did run a story on Jack and Inga.

Her conversation with Jack left Inga unsettled and so, as was her habit, she wrote him a letter to further expand on her feelings. She asked him if he had ever considered the meaning of the word *home*, which Inga called a "beautiful" word that "when pronounced in the right way somehow it nearly reaches mother, father and love."

"At our age—at mine at any rate—it probably should mean with a man and some children," Inga said. Against that standard, and now separated from Jack, her familiar apartment at 1600 16th Street NW now felt like "anything but a home. It is an oblong, ugly modern place where I sleep, cook my quick breakfast, entertain very rarely, and never put my heart into." Because she had been with Jack, the man she loved, Room 132 in the Fort Sumter felt more like a home than the place she lived.

It had been even harder for Inga to say good-bye to Jack this time than on her previous visit to Charleston two weeks before. "In that lies the danger," Inga wrote. "That is where the tears, grief and misery lies buried. Not only in loving, which to me is the freest most exhilarating of all feelings, but in missing and being quite lost. I told you about it months

---

*Cassini had begun his career in America as a political cartoonist in Washington, and his brother, Igor, still worked at the *Times-Herald*. Cassini would become Jackie Kennedy's favorite fashion designer and designated "Secretary of Style." Jack didn't make the Patterson party but met Tierney in 1946 and began a brief romance with the star after she separated from Cassini. When Kennedy told Tierney, as he had told Inga, that he could never marry her because she was a divorcee, Tierney ended the relationship.

ago and you looked very puzzled, maybe you don't even understand me now."

Belying his own carefully cultivated image of being emotionally detached, Jack did understand Inga, but he was as lost as she was. There is little doubt that he loved her. At twenty-four, as increasing numbers of his friends had married, he thought about marriage, too. The war and the possibility of premature death made marriage to Inga seem romantic, especially in contrast to the pedestrian institution modeled by his parents.

Jack doubted he would ever find someone to whom he was so perfectly mated as Inga. She would be the ideal wife for a politician, except that he could not marry her and still have a political career. And while he had not yet fully made up his mind what to do, and still harbored some small hope that he might have both Inga and a political future, deep down he knew which direction he was leaning if he had to make a choice.

Jack realized that scandal would impact not only his own career but also the family image Joseph Kennedy had worked so hard to cultivate. Marrying Inga would not only cripple his own political aspirations, they could damage those of his brother, and that, Jack knew, would be unforgivable within the family. The quest for the White House was not an individual trek; it was a family quest, for the Kennedys were now a completely political family. None of the Kennedy children aspired to follow their father into business; Joseph Kennedy's business holdings were now only the means to finance and further the family's political interests.

Two decades later, New York governor Nelson Rockefeller torpedoed his presidential aspirations by divorcing his wife and marrying a young divorcee and family friend. Jack, whose last genuine romantic impulse ended when his relationship with Inga ended, shook his head. "I don't believe it," he told *Washington Post* publisher Katherine Graham. "No man would ever love love more than he loves politics."

Loyalty to family had also cost Inga an important ally in her fight to keep Jack. Having received and understood the signals sent by her father, and even though she still adored Inga, Kick was no longer a cheerleader for the relationship. In fact, according to Inga, Kick now confessed that she was "jealous" of Inga's relationship with Jack, though perhaps the more proper word was "circumspect."

Kick, Inga told Jack, is "more afraid of the pain that I shall cause you in the future then [*sic*] she is concerned with the happiness we may enjoy at present." Inga dismissed Kick's concerns, noting, "She is young and as yet intolerant." Inga admitted that she should "have one eyelash" focused on the future, but admitted that when it came to imagining a future without Jack "I closed my eyes tightly." It made no sense to ignore the obvious, Inga acknowledged, but she said she felt as rum dumb as a man "after emptying three quarts of Haig whiskey."

This disorientation helps explain why Inga, on the same day she wrote Jack her latest love letter, told Nils Blok that he could come to Washington and sleep with her.

Blok had not been a part of Inga's life since she had met Jack. Intimate when Inga was attending Columbia University and lonely for a husband three thousand miles away, Inga and Blok continued to see each other for a short time after Inga moved to Washington. On a drive through the West Virginia countryside on June 28, 1941, they were involved in a car accident that left Inga with a broken nose, chipped teeth, numerous bruises, and two black eyes.

Inga had been driving, despite being several years out of practice, but when they filed an insurance claim, Blok claimed to be the driver as he had insurance and Inga did not. Inga sued for a generous settlement for her injuries, claiming that she intended to resume her acting career and "this mar to her beauty will militate against" her chances in Hollywood.

Inga treated Blok in the same way White claimed Jack treated her—like linoleum—and so expressed her gratitude to Blok for allowing her to file a (fraudulent) insurance claim against him by cutting off most communication once she met Jack. The break had been so complete that Blok was genuinely surprised in late January 1942 when Inga contacted him to ask if he would like to dine with her while she was in New York City visiting with Fejos about their divorce. "Now and then you have a queer way of imposing," said Blok, but grateful to once again be in her company he added, "but I have forgotten that now."

Having heard from Inga that she was divorcing Fejos and that her relationship with Jack was crumbling, Blok actively pursued Inga once more. Blok telephoned Inga to say he wanted to come to Washington to see her. At first, the idea pleased Inga, telling Blok it would be "cozy" to see him, but then she had second thoughts. Blok persisted but told Inga he would come only if he could "go to bed with her." Inga refused—at first.

Blok called Inga again thirty minutes later and begged her to reconsider. Inga expressed frustration that "she can't tell him 'no' sometimes," yet she also felt cheap agreeing to sleep with Blok while she was still in love with Jack—even if Jack was likely contemplating a break with her. "I don't want to sleep with a dozen men at one time," Inga protested. But Blok was undeterred. He hoped to push Jack out of the picture and flew to Washington that very night.

Blok spent most of the night at Inga's apartment. Watchful FBI agents saw the lights in Inga's apartment go off and on throughout the night until Blok left in the early morning hours and checked into the Lafayette Hotel. Almost immediately, Inga was filled with regret and was anxious for Blok to go on his way.

The next morning, Blok called to invite Inga to breakfast, but she said she had business appointments until late afternoon. Blok was upset. He reminded Inga he had come to Washington only to see her, but as was her habit, she now found excuses to avoid him. They quarreled, and Blok returned to New York that evening while Inga went to a dinner party hosted by an attaché at the British embassy. Blok's feelings were hurt, but he was consumed with desire.

Inga, however, was again thinking only of Jack. After returning home at 1 a.m., Inga wrote Jack, telling him she had run into Arthur Krock, whom Inga knew was "a general agent for Palm Beach"; that is, a spy for Jack's father. Krock, Inga told Jack, "has been entertaining Washington dinner parties about me—maybe you too." It was a short letter. Inga wrote that she was too tired to write more—without explaining to Jack why she had gotten so little sleep the night before.

What irony! For perhaps the only extended period of time in his adult life, Jack Kennedy had maintained a monogamous relationship. Yet the woman to whom he remained faithful had now been unfaithful to him, though he did not know that at the time and, apparently, never found out.

Inga, Olga, Anton. Inga as a toddler with her mother, Olga, and father, Anton, who would die of complications from malaria when Inga was only four. (Courtesy Ronald McCoy)

Inga at about eleven. Inga as a preteen in Copenhagen at about the age she began to study ballet and was told she had the potential to be "the next Pavlova," but she gave up dancing and instead studied to become a concert pianist. (Courtesy of Ronald McCoy)

Inga at Miss Europe. Inga wearing an extravagant gown while in Paris for the 1931 Miss Europe contest. Inga did not win but was such a popular contestant she was offered commercial endorsement opportunities and a chance to perform at the Folies Bergère. (Courtesy Ronald McCoy)

Inga cover photo. While her film debut in Denmark had not gone well, Inga still hoped to get into movies while she worked as a gossip columnist in Hollywood. Here is a glamour shot taken during her 1945 screen test. (Courtesy Terence McCoy)

Inga in Paris. When she competed for the Miss Denmark title in 1931, acquaintances said Inga had the appearance of a healthy farm girl. Competing in the Miss Europe contest a few months later, she developed a much more sophisticated look. (Courtesy Ronald McCoy)

Nabi with Olga. Inga with her first husband, the suave Kamal Abdel Nabi (far right), her mother, Olga, and an unidentified family friend. Egypt proved too exotic for Inga, so she concocted a story that she was ill and needed treatment in Switzerland to escape. (Courtesy of Ronald McCoy)

Inga in Flugten. Inga in a publicty shot for 1934's *Flugten Fra Millionerne* ("Millions in Flight") with her costar Erling Schroeder. The two had no chemistry; the sparks on set were between Inga and the director, Paul Fejos. (Courtesy Ronald McCoy)

Inga adult smile. Inga circa 1941. A British reporter who interviewed her said what drew you to Inga was her eyes—"so candid and interested, so questioning, with a twinkle lurking in the corners." (Courtesy of Ronald McCoy)

Inga with Fejos in apartment. Inga clowning with her second husband, filmmaker Paul Fejos, in their Copenhagen apartment. Just behind Fejos's right elbow is the inscribed photo Adolf Hitler gave to Inga, proudly displayed on the grand piano. (Courtesy Ronald McCoy)

Miss Denmark. Inga's official photo for the Miss Europe contest after having been crowned Miss Denmark of 1931. Several of Inga's aunts were upset she had entered the contests, as beauty pageants in those days were considered radical affirmations of women as sexual beings. (Author's photo)

Inga on Sipura. Inga loved the Mentawai people in the East Indies, and one little boy named Peipepteoman loved Inga, calling her "Darling" as he thought that was her name since that was what Inga's husband, Paul Fejos, always called her. (Courtesy Ronald McCoy)

Inga playing piano. Inga was accepted to study piano in Paris under the world's leading authority on Chopin, but she married instead and later gave up the piano entirely when she developed severe rheumatoid arthritis before she was thirty. (Courtesy Terence McCoy)

Inga in Copenhagen apartment. Classmates at the Columbia University Graduate School of Journalism said Inga seemed to enjoy playing the part of a *femme fatale*, often wearing all black and using a cigarette holder. (Courtesy Ronald McCoy)

Kick Kennedy. Kathleen Kennedy, whom everyone called "Kick," was three years younger than Jack, but they were so close some people thought they were twins. Kick and Inga became very close friends, which was key to Inga's attraction for Jack. (Courtesy of Ronald McCoy)

Cahan. Dr. William Cahan, who would go on to a brilliant career fighting cancer and smoking, promised Inga he would divorce his wife and marry her. Inga's skepticism was confirmed as Cahan stayed married five more years after his and Inga's romance ended. (Courtesy Terence McCoy)

Times ⚓ Herald

WASHINGTON, D. C.,
THURSDAY, NOVEMBER 27, 1941

Did You Happen to See---

JOHN F. KENNEDY?

An old Scandinavian proverb says the apple doesn't fall far from the tree. No better American proof can be found than John F. Kennedy.

If former Ambassador Joe Kennedy has a brilliant mind (not even his political enemies will deny the fact), charm galore, and a certain way of walking into the hearts of people with wooden shoes on, then son No. 2 has inherited more than his due. The 24 years of Jack's existence on our planet have proved that here is really a boy with a future.

Young Kennedy — don't call him that, he will r e s e n t it greatly—did more than boot the football about at Harvard. He was extremely popular. Graduated cum laude, was a class officer, sailed on the intercollegiate sailing team during his sophomore year, and most important, wrote a thesis.

Arthur Krock, from the New York Times, read it and suggested it be put in a book. Henry Luce, of Time, Fortune and Life, must have thought the same, because he wrote the foreword, and by putting in 12 hours a day, cooled off with as many showers, Jack polished it off during the summer and the much-praised book, "Why England Slept," was the result. It sold like wildfire.

"Yes, I certainly still have the same opinions as in the summer of 1940," says Jack Kennedy.

"You must understand that the reason I did not editorialize was because nobody is going to listen to a boy of 23. Besides it was not the idea to say I, I, I. The book is based on facts, and

JOHN F. KENNEDY

I did a lot of studying in order to be able to write it. I couldn't say if I am going to write another book. Now, I am in the Navy, that is the most important, but I have many plans for the future. Some day, when I have time, I am going to study law."

Jack hates only one subject—himself. He is the best listener I have come across between Haparanda and Yokohama. Elder men like to hear his views, which are sound and astonishingly objective for so young a man. — INGA ARVAD.

Compliments of the Times-Herald

"Did You Happen to See?" Inga's column on Jack Kennedy for the *Washington Times-Herald* was mounted on a plaque and presented to Jack as a gift from the newspaper, but he insisted Inga keep it as a memento. No photo of Jack and Inga together has been found, a signal of how discreet they kept the relationship. (Courtesy of Ronald McCoy)

Robert Boothby. Following "a whirlwind courtship in an orange grove," as it was described in hostile British newspapers, Inga became engaged to British MP Robert Boothby until newspapers uncovered Inga's past connections to Hitler. Boothby said he would have been prime minister if he had married Inga. (Courtesy Ronald McCoy)

Inga typing *Duel in the Sun*. Her mother chided her for her extravagance when she bought a Royal typewriter after arriving in America, but the typewriter paid for itself a hundredfold, such as when Inga promoted the David O. Selznick film *Duel in the Sun*. (Courtesy of Ronald McCoy)

Jack's photo with 109. Jack Kennedy posed for this jaunty photo to accompany Inga's story of how he saved most of his crew on the *PT-109*. Inga's story was the template for the story of Kennedy's heroics that was central to every one of his political campaigns. (There is no photo credit with the article)

Hitler's Ideal

Considered by Chancellor Hitler to be the paragon of Nordic beauty, he has honored Inga Arvad (above), beautiful, blonde newspaperwoman, with appointment as chief of publicity for the Nazis in Denmark. It was as a newspaper woman that Miss Arvad met Hitler.

Inga with WC Fields. Inga admitted she did not have enough "bitchiness" to be a good Hollywood gossip columnist, which actually made her popular with stars who were grateful that she wasn't always digging for dirt. Here she is with W. C. Fields. (Courtesy Ronald McCoy)

Inga's 1936 INS photo. Inga swore that she knew nothing about this photograph. Distributed by the International News Service, it appeared in scores of American newspapers in 1936 with the caption that claimed Inga had been appointed "chief of publicity for the Nazis in Denmark." (This version appeared on the front page of the Shemokin, Pennsylvania, *News-Dispatch*, which has been defunct since 1967)

Fejos W-G in Peru. Billionaire Axel Wenner-Gren, "the Swedish Sphinx," (seated) visits one of the Incan ruins discovered by Inga's second husband, Paul Fejos (standing). Despite these headline-making discoveries, the FBI was certain the expedition was a front for the Nazis' incursion into South America. (Courtesy Ronald McCoy)

Inga with boys. Inga's greatest desire was to have a home with children, which she finally realized with her marriage to movie cowboy Tim McCoy. Here she is with her two sons, Ronald (left) and Terence while living in La Cañada, California. (Courtesy Ronald McCoy)

Tim, Inga on *Gunfighter* set. Inga was not head-over-heels in love with movie (and real-life) cowboy Tim McCoy, but she admired his work ethic and his "guts." Here they are pictured on the set of Tim's last motion picture, *Requiem for a Gunfighter*, made in 1965 when Tim was seventy-four and Inga was fifty-two. (Courtesy of Terence McCoy)

CHAPTER 49

"OBSCENE"

JACK AND INGA MIGHT HAVE HAD MORE LUCK IN PRESERVING THEIR relationship had they not become increasingly aware that government investigators were recording every word they spoke or wrote to each other. In addition to having her phone tapped, Inga told Kick that she and Jack felt unable to discuss anything of substance by telephone because Jack's landlady listened in on all of Jack's conversations. Jack further told Inga that he had discovered that "the fellow in the next room" (it is not clear if this was at work or the boarding house where he lived) was copying all of his mail.

Despite that, Jack wrote Inga more often, having been stung by her previous criticism of his inattention. Jack seldom bared his soul in any letter, but now he knew that his letters might be read by prying eyes. His writings, therefore, are banal, and it is only because Jack was usually so reserved that his occasional affectionate remarks stand out.

In a February 13 letter, Jack, as he often did, blasted the sorry state of American politics. He was upset that with all the great issues facing a world at war, the buzz in Washington was over a minor scandal in which a "fan dancer" had been hired to work on a government physical fitness program. "I think that everything up there has gotten too complex for the average Congressman," Jack wrote. "Nero had better move over as he is getting plenty of company." Jack closed the letter to Inga with this sentiment: "The only thing that continually measures up to expectations is you. I hope you fully understand your responsibility. Ever, Jack."

Inga was undoubtedly appreciative of this loving line, but Jack was not her only suitor. Blok had also written her a letter, in Danish and considerably more passionate than the one sent by Jack. Blok was still in a state of postcoital bliss. He rhapsodized to Inga about "how round and luxurious, warm and lovely your breasts are; how I have even felt that I was kissing your soul when your breasts heaved." Her breasts, Blok wrote Inga, "have told me much more than you have ever expressed with words . . . and taught me more about you, about life, and why one should get up in the morning . . . why a man can be glad to be alive."

"I want you," Blok told Inga. "Not because I wish to receive—I have already received—but because I want to give. That is the deepest feeling, the deepest need of man. It is the only thing that makes real happiness." Blok realized he was not Inga's first choice, but told her that even if she were to marry "300 times and sleep with every man 1,000 times . . . no one will relish your whims, your kindness, and the things you think I am the antithesis of more than I."

Blok followed up his letter with a telegram that begged Inga to come to New York, but she declined. She wished to disentangle herself from Blok for the time being, but instead of telling him so she simply said that she needed to work and also planned to visit her mother in Maryland, where Olga was now employed as a caregiver/companion for the Sanger family matriarch. Inga had not seen her mother in almost two months.

Blok then sent Inga flowers on Valentine's Day and telephoned to ask Inga what she had thought of his amorous letter. It was "positively wonderful," Inga told him. She had read it twice the day it arrived and twice more the following morning, but then she put it in the incinerator, as it was not the type of letter she felt should be left laying around her apartment.

FBI agents, however, retrieved the letter from Inga's trash, had it translated, and then circulated and filed it in a plain brown envelope that was marked "OBSCENE" in large capital letters to warn away any unsuspecting secretary who might wilt upon reading Blok's rather mild attempt at erotica, oblivious that the real obscenity was retrieving private love letters from a person's garbage.

Reflecting her ongoing confusion, her emotions were changing like the weather. Inga now felt some regret that she had not invited Blok to come to Washington. They could have spent the night together and had breakfast before she went to Baltimore to visit Olga. She asked Blok to write her more letters and asked, "Sweetheart, do you love me?" Blok said that he did. "I just wanted to hear you say so," Inga said. "It sounds so nice." A week before, Blok had asked Inga if she loved him. "I guess so, sweet," she replied. It was a good thing that Inga's breasts spoke to Blok because her mouth was stingy with affectionate words.

Perhaps Inga did not say she loved Blok because she knew she would not have meant it. But she was also distracted and worried—distracted because she still loved Jack and hoped to keep him, worried because she feared that she was pregnant with Jack's child even as she felt she might be losing him. The FBI dutifully noted that Inga had contacted two Washington clinical laboratories to run a pregnancy test.

Fearing that she was carrying the child of a man she could not have while being pursued by a man she wasn't sure she wanted, Inga was further depressed that her work that weekend entailed attending Cissy Patterson's party in honor of the dashing and beautiful near-newlyweds, Cassini and Tierney—and on Valentine's Day at that. It was another reminder to Inga of what she still did not have in her life.

She wrote Jack a long letter, noting that she had learned Valentine's Day was the feast day of St. Valentine, "the patron of lovers and the help[er] of those unhappy in love. Certainly, that doesn't leave anybody out, does it dear? So we can all take part and choose the role we prefer to play. Some take the leading parts, but we can't all be lords and masters, there have to be some who serve, some who wait, and often the servant is happier and more content than the master. It is a matter of finding the right place."

"The right place"—Inga wondered where that was for her and Jack? Jack may have felt chained to a dull and hated desk job at the Charleston Navy Yard, but Inga sensed he would soon be going away. She said she had felt it for many months. Jack always craved to be where the action was. Staying in Washington among all the major decision makers for the duration of the war might have once satisfied that craving, but now he was stuck in Charleston far from politics, far from the war, far from everything. Inga knew Jack well enough to know that he craved excitement.

Now essentially banned from Washington, that seemed to mean getting into combat.

Inga said she should be like most women and proudly urge Jack, "Go and defend your country." Inga knew she should do that, "but somehow the pride is not there." All she could think of was that she wanted God to "keep His hand safely over you," so that Jack would return "with your handsome body intact" and the chance to be all that he wished to be—"a White-House-man and wanting the ranch—somewhere out West."

Asking God to watch over Jack led Inga to ruminate on faith. "You always say you have faith," Inga told Jack. "Sometimes I wonder if you believe it yourself. To me it seems that the faith you are born with is an empty one. The one you acquire later in life, when God has risen [*sic*] the curtain and showed you life, showed you all its beauties and many of its miseries—well, if you have faith then—that is worth something."

As the helper of those unhappy in love, Inga needed St. Valentine that day. Imagining the day when Jack would come home from the war, Inga said, "let us have lunch on the first day you are ashore, shall we? That, of course, provided that you are not married, [as] your wife maybe wouldn't understand. It is always hard to understand if you are very young and in love, and that is probably what she will be." It was increasingly clear to Inga that she would not be Jack's wife, but she did not blame him; she blamed herself. Twice already she had been another man's wife, but had she known marrying Nabi and Fejos would mean that she could not marry Jack, "I would still be a spinster."

CHAPTER 50

"Every pleasure of youth but not the responsibility"

ON THE MONDAY AFTER VALENTINE'S DAY 1942, INGA WAS BARRAGED with attention from admirers. A drunken Blok called to ask Inga if she would come to New York or if he could come to Washington. Inga declined but was vague on her reasons, knowing she intended to go to Charleston to see Jack. Then Bernard Baruch called to flirt by complaining that Inga had not kept in touch and then asking her if she was living alone. "Yes," Inga said. "Perfectly immoral and dreadful, don't you think?" Baruch said it sounded dull. Inga said it was, but that it was also healthy. When Baruch persisted and became more suggestive, Inga ended the call.

The phone rang again and Inga, assuming it was a persistent Baruch, answered in a way that made Jack suspicious that she had been expecting someone else. "I have no suitors," Inga lied, "and I haven't got you either." Inga told Jack she knew he was agitating for sea duty, but Jack said his request for a transfer to Pearl Harbor had been denied. She then asked about "the church stuff" (presumably about whether her prior marriages could be annulled if she converted to Catholicism), and Jack replied that he had both spoken to a priest and requested a book on church doctrine. But he seemed displeased that she had brought the subject up.

Inga was in an affectionate mood and, according to the FBI, referred to Jack throughout the call as "Honey, Darling, Honeysuckle [and] Honey Child Wilder."* Jack asked Inga when she was coming to Charles-

---

*Patricia "Honeychile" Wilder was a Georgia-born showgirl infamous for her New York nightclubbing, and was allegedly the model for the character of Holly Golightly in Truton. "In three or four months," Inga teased, "or when you really want me to come." Jack said that was right away. Jack complimented one of Inga's recent columns, but Inga said she thought it had been "terrible." Jack said, "You don't know what is good and what is bad." Inga, still feeling playful, replied, "I know that *you* are good—and damned bad." Such talk made Jack wish Inga was in Charleston *now*. Inga promised to arrive on Friday.

Given the problems encountered at the Fort Sumter Hotel, Inga planned this time to stay at the Francis Marion. But if Inga and Jack expected this would prevent unwanted snooping, they were wrong. The FBI, which knew all of Inga's plans because they had tapped her phone and bugged her apartment, again made arrangements with patriotic hotel staff to bug her hotel room.

Before she left for Charleston, Inga had the opportunity to meet Jack's maternal grandfather, the legendary former congressman and mayor of Boston, John F. "Honey Fitz" Fitzgerald. Inga and Kick joined Fitzgerald for lunch in the House Dining Room where "Honey Fitz" broke into song, as he often did, singing his signature tune, "Sweet Adeline." Inga was quite taken with Fitzgerald, devoting one of her columns to him and proclaiming, "Where he is, there is eternal sunshine." Unsurprisingly, Fitzgerald, who while mayor had had an alleged and highly publicized dalliance with a busty cigarette girl named "Toodles" Ryan, was also taken with Inga. He asked Kick if Inga was married. Kick replied that she knew nothing about Inga's personal life.

Inga called Jack that night to tell him how much she adored his grandfather. As they finalized plans to meet in Charleston the following day, Inga asked Jack when he could return the favor and come to Washington. Jack said he had no idea when he might get permission to travel because, "You know how things are." Inga replied, "No, I don't know. You are always so damned secretive, and I am the only person who doesn't know a thing." The testy exchanged augured that her next visit to Charleston would be less pleasant than the previous two.

Jack was increasingly concerned about the impact his romance with

---

man Capote's *Breakfast at Tiffany's*. The joke behind why Inga called Jack "Honeychile" is unknown.

Inga was having on his reputation, and he was becoming increasingly anxious to get into the war. Lem Billings gave him the surprising report that his affair with Inga was more widely known than Jack realized. Billings said that his mother, who lived in Baltimore, had heard from a friend about "the big Romance that has been rocking Washington circles—that one of the Kennedy boys is madly in love with a very beautiful & ravishing Danish reporter—but that unfortunately the gal has been married several times—so that it will be difficult for her to marry him." If Jack entertained the idea that Inga could quietly have her two marriages annulled and that they could then marry with no one the wiser, this information from Billings made him realize that would not be possible. Too many people knew about Inga's past.

Jack was also surprised and delighted to hear that Billings would soon be traveling to Africa to serve in the American Field Service, a paramilitary ambulance corps that recruited college graduates who had been rejected as unfit for military service. Billings had poor eyesight. While Jack was happy for Billings, it irked him that even a friend judged 4F for military service (which should have happened to Jack) was getting into a combat zone while he was stuck in a "boring, lousy, stinking" desk job in Charleston. "He wanted active duty," Billings recalled.

Jack's desire for sea duty increased even more after seeing a letter Clare Boothe Luce had sent his father. Luce had had a lengthy affair with Joseph Kennedy when Joe Senior was the U.S. ambassador in London, and Luce, like Gloria Swanson before her, almost became an auxiliary member of the Kennedy family. Inga believed that Luce was attracted to Jack and Jack to Luce—and she was correct. Luce once arranged for Jack to date her daughter, Ann, but when Jack came to pick Ann up "he showed more interest in mother than in daughter."

Luce and her husband, Henry, publisher of *Time* and *Life*, owned a plantation about fifty miles north of Charleston. Since this was within his seventy-mile restricted travel zone, when Jack found out Luce was wintering at the plantation he went to visit her. What Jack said about his father's defeatist attitude toward the war alarmed Luce enough that she wrote Joseph Kennedy almost immediately.

Jack, Luce told Joe, was "vaguely unhappy about your pessimism. It alarms him ('so unlike Dad') and dispirits him." America could successfully prosecute the war only if millions of young men like Jack did their duty by following orders from their commanders, Luce said, "and we hadn't oughtta make them feel that [those] orders are too mad, and too vain." Joe was so disturbed by Luce's admonition that he forwarded her letter to Jack with a note: "Heaven knows, I don't want any pessimism of mine to have any affect on you, but I don't know how to tell you what I think unless I tell you what I think."

Inga arrived in Charleston by plane Friday night to find Jack in a subdued mood. She later worried that perhaps she had talked too much during the visit, but instead told Jack later that she realized that she had only been trying to fill the "big silence on your part." Of course, what Inga wished to talk about, Jack wished to avoid.

Their first night together, Inga told Jack she was worried that she was pregnant. She also talked to Jack again about the possibility of getting her marriage annulled. "It was noted that Kennedy had very little comment to make on the subject," read a report made to J. Edgar Hoover. Inga returned to the topic of her possibly being pregnant a day later, and when Jack again tried to change the subject Inga accused him of "taking every pleasure of youth but not the responsibility."

Jack wisely made no mention of terminating the pregnancy. He knew Inga well enough to know that such a suggestion would have infuriated her. He knew that Inga, now twenty-eight, wanted to have children—his children. He also likely recalled Inga's story of how grateful she was that her mother had rejected counsel to abort her.

There were rumors that Jack had gotten a girl pregnant while a freshman at Harvard, and it was supposed that his father's agents had arranged for the girl to get an abortion. There would be other, similar stories later in Jack's life, including while he was president, but he treated Inga differently from other women he knew. If she truly had been pregnant, we cannot know for certain whether Jack would have pressured her to have an abortion. He hoped that he would not have to do anything and prayed that it was a false alarm, which it turned out to be.

Jack showed Luce's letter to Inga. Aware that the letter, with its call for action, had had a big impact upon Jack, Inga held her jealousy of Luce in check and instead praised the older woman's wisdom (Luce was thirty-eight) in endorsing Jack's growing ambitions. "You will get there," Inga later wrote. "As Clare says, 'He has everything to make a success.' Right she is, and I like her for discovering it so quickly."

Even though this was only their third weekend together in Charleston, Inga and Jack had established a routine. They dined twice at their favorite restaurant, Henry's, again went to Mass at the Cathedral on Sunday, and they discussed world affairs.

They took particular aim at the British. Jack said Prime Minister Winston Churchill had been responsible for maneuvering America into the war (though how Churchill orchestrated Pearl Harbor, Jack did not say). Kennedy questioned Churchill's judgment, noting that writer John Gunther had quoted Churchill as incorrectly predicting "the Japs would fold up like the Italians." Jack also forecast that the war would be the end of the British Empire, and Inga concurred that Churchill's most recent speech reeked of "defeatism" and added that British soldiers were "no damn good."

Jack also told Inga that he believed his father's greatest political mistake had been not explaining his position on the war in detail. Jack said his father's position was nuanced and not appeasement, but he "stopped talking" and did not "present his side of the question fully" because he was worried any remarks he made would harm Jack's and Joe Junior's political careers. The FBI made no note of what Inga said to that.

As was also Inga and Jack's custom—and despite Inga's fear that she might be pregnant or, if not, that she might *become* pregnant as Jack declined to wear condoms—they again "engaged in sexual intercourse on a number of occasions," the FBI noted.

Inga also again asked Jack about when he might go off to combat, and whether he would tell her before he did. "Why wouldn't I tell you?" Jack asked. But Inga knew that Jack enjoyed keeping secrets. "I don't know, maybe you would," she replies. "You wouldn't tell me ahead of time; you would tell me when you left."

Inga knew Jack and his predilection for subterfuge well. The following week, in fact, he did not tell Inga he was coming to Washington to tell her he had made a decision about their relationship.

CHAPTER 51

"The unequalled highway to the White House"

PERHAPS MAKING UP FOR HIS ALOOFNESS DURING THEIR WEEKEND together, Jack presented Inga with a rare gift, a pair of antique hurricane lamps that Inga found "perfectly beautiful," adding, "I feel deeply attached to them already and have sworn never to leave them." Inga acknowledged they were an unusual token of affection, but they meant everything to her "because I am slightly crazy about the person who gave them to me. A mink coat from FDR would leave me cold and a violet from my sailor-boy throws me into raptures."

Jack's lack of effusive expressions of love did not bother Inga. She was annoyed how casually Americans expressed affection, calling everyone "Darling . . . just to be sort of friendly," and using the phrase "I love you" cavalierly. "I like people who use that phrase very rarely and then mean it, when it actually crosses their lips."

But Inga was no fool. She had noticed Jack's changed demeanor in Charleston and had gotten a sense that he had made a decision. In a letter she wrote immediately after arriving home, Inga told Jack, "Every time I see you I learn something new. As I told you yesterday I know you pretty well, and still I like you. You know, Jack, that is a hell of a compliment, because anyone as brainy and Irish-shrewd as you can't be quite like a white dove."

Fejos and others may have claimed Inga cared nothing for politics, but she understood politics, especially that it is a tough, nasty business, and if Jack intended to go as far as he planned to go in the profession

257

then sentimentality was a luxury he would not indulge. Inga could see her dream for her and Jack slipping away, but always generous, she offered encouragement instead of self-pity. "Put a match to the smoldering ambition," Inga told Jack, "and you will go like wild fire. (It is all against the ranch out west, but it is the unequalled highway to the White House.) And if you can find something you really believe in, then my dear you caught the biggest fish in the ocean."

Even though promoting Jack's public career was against her interests, Inga told Kick that she had talked to Patterson and Waldrop about hiring Jack to do book reviews for the *Times-Herald*. This would allow Jack to "keep his face and name alive in Washington, as Charleston and Norfolk are so dull."

While marrying Jack seemed more unlikely than ever, Inga was still committed to divorcing Fejos. She asked Cissy Patterson for a leave of absence to travel to Reno, promising that while there she would write articles about famous people in town for the same purpose. Patterson agreed to give her the time off.

Olga asked to come, but Inga initially did not want her to tag along. She told Olga that she was tired and feeling nervous. She needed a vacation, and perhaps the trip to Reno, despite the reason she was going there, might offer the relaxation that she needed. If only Jack could be transferred closer to Washington, she added, "things will be easier."

Inga also complained of being in pain. "I feel like hell," she told Fejos. She worried it might be appendicitis. It was more likely the onset of rheumatoid arthritis that would trouble her the rest of her life. Despite not feeling well, Inga flew to New York to finalize arrangements with Fejos regarding her trip to Reno, and while in town she also briefly saw Blok. When she got back to Washington, Blok called and Inga confessed that she was "very lonesome." Blok told her again how much he loved her and asked if she would go to bed with him again. "Of course I will go to bed with you," Inga replied.

If Jack was restless in Charleston, so was Inga in Washington. She was tired of doing her column for the *Times-Herald*, dissatisfied that she had no role to play in the war "to defeat the Axis," and annoyed with herself for not being more ambitious, or as she phrased it, "to put my head above that of the crowd." She still daydreamed about moving "out West" where she would live in a small house with lots of books and a place to write. "And before I left," she told Jack, "I would make sure that I had your baby along with me . . . because you are the kind the world ought to swarm with."

Inga admired Jack because he had the wonderful balance of "brains and goodness" to make the world a better place, but also the "sufficient meanness" to get these good things done. She had only one complaint: "Maybe your gravest mistake handsome . . . is that you admire brains more than heart," though Inga acknowledged that "heart never brought fame—except to Saints—nor money—except to the women of the oldest profession in the world, and that must be hard earned."

Inga continued, "You once said—as a matter of fact last Sunday—'To you I need not pretend, you know me too well.' I do, not because I have put you on a pedestal—you don't belong there, nobody does—but because I know where you are weak, and that is what I like. A man or woman who thinks and makes others believe that he has no weakness in him or her, well they are like diamonds cut by the unskilled hand."

The war would be over one day, and then Jack would show the world what he could do, Inga said, unaware how the war would come to shape Jack's future. If Inga was still a part of Jack's life then, she wanted him to know that he could always turn to her, whatever his need, and she would be there "always with an outstretched hand with a warm grasp of love and understanding." And then she made an analogy between herself and Lot's wife, who turned into a pillar of salt when "she looked back, the curious creature," as God destroyed Sodom. The Bible is unclear why God punished Lot's wife in this way. For Inga, the story was simply an always appropriate reminder for how to live: never look back; always move forward. This philosophy would be sorely tested in just a few days.

CHAPTER 52

"Totally dead inside"

INGA SENT JACK A TELEGRAM THAT SHE WOULD BE UNABLE TO TRAVEL to Charleston until March 6, as she had to work on Saturday, February 28. Being discreet, Inga signed the cable "Love, Barbara." On the 28th, Jack called Kick to tell her he was flying to Washington that night, but he begged her not to tell Inga. Kick told Inga anyway. Inga, hoping for the best but expecting the worst, decided not to meet Jack's plane.

On landing, Jack went straight to Inga's apartment, wearing a "mixed uniform" of an ensign's cap and a navy raincoat over his civilian's suit. Even though both Jack and Inga seldom drank alcohol, Inga had a bottle of Haig whiskey delivered from a local liquor store. But Inga did not need a stiff drink that night. Jack delayed telling Inga whatever it was he had come to Washington to tell her.

We do not know what reason he gave Inga that night for his sudden decision to travel to Washington, because the bug the FBI had placed in Inga's apartment was malfunctioning. The FBI learned from Inga's landlady, however, that Jack spent Saturday night in Inga's apartment. Jack may have told Inga that he had traveled to Washington to see Billings before he left for Africa, because he brought Billings to Inga's apartment on Sunday to say hello.

But Sunday afternoon, Jack and Inga were alone in her apartment and began to have the delicate discussion that was the real reason for Jack's visit. Jack told Inga they needed to end their romance.

Exactly how Jack broke this news is unknown. The FBI's microphone was still not working properly. "The set-up was such that they [the agents listening in] got noises from adjoining rooms," an FBI agent explained. This failure of technology afforded Inga and Jack a modicum of privacy and dignity that the FBI had denied them many times previously. All the FBI noted was that the conversation was short as Jack "did not stay very long, which is unusual."

Sam McKee, the special agent in charge of the FBI's investigation of Inga, listened to the tape several times. He could not make out most of what was said, but reported that Jack told Inga "Naval authorities were watching him and apparently had a microphone in her room. This seemingly was the reason given by Jack in breaking off these relations with Inga."

How Jack learned that Inga's apartment was bugged is unknown. Perhaps a colleague at ONI tipped him off (ONI was still cooperating with the FBI), but the better guess is that someone at the FBI, perhaps Hoover himself, alerted Joseph Kennedy, who then alerted his son.

Aware that he had nearly been sacked already because of his relationship with Inga, Jack panicked. He now thought less about his long-term career and more about the short-term danger of being thrown out of the service to the shame of his family. It was one thing to think that a few busybodies were peeking through keyholes, but audio recordings that included conversations he had had with his father raised the risk to a much higher level.

Just before he left Inga's apartment at about 6 p.m., Jack called Kick to tell her he would be over for supper shortly but that Inga would not be joining him, claiming that she had work to do. Remarkably, Jack returned to Inga's apartment later that night. Kick had gone out, and Jack needed a ride to Washington's National Airport to catch his plane back to Charleston. We do not know that Inga gave Jack the ride he needed, but since Kick had scolded her for being too "warmhearted" and too giving of herself, it is almost certain that she did.

A depressed Inga called Fejos shortly after returning from the airport.

"I hear our friends, those that have been looking for me the whole time, you know whom I mean, they are still on my trail," Inga told Fejos. "Very much so apparently. I hear they have a Dictaphone in my room. I hope they have so they can listen to my interesting conversations."

"Don't be listening to such silly talk," replied Fejos, who declined to admit what Inga already knew, that he, too, had hired a private detective to spy on his wife.

Inga knew it wasn't silly talk. "That is what I hear and from very reliable sources on account of my attachment to the Naval Intelligence Service," she said, referring to Jack. "So I'm quitting that acquaintance."

"What?" a surprised Fejos said. "I don't get that."

"I am not going to see that person anymore," Inga said. "I'm tired of all that nonsense. I want peace for God's sake."

Fejos pestered Inga to tell him what happened, but Inga said nothing had happened; she lied and said the decision to break it off with Jack was hers.

McKee, who knew more than even the main participants themselves, noted with perhaps the slightest pang of regret that "Inga Arvad, up until the time of this conversation, was apparently madly in love with Jack Kennedy and was planning to go to Reno to divorce Fejos so she could marry him."

Inga still planned to go to Reno to get her divorce. Despite what McKee wrote, she was still madly in love with Jack. But now she knew without any doubt that there was no chance he would marry her. As she had predicted, Jack had relied on his brains more than his heart. She told Kick that she had decided it would be best if she did not contact Jack again, "even though she feels lousy about it." Kick told Jack, "Inga seemed very sad . . . I haven't inquired into the story but I certainly would like to."

Inga was still in shock from her breakup with Jack when she came home three days later to discover her apartment had been burglarized. She reported to the District of Columbia police that $450 in money orders and several pieces of jewelry, including a diamond ring that Inga valued at $400, were missing.

Unknown to Inga, the burglar was the second break-in of the day, for the FBI, aware that Jack had told Inga she was under electronic surveillance, had also entered her apartment earlier on March 4 to remove the malfunctioning bug they had installed in her apartment.

Agents refused to believe Inga's apartment could have been burglarized without their knowledge while they were still staking out her residence. They told Hoover Inga must have faked the burglary as "a plant to determine if she is being investigated." Agents also found Inga's "lack of anxiety" at having been robbed suspicious, discounting the notion that she might simply still be numb from the encounter with Jack that they themselves had overheard.

McKee developed a plan to call Inga's bluff. He would urge police detectives to revisit Inga and advise her that police knew about the "men coming from her apartment in the morning," and demand to know who these men were, where they lived, and "tell her [the detective] wants to talk with them." Certain that Inga would be humiliated by such a confrontation, McKee told Hoover that he believed "this treatment will shut her up."

There is no record that this brilliant piece of detective work was tried, but the FBI was no doubt surprised when, nine months later, the Bureau learned that District police had arrested a suspect in Inga's not-fictional burglary. A former neighbor of Inga named Coffey, who by then was in the Coast Guard, had tried to cash a money order that was made out to Inga. Coffey must have been unfamiliar with the gender of Scandinavian given names, for he tried to cash the money order using a phony Coast Guard ID belonging to "Inga Fejos."

That Coffey had lived in an apartment on Inga's floor helped explain how the burglary could have occurred under the nose of the FBI; it was an inside job. It is possible that Coffey had surreptitiously observed FBI agents entering Inga's apartment, thought they were common thieves, saw that entrance into the apartment was easy, and concluded that if two break-ins occurred on the same day, it would make it more difficult for police to conclude which burglar stole what.

Three days after the break-in, Inga received her third great shock of the week when she received a telephone call from Jack on March 7. It had not even been a week since the breakup.

"Surprised to hear from me?" Jack asked. "A little maybe," Inga replied, though Kick had told her that her brother intended to call. Jack said he would have called sooner, but his bad back was acting up again.

Inga told Jack she was still reeling from the discovery that her apartment had been burglarized. Inga then told Jack she had canceled her plane reservations to Charleston.

"Why didn't you come?" Jack asked.

"What a question!" Inga replied. "Don't you remember that we talked it over Sunday?"

"I know it," said Jack.

"Oh, you don't think it's going to stay?" Inga asked.

"Life's too short," Jack said.

"Oh, Kennedy!" Inga groaned. "You're not giving up what we promised last Sunday, are you?"

"No, not until the next time I see you," Jack said. "I'm not too good, am I?"

"I think you're perfect dear," Inga said. "We'll probably meet again."

"You mean next week?" a hopeful Jack asked.

"I'm not coming," Inga said. "I don't know. I'm not trying to be stubborn. I'm only trying to help you. You know that, don't you? . . . Did you think I was coming to Charleston?"

"I had high hopes," said Jack.

Warned away from Inga by his father, Jack remained curious just how much trouble Inga was in. Even though he had in theory broken off their relationship, he still had questions about the "ugly rumors" and "all this gab going around." Inga knew why she was a person of interest to the FBI, but she also knew she was not a spy. She told Jack that his father was just "trying to scare you." But Jack pushed back, saying that his father had heard from a reputable source, an old acquaintance in the Roosevelt administration, Maritime Commissioner Max Truitt, "the thing isn't O.K. for some reason. You are mixed up in something. . . . You're not holding out on me, are you?"

Inga should have been furious at this lack of trust from her now former lover, but by now she had become resigned to being the object of innuendo, so she let it pass. She told Jack that she was innocent of all but one thing: "There's nothing illegal they can put their hands on. What's illegal about being in love?" Inga expressed hope that her divorce from Fejos would disassociate herself from Wenner-Gren and end the suspicions.

She also said she was trying to set up an appointment with J. Edgar Hoover himself to try to straighten things out. She had called Helen Gandy to set up an appointment for the following week. What, Jack asked, did she intend to tell Hoover? "I'm going to say, 'Now, look here Edgar, J. [*sic*], I don't like everybody listening in on my phone,'" Inga replied. "I'm going to tell him that I would like to know a little bit about the whole thing myself because I hear nothing but a fantastic amount of rumors from everybody and I am after all the chief actress in the play." As far as can be determined, Hoover never met with Inga.

Jack also asked Inga whether she still intended to divorce Fejos. "I just wanted to be sure that this is what you want to do," Jack said. "From what you have said, I didn't have anything to do with you getting the divorce." Inga said falling in love with Jack had convinced her that she no longer loved Fejos, "but that doesn't hold you responsible for anything." Inga told Jack she still loved him as much as ever, but she accepted that their romance was over and that she and Jack would never marry, so "you don't figure in my plans whatsoever." A somewhat chastened Jack could only reply, "O.K."

It was, of course, not that simple. She and Jack promised to keep writing one another, and a few days later Inga wrote Jack to express concern about his bad back. She wished she could come to Charleston, "Not because I want you to make love to me and say charming things. Only because I wish more than anything to be with you when you are sick. . . . Maybe it is the maternal instinct."

Inga was still dissecting all that had happened. She had always thought of the human heart as a cage where a bird sits, she said. Some birds mourn and some are nasty, but "mine always sang. It did especially for a few months this winter. In fact, it sang so loudly that I refused to listen to that other little sensible creature called reason. It took . . . the FBI, the US Navy, nasty gossip, envy, hatred and big Joe, before the bird stopped [singing]."

Inga worried that perhaps she had let Jack win her over too easily, and that was the root of their problem. Or perhaps she should fight harder to keep Jack, though she doubted that would be enough. "You belong so wholeheartedly to the Kennedy-clan, and I don't want you ever to get into an argument with your father on account of me. As I have told you a dozen times, if I were but 18 summers I would fight like a tigress for her young in order to get you and keep you. Today I am wiser. Nevertheless I may as well admit that since that famous Sunday evening I have been totally dead inside."

PART IX
From Tulagi to Hollywood

CHAPTER 53

"Reno-vating" Inga's marriage

Kick Kennedy had said once she would scream if Inga did not stop talking about Jack, but now she had to listen as Jack "talked for hours" about his continued longing for Inga. But Inga remained obstinate—understandably so given that Jack had clearly ruled out marriage—and would not travel to Charleston to see Jack again.

Jack was soon distracted from his hopes to continue his amour with Inga by his poor health and the foul mood of his father, who was being ostracized by President Roosevelt. This ongoing feud between Roosevelt and Kennedy seems to have played a role in FDR personally directing the FBI to continue its investigation of Inga even after FBI officials, including Hoover, had concluded the investigation had run its course.

Jack aggressively encouraged Joe Senior to take steps to rehabilitate his public reputation, sullied by accusations of cowardice because of Kennedy's defeatist attitude while ambassador to Great Britain. Jack's admonitions inspired his father to write Roosevelt on March 4 and again offer his services like any other dollar-a-year man. "Joe [Junior] and Jack are in the service and I feel that my experience in these critical times might be worth something in some position," Kennedy told Roosevelt.

Roosevelt, always comfortable with ambiguity, wrote back what Kennedy perceived to be an encouraging note, which led Kennedy to fly straightaway to Washington on March 12 for a meeting with the president. But when word leaked out that Roosevelt was contemplating appointing Kennedy to anything, the White House received an avalanche of letters protesting the idea. The backlash was such that Roosevelt knew he could not offer Kennedy any position of sufficient prestige that it would require congressional hearings or approval.

FDR, therefore, offered Kennedy only a modest post with the Maritime Commission where he would be tasked with ending bottlenecks in shipbuilding. Jack advised he take it, do the job well, and parlay it into something more, but his father was offended he was not offered something with greater authority and turned it down. Roosevelt "was not pleased" that Kennedy was being so hardheaded.

Kennedy's refusal to rehabilitate his reputation on his own made Jack and Joe Junior (whose flight training to become a naval aviator was nearly complete) all the more determined to get into combat, and as quickly as possible, to dispel the notion that Kennedys were cowards. Jack's old friend Torbert Macdonald, now in the service and as bored with a desk job as Jack was, hoped to join them. "We're rapidly joining the ranks of the young middle-aged . . . let's get the hell out of jobs that were deemed for older men," Macdonald wrote.

But Jack faced a major impediment to getting into the war. To alleviate his chronic back pain, Jack had been following a Charles Atlas fitness program, writing Billings that "[I] believe I am well on my way to HEALTH, STRENGTH and PERSONAL POWER, whatever personal power is." But the exercises were of modest benefit, and by late March his back pain and stomach cramps were so severe that he was granted ten days leave to see specialists at the Mayo Clinic and in Boston.

First, however, Jack flew to Palm Beach to further console his father and also to see a friend from his brief time at Stanford University named Henry James. It was on this visit that Jack intrigued James with his description of Inga as beautiful, warm, sexy, and possibly a spy. James was astonished that Jack had not run as far and as fast from Inga as he could, warning Jack he was risking jail if it turned out Inga was a foreign agent. But when James pressed Jack about whether he had truly ended his relationship with Inga, "He just looked at me. Wouldn't say anything—wouldn't say yes, wouldn't say no."

Sans Inga, Jack dated a few women, including old girlfriend Charlotte McDonnell—until he discovered McDonnell still did not believe in sex before marriage. Despite reports in some Kennedy biographies, McDonnell said Jack never proposed to her because "he was never in love with me. He liked to think he was, when things were going bad and he didn't have anyone else, but he really wasn't."

Inga was worried to learn about Jack's poor health and that he was, on the advice of the specialists he had seen, contemplating having risky disc fusion surgery. But Jack's request to have six months leave to have the operation was denied, and instead he was ordered to undergo more tests at the Charleston Naval Hospital.

Aside from sympathy and the distraction from pain that lovemaking might provide, Inga doubted there was much she could do to help and plenty that her presence might do to hurt Jack's career. So, she only sent words of concern coupled with the irreverent tone that Jack found so appealing: "Those we love we never want to suffer, but as [surgery] will make a better golfer out of you it will probably make you happier in the end, even if it's going to be very uncomfortable for the time being."*

The FBI, based on reports from Inga's landlady, thought Jack spent the Friday and Saturday nights before Inga left for Reno at her apartment, but that was not possible. Jack was in no shape to travel as he prepared to be admitted into the Charleston Naval Hospital the same day (April 12) Inga left for Reno. More likely, if a man spent the night in Inga's apartment, it was Nils Blok, who in terms of height, weight, and coloring bore a slight resemblance to Jack if seen in the dark and through a peephole.

Reno, Nevada's largest city with a population of less than twenty thousand (Las Vegas at the time was a hamlet with fewer than five thousand residents), was the divorce capital of America. It was an economic development initiative. In 1930, Nevada was by far the least populous state in the nation with barely ninety thousand residents—considerably less than half the population of Wyoming, the next least-populous state. Desperate to lure new businesses and residents, the 1931 Nevada Legisla-

---

*Kennedy was an avid golfer, but during the 1950s the sport was so associated with President Eisenhower, who was nearly thirty years older than Kennedy, that as a candidate and as president Jack took pains never to be seen playing golf; claiming to represent a "new generation" of leadership, he wanted to be associated with more vigorous and youthful sports like touch football.

ture passed two laws; one legalized gambling and the other reduced the residency requirement needed to obtain a divorce to six weeks.* Initially, divorce was the greater growth industry.

By 1940, 5 percent of all divorces in the United States were granted in Nevada, even though the state had less than one-half of 1 percent of the nation's population. The name of "The Biggest Little City in the World" became a verb; those getting a divorce there were said to be "Reno-vating" their marriage, as was noted in the 1936 play and 1939 movie *The Women*, authored by the multitalented Clare Boothe Luce.

After a 2,500-mile train trip, Inga checked into Reno's Riverside Hotel located along the Truckee River, conveniently one block from both the Reno train station and the Washoe County Courthouse. The red brick, six-story building covered half a city block and catered almost exclusively to those establishing residency for a divorce, as clear a sign as any just how good business could be catering to the brokenhearted (or hardhearted, as the case might be).

Meanwhile, doctors at Charleston had evaluated Jack and recommended against back surgery, but sent him to the Chelsea Naval Hospital in Boston for yet more tests. He reported there on May 18.

Inga was only marginally happier in Reno than Jack was in the hospital. While she said the city was beautiful, lodged at the foot of the Sierra Nevada Mountains, it was a place "you wouldn't send your worst enemy to." The problem, Inga told Jack, was that "the place seems silly, dreadfully money conscious, and full of cowboys who look like Bob Addie (our sports writer) when he says about one of the elder girls in the office, 'You know what she needs? A roll in the hay.' To me that is about the tops of horrible expressions for a thing which ought to be beautiful."

Inga found Reno with its "bars [of] uninviting names" so boring that she changed her mind and invited Olga to join her for several weeks. "She

---

*Before Nevada changed its law, South Dakota, of all places, was a popular place to get divorced as it had only a ninety-day residency requirement. Because of the fluid population, states on the western frontier had a lower threshold for residency than the older, established eastern states. (April White, "The Divorce Colony," *Atavist Magazine* 55 [December 11, 2015])

is going to be my salvation," Inga said. In the meantime, Inga spent her time reading and writing letters. She wrote Jack, but said she would maintain the correspondence only if he wanted to hear from her.

She knew Jack wasn't feeling well and also wasn't sure if he had emotionally moved on because of her continued refusal to sleep with him. In her note, Inga told Jack she hoped to see him at least once more. "Some day we will have a steak, mashed potatoes, peas, carrots, and ice cream again," Inga said. "It won't ever be like the old days, somehow the past is gone, but you have a great future—don't ever let anybody make you believe anything different."

CHAPTER 54

"Hearts beating in the same rhythm"

JACK WAS DELIGHTED TO RECEIVE INGA'S LETTER. HE MISSED HER A great deal, and with the lines of communication reestablished he immediately telephoned her in Reno. As Inga recalled, one of the hotel staff came and knocked on her door, saying someone on the telephone "wants a person called Inga Binga. Is that your married name?" When Inga went to the phone, "a very optimistic voice said, 'Will you pay for a collect call from John F. Kennedy in Chelsea, Massachusetts?' Well! Nobody knocked me with a hammer on the head, but compared to that news it would have been mild."

Their conversation made it feel like the old days—as in three months before—and Jack begged Inga to follow up with "a good long letter." She complied with a letter so long it was the equivalent of about ten "Did You Happen to See?" columns. She told Jack about the many sad tales in Reno, such as the husband who traveled from the East to beg his wife to reconsider the day before their divorce was to be final. But the wife said he was wasting his time; she intended to marry the one she "really loves," who was by chance in Reno and surreptitiously spending each night in the woman's room. "That is what drifts in through the door," Inga told Jack. "I try to keep it shut so as not to hear or see too much. Not that I am a prude, just a tired girl who wants to look like a million again."

Inga was glad that Olga had come after all. "She takes care of me like a mother-hen of her only chick," said Inga, who was, in fact, Olga's only chick. They took walks, talked, took rides in the countryside, read books, and were in bed every night before ten o'clock. The war seemed far away there, Inga said, especially since "I haven't got somebody who loves me enough to explain the whole matter." And since Jack was not there to offer his own insights into the geopolitical situation, Inga had been reading to learn more.

She read *The Japanese Enemy* in which British journalist Hugh Byas argued that the Allies should not underestimate Japan, and predicted the war in the Pacific would be a long and bloody conflict. Jack would soon find out how accurate that prediction was. The book was informative but dry, Inga said; it made *Why England Slept* seem like "a thrilling murder-story" by comparison.

Inga also reported to Jack that she had read *The Last Time I Saw Paris* by Elliot Paul, "which delighted me, perhaps [because] I loved France and her capital, where I spent so much time," and also *Lanterns on the Levee* by William Alexander Percy (Walker Percy's uncle) because her time in Charleston had made her fall in love with the South.

But the book that particularly resonated with Inga was the Daphne de Maurier historical romance *Frenchmen's Creek* about a seventeenth-century married English noblewoman named Dona who despises her shallow and mundane life in court society and falls in love with a French pirate named Aubéry and joins his crew. When her pirate lover is captured, Dona kills a man to aid his escape, but then decides her place is with her husband and children and bids her pirate lover adieu.

The story appealed to Inga's "romantic soul, which I have to hide in the God's year of 1942, because it simply isn't the thing to have. Only on very special occasions, and then a girl is too bashful to show that she loves a moon hanging low in the sky and stars which twinkle above her head." In case Jack had not already understood the hint, Inga said Dona and Aubéry had what she and Jack once had: "Two who for just a few seconds have their hearts beating in the same rhythm. Rare I hear it is, but probably what they mean, when they say, 'Heaven on earth.'"

As if shaking herself out of a dream, Inga then told Jack, "We really should take up another subject," and congratulated him on his upcoming twenty-fifth birthday on May 29. "Responsibility and life is just starting," wrote Inga, playing the sage who was four years older. "Happiness and pain. Hopes and failures. Love and hatred. And as I know you, you will have plenty of it all. That golden goblet which contains the elixir of life will be drunk greedily by you."

She still wondered about Jack's plans and whether he would ever tell her all of them "because you always have a hundred. The 99 you tell me, and the one you really hope will materialize you keep to yourself. Maybe wise. Maybe right. And I believe that a person ought to live; we can't monopolize each other, even if we are the best of friends. Even lovers shouldn't and too often do."

Inga's plans were uncertain. Once the divorce was final, she would go back to the *Times-Herald*, but probably not for long. "I would like to do something for these United States," Inga said. "I can't enlist in the armed forces and would most likely be a dreadful soldier . . . but there are many ways of winning. And I am not going to sit and do nothing at all."

Another *Times-Herald* employee had also resolved to do her bit for the war effort, which not coincidentally would allow her to follow her heart's desire. Kick confided to Jack that she had come to realize how much she loved Billy Cavendish, the Marquess of Hartington, and wished to be his wife. She was scheming to get back to Britain as a worker for the Red Cross, but Jack urged her to forget Hartington. "I would strongly advise against any voyage to England to marry an Englishmen," Jack wrote. "It has come time to write the obituary of the British Empire." Why Jack thought the future of the empire should be a key factor as to whether two people in love should marry is unclear, but Inga said Jack relied too much on brains and not enough on heart.

On June 3, 1942, the Second Judicial District Court of Nevada granted Inga's divorce from Fejos on the grounds of "willful desertion" for a period of more than one year; Fejos had been away from Inga in Peru for more than two years. Inga, whose attorney in the case was Bert Goldwater, a distant cousin of future Arizona senator Barry Goldwater, sought no alimony, and she and Fejos had agreed how to divide their property and possessions months before.

In its decree, the court noted that with the divorce now final, there were no restrictions on remarriage. Fejos took this provision to heart. On June 22, less than three weeks after his divorce from Inga was complete, he married his companion of the previous six months, Marianne Arden, in a ceremony in Baltimore.* Walter Winchell took note in his column, describing Arden as "the lovely Viennese pianist-singer," and noting that Inga "the Washington interviewer . . . made it possible by going to Reno." It was Inga's second appearance in a Winchell column, but now Fejos, too, had also made it into what he had sarcastically referred to as "the greatest institution of newspaper writing in the US."

---

* Like Inga, Arden was a remarkable woman, who would compose more than one hundred songs and who released a new album of recordings in 2012, when she was ninety-nine years old!

CHAPTER 55

"He looks like a limping monkey"

INGA HAD HOPED HER DIVORCE FROM FEJOS, WHICH CUT HER TIES TO Axel Wenner-Gren, would end the FBI's interest in her case. As Jack had predicted, she was soon disappointed. The FBI did consider dropping its surveillance of Inga, but President Roosevelt had other ideas.

Several agents assigned to Inga's case and J. Edgar Hoover himself were beginning to doubt the utility of continuing to monitor Inga. They had now been keeping her under observation for nearly five months, and while Inga's exotic background and active social life always seemed to hold promise that something would break, there had been no concrete evidence of espionage at all.

In addition to her divorce from Fejos (and by extension Wenner-Gren), Inga's affair with Jack now seemed over, which meant she was no longer sleeping with an ensign in ONI. Anyone listening to the tapes (or reading the transcripts) of Inga's conversations regarding these events would know that these were difficult and heartfelt decisions, and not a cold-hearted ruse implemented by a master spy to throw her pursuers off the scent.

Edward Tamm, the Bureau's deputy director, thought so and recommended to Hoover that the investigation into Inga "cease" and that "a closing report be submitted to the Bureau." Hoover initially agreed with Tamm's recommendation. Frank Waldrop never understood why the FBI believed that Inga was a viable suspect in the first place. "I'll say this, I never thought Hitler had any too great an organization around here, but if he was depending on Inga, he certainly didn't seem to know his business."

The FBI, however, was still the agency responsible for counterintelligence in Latin America. In late April, Hoover provided Roosevelt with an overview on the Bureau's latest thinking regarding Nazi infiltration in the Western Hemisphere. Hoover included one FBI informant's rather extraordinary belief, given the logistics involved, that "any attempted German invasion of South America would strike first at the Upper Amazon because an expeditionary force, once established there, would be very difficult to dislodge."

Fejos, of course, had spent most of the past two years in the Upper Amazon, and Hoover told Roosevelt that the FBI continued to believe that Fejos was a Nazi agent and that Fejos's Peruvian expedition, funded and directed by Wenner-Gren, was phony, despite the discovery of lost Incan cities. "His wife, who is divorcing him, is reported to be a former favorite of Hitler," Hoover reminded Roosevelt. "At present she writes a column for the *Washington Times-Herald* under the name of Inga Arvad."

The question was whether Inga's impending divorce from Fejos freed her of further suspicion. Roosevelt's answer came quickly in a confidential memorandum dated May 4 to Hoover that read: "In view of the connection of Inga Arvad, who writes for the *Washington Times-Herald*, with the Wenner-Gren Expeditions' leader, and in view of certain other circumstances which have been brought to my attention, I think it would be just as well to have her specially watched."

Roosevelt did not elaborate to Hoover on what he meant by "certain other circumstances" warranting a continued investigation of Inga. There seem to be two possibilities, neither of which speak well of the president.

The "other circumstances" cited by Roosevelt may mean the political gossip being gleaned from the surveillance of Inga that FDR found both useful and entertaining, but which had no relevance to whether Inga was a spy. As William Sullivan, who had once led the FBI's intelligence operations, noted, "Roosevelt unfortunately established the precedent of using the FBI as the president's personal political tool."

Hoover had undoubtedly shared with FDR the conversations between Jack and Joseph Kennedy where they discussed how Joe Senior might get back in the good graces of the president. FDR was also likely told that Bernard Baruch, whose love life had long fascinated Roosevelt, was audaciously flirting with Inga, a woman less than half his age. Roosevelt considered both Kennedy and Baruch troublesome men and perhaps hoped that continued surveillance of Inga would provide useful information on them as well as on Inga's boss and FDR's nemesis, Cissy Patterson.

But the wording of FDR's memorandum to Hoover ("other circumstances which have been brought to my attention") implies that perhaps the president had also received information about Inga from sources other than the FBI.

Roosevelt had established his own private political investigating unit within the White House, led by journalist John Franklin Carter. Carter was paid for his covert work from a secret White House fund even as he still wrote a nationally syndicated newspaper column titled "We, the People."

Hoover had considered Inga a plausible spy because he deduced that working as a journalist would be perfect cover for a foreign agent engaged in "a most subtle type of espionage." Similarly, FDR had hired Carter as his personal spy because, as historian Joseph Persico noted, he "grasped that Carter's profession offered the perfect cover for delivering intelligence, a Washington journalist coming to the White House occasionally to interview the President."

Less egregious, since there is no evidence burglaries were committed to collect political intelligence, Carter's tiny group was still certainly a forerunner of the notorious "Plumbers" unit established in the Nixon White House. Carter's "fact-finding unit" helped satiate Roosevelt's "weakness for the gossipy products." The problem was that Carter was very credulous. Among the tidbits he passed on to FDR were that Free French leader Charles de Gaulle was plotting with American labor leader John L. Lewis to seize control of the U.S. government. Another was that American seismologists had recommended bombs be dropped on active volcanoes in Japan in hopes of spurring an eruption. "One can only wonder at some of the notions Carter relayed to the President from his nebulous sources," Persico said. This may have included notions about Inga.

It is possible that Carter, who worked briefly as a journalist in Nazi Germany in the 1930s, may have himself met or at least heard of Inga while there. If not, he knew someone who did. One of Carter's covert duties was to manage German defector Ernest "Putzi" Hanfstaengl, the gregarious, American-educated, inveterate gossip and blowhard who had been a member of Hitler's inner circle and who had been tasked in the mid-1930s with managing relations with American reporters in Germany. Hanfstaengl defected after he fell out of favor with Hitler in 1937, partly because his wife, Helen, whom Hitler adored, had divorced him. FDR agreed with Carter that Hanfstaengl might provide valuable insights into Hitler's and the German people's psyche.

As early as February 1942, Carter urged the FBI—"in passing," according to Hoover—to interview Hanfstaengl about Inga. Hoover vaguely recalled that Hanfstaengl was in Canada in an internment camp, but there is no record of the FBI ever following up on Carter's tip or what Carter believed they would learn about Inga from Hanfstaengl. Carter put few things in writing.

Whatever Roosevelt's inscrutable motivations and whatever their impetus, Hoover immediately put the FBI back on Inga's case. The Bureau wasn't sure where she was, so Hoover directed his agents to "immediately determine the subject's whereabouts and activities and resume coverage in this case similar to that previously in effect."

Hoover was therefore irritated to learn that Inga had been back in Washington for nearly a week before the Bureau knew of her return, and then only because her byline had reappeared in the *Times-Herald*. Flummoxed agents explained that Inga had not returned to her residence, which was where they had focused their stakeout, but was living with Kathleen Kennedy while her own apartment was being freshly painted. This did not prevent Hoover from sending a sharp rebuke to his subordinates that "it was apparent this matter was not receiving appropriate attention on your part. I desire that this matter receive more careful consideration in the future."

The FBI once again tapped Inga's phone, which allowed agents to hear Inga tell Kick's new roommate, Betty Coxe, how "she was very disgusted with the F.B.I. business and how the F.B.I. and the Navy handled Jack." Inga told Coxe the situation was "awful and that at cocktail parties it seemed as if each person was looking at her and trying to decide if she was a spy or not."

Inga said she had lost interest in her work at the *Times-Herald* and had come to hate Washington. She was contemplating moving to New York City, partly to be with Nils Blok and partly because she believed she would be able to land a job in the Office of War Information (OWI) and earn a salary of $10 more per week than she was earning at the *Times-Herald*.* Blok was already employed there, writing scripts for broadcasts into the Scandinavian countries (OWI began Voice of America in 1942).

On the other hand, Inga said, she hated to walk out on Cissy Patterson, who had been good to her and who she feared would be angry at her for leaving. Coxe, however, disagreed that Inga owed the paper anything and counseled that she should move to New York and take the job at OWI, where she would be doing something for the war effort. But Coxe told her that she should not marry Blok or anyone else for at least three or four months until she was sure it was right. Inga was so anxious to be a wife and mother, Coxe said, "she would probably marry anything with pants on right now." Inga acknowledged that she was no more than "fond" of Blok and was still in love with Jack. Inga complained about Kick's plans to move to London, which would sever an important connection to Jack.

Inga then made two very strange statements. She said she did not blame the FBI for investigating her. She knew some powerful people had pushed the Bureau to do so, and she believed that anyone under suspicion needed to be investigated in a time of war. She blamed her predicament on "Washington bad luck." Then, exhibiting rare bad taste, Inga compared her plight to that of the Jews in Germany. There were "damned dirty Jews" in Germany, but there were also good ones, Inga said, yet these good ones "got hit on the head the same as the nasty ones."

It was an appalling thing to say and demonstrated that for all her

---

* In the FBI transcripts, Inga incorrectly refers to the agency as the Coordinator of Information (CIO), which was another agency entirely, run by William Donovan to coordinate U.S. intelligence, not disseminate American information and propaganda around the world.

Jewish friends, such as Lothar Wolff and Bernard Baruch, Inga still possessed the ingrained anti-Semitism of the time and still failed to grasp the enormity of the crimes being committed in Nazi Germany. Seeing herself as a martyr, it was clear she was also tired, stressed, and in need of a change.

After returning from Reno, Inga told her former *Times-Herald* colleague John White, who had enlisted in the marines, that she had had lunch with Joseph Kennedy. Papa Joe likely wanted to discern Inga's intentions regarding his son now that she was a free woman, but he also peppered Inga with questions about Kick and White, including whether Kick was in love with White and what kind of person White was. Inga told Kennedy that White was "a grand fellow," adding mischievously, "of course, it isn't every boy who likes to live on a girl's money." Inga did not say whether Kennedy laughed at her joke, but White roared when she recounted the conversation to him.*

If Joseph Kennedy thought a now-divorced Inga would aggressively pursue Jack, he had it the wrong way round. On June 24, the same day Inga spoke to Coxe, Jack stopped in Washington on his way back to Charleston after his hospital stay in Boston. He called Inga in the middle of the night—shortly after 1 a.m.—to ask if he could come to her apartment and spend the night. Inga refused, but as the FBI noted, she repeatedly called Jack "darling and both were affectionate." She also declined to see him off at the airport later that day, but she and Jack promised to stay in touch.

The specialists at Chelsea Naval Hospital in Boston had diagnosed Jack's back problems as muscular strain rather than a ruptured disc. Bored by more than two months of inaction, Jack wholeheartedly agreed to avoid surgery and pursue far less drastic treatment measures that would allow him to get into combat more quickly.

Jack had received a "superior" rating from his commander in ONI, but both the commander and Jack knew he had no future there and no

---

*It may have been at this lunch where Joseph Kennedy made a play for Inga, much to her chagrin. That a father would try to sleep with his son's girlfriend led Inga to believe "there was something incestuous about the family," she told her son, Ronald McCoy. (JCBP)

chance for promotion because of the brouhaha surrounding his affair with Inga. So Jack applied to attend midshipmen's school, a requirement for any naval officer hoping to go to sea. ONI, however, could not get a replacement for Jack in Charleston, so his application was turned down. Fortunately, demand was such that a second midshipman's school in Chicago was organized, and this time he was accepted and his transfer approved.

Jack left Charleston for Chicago on July 22. He again stopped while traveling through Washington and called Inga to ask if he could come to her apartment and spend the night. Excited that he was finally on his way to the front, perhaps also understandably frightened about what might lay ahead and realizing he might not see Inga again, Jack may have thought of a song from the 1930 musical *Three's a Crowd* that had, for understandable reasons, become popular once more with its plea to "give me something to remember you by when you are far away from me."

But the something Jack wanted from Inga to remember her by Inga still declined to give. She again refused to sleep with Jack, but she did see him while he was in Washington and was shocked by what she saw. As she later told a friend in a call monitored, of course, by the FBI, Inga said, "He went through town and just a few minutes ago he was here and then he is going on active seat duty. Only you know, his back—he looks like a limping monkey from behind. He can't walk at all. That's ridiculous, sending him off to sea duty."

Even more ridiculous, from the standpoint of his health, was Jack's decision to apply for command of a PT ("patrol torpedo") boat. The squat but fast eighty-foot-long boats had been glamorized in the book and film *They Were Expendable*, which documented how MacArthur had been evacuated from the Philippines. PT commanders tended to come from wealthy families as they were among the few Americans with experience piloting powerboats. But since PT boats bounced across the surf at speeds of forty knots—the equivalent of forty-five miles per hour on land—and commanders rode the boats standing up, Jack's back would take a terrific pounding.

A bad back could heal, however, and Inga was worried about a more fatal outcome. "Be brave," she told Jack. "I don't even mind to see you a

Navy-hero. But duck when the Japanese or German bullets aim at the handsome chest or bright head. You are just too good—and I mean good—to be carried home."

Inga was prescient; Jack would become a "Navy-hero" barely a year later—and just avoid being carried home. A lot could happen in a year, as Inga was about to find out.

CHAPTER 56

"Inga Binga got married—and not to me"

DURING THE SUMMER OF 1942, INGA MADE SEVERAL TRIPS TO NEW YORK City. She had seen Nils Blok on multiple occasions, but she had primarily been seeking work at the OWI where Blok was also employed. A former *Times-Herald* colleague, Dick Hollander, was a supervisor in the agency and had all but promised Inga a job. Hollander had not thought to check with J. Edgar Hoover, however.

Why Hoover went out of his way to torment Inga, especially given his own doubts that she was a spy, is unknown; perhaps it was just because he could. More likely, he wanted to provide Roosevelt with tangible proof that he was faithfully following FDR's May 4 directive to have Inga "specially watched."

Having been made aware of Inga's impending offer of a job at OWI, Hoover wrote Roosevelt's secretary, Marvin McIntyre, reminding McIntyre that the president had sent him a "personal note" asking to be apprised of Inga's activities. "In view of the general background concerning this woman," Hoover told McIntyre, he thought the president should know about the OWI job offer. Hoover did not contact OWI himself because of "the very confidential character" of the investigation of Inga, and told McIntyre, "I thought you might wish to do this in your own way."

Inga, of course, had no way of knowing that Hoover had signaled the White House to intervene to prevent her employment at OWI, although it is not clear this would have dissuaded her from moving to New York. Lonely without Jack, she had had enough of Washington and sincerely wished to do something to assist the war effort. Working at OWI would make her feel as if she was making a contribution, however small.

She was not deeply in love with Blok, if she was in love with him at all, but he was a genial companion and a warm body for a woman who did not want to grow old alone. It is hard to believe Inga contemplated having children with Blok, given her lukewarm feelings, but she wanted to be a mother and worried time was running short. By the standards of 1942, when most women married by age twenty-one, twenty-nine was getting old to have a first child.

While Inga was still mulling over whether she would actually marry Blok, she realized that saying she was planning to wed would provide a graceful exit from the *Times-Herald*. Vague explanations about ennui and "Washington bad luck" would not have set well with Patterson, particularly after all the favors Patterson had done for Inga, but romance was an acceptable out. A number of women at the paper were offering sudden resignations to marry before their soldier or sailor was shipped overseas. Even career-minded Page Huidekoper got married to a young soldier who had no money, which led Kick to chide, "But Page, I thought you were *ambitious*."

In her resignation letter, Inga thanked Patterson for "all that you have done for me," but added, "however, as I am getting married in the very near future and my husband-to-be is working in New York, I see no possibility of combining a job here in Washington with a home in New York." Not only was Patterson not angry with Inga, she gave her a generous cash wedding gift and two strong letters of recommendation.

Kick herself toyed with the idea of marrying John White—they had finally at least shared a passionate kiss (the marines having made White bolder)—but Kick realized she could not marry someone of no social standing. Instead, she pined for Billy Cavendish, but until she could get to London, Kick took over the duty of writing "Did You Happen to See?" from Inga.

Kick believed Blok was no better a match for Inga than White was for her. When Inga telephoned Kick to invite her to a farewell lunch, Kick asked Inga whether she really intended to marry Blok. As the FBI recorded, "Arvad said that she didn't know, that she would tell her when it was over." Kick later explained to Lem Billings that Inga "is going to marry a Dane," the reason being "she admits that Jack was the only person she cared for really and when she couldn't have him there was no sense to sit around waiting for someone else who might never come."

Not long after Inga had left Washington, Kick traveled to New York to see White, who was stationed nearby, and together they drove into the city to see Inga at the apartment she shared on Riverside Drive with Blok. Kick recalled that her visit caused a great deal of tension, as Blok seemed threatened to have anyone present who reminded Inga of Jack. While White engaged Blok, Inga drew Kick aside and told her that she still loved Jack. Kick and White agreed that if Inga and Blok did wed their marriage would not last six months.

That might have been a generous estimate, for before she was even really engaged to Blok, Inga was seeking advice about divorce. She went to see her attorney, a former FBI counselor named Lyle O'Rourke who had been one of her column subjects. She asked O'Rourke if it mattered in what state she was married "from the standpoint of possibly wanting another divorce some time." O'Rourke asked if Inga was planning to marry Kennedy. "No," Inga replied. "Kennedy will be on the high seas in a week or two and one should not marry anyone in the armed services because this separation business does not work. My [previous] husband was away for two years." When Inga told O'Rourke that she was thinking of marrying Blok instead, O'Rourke replied, "Why get married at all? There is no point to be gained."

Inga kept receiving this advice from multiple parties, particularly since she made no great effort to hide her lack of enthusiasm for Blok. Just before she left for New York on August 7, Inga called Bernard Baruch's office. Unlike his treatment of Joseph Kennedy, Roosevelt had finally relented and given Baruch an assignment with genuine responsibility. The day before Inga called, FDR had placed Baruch in charge of a commission devoted to ensuring the United States had all the rubber it needed for war production.

The suddenly busy Baruch was out, so Inga conversed with his secretary, a Miss Higgins. Having learned that Inga intended to move to New York to marry Blok, Higgins asked, "Is he nice?" Inga replied, "Well, that's all a matter of taste." Alarmed at this unusually blasé attitude for a prospective bride, Higgins urged, "Well, for goodness sakes now; don't jump into anything. You're too pretty."

Inga did not jump into marriage with Blok. While Nils had hoped to marry Inga as soon as she arrived in New York, Inga kept putting him off and never married him, although they lived together and most of her acquaintances in Washington assumed they had married, including Jack. "As you have probably not heard—Inga Binga got married—and not to me," Jack mournfully wrote Billings. "She evidently wanted to leave Washington and get to NY—so she married some guy she had known for years who loved her but whom she didn't love. . . . Anyway she's gone—and that leaves the situation rather blank."

Jack had lost what Frank Waldrop said was the love of his life, but at least Jack knew what he would be doing for the foreseeable future. He was off to war, in part to redeem the Kennedy name. Inga had also lost the love of her life, had decided against marrying Blok, and had no idea what she was going to do with her life. Her situation was blanker than Jack's.

Inga discovered that her job offer at OWI had been withdrawn, though she didn't know why. Hollander, her former colleague at the *Times-Herald*, had been reassigned, and when she contacted OWI after his departure Inga was told that OWI had no current openings. The reason Inga had called Baruch when she arrived in New York was to seek help finding work, for as she told Miss Higgins. "I don't know what I'm going to do."

CHAPTER 57

"Adolf Schickelgruber knows
nothing of love"

WHILE INGA STRUGGLED TO FIND WORK, THE FEDERAL GOVERNMENT struggled anew in August 1942 with the question of whether to arrest Inga. This time it was Assistant Solicitor General Oscar Cox who queried Hoover on "the advisability of interning Inga Arvad as a dangerous alien." Once again, as he had done for Edward Ennis six months before, Hoover prepared a dispassionate report on Inga's background that evinced no particular enthusiasm for her arrest, and Cox let the matter drop.

The FBI had lost interest in Inga's case. It had seemed full of possibilities at the beginning of 1942, but after months of surveillance they had found little of interest beyond Inga's complicated love life.

In the days after Pearl Harbor, with paranoia high, government officials and average citizens alike felt the urge to do something—anything —to counter the Axis menace. Anything out of the ordinary—like Inga— attracted notice, and during the first half of 1942, Americans were kept on edge by a German U-boat campaign that sank hundreds of ships off the East Coast, sometimes in full view of horrified beachgoers.

There were also very real dangers onshore. In June, submarines landed eight German agents on American beaches, but two of the saboteurs had a change of heart and tried to turn themselves in to the FBI. Evoking the William Sebold case the year before, the FBI initially thought the turncoats were cranks (the FBI's New York office had a large, three-drawer file cabinet stuffed only with false reports and phony confessions). Only when one of the would-be saboteurs traveled to Washington and showed agents $82,350 in cash he had been given by the Abwehr was the FBI convinced to act and arrest the six saboteurs still at large. The two Nazi defectors received prison terms; their six colleagues were executed on August 7, the day Inga arrived in New York.

With such tangible threats afoot, it no longer seemed sensible to focus FBI resources on Inga, whose case had produced no credible evidence of espionage. And so, for the first time in months, now that she was out of Washington, Inga's phone went untapped. The FBI did not bug or break in to her New York apartment, nor did they have agents watching her round the clock. She was as free as she had been in ten months. Her file, however, was not closed. Aware that President Roosevelt might again request an update on Inga, the FBI continued to periodically note her whereabouts, and her past association with Hitler and the Nazis would soon cause more problems.

Inga, however, was anxious to be freed from the FBI's web entirely. It is unknown what triggered this lingering anxiety, but on January 27, 1943, Inga wrote a letter to FBI Deputy Director Clyde Tolson, begging him to arrange for her to meet with Hoover "for five minutes," Inga said. "I would like to talk to Mr. Hoover about a personal matter, in which he is the only person who can help me."

Inga believed she had made a friend of Tolson because of her laudatory profile of him in the *Times-Herald*. In her letter, she even teased Tolson about his supposed love of candy bars. Tolson's secretary sent Inga a cursory acknowledgment that her letter had been received, but there is no record Tolson himself replied or that he tried to arrange a meeting with Hoover for Inga—or that Inga ever followed up on her request. Twice rebuffed in her efforts, she clearly was persona non grata to Hoover, who would, of course, certainly have declined to acknowledge that Inga was under investigation.

No longer under constant surveillance by the FBI, there is no detailed, nearly hourly record of Inga's activities and words during her time in New York City. We can surmise that the first few months were a stressful time. Olga, who no longer worked for the Sanger family, was back in New York and no more pleased than she had been before that Inga was with "a wreck of a person like Nils Blok."

Blok could not have been pleased that Inga declined to marry him, probably because she still carried a torch for Jack. As Inga told Kick Kennedy, she could no longer write Jack because "Nils will turn green and tear the ceiling down" if she did. Inga had received a letter from Jack, full of his views on the world situation. She told Kick that she was saving it "for my great-grandchildren—whom I hope will look like him—to see what a man he is . . . he hasn't changed a bit, and I hope to God he never will."*

Kick told Jack that things between Inga and Blok were unsettled. In a letter to Billings, Jack said he was heartened to hear that Inga was "cooling towards her new husband." Jack said it sounded as if Inga "should be back in circulation again so maybe I'll grab her this time." If not, he sighed, he would "probably end up with Charlotte [McDonnell]," which not only sounded insulting of McDonnell but also as if Jack believed the world contained a very finite number of eligible women.

There was also sad news. George Mead, a friend of Jack whom Inga had met, was killed in the battle on Guadalcanal, the first war fatality that each of them knew personally. Inga had thought Mead was "such a nice boy," incapable of killing a fly, that his death placed "a firm grip on my heart." She told Kick, "You were sweet when you said, 'Pray for him.' That faith, little Miss Moffett, I envy you."

Despite Blok's jealousy, Inga and Jack did have a few brief phone calls while he remained stateside, and Inga told Kick she would probably write Jack again someday, but in the meantime she asked Kick to tell her brother that "writing isn't so important because the Navy marches by twice a day here, and I see their uniforms and only one face—a happy cheerful young one who expects 100 percent from life and probably will get 99—that I pray for."

Blok's jealousy was not the only reason Inga refrained from writing Jack. She was also depressed about being unemployed. It was a terrific weight upon her, given her obsession with being self-sufficient and her worries that Blok never had money. Finally, in December 1942, Inga got

---

* Kick apparently forwarded the letter to Jack because Jack kept it in the same scrapbook where he saved most of his letters from Inga.

back into journalism when she was hired to be a reporter for the North American Newspaper Alliance (NANA). Similar to the older and more established Associated Press, NANA was a union of about eighty newspapers, including some of the largest in the country, which had attracted some of the finest writing talent in the world. Ernest Hemingway had worked as a correspondent for NANA when he covered the Spanish Civil War.

Inga, too, was covering a war but from the stateside perspective. For perhaps the first time since arriving in the United States, her experience in Nazi Germany was an asset. Inga's first article for NANA was posed as a former close observer's appraisal of the Nazis' strange attitudes toward love, marriage, and childrearing. To establish Inga's credentials for this type of analysis, the article led with an introduction that recounted how, as a Danish reporter, she had earned a scoop on Göring's wedding, and then interviewed Hitler, Goebbels, "and many more" leading Nazis.

Inga had told Jack that she wanted to do something for the war effort. Bashing her former Nazi acquaintances made her feel part of that effort; Inga also no doubt hoped it might help dispel any lingering suspicions that she was a spy. In an ironic twist on her own dilemma, Inga noted with disgust that official German policy prodded young women to quickly marry soldiers, not out of love, but so that they could birth "new cannon fodder" for Hitler's armies. Where she had once rhapsodized about Göring's devotion to his bride, Inga now described the Reichsmarschall as "pompous . . . hard-hearted, cruel." She once admired Goebbels's magnetic personality; now she derided the lecherous propaganda minister as a "dwarf with the club foot, who looks rather repulsive." And barely two years after she refused to badmouth Hitler to her Columbia classmates, Inga now mocked him as "Adolf Schickelgruber,"* who had no idea what love "is all about."

When it came to hatred of the Nazis, Inga had become more Catholic than the pope. Her articles exhorted Americans on the home front to do

---

* Schickelgruber (actually spelled Schicklgruber) is the surname of Hitler's grandmother who gave birth to his father out of wedlock. Inga, then, is essentially calling Hitler "son of a bastard."

their duty, emphasizing they played a role as key as soldiers and sailors in battle. Reporting on the problem of worker absenteeism, Inga wrote, "Dodging your duties in a war factory is not just letting down the boss; it is giving the Germans and Japs a chance to turn out more ammunition to kill the boys serving Uncle Sam." To reduce absenteeism, Inga pushed the idea that factory owners should provide day care for women workers with children.

All this jingoism did not convince the FBI to close Inga's file. The surveillance had ended, but the Bureau continued to take note of Inga's activities. When Inga wrote a small feature that appeared in the *Boston Globe* about a used car dealer from Texas who was looking for volunteers to drive some of his newly purchased inventory from New York to Dallas, an FBI agent alerted Hoover. If Inga was a spy, the agent said, perhaps she was using her articles to convey messages to fellow operatives, and this item might have been designed to "convey instructions to such individuals as escaped prisoners of war how to obtain transportation to Texas in order to escape through Mexico."

From what can be determined from her file, the FBI found no nefarious intent in any of Inga's stories, such as one that condemned the growing black market for rationed food items like beef (Inga tried the horsemeat that many carnivorous Americans were turning to as a supplement), or another that complained that New York City's high-end restaurants did not seem subject to the rationing requirements that applied to the hoi polloi. An El Morocco spokesman justified the disparity in menu offerings between rich and poor this way: "[Most] Americans don't care too much for champagne. They prefer hard liquor."

Always interested in the plight of women, Inga knocked down rumors that members of the Women's Army Corps had been sent home in large numbers because they had become pregnant out of wedlock (none had), and Inga interviewed refugees who exposed the brutality of the German and Japanese occupations. She focused on the plight of women who were raped, forced into prostitution for use by enemy troops, and who were tapped for inhumane medical experiments—the latter one of the earliest published reports in the American press about such Nazi atrocities.

And as she did with "Did You Happen to See?" Inga specialized in profiles of interesting women, such as the pioneering Chinese aviatrix and actress Lee Ya-Ching, who was touring the United States to promote the war effort in the Pacific. Inga labeled her "The Flying Tigress of China" and wrote, "When she sits down on a huge pastel blue couch and leans her head with the large intelligent eyes, the arched eyebrows and her crowning glory of blue-black hair against a pillow, it is hard to believe that those eyes have for hours at a stretch been glued to an instrument board. Or that the tiny hands with lacquered nails have been grimy with the dirt of a mechanic."

This writing style had drawn guffaws in Washington, but her bosses at NANA loved Inga's ability to capture the essence of a person's character through a few well-observed details about their appearance or mannerisms. They decided Inga might be a great fit for an extraordinary opportunity.

Sheilah Graham, one-third of Hollywood's great triumvirate of gossip columnists that also included Louella Parsons and Hedda Hopper, was abandoning her *Hollywood Today* column to return to her native Britain. On August 17, 1943, NANA general manager John Wheeler offered Inga a six-month contract that paid $75 per week to write Graham's daily column plus "any special news story you may develop or we may request to be filed." NANA had an option to extend Inga's contract for a year, but if Inga did not pan out all she would receive was "reasonable notice and pay [for] your railroad fare back to New York."

Inga Arvad, who could not find work a year before and who was facing possible arrest as an "dangerous alien," was now to be one of the three most powerful women in Hollywood. No wonder she loved America.

CHAPTER 58

"I am a lousy gossip columnist"

TWENTY MILLION AMERICANS READ SHEILAH GRAHAM'S *Hollywood Today* column in NANA newspapers. Now, those twenty million loyal readers would get their Hollywood gossip from Inga Arvad.

Graham's stated goal in returning to England was to cover the "human interest side of the war" for NANA, but in reality she was still grieving over the death of her lover, writer F. Scott Fitzgerald. Fitzgerald's wife, Zelda, had been institutionalized in an asylum, and Graham became Fitzgerald's constant companion and muse while he worked as a screenwriter and struggled to finish his final novel, *The Last Tycoon*. After he died from a heart attack in 1940, Graham wrote, "The fact is, I will never get over Scott Fitzgerald."

Graham was a tough cookie who had grown up in Dickensian poverty after her father, a Ukrainian Jew, died while Graham was an infant, and her mother, a cleaning woman, was forced to place Graham and her five siblings in an orphanage. Graham blossomed into a beautiful blonde and was rescued from poverty at age eighteen when she married an older benefactor who arranged for her to study at the Royal Academy of Dramatic Arts. Graham later became a dancer, a failed novelist, and finally a reporter.

In Graham's story there are parallels to Inga's life, but while Inga was resilient, she never became hard like Graham—or Parsons or Hopper, for that matter. That trio reveled in the foibles of the famous, and a bad word from any of them could end an actor's or director's career almost immediately, a power they used generously. Hopper happily gave herself the nickname "the Bitch of the World."

Inga liked being nice to people and confessed, "I hate gossip, and I am a lousy gossip columnist, there is no doubt about it." In contrast to Hopper, she added, "I couldn't seem to work up enough bitchiness."

John Wheeler expected Inga's tenure would be short-lived, not because he doubted Inga's temperament, but because he expected Graham to quickly become bored in war-torn England. Until then, he liked Inga's writing style and that she, like Graham, was a beautiful blonde whose byline photo would help draw in readers. Her looks also helped her in Hollywood, whose denizens made fun of Parsons's matronly appearance.

Graham provided Inga with virtually no help getting started beyond the faux advice included in her final column. Among her helpful "tips" was that the stars were seldom good sources of gossip but their friends were, and that Inga should assume the studios would not tell her the truth about anything. Other sage advice included the warning that "Errol Flynn will try and flirt with you. (I'll bet a dollar on that right now.) . . . It is better not to approach Bette Davis when she is feeling moody . . . [and] Bing Crosby will try his hardest to avoid an interview."

Inga did not need this "wisdom," as she quickly fit in with the social whirl in Hollywood as easily as she had in Washington, Berlin, and Paris. Even Graham acknowledged Inga was "popular in Hollywood" because Inga was not looking to dish dirt. Her column contained few blind items about affairs, pending divorces, or other unpleasant news. Most were upbeat, unless they were just pedestrian, which also meant they were seldom revelatory or exciting for the reader.

Typical was Inga's first column, which appeared in papers on September 16, 1943, and which noted that Dorothy Lamour, "minus sarong," had signed up for another "road picture" with Crosby and Bob Hope; that Judy Garland had been cast in *Meet Me in St. Louis*; and that Bette Davis was mourning the death of her second husband, Arthur Farnsworth. Inga also noted the oddity that Hollywood had cut back on war pictures because moviegoers, including those in uniform, wanted "'light entertainment' before we get down to skinning the Japs." Inga's jingoism was unabated.

Future columns were equally innocuous, but Inga had clout. A positive word in her column allegedly helped young Elizabeth Taylor win the lead in *National Velvet*. No wonder she received more thank-you notes than hate mail, such as the note sent by Anne Baxter after Inga had done a profile of the young star of *The Magnificent Ambersons* and *The North Star*. "It was a swell job of reporting," Baxter wrote. "Remember my cool pool on a hot day—definitely a standing invitation!"

Inga had asked Baxter if rumors she intended to marry soon were true, and Baxter replied with a bit of wisdom that Inga had also just taken to heart. "Not during the war," Baxter replied. "It would not be fair to the boy, and it certainly would not be fair to myself. I know a lot of boys in the service and do you notice how much they change after they have been away for a while? If I married, it would not be the same boy who came back. And maybe I wouldn't be the same girl to whom he came back."

Inga had discovered the truth of Baxter's observation just a few months before when she was reunited with Jack for the first time in a year and a half. Jack had returned from the South Pacific a war hero after surviving an incident that had killed two of his crew, but he had demonstrated extraordinary courage and a resolve to live in saving the lives of the other ten men on his boat. Inga found the tale astonishing, but not surprising, as she had always told Jack this was the stuff of which he was made and why he could become president, if that is what he wished.

Jack had high hopes of rekindling his romance with Inga but would learn that Inga had a new beau, while Inga discovered that the Jack she knew and loved had changed.

CHAPTER 59

"A hell of a letter"

JACK FACED DIFFICULTIES GETTING INTO COMBAT EVEN AFTER GRADUAT-
ing from midshipmen's school. An avid and skilled sailor since childhood,
he turned out to be an exceptional instructor, and the navy wanted to
keep him in Chicago to teach other prospective PT commanders. Jack
appealed to his father for help, and, per normal, Joseph Kennedy made a
few calls and reluctantly secured Jack's orders to go overseas.

Eventually shipped to the Solomon Islands, Jack found the South
Pacific no paradise. Dreams of a sitting on a sandy beach with "a warm
Pacific maiden stroking me gently but firmly while her sister was out
hunting my daily supply of bananas can be filed under bubble-bursted
[illusions]," Jack wrote Inga in April 1943.

If war is mostly tedium broken up by moments of terror, for Jack, so
far, it was mostly tedium, which is why he begged Inga for a letter. "If an
appeal for a report from you on the basis of our former friendly association
leaves you cold," Jack wrote, "I will put it purely on the basis of a contribution to the war effort—and you can write it instead of knitting a pair of
socks."

Inga was not the only woman to whom Jack sent letters, but she was
the only one he desperately wanted to hear from. In an incident that
Sigmund Freud would have found revealing, Jack sent letters to two
female acquaintances but was so careless he mixed up the envelopes so
that each woman got the letter intended for the other. This explained
why, Jack told Lem Billings, "I have heard from neither for 3 months."
Jack told Billings that because they were regularly rotating personnel, he

hoped to be back stateside by fall, though he added the melancholy note that coming home was not as exciting as it might be because "Inga Arvad's husband will still be there."

If Jack believed Inga was married, it is remarkable that in April 1943 he wrote her such a long, affectionate letter (easily one of the longest letters he ever wrote), except that she was perhaps the only person—with the exception of Kick—with whom he could completely drop his guard and let his emotions show. He told Inga he had taken time to visit George Mead's "very simple grave," just off the beach on Guadalcanal. The marker was only an aluminum plate, which was inscribed: "Lt. George Mead, USMC, Died Aug. 20, a greater leader of men—God bless him." Jack told Inga, "The whole thing was about the saddest experience I've ever had and enough to make you cry."

Despite such sadness and a litany of complaints about admirals, generals, politicians, and the dedication and skill of his fellow fighting men, Jack said, "Well Inga Binga, there is a brief outline of the general situation. I'm extremely glad I came—I wouldn't have missed it for the world, but I will be extremely glad to get back."

He gave this letter to fellow officer and friend Henry James to mail to Inga when James returned to the states in a few weeks, but James was intent on hand delivering the missive. Inga did not receive it for months, and so, to Jack's growing irritation, she did not respond. However, he waited some time before complaining, as he was preoccupied with new duties.

Jack was given command of the *PT-109* and won the respect and admiration of his crew not only for his abilities as a skipper but also for the stoicism he displayed in regard to his painful back. "He was in a lot of pain . . . I don't remember when he wasn't in pain," a fellow officer said. Jack would soon prove just how much he could endure.

On the night of August 1, 1943, the *PT-109* joined fourteen other PT boats dispatched to intercept and harass a Japanese convoy that was expected to travel through Ferguson's Strait in the Russell Islands (about seven hundred miles east of New Guinea). In addition to Jack, aboard the *PT-109* were his crew of eleven and a friend, Ensign Barney Ross, who had volunteered to come along to help man the boat's machine gun.

The mission was troubled by poor communication and coordination and a moonless sky that made it difficult to see even a few feet into the black night. At about 2:30 a.m., a Japanese destroyer appeared out of the darkness. With only a few seconds of warning, Jack, for reasons still unclear seventy years later, was unable to maneuver the *PT-109* out of harm's way. The destroyer struck the boat, slicing it in two. Two members of Jack's crew were killed instantly, a third, thirty-seven-year-old Motor Machinist Mate Patrick McMahon, was badly burned, and all the survivors were adrift in the ocean.

It was the only occasion during the entire war when a nimble PT boat had been rammed by an enemy craft. Whether the incident was the result of faulty seamanship on Jack's part or was just a freak accident in unusually dark conditions remains unresolved. Jack heatedly disputed charges that he had not been following proper procedures, but he later acknowledged that the story of the *PT-109* was "fucked up."

What particularly angered Jack was that none of the other thirteen PT boats in the area came to the *PT-109*'s rescue at the time of the collision, nor was a search party dispatched the following day. Men on the other boats had seen a ball of fire when the Japanese destroyer struck the *109* and had assumed all hands on board had perished. Jack and his men were on their own.

Having tread water for more than ten hours, Jack realized no help was coming and led his men on a three-and-a-half-mile journey to tiny Plum Pudding Island. McMahon was so badly injured that Jack placed the rope of McMahon's life preserver in his teeth and had McMahon ride atop his back while Jack did the breast stroke for the more than four hours it took to swim to the island.

Despite exhaustion and having been without sleep for thirty-six hours, Jack swam out into Ferguson's Strait that night in hopes of flagging down an American ship, unaware that the navy had presumed he and his crew were dead and also that American operations that night had moved further north.

The next day, Jack, once again towing McMahon on his back, led his men to a larger nearby island in hopes of finding food and water. Finding neither, Jack and Ross swam to yet another island where they found a one-man canoe loaded with a drum of water and some crackers and candy. Jack used the canoe to return to the crew and was astonished to find that two islanders who worked with a nearby Allied watch station had stumbled upon Jack's men.

Jack carved a message on a coconut shell for the islanders to deliver to the watch station, which passed on the remarkable news to the PT base on Tulagi that most of the *109* crew had indeed survived. Seven days after his boat had been sunk, Jack and his men were finally back at base receiving medical treatment and rest. Grateful for rescue, Jack was still bitter that the navy had given up on him and his crew so easily.

Word that former Ambassador Joseph Kennedy's second oldest son was missing and then found in the South Pacific made headlines in the United States, but few details of the remarkable ordeal were known until Jack was reunited with Inga, who would write about it for NANA.

Before that, stuck out in the South Pacific, Jack had begun to lose hope that he would ever be reunited with Inga. While recuperating from the *PT-109* ordeal, he wrote Inga a gently scolding note because he had not received a letter from her, "not even a rejection slip," though he acknowledged some blame fell on James for not delivering his earlier letter to her in a more timely manner.

"Well," Jack said resignedly, "I suppose the War brought us together—that and Miss K—and it's doing an excellent job of separating us—lately, it appears permanently. However, I'll be back—and we can discuss then over the break-fast table how you shattered my morale out here."

Days after Jack wrote these words, Inga repaired Jack's morale when her letter arrived with the revelation that she hadn't married Nils Blok after all. Jack noted that Inga always had a knack for "making me feel one hundred per cent better," and apologized for his previous "indignant, incoherent letter" that he blamed on having written while under the influence of strong drink consumed during a "small celebration" on the base.

Jack marveled to Inga at how willing the Japanese soldiers ("the greatest jungle fighters in the world") were to kill and die to defend "God damned hot stinking corners of small islands in a group of islands in a part of the ocean we all hope never to see again." The American soldier, on the other hand, while willing to kill in the line of duty, was also "trying desperately to prevent himself from being killed." All in all, Jack said, the war was "a dirty business," and he was disgusted with politicians and pundits who pushed for Japan's total defeat, whatever the cost, and made "thousands of casualties sound like drops in the bucket. But if those thousands want to live as much as the ten that I saw, the people deciding the whys and wherefores had better make mighty sure that all this effort is headed for some definite goal, and that when we reach that goal we may say it was worth it, for if it isn't, the whole thing will turn to ashes, and we will face great trouble in the years to come after the war."

Jack then told Inga about a letter he had received from McMahon's wife. She wrote him, "I suppose to you it was just part of your job, but Mr. McMahon was part of my life and if he had died I don't think I would have wanted to go on living." All the men wanted to live, Jack said; too many would die. He worried he might yet be one of them. Jack had once been sure he would get through the war "no matter what happened," but "I've lost that feeling lately, but as a matter of fact I don't feel badly about it."

Inga had suggested Jack think about writing a book about his wartime experiences, but Jack now said, "I wouldn't go near a book like that." He found war "so stupid," that while it "has a sickening fascination . . . I want to leave it far behind me when I go."

"Inga Binga, I'll be glad to see [you] again," Jack wrote. "I'm tired now. . . . Now that I look back, [this] has been a hell of a letter. It isn't what I was going to say at all." Jack closed by wishing Inga well with her new job as a gossip columnist. He thought she would be "just right for the job." He had a new boat to command now, he said, but soon he would be home, and when he was, he told Inga, he would travel to Los Angeles to see her, and signed his letter, "Much love, Jack."

It would be nearly another four months until Jack returned to the United States. He had fulfilled his mission, but it was his constant back trouble that finally led to his detachment from active duty. Arriving in San Francisco on January 7, 1944, Jack quickly made a sharp right turn south toward Los Angeles. He told his father he would soon come to Palm Beach to lounge by the family pool. But first he wanted to see Inga.

CHAPTER 60

"Life is so cruel"

INGA HAD BEEN SHOCKED BY JACK'S APPEARANCE *BEFORE* HE WENT TO war. Now, after a year overseas and the *PT-109* ordeal, she was completely appalled. Jack's determination to go into combat, particularly on a PT boat that gave his back a daily pounding, had "wrecked his health," Inga noted at the time. But she also observed something that in many ways was worse than poor health: he had come back "embittered."

The man who had always given "the impression that his big white teeth are ready to bite off a huge hunk of life" was now "thin and drawn and out of it." Later in life, Inga told one of her sons that Jack had joked about the sinking of the *PT-109*, telling her the navy could not decide whether "to give him a medal or throw him out." But "that was the only thing he joked about. His sense of humor was gone."

The Jack whom Inga had loved had not completely disappeared. Many of the qualities that had drawn her to him the first place—his intellect, his wit, his "animal magnetism"—were still there, but there was now a hard layer covering those things that made Jack, who had always been emotionally distant, all that much harder to reach. Inga had once called Jack her "sailor-boy," but he was no longer an amiable, impetuous youth. He had led men into battle and some to their death. If he now seemed grim, he had reason to be. As Anne Baxter had said about the wisdom of marrying in wartime, war changes everyone who is part of it.

Certainly the war was the main cause of the changes in Jack, but it was not the only one. The loss of Inga had hardened him, too. Even though he had initiated the breakup, he had done so under duress and remained extremely ambivalent about it. He had begged Inga to come stay with him less than a week after he told her they were through. He continued to write and call, to fantasize about her all those months at sea, to say that all the other women he knew "merely filled the gap" in her absence, and to try, so far without success, to seduce her once more.

And while it was not immediately obvious, his general attitude toward love and romance had changed. As his peers did, Jack had once spoken of marriage as an expected and desired life's goal, but after his reluctant separation from Inga, he abandoned interest in marriage—certainly as an institution based on sentiment. Had the presidency not been his goal, he might never have married. When he did wed a decade later, it was done with cold political calculation, not because he sought the type of emotional intimacy he enjoyed with Inga.

Arriving statewide, he might have gone straight to Palm Beach to see his mother and father. They had endured, after all, the shock of thinking for a few days that their son had died. But he did not. Inga was the first person he wanted to see when he came home, and he had been in such a rush to see her that he broke a promise to a good friend, Red Fay, that he would stop first in San Francisco to see Fay's parents.

He felt great anticipation, yet when Jack arrived in Los Angeles, even though he spent several days with Inga, he found "the romance was over." Inga still loved Jack and still wished that they could marry. But she knew that would never happen. All the objections Jack's father had raised and Jack's own qualms were still valid.

Inga had divorced Fejos and not married Blok. Perhaps Jack, in a fever to be with Inga, imagined this had changed things, but Inga knew better. She was a twice-divorced Protestant still under investigation by the FBI, and she knew that if they renewed their romance then down the road Jack, the ambitious Catholic politician, would once again conclude, as he had twenty-one months before, that he could never marry her.*

---

*Interfaith marriage remained taboo to many people in the 1940s. When word reached Joe and Rose Kennedy that Joe Junior was dating a Protestant while in training as a naval aviator, the family asked a local priest to intervene. Rose purchased him a year's subscription to *The Catholic Digest*, and Joe Senior warned his son in a long letter that a Catholic candidate for the U.S. Senate in Massachusetts named Joe Casey was facing intense criticism from Catholic voters, especially women, because he had married a Protestant. Faced

"She just didn't want to go through it again," said Inga's son, Ronald McCoy. But if Inga knew she would never be Jack's wife, she still wished to be his helpmate. As Jack told Inga the story of the sinking of *PT-109*, she realized that Jack's actions in saving his crew had been even more heroic than the initial contemporary news reports had indicated. Inga insisted on writing up a story on Jack's heroics for NANA, though she quoted him as demanding, "None of that hero stuff about me. The real heroes are not the men who return, but those who stay out there like plenty of them do, two of my men included."

Inga described Jack as being "reluctant" to talk about himself, but was "outspoken" when lauding his crew. "I never could praise them enough," he said. But the crew had plenty of praise for Jack. Inga sought out the wife of Patrick McMahon, since she lived in Los Angeles, and went to visit her. As Inga reported, Mrs. McMahon "with tears in her eyes and a shaky voice . . . said, 'When my husband wrote home, he told me that Lieutenant Kennedy was wonderful, that he saved the lives of all the men and everybody at the base admired him greatly.'"

"Then you are a hero," Inga told Jack, but "Lieutenant Kennedy looked reproachfully at me as he answered, 'the job of a PT boat officer is to take the men out there—and just as important—to bring them back. We took them out—we just had to get them back.'"

Inga's story on Jack appeared in dozens of papers nationwide, including on the front page of *The Boston Globe* where Jack's future constituents would read it. While Jack had not revived their romance, Inga had once more provided important help to Jack's future political career. She had already had bucked up his confidence and given him the courage to reveal his aspirations to his father. Now, she had widely publicized the war heroics that would be the bedrock of all Jack's future political campaigns, with her article a template for future articles that would be even more widely read.

After Jack left Los Angeles, he spent time with his parents in Palm Beach and then traveled to New York City for some rest and relaxation.

---

with this onslaught, Joe Junior quickly assured his parents the romance was not serious. (Goodwin, p. 625)

While at the Stork Club, he ran into an acquaintance, *Life* magazine writer John Hersey, who was married to one of Jack's former girlfriends, Frances Ann Cannon.* Over drinks and during breaks in Zero Mostel's floorshow, Jack elaborated to Hersey on what had appeared in Inga's story. Hersey was fascinated and obtained Jack's permission to write a lengthier article about the ordeal, though Jack insisted Hersey talk to his crew before proceeding. Hersey did and discovered Jack's men "were wildly devoted to him, all of them."

Life magazine, however, took a pass on the article, and so it appeared instead in the June 17, 1944, edition of *The New Yorker* under the title "Survival." Joseph Kennedy then strong-armed *The New Yorker* into granting a generous reprint permission to the *Reader's Digest*, and it was this version that was reprinted again and again and widely circulated during every one of Jack's political campaigns—but its basis was the article that Inga had written months before.

The week that Hersey's article was published in *The New Yorker*, Jack acceded to back surgery for a ruptured disk at the Chelsea Naval Hospital in Boston. The operation did not go well. Painful back spasms and constant abdominal pain were among the postsurgical complications, which led Jack to suggest, "The doc should have read one more book before picking up the saw." More surgery and months of recuperation offered little respite, and by the end of 1944 doctors concluded Jack could never return to active duty. He was scheduled to exit the navy on March 1, 1945.

Jack's poor health prevented him from attending Kick's wedding to Billy Cavendish, the Marquess of Hartington. Kick had left the *Times-Herald* and gone to London in 1943 to work for the Red Cross and resume her romance with Cavendish—to the mortification of her parents, demonstrating that Kick had greater courage and independence of spirit than Jack.

---

*To underscore once more just how small and incestuous was the social circle in which Jack Kennedy traveled, Frances Ann Cannon later divorced Hersey and married Fraser Dougherty, the first husband of Page Huidekoper, Inga's *Times-Herald* colleague who had told the FBI she worried Inga might be a spy.

Kick and Inga maintained a regular correspondence, but the roles were now reversed from their time in Washington, and it was Kick who was now offering Inga advice on romance. "Inga, what has happened to Nils?" Kick wrote in late 1943. "Has another husband bit the dust? You are a funny girl. I miss you lots and wonder if you are happy at the moment. I hope so. But don't make any more mistakes. You are still young and it just isn't worth it. Listen to old granny's advice."

After Inga saw Jack in Los Angeles, she apparently wrote Kick and expressed concern for how Jack had changed. Kick wrote back, asking Inga to forward a copy of the article she had written on Jack, but agreed, "I have seen enough of these boys who have returned from real fighting to know what it does to them." Despite this, or perhaps because of it, Kick then told Inga she had made up her mind to marry Hartington "and if it wasn't for this religious difficulty I'd be married to him now."

Kick did marry Cavendish on May 6, 1944, but the "religious difficulty" meant that Joe Junior was the only member of the Kennedy family who attended the wedding, which was a civil ceremony at the Chelsea Town Hall. Her parents boycotted the ceremony, though Joe Senior sent a telegram of blessing. Rose Kennedy, aware that Kick had capitulated to Cavendish and agreed to raise any children they had as Anglicans, told Kick she was "heartbroken and horrified," and worried that other Catholic girls who looked up to the Kennedys would now think it fine to marry outside the faith. "What a blow to the family prestige," she said. Rose was so distraught that she checked herself into a hospital to avoid speaking to reporters.

The "tragedy" of Kick's marriage, however, was superseded by a genuine calamity when Joe Junior was killed on August 12, 1944, while flying an incredibly dangerous mission over the English Channel. Whether driven by envy of the attention Jack received for his heroics (and determined to best his little brother once more), or the ongoing desire to rehabilitate the Kennedy name, or genuine patriotism, Joe Junior volunteered for an extraordinarily hazardous mission.

He was to fly a bomber packed with twenty-two thousand pounds of explosives toward the French coast and then parachute out while the plane was then remotely piloted toward its target, a German V-1 missile base.

But there was a mishap and the plane exploded shortly after takeoff. It was said to be the largest human-caused explosion in history until surpassed by the atomic bomb. It was so immense that "not a single part of Joe Kennedy's body was ever found."

Joe Senior was inconsolable and locked himself in his room for days, yet it was Jack who was most impacted. He had spent his entire life measuring himself against his older brother, and now that yardstick was gone. Further, even though his parents had begun to appreciate Jack's virtues, their hopes and dreams had always fallen primarily on Joe Junior. In that regard, as Doris Kearns Goodwin noted, Joe Junior acted as a shield for his younger brother, who had been relatively free of crushing family expectations. It would take time, but those expectations would now shift heavily onto Jack's shoulders.

Before Joe Junior's death, Kick had written Inga to tell her how happy she was with Billy, noting with her typical irreverence, "My new name, although it ain't necessary, is The Marchioness of Hartington. Aren't I lucky?" In an earlier letter, Inga had congratulated Kick for following her heart and marrying Cavendish, a message of support that Kick was "so pleased" to receive. Kick congratulated Inga on her new life as a Hollywood columnist, but begged her to become a foreign correspondent so that she could come to London and meet Cavendish. "He's a shy old thing but I think you'd love him," Kick said.

Kick gently brought up the subject of Jack, although the tone of all her letters to Inga suggest Kick was as sure as Inga was that she and Jack would never get back together. Kick told Inga she had "blubbed for the 1st time in many months" when Jack wrote her a letter supporting her decision to marry Cavendish and telling Kick "of course you know you have always been my favorite in the family."

But as was true for all too many war brides, Kick's happiness was short-lived. Because of Cavendish's military duties, he and Kick had spent a grand total of six weeks together during their four-month marriage. A German sniper in Belgium killed Cavendish, a major in the Coldstream Guards, on September 10, 1944, less than a month after Joe Junior's death. Little wonder that in her diary entry for September 20 a disconsolate Kick wrote, "So ends the story of Billy and Kick. . . . Life is so cruel."

CHAPTER 61

"The way her zygoma met her maxilla"

INGA MAY HAVE THOUGHT SHE WAS A LOUSY GOSSIP COLUMNIST, BUT the editors at the various NANA newspapers apparently felt she was doing fine, for *Hollywood Today* continued to run in just as many papers as it had when Sheilah Graham was its author. In March 1944, NANA exercised its option to renew Inga's contract for a full year.

Inga liked Hollywood. She rebutted the popular image of Hollywood as a den of iniquity by declaring, "It is not a place where debauchery is prevalent." Instead, it was a relatively "small community . . . where there is more talent by the square inch than anywhere else in the world."

Hollywood liked Inga. She was generous with praise, and her determination, in contrast to Hopper, Parsons, or Graham, not to dig up dirt or ruin careers endeared her to most Hollywood stars. Her warm personality and startling good looks especially appealed to leading men who favorably compared Inga with their costars, who were some of the most beautiful women in the world.

Vincent Price, fresh from working with the magnificent Gene Tierney in *Laura*, inscribed a photograph for Inga that read, "What do you write for someone you admire devoutly and think one of the most beautiful women in the world?" Joseph Cotten, who had just costarred with Ingrid Bergman in *Gaslight*, called Inga "the girl I love," and Turhan Bey, who had starred in *Ali Baba and the Forty Thieves* with the exotic Maria Montez, told Inga, "My body and soul is yours for the taking."

Inga did not take Bey's body or soul, nor did she have an interest in dating any famous actors, no matter how handsome they might be. She did have an especially warm relationship with Walter Pidgeon, but it remained platonic. When it came to romance, with her extraordinary ability to discern talent and potential, Inga instead fell in love with a brash, handsome, and young Jewish Army Air Force surgeon from New York named William G. Cahan. The romance came with a twist that renewed Olga's lament that her daughter had a blind spot when it came to men— Cahan was married.

Cahan's father had been an illustrator for books and newspapers, but Cahan decided to become a doctor at age fourteen as he watched his beloved grandmother die. "Never again as long as I lived," Cahan wrote in his memoir, "would I feel helpless and ignorant while someone I loved was in acute distress." Cahan went to Harvard as an undergrad, encountered the anti-Semitism typical of the period (although Cahan himself was not religiously observant), and later graduated from the Columbia College of Physicians and Surgeons.

It 1941, Cahan married Pamela Gordon-Howley, the vivacious daughter of the renowned British and American stage actress Gertrude Lawrence. Shortly after Pearl Harbor, Cahan entered the Army Air Corps, but received permission to defer active duty until he had completed his one-year surgical residency, which was when Cahan began his pioneering work in treating cancer.

In September 1943, Cahan was ordered to report for duty just a few blocks from where he grew up. He was to serve as company doctor for a unit within the Army Emergency Relief Fund that was assigned to stage a Moss Hart play titled *Winged Victory*, the story of pilots in training for what was then called the Army Air Force. It was not uncommon for the armed services to use personnel with experience in the entertainment business to put on shows or make films designed to raise both morale and money. One of the most popular films during the war was Irving Berlin's *This Is the Army* starring Ronald Reagan. Among the three hundred men in Cahan's unit who performed in *Winged Victory* were such emerging stars as Karl Malden, Lee J. Cobb, and Mario Lanza.

Cahan himself had little to do except regularly check the men for signs of lice or venereal disease, but the play was such a hit that the company, including Cahan, were sent to Hollywood to turn the play into a movie. Inga visited the movie's set on June 7, 1944—the day after D-Day—to do an item for *Hollywood Today*.

Cahan was immediately "struck" by Inga's beauty, including being "enthralled" by what he described, being a physician, as "the way her zygoma met her maxilla—O.K., her high cheekbones." There was a complication. Cahan's wife, Pam, had joined her husband in California where they shared a rented house in the Hollywood Hills. Wishing to hide his infidelity, Cahan confined his rendezvous with Inga to the daytime hours. The affair continued for five months until Cahan was shipped overseas, and then he and Inga maintained a regular and often passionate correspondence.

It was out of character for Inga, who articulated traditional values when it came to home and family, to contribute to the breakup of another woman's marriage, but she was smitten with Cahan, who assured her his marriage was already "crumbling."

As she did repeatedly in her life, Inga wrote down her thoughts in fictional form, this time in what appeared to be a screen treatment when she later worked at MGM where a female reporter falls in love with an army surgeon who is described as "6 feet, broad shouldered with dark hair [and] a sure, quick, yet charming manner." But what really appeals to the reporter/Inga is the "genuine" interest the surgeon shows in each of the men under his care. When she took the surgeon's hand to shake it, she felt an electric charge. "They are head over heels in love, though none [*sic*] of them know it yet."

In Inga's story, the debonair surgeon avoids talking about his personal life but instead spends his time opening up the woman's world to new ideas and experiences. In real life, Inga had always loved to hear Jack talk about world affairs and politics. Now, she enjoyed listening to Cahan talk about everything from classical music to racial injustice. Unlike Jack, Cahan was terribly romantic, writing her love poems and taking her to glorious locations for picnics, such as a cliff overlooking the beach at Malibu. Also unlike Jack, Cahan, as portrayed, is not quite so focused on sex; if Inga's fictionalized account is to be believed, they did not even kiss on their first date.

When they did become intimate, Inga was enraptured. Cahan had a medical explanation. "After making love, [Inga] would often comment that her painful rheumatoid arthritis was dramatically relieved," Cahan later wrote. "How much of this was due to psychological factors and how much to a sudden surge in her adrenal hormones (of which cortisone is one), was hard to say." Cahan said similar observations led to steroids such as cortisone becoming standard treatment for arthritis.

Inga had hopes she and Cahan would marry, and they discussed the topic regularly. He was the first man Inga had met who seemed Jack's equal in terms of intellect and vitality. As Jack had, Inga believed Cahan was making her a better person. Inga had stopped playing the piano because of her arthritis, but Cahan rekindled her love of music by insisting she listen to recommended recordings of opera. She had read American history to please Jack, now Cahan had her reading books that raised her social consciousness, such as *Earth and High Heaven*, a best-selling novel about mixed marriage, or *Freedom Road*, the story of an ex-slave who rose to become South Carolina's senator during Reconstruction. "My blood was boiling, and my tears were hot in my eyes," Inga told Cahan after she had read the book. "What injustice, what life, and what can be done about it?"

Inga could see that Cahan, who would later do pioneering research in the treatment of lung and breast cancer and become a significant leader in the national antismoking campaign, "was on the edge of brilliance." But more than that, Cahan had renewed Inga's enthusiasm for life. The harassment by the FBI, her divorce, the loss of Jack—all this had left her beaten and battered. It was as if "a fortress is built around me, or maybe I am like a clam," Inga said. Now, Cahan, like the painter of a ship, was "chipping off the old paint." Inga said, "There is something nice and clean about a naked ship, it is all ready for a new coat."

As with Jack, she wished to have Cahan's child. "I think you are the greatest human being I have met," Inga told him, "and when I say great, I mean within yourself and your relationship to the rest of mankind."

Inga had a chance to compare Cahan directly with the man she had previously thought the greatest she had ever known. When Jack made another visit to Los Angeles in late 1944 after his botched back surgery, he immediately called Inga. But when Jack arrived at Inga's apartment, he found that she had arranged for Cahan to be there to meet the man Inga still believed would be a future president.

"He and I talked Harvard, football, show business, and so on," Cahan recalled. "After a while, however, it became clear that one of us would have to leave. To my great relief, he did." Yet Cahan would soon depart, and Jack would return.

CHAPTER 62

"Not pro-Nazi in any respect"

CAHAN SO STIMULATED INGA'S INTELLECT THAT SHE NOW FOUND HER gossip column unbearbly trite. Now, when dining with Hollywood insiders, Inga "practically threw up my Romanoff dinner right on the table hearing about what they consider important," she told Cahan. "There wasn't a thing which I would give a fig for today." Even so, always worried about how to make a living, Inga was distressed that Sheilah Graham, as predicted, grew bored in London, returned to Hollywood, and in late 1944 demanded her column back.

Graham agreed with Inga's own assessment of her shortcomings as a gossip columnist. "I heard, mostly from the editors, that her column was too nice," Graham said. "Unless you are a brilliant writer, you cannot adore everyone so much. It makes for dull reading." Graham also considered Inga a phony. "She was as sharp as I was in real life—sharper—but in print she was all sugar," she said.

Graham knew that Inga still had hopes of breaking into the movies as an actress. Inga's good friend Walter Pidgeon had arranged for a screen test at MGM, which Inga thought had gone very well. Graham was at the MGM lot and ran into Inga as she was reviewing still photographs from her test. Graham peered at a few of the photographs and, "without intending to be rude or annoy her, I said flippantly, 'You look like a younger Gloria DeHaven.'" DeHaven was a contract player at MGM who at nineteen was twelve years younger than Inga. Whatever Graham intended, and it is doubtful that there was no malice intended, Inga took the quip as an insult and told Graham, "Everybody told me you were a bitch, and now I know you are."

Inga's contract was effective until March 11, 1945, but when Graham threatened to start a rival gossip column with another syndicate, NANA advised Inga in October 1944 that Graham would be taking back *Holly-wood Today* in December—at $200 per week, nearly three times Inga's salary. Inga may have lost interest in writing gossip, but she was competitive enough that the circumstances of her ouster riled her. She was also perturbed that she had turned down an offer a few months before to work at MGM because of her loyalty to NANA. After considerable wrangling, NANA agreed to pay Inga for the three months remaining on her contract, and freed her to do freelance work for other publications in the meantime.

At the same time Inga was wrangling with NANA, the filming for *Winged Victory* ended and the service members associated with the production received new orders. Cahan was being sent to New Guinea. He and Inga celebrated Christmas together and then said good-bye, their situation unresolved. Inga professed to love Cahan "with much more than just my heart," but he was still married and was now off to war. In a farewell note, he told her, "How incomplete my existence might have been without you—like an artist, born color-blind, looking at a sunset." They were the words of a romantic and an idealist, but it certainly crossed Inga's mind whether war would do to Cahan what she had seen it do to Jack. She adopted a fatalistic attitude. Inga, who spent a great deal of time thinking about what it meant to have faith, told the nonreligious Cahan, "I put it in God's hands. I know that makes you laugh."

For Inga, the next several months were so chaotic that she told Cahan "I often doubted if I stood on my head or my feet." The combined stress of fighting with NANA and saying farewell to Cahan (and without love-making to ameliorate her condition) put Inga in bed with a particularly bad flare-up of her arthritis.

She was cheered when she received a phone call and heard a familiar voice on the line asking for "Inger-Binger" in his Boston accent. Whatever her problems, Inga knew that Jack had had a far worse year with Joe Junior's death, Kick becoming a young widow, and his deteriorating back. Inga immediately followed up their conversation with a letter. "It was so wonderful to hear your voice, it was nearly like years ago, before so much too much had happened in your life," she wrote.

Noting how Jack "suffered" with his back, Inga hoped he could understand how scared she was to feel debilitated by her arthritic condition, which no one seemed to know how to treat. One doctor suggested removing Inga's tonsils as a cure. "It scares me because I depend upon one person in this world, and that's the undersigned," Inga told Jack. She added, "I still wish we could sit down and talk for a couple of hours [as] there are hundreds of things I would like to discuss with you and somehow you seem one of the nearest friends I have." She begged Jack to call again soon.

Jack's call preceded by a few weeks a call from another old acquaintance: the FBI. The FBI had mostly ignored Inga the previous two years. For all of 1944, there is only one entry in her file that noted she had been writing a "a column of movie gossip," and the Bureau also asked her friend and former filmmaking colleague Lothar Wolff to prepare a statement that outlined what he knew about Inga. Wolff had little to add that the Bureau did not already know, but repeated that Paul Fejos had always insisted that Axel Wenner-Gren "was neither a Nazi nor does he have any Nazi sympathies."

Wenner-Gren was the primary reason the FBI came to visit Inga in late February 1945, justifying the suspicion Inga held all along that it was her ties to the Swedish industrialist more than any other fact that had held the attention of the FBI. The latest theory put forth by Assistant Attorney General Herbert Wechsler was that Inga was not a spy working directly for the Germans, but that she was a "private" agent working for Wenner-Gren, who may have been working at the direction of Nazi Germany.

Wechsler, who would be hailed as a "legal giant" in his 2000 *New York Times* obituary, was head of the Justice Department's War Division, and in early 1945 was beginning to develop the framework by which war criminals would be tried when hostilities ended. As he contemplated postwar justice, Wechsler was determined to clarify once and for all whether Wenner-Gren was a Nazi agent during the war. If he was, Wenner-Gren might find himself in the dock at Nuremberg.

Given what was at stake, Wechsler asked the FBI to conduct extensive "interrogations" with Inga and Paul Fejos that Wechsler envisioned would last several days, while other agents flew to Mexico City to conduct a similar examination of Wenner-Gren. "Miss Arvad's social and political activities both in Europe and this country are so related to the theory that she was Wenner-Gren's agent that it would seem desirable to explore her entire adult life in considerable detail," Wechsler told Hoover.

To underscore just how much detail he expected, Wechsler sent a four-page list of dozens of suggested questions for Inga around fifteen general lines of inquiry. Wechsler sent his memorandum to Hoover on February 26, but it did not arrive at the FBI field office in Los Angeles until February 27; the Los Angeles agents had already interviewed Inga on February 26. From beginning to end, such snafus were a regular occurrence during the Bureau's investigation of Inga.

It is remarkable that this February 26 interview was the only time the FBI ever directly asked Inga questions, excepting her initial interview in December 1941. Since then, the FBI had gathered information from Inga only via various eavesdropping techniques, never giving her the chance to explain anything, even though she had twice begged Hoover for the chance to be heard.

This latest "interrogation" ploughed no new ground. Inga again explained that she had been a professional journalist, interviewing prominent Nazis as part of her job, and that "she was not pro-Nazi in any respect." Inga repeated that her only connection to Wenner-Gren was through her ex-husband, Fejos, and his and Wenner-Gren's "business association" based upon anthropology and nothing else. Any funds provided by Wenner-Gren were simply the salary paid Fejos for his work. Any other relationship she had with Wenner-Gren or his wife was "purely social," but Inga added "that she believed she would have known from her social contact with Wenner-Gren if he had any pro-Nazi views." She emphasized she had not seen Wenner-Gren since 1942, and that Fejos was "an ardent American" who would never do anything to harm the United States.

Inga never mentioned Jack during her interrogation. When asked if she had ever used the alias of "Barbara Smith," Inga "denied it categorically." It was the truth; the alias she had used in Charleston was "Barbara White." To further dissuade agents from pursuing her case further, Inga made a point to note that she intended to marry Cahan, who was described as "a member of the American armed force who was in an active theater at the present time."

While mildly chagrined that they had not received Wechsler's memorandum prior to interrogating Inga, Hoover believed the agents had been thorough and had touched on most of the points Wechsler hoped to cover. The FBI did not interview Inga again, nor did Wechsler push them to do so.

Fejos was interrogated at greater length than Inga, over the course of two days in early March in New York City. As Inga had done for him, but with less gallantry, Fejos, too, sought to clear Inga's name, agreeing that her relationship with Wenner-Gren was "strictly social and of no possible significance." Highlighting how little he knew his wife and why they were mismatched, Fejos described Inga as "frivolous," and said of her time in Nazi Germany, "She would be utterly unable to write an article of a serious nature."

Fejos, too, was not reinterviewed by the FBI. Wenner-Gren was removed from the blacklist when the war ended and faced no charges after the war. In 1960, an FBI memorandum was added to the record that stated "the real reason" why Wenner-Gren was placed on the blacklist was that Wenner-Gren had attained such influence that, unfettered, he would have essentially become "the economic Czar of Mexico," which was contrary to U.S. business interests, not national security.

Inga heard no more from the FBI after that. The war was winding to a close, at least in Europe. A few news clippings were added to her file over the next decade or so, but there were no more wiretaps or bugged rooms. But that did not mean that Inga was free from her past. Her time in Nazi Germany continued to haunt her, and in 1945 it would cost her another chance at marriage—not to Cahan, but to a man once tapped as a future prime minister of Great Britain.

PART X

Prime Ministers and Cowboys

CHAPTER 63

"Bachelor girl"

WHEN INGA PURCHASED A ROYAL TYPEWRITER SHORTLY AFTER ARRIV-ing in America in 1940, Olga chided her for her extravagance, but that typewriter paid for itself a hundredfold. Having lost *Hollywood Today*, Inga began making good money as a freelance writer.

Inga received $200 to $400 per article from magazines such as *Collier's*, *Liberty*, and *Pageant* for profiles on such people as legendary Hollywood talent scout Billy Grady, prolific costume designer Walter Plunkett, actress/supermodel Anita Colby (whom Inga described as "the most photogenic face in the history of cameras"), and Inga's best friend in Hollywood, the petite, red-haired Swedish actress Signe Hasso.

Hasso, who had been billed as "the next Garbo" and would later be godmother to Inga's youngest son, Terence, was, like Inga, a divorcee. Inga's profile focused on the pros and cons of being a beautiful, single woman in Hollywood, a "predicament" shared by Inga. Being a "bachelor girl," as Inga phrased it, "has loads of advantages. She gets up when she wants, goes where she wants, chooses her own friends, throws parties for whom she wishes, and when she chooses. She runs her home the way it suits her." On the other hand, "wolves" constantly pursued bachelor girls, which made single women fodder for gossip columnists, as Inga would soon be reminded.

While freelance writing paid well, Inga was disappointed her screen test had not led to an acting contract. Inga believed MGM studio head Louis B. Mayer had blocked her chances to be on screen because she was once guilty of "cussing him" during an unspecified confrontation. Mayer must not have been too angry, however, because on March 26, 1945, Inga received a six-month contract to work as a screenwriter at MGM for $125 per week.

Inga wrote several draft screen treatments, but most, including those based on the Wenner-Grens and her romance with Cahan, are not particularly compelling, and she never earned a screen credit. "Fiction is something absolutely alien to me," Inga confessed, although one of her ideas seemed perfect for the film noir movement sweeping postwar Hollywood. It was a macabre tale of a small-town druggist and serial killer who schemes to be elected county coroner to cover up his crimes. When she had been a reporter at the *Washington Times-Herald*, Inga said the few times she helped cover a murder were "terribly exciting."

Once again employed and making a generous salary, Inga received more good news when she became a U.S. citizen on April 27, 1945. Hasso threw a party to celebrate. Back on December 12, 1941, Inga had asked Agent Hardison if the FBI could provide her with a certificate to show that she had been investigated and proved not to be a spy. Hardison said it was impossible for the Bureau to provide such a "diploma," but Inga certainly could argue that she could never have become a citizen if the FBI or any other agency had a genuine concern about her loyalty to the United States.

Inga seemed to have everything except the one thing she really wanted. As she noted in her profile of Hasso, there were many men in Hollywood who would have been more than pleased to provide a "bachelor girl" with sex, but few of the wolves were ready to provide marriage, a home, and children.

Inga was still engaged in a passionate correspondence with Cahan, who was stationed in New Guinea, but how long might he be away at war? In the spring of 1945, with no public hint America was developing an atomic bomb, many experts believed the war with Japan might last until 1947—at least. As Inga noted many times: absence does not make the heart grow fonder. There was also the question of whether Cahan would fulfill his promise to divorce his wife to marry Inga, and Inga, for all her declarations of love, seemed uncertain whether the cocksure Cahan was the man for her.

"It is a big task to marry anyone," Inga told Cahan. Cahan himself noted that their conversations about matrimony had been one-sided. "We always talk about, if you would make me a good wife—but we haven't yet questioned, would I be a good husband for you?" he said.

Inga liked confident men, but the jaunty Cahan, who often signed his letters to Inga, "Your Bill, Steak, New York Cut," was beyond self-assured. "You were sweet the last day when we drove home and you told me all the things you had done for me," Inga wrote Cahan. "I had to smile, because it was like a pigeon blowing out its chest and yet, how true, how very, very true." While Inga liked men from whom she could learn things, she also wanted an equal partnership. "Mutual respect," Inga said, was perhaps the most important ingredient in making love work. A lack of mutual respect "is why I never could love any of my [previous] husbands."

While Inga's future with Cahan was uncertain, she was not prepared to revisit the past when Jack Kennedy again came calling. In early 1945, Jack was seeking relief for his troubled back at Castle Hot Springs, Arizona, a health resort near Phoenix. He was supposed to stay for six months but got bored after five weeks and left for Hollywood. While there, he told Billings, he planned to "tangle tonsils with Inga Binga among others. She has gone to work for MGM. With that sensational bit of news I will close."

Inga had had her tonsils removed a few weeks before, but that was not the reason hers did not tangle with Jack's. In part, it was loyalty to Cahan, whose absence made her visit with Jack less awkward this time, but mainly there was just no future in it. Jack shared the news that he had decided to run for Congress the following year. He was taking his first step toward the White House, meaning that a renewed relationship would still go nowhere. The recent visit by the FBI also reminded Inga that, as much as she loved Jack, she needed to move on for her own sanity, if nothing else.

With Inga declining to renew their previous intimacy, Jack pursued some of Hollywood's other most beautiful women with mixed results. He successfully seduced Sonja Henie and Peggy Cummins, but despite pouring on the charm struck out with Olivia de Havilland, in part because while intending to use the bathroom at her house he mistakenly walked into a closet, leading to an avalanche of tennis rackets and balls falling on his head. "Do you think it was me walking into the tennis closet?" Jack later mused about such a rare failure at seduction. "Do you think that's what really did it?"

In addition to seducing starlets, Jack spent his time in Hollywood trying to learn what elusive qualities turn an actor into a star, and whether those qualities could be replicated to turn a politician into a president. Jack roomed with young actor Robert Stack and palled around with old friend Chuck Spalding who, following the success of his book, *Love at First Flight*, was now, like Inga, a screenwriter.

Gary Cooper had purchased the film rights to Spalding's book (though the wartime tale never was made into a movie), and one night Jack joined Spalding and Cooper for dinner to try to fathom the great star's allure. Jack left "mystified." Cooper's laconic image was no act, Jack discovered, as Cooper said almost nothing during dinner. How, Jack wondered, could anyone so "yawn-inducingly boring" still be mobbed by adoring fans when they left the restaurant?

But Jack was a quick study. After spending time with other stars such Spencer Tracy and Clark Gable, Jack realized that the great ones always play themselves, or more accurately, they play the persona they have developed for themselves. Just as the poor young Cockney acrobat named Archie Leach made himself into the suave Cary Grant, so, too, Jack would recast his image. The genial but insecure youth who had been dominated by his father and late older brother would, through conscious effort and practice, slowly but surely project a captivating mix of warrior and philosopher, youth and wisdom, courage and humor, and in doing so become America's first movie star president.

Shortly after Jack left Hollywood, he received an offer from Hearst (orchestrated by his father, of course) to cover the opening organizing session of the United Nations in San Francisco, beginning in April, as a journalist. Jack was to report on the proceedings from the perspective of a military veteran.

Jack was not the only politician who finagled a trip to the UN meeting by working as a correspondent. Another was a member of the British Parliament named Robert Boothby, a dashing aristocrat who had once been Winston Churchill's right-hand man and considered a likely future prime minister of Great Britain. Shortly, he would be Inga's fiancé—for about a week.

CHAPTER 64

"Whirlwind romance in an orange grove"

ROBERT BOOTHBY WAS A DOZEN YEARS OLDER THAN INGA, BUT IN MANY respects other than age he was a stocky, English version of Jack Kennedy. Tall and handsome, he had the same infectious grin, the same mop of unruly hair (though Boothby's was black, not chestnut), and the same "enormous appetite for life." He loved opera, jazz, Hemingway, and gambling, drove a Bentley two-seater (usually at great speed), and ran in the British version of café society where to be a bore was the greatest possible sin; among his dearest friends was the playwright and composer Noel Coward.

As with Jack, women found Boothby devastatingly attractive and, also like Jack, he took great advantage of this fact. Unlike Jack, Boothby was bisexual, though discreet, and most of his flirtations with men occurred when he was young; later in life, his sexual partners were almost exclusively women, and in the 1960s he won a lawsuit against a newspaper for suggesting he had an affair with "mod" mobster Ronnie Kray.

When he met Inga, Boothby had been married and divorced and was in the middle of a life-long affair with the wife of a good friend, future Prime Minister Harold Macmillan. Like Jack, Boothby would eventually demonstrate to Inga that he, too, loved politics more than love.

A natural politician who got along as well with fishmongers as he did dukes and duchesses, Boothby was first elected to Parliament at age twenty-four. The son of an Edinburgh banker, he was witty, eloquent, often intense, and had a deep and powerful voice that one admirer termed "golden gravel." Winston Churchill was impressed by Boothby's maiden

speech in Parliament, and a year later when Churchill was named Chancellor of the Exchequer, he asked Boothby to be his chief aide, his parliamentary private secretary, and treated Boothby practically as a son for
several years.

Boothby's antagonism toward Nazism predated Churchill's, for
Boothby, like Inga, spoke fluent German and traveled often to Germany,
usually to enjoy Wagner festivals. He met Hitler in 1932 and immediately
sensed the danger that Hitler's coming to power represented to Germany
and the world, although his fiery appeals to British audiences to prepare
for another war were usually met with stony silence. When a journalist
wrote of Boothby that he was "always ahead of his time and always right,"
Boothby, no more modest than any of Inga's lovers, replied, "From this
conclusion, I cannot dissent."

The career of this self-described "rebel" looked very promising
indeed. "I found myself generally regarded as a coming young man, if not
the coming young man, in politics," Boothby recalled in his memoir. "All
doors were open to me." In the mid-1930s, a betting man, as Boothby
was, would have laid odds that Boothby had a far better chance to become
prime minister than did his aging mentor, Churchill.

But Boothby's star began to dim with the onset of war. Where he had
once enjoyed arguing with his protégé, Churchill now became increasingly irritated by Boothby's temerity in offering unsolicited criticism and
advice. Churchill then broke with Boothby when Boothby became
embroiled in a relatively minor financial scandal.

Boothby was head of the Ministry of Food in Churchill's government,
but also led a government commission charged with managing Czecho-
slovakian assets frozen in Britain following the Nazi occupation of that
country. Boothby failed to disclose that he had also been hired to personally represent an individual with a claim on some of those assets. When
this failure to declare a conflict of interest was discovered, Boothby was
sacked as Minister of Food and was not offered any other position in
Churchill's cabinet for the remainder of the war. Churchill could be generous with those he saw as peers, but was often harsh with those he considered subordinates. Boothby's constituents in East Aberdeen, however,

considered the scandal much ado about nothing and returned Boothby to the House of Commons for another two decades.

Now primarily a back-bencher, Boothby amused himself in other ways, such as writing for British newspapers, and so he was sent to America in April 1945 by *News of the World* to cover the opening session of the United Nations in San Francisco, where Jack Kennedy was doing the same for the Hearst newspapers. It is unknown if Jack and Boothby met during the conference, but they took a similar approach to their jobs.

Boothby reported that on the lengthy train ride from New York to San Francisco, "We were all tight all the time," and this behavior continued when he arrived, noting one dinner "consisted of aspirin and champagne." Jack was also a bon vivant correspondent. One night, Arthur Krock recalled seeing Kennedy propped up on the bed in his Palace Hotel room, dressed in evening clothes, "a highball in his hand" and telephoning his editor to say, "Kennedy will not be filing tonight."

When the opening session of the UN conference ended, Boothby went to Los Angeles in May to attend a party hosted by British diplomat Sir Charles Mendl and his wife, the former Elsie de Wolfe, who had become famous for creating the profession of interior decorating. Also invited to the party was another of the Mendls' good friends, Inga, whose beauty and charm astounded Boothby.

Boothby "was forever falling in love and asking women to marry him," an acquaintance said, and now he conducted with Inga what was later described by a hostile British newspaper as "a whirlwind romance in an orange grove in California."

Inga and Boothby had much in common. Inga had spent a good deal of her childhood in England; she and Boothby had both enjoyed Germany in happier times; while Inga no longer played the piano, Boothby's enthusiasm for music enthralled Inga; and they had some mutual acquaintances. Boothby had recently dined in New York with Inga's old admirer Bernard Baruch, whom Boothby called "perhaps the closest friend Winston Churchill ever had."

Even though he and Inga spent fewer than three days together, Inga had swept Boothby off his feet. He proposed. It was now Inga's turn to be dumbstruck. The idea was appealing. She found Boothby charming and seductive, as many women did. Inga wished to marry a man with ambitions who was looking for a partner who could help him achieve those ambitions. Like Nabi, Fejos, Kennedy, and Cahan, Boothby was a brilliant man and still only forty-five years old. Inga had once daydreamed about being first lady of the United States. Unaware that Boothby's political star was no longer rising, Inga could daydream of being the prime ministerial consort.

Inga was also thirty-one years old. If she still hoped not only for marriage but also children (and Boothby said he wanted a family), she knew she had better get going. Cahan was across the Pacific and still married. Jack had breezed through town again, which only brought back memories of what might have been. She recalled the logic that justified her moving from Washington to New York: Why wait for someone who might never come? Boothby had made a proposal, and it seemed to offer Inga the type of life for which she had been groomed from birth.

Boothby returned to England to prepare their nuptials, but he worried that Inga might have second thoughts during his absence, so he wrote her a florid twenty-page letter in order to assure her definitive ascent. Much of the letter was a torrid profession of love and a further case for why she would be happy as Boothby's wife, but a large portion was also devoted to Boothby's explanation to Inga why, even as his spouse, she would not be the only woman in his life.

Inga's oldest son, Ronald, was one of the few to have seen the later-destroyed letter, but he said it detailed Boothby's then fifteen-year relationship with Lady Dorothy Macmillan, whose maiden name was Cavendish and who, proving once again what a small world it is, was the aunt of Kathleen Kennedy's late husband, Billy Cavendish, Marquess of Hartington.

Harold Macmillan and Boothby were political allies but were personally complete opposites. Boothby was a rake, while Macmillan was so dreadfully dull that Dorothy's sisters fought over who had to sit next to him at family dinners. Dorothy was a handsome but far from beautiful woman, but she loved sex and craved excitement. When she met Boothby a few years after her marriage, she said she felt awakened from a sleep that had consumed her previous life. She and Boothby quickly became lovers.

Elizabeth, queen under King George VI and known as the Queen Mother during her daughter Queen Elizabeth II's reign, once said that Boothby was "a bounder, but not a cad." And it was true that Dorothy was the pursuer, though Boothby enjoyed being pursued. Dorothy wished to divorce Macmillan so she could marry Boothby, even telling Macmillan that their youngest daughter, Sarah, was Boothby's child, not his. But Macmillan, amazingly, still loved Dorothy and realized a divorce would destroy his political career. It was the policy of the Conservative Party in Britain at the time to disallow those who were divorced from standing for election.

Unable to wed, Boothby and Dorothy began what was a marriage in everything but name. They lived together and did nothing to hide their affair. The romance was common knowledge among the aristocracy, but in a day when journalists deferred to the influential, it was not commonly known to the public. Boothby once tried to end the affair by marrying Dorothy's cousin, Diana Cavendish, but Dorothy hounded the couple and the marriage lasted only two years. Even though she had a husband, Dorothy was unwilling to share her lover with anyone else.

Remarkably, even after receiving this letter—perhaps she admired Boothby's candor—Inga confirmed to Boothby that she still accepted his proposal of marriage. Boothby was under the impression that they had agreed to keep the engagement quiet for now, perhaps to give him time to break the news to Dorothy. Inga, however, was too excited to keep the news to herself. She told friends who told friends and soon word reached the press, including the gossip columnists.

From experience, Inga realized denying the rumor would make things worse. "The more you stir in dirt, the more it smells," Inga said. Having received several inquiries from reporters, Inga announced her engagement to Boothby on May 22, noting that they intended to wed in September and that the proposal had come after knowing Boothby only three days.

The item was published in newspapers around the United States and in Great Britain, where Inga's name rang a bell with some editors who had good memories: Wasn't Inga Arvad the woman who had had exclusive interviews with Adolf Hitler back in the 1930s? They checked their old files.

CHAPTER 65

"What had been a halo fell down and became a noose"

ROBERT BOOTHBY WAS "BEWILDERED AND UPSET" TO LEARN THAT INGA had made their engagement public. He cabled her immediately and told her to give "no further interviews to press. They are invariably distorted and seldom do good." Boothby would stand for election as a Conservative in July and worried that publicity around such an impetuous engagement "might do me considerable political damage." It was the first of five telegrams he sent Inga that day.

Having told Inga to say nothing more, Boothby changed his mind a few hours later and cabled Inga to beg her to call the press and clarify that "at present [there is] no definite arrangement for marriage"; they would decide whether to marry only after Inga had visited England and, presumably, Boothby's constituents in East Aberdeen. Worried that Inga would not take kindly to being handled, Boothby sent another telegram to assure her that this was not a serious problem between them, and represented only the "penalty of becoming involved with [a] public man."

Boothby's equanimity lasted only a few hours. The morning papers were out in London, and for Boothby the coverage of his engagement to Inga left him "absolutely shattered." He predicted the incident "will almost certainly lose me [the] election." First, he was an object of ridicule for having become engaged to a woman he had known less than three days. The *Daily Mirror*, a strong supporter of Labour in the upcoming election, mocked that Boothby had been overcome by "the scent of orange blossoms."

Worse, elements of Inga's past were emerging. The chief culprit was Inga's former rival in the gossip business, Louella Parsons, who had promised Inga "a very nice story" about the engagement in her Hearst column, but who instead dredged up the notorious INS photograph from 1936 (INS was owned by Hearst), which proclaimed that Hitler had named Inga chief of publicity for the Nazis in Denmark. Hitler had committed suicide in his bunker just three weeks before. The wounds of war were far too fresh for any perceived association with the Nazis to be easily forgiven. A panicking Boothby cabled Inga once more and told her the only thing they could do now was to "call the whole thing off until [the] election is over."

Inga, dizzy from this remarkable flurry of telegrams and perhaps more than a little irritated to once again be haunted by her past and to again play a passive role while her erstwhile lover made all the decisions, obliged. She called several reporters whom she believed would be sympathetic and announced the two-day-old engagement was already over. "Ironically, I have broken my engagement to Mr. Boothby because I love him," Inga said. "I love him very much."

Although she was thirty-one, Inga gave her age as twenty-seven to reinforce her story that she had interviewed Hitler while still in her naïve teens, and emphasized again that any contact she had with the Nazis was solely in her role as a professional journalist. She said reports that she had been named the Nazi propaganda chief in Denmark were ridiculous. "Do you imagine I would have been permitted to become an American citizen last March if these things were true?" she "snapped" (this was UPI's description). Inga blamed the brouhaha on Boothby's enemies in the British press, and added, "I do not wish this ridiculous publicity to hamper his career."

Privately, Inga was livid with Parsons and thought about filing a lawsuit, but on what grounds? The question that haunted Inga, as it had in Washington three years before, was "clearing myself. Now how do you go about doing that?" It dawned on Inga that wherever she went and whatever she did right up until and including her obituary, her association with Hitler and this photograph proclaiming her chief of publicity for the

Nazis in Denmark would almost certainly be mentioned. "The question is what will it shatter the next time?" she asked.

Inga took stock of all her brief association with Hitler had cost her so far in life. Forgetting the also relevant fact that she was a Protestant divorcee, Inga blamed her association with the Nazis for her inability to marry Jack Kennedy. Her relationship with Jack led to his eventual transfer overseas to combat where "he became a big hero, and saved several lives at the expense of his own health which will never be regained." Now, it would prevent her from marrying Boothby and might cause Boothby his seat in Parliament. She noted that when Boothby entered the House of Commons after the stories of his engagement appeared in London's newspapers "he was greeted with a mixture of laughter and pity and even the Prime Minister (Churchill), whom he's a great friend of, cut him short."

Inga recalled the pride she had once felt in securing two exclusive interviews with Hitler, then the most fascinating figure in the world, and the praise she had received for such a journalistic coup. But once she became "a suspicious character to beware of. . . . What had been a halo fell down and became a noose."

Boothby, the masterful politician, managed to turn the incident to his advantage. When an elderly constituent asked during a rally whether it was true, as the *Daily Mirror* claimed, that Boothby had become engaged "after a whirlwind courtship in an orange grove," Boothby pounced. "Madam, I can truthfully tell you that I don't know whether I am engaged or not. You had better ask the Editor of the *Daily Mirror*. But, without any disloyalty to my fellow-candidates in this election, I must now ask *you* a question. Take a look at them in the north of Scotland, and tell me which of them, with the exception of myself, is capable of conducting a whirlwind courtship in an orange grove." Boothby sat down to "a storm of laughter and applause" as his campaign manager leaned over and whispered, "That's worth a thousand votes."

From then on, Boothby treated his supposed engagement to Inga as a joke made up by a malicious press. He claimed he called the editor at the *Daily Mirror* to "inquire about the progress of my romance with Miss Arvad and I'm making the inquiry of you because I know nothing about it and you seem to know everything. Just tell me confidentially—how'm I doing?" Faring poorly in romance, politically Boothby did well. He won reelection by a solid majority, a feat all the more remarkable because the Conservative Party and Churchill as prime minister were voted out of power by a wide margin.

That Churchill, symbol of British defiance during the darkest days of the war, had been turned out of office surprised most observers, though not one, a young man writing for Hearst named Jack Kennedy. Following the UN conference, Jack had been sent to Britain to cover the election. He almost certainly read about Boothby's engagement to Inga and the subsequent debacle. While he left no written record of his thoughts, it seems plausible, given that he would soon embark on his first political campaign, that Jack now saw his father's wisdom in insisting he break ties with Inga, no matter the heartache it may have caused them both.*

Having won reelection in July, Boothby now attempted to repair his relationship with Inga. He claimed that even Lady Dorothy had felt Inga was mistreated, though that seems unlikely. Dorothy would almost certainly have done her best to break up Boothby's marriage to Inga—or anyone else. Boothby would not marry until 1966, the year after Dorothy died, wedding a beautiful brunette thirty-three years his junior named Wanda Sanna.

Immediately following their botched engagement, Boothby and Inga periodically made plans to meet in England or California or some point in between, but it never happened. They remained on friendly terms, and Inga went to visit Boothby more than a dozen years later.

After Inga's death, her son, Ronald, sent Boothby the infamous twenty-page letter that confirmed Boothby had professed to be head over heels in love with Inga when he asked her to marry him, but which more importantly detailed his strange and in many ways tragic relationship with Dorothy. Boothby was happy to retrieve the letter, which he then burned

---

*While Boothby and Jack never met in person, they did appear together on television, although in separate studios, in 1958, when Jack was a senator, to discuss their perspectives on the Cold War during the short-lived Edward R. Murrow program *Small World*. In his memoir, Boothby said he agreed with columnist Walter Lippmann that Kennedy as a president was "vastly overrated." (Boothby, *Recollections of a Rebel*, p. 250)

along with the hundreds of love letters he had received from Dorothy over the years. "Letters intended for one pair of eyes only should not be seen by others," he told his biographer.

Two more postscripts: Although Boothby had allegedly fathered children out of wedlock, nearly a decade after Dorothy's death Boothby assured Macmillan that Macmillan's daughter, Sarah, was, in fact, Macmillan's daughter; Boothby explained that he always wore a condom when having sex with Dorothy. Why he did not ease Macmillan's doubts (not to mention Sarah's) decades before, he did not say.

The episode between Inga and Boothby may also explain one of the stranger anecdotes of the Kennedy presidency. In March 1961, when Macmillan was prime minister and Kennedy was president, they met in Key West to discuss nuclear arms policy. During a break in the discussions, Kennedy suddenly turned to Macmillan and said, "I wonder how it is with you, Harold? If I don't have a woman for three days, I get a terrible headache."

This is usually portrayed as further evidence of Jack's rampant promiscuity, but it is also possible, because of the gossip flowing around Inga and Boothby, that Jack had learned of the affair between Lady Dorothy and Boothby. As Macmillan and Dorothy no longer had sex and Macmillan famously refused to engage in affairs himself, perhaps Jack knew the prime minister had likely been without a woman for three decades, let alone three days, and was testing Macmillan's reaction to a sensitive subject. The only reaction Jack received was Macmillan's astonished silence.

CHAPTER 66

"A mild drizzly moon"

INGA'S SHORT-LIVED ENGAGEMENT WITH ROBERT BOOTHBY CREATED such a kerfuffle that even Olga, who was living with Inga in West Hollywood, made the gossip columns. Harrison Carroll, famous for giving a young actor named Marion Morrison the new moniker "John Wayne," put this item in his column: "Everything happens to Inga Arvad. The same night that she broke her engagement to Bob Boothby, her mother received second and third degree burns on face and arms from flaming paraffin."

Across the Pacific in Brisbane, Australia, rather than fire, William Cahan was overcome by "an internal iceberg" when he read the item about Inga's engagement to Boothby. The still-married Cahan begged for an explanation as to how Inga could break the "unwritten, unspoken faith we have in each other." When he did not hear from Inga right away, he wrote again, saying he had reread Inga's most recent letters (one sent as recently as May 5, the day before she met Boothby), and he could find "no faltering, no uncertainty in your outspoken love for me." Cahan was baffled. "Good heavens, baby, how does your love swing around so fast?"

In addition to being thrilled by Boothby's attention, Inga had simply grown tired of waiting and tired of promises that might never be kept. Inga remained friendly with Cahan (Olga continued to seek out Cahan's medical advice for several years), but this was the beginning of the end of their romance. When Cahan finally returned to the States in December 1945, Inga met his boat in San Francisco. The only person standing on the dock, she was "a silhouette out of some sentimental wartime movie,"

337

Cahan remembered. They spent one last romantic night at the St. Francis Hotel, but the next morning Inga went back to Los Angeles and Cahan traveled to New York City to resume his medical practice.

They continued to correspond, with Cahan telling Inga she was still haunting his thoughts. In March 1946, he wrote to say, "Please trust me and hold your impatience in rein for just a bit longer." Inga traveled to New York so that she and Cahan could discuss their future. As they talked, they realized they did not have one together. Cahan was still married—he would not divorce Pam until 1950—and was in the middle of his residency "with a salary too small to support us." Inga and Cahan kissed good-bye.*

Inga, never looking back, had recently met another man whom she was interested in marrying—John Gunther, one of the best-selling authors of the twentieth century. Gunther had been a foreign correspondent for the *Chicago Daily News* in the 1930s and had written a provocative and insightful book on the rapidly changing political situation in Europe titled *Inside Europe*.

"Translated into 12 languages—Suppressed in 3 countries," as the dust jacket of a later edition boasted, it was a book read and analyzed by world leaders and those hoping to become world leaders, such as Jack Kennedy, who used the book as a tour guide when he traveled through Europe in 1938. It was, according to Gunther's publisher, the best-selling nonfiction book in America in the twenty years after World War I.

In 1945, Gunther was working on a new book, also destined to be a best seller, titled *Inside U.S.A.*, a series of sharply drawn profiles on the politics and characteristics of each of the then forty-eight states. The book was such a hit that, bizarrely, it inspired a Broadway musical review.

Gunther was in California doing research when he was invited to a party attended by Inga in October 1945. Like Boothby, Gunther was divorced and a dozen years older than Inga, and also like Boothby, he was immediately smitten. Inga, Gunther said, had "an eye toward the right things and much sunshine in her hair and smile." Neither Inga nor Gunther left the details for posterity, but their romance progressed by the

---

*Cahan later married Grace Mirabella, founder of the eponymous fashion magazine.

light of what Gunther repeatedly and fondly described in love letters to Inga as a "mild drizzly moon."

Inga, a lover of books and intellectual discussions, was enamored with Gunther, whom she considered a "wonderful gentleman." Later in life, she said that one of the worst mistakes she ever made was not marrying Gunther. On the other hand, she did not have much of an opportunity to do so. This time, the complication was not that her lover had a wife, another lover, or an antagonistic father, but was instead Gunther's only son, Johnny, who developed a brain tumor in the middle of Gunther's long-distance courtship of Inga.

Inga and Gunther had already had difficulty finding time to be together while Gunther was under deadline to finish the half-million words that would complete *Inside U.S.A.* (In the book, Gunther called the new congressman from Massachusetts, John F. Kennedy, "an attractive youngster of twenty-nine.") Still, Gunther made time to maintain a regular romantic correspondence with Inga, telling her, "You flirt so nicely & tantalizingly (I think flirtation is an admirable habit all in all)."

Then, in April 1946, Johnny, sixteen, was diagnosed with a brain tumor and had immediate surgery. The surgeon reported to Gunther that Johnny's tumor was "about the size of an orange. I got half of it." Johnny survived another year and two months, his condition ebbing and occasionally improving as Gunther sought every possible treatment.* It was, Gunther told Inga, "a period of strain and crisis without interruption," which made him all the more grateful when Inga called to perk up his mood with "gay talks."

"You are a warm creature," Gunther told Inga, "kind, with an exciting voice, human and with much vitality and I imagine fundamentally serious-minded just as I am, intelligent but not an intellectual thank God, and with a nice devil-may-care instinct to have fun." Inga must have mentioned her dream of owning a ranch in the West, for Gunther asked, "When do we move to Arizona?"

Despite the turmoil around Johnny and their separation, Gunther told Inga, "No, I have not given you up!" But he admitted that love only

---

* Gunther chronicled the ordeal in his book *Death Be Not Proud* (1949)

by correspondence "gets to be somewhat barren, to put it mildly." Great affairs conducted only by mail were usually shams that involved people like George Bernard Shaw, "a kind of miraculous vegetable" who corresponded with the actress Ellen Terry, or Tchaikovsky, who allegedly courted a patron named Nadezhda von Meck by letter for thirteen years, "but Tchaikovsky was a fairy, I believe, which I have the honor to report I am not," Gunther wrote.

Gunther freely admitted that he longed to again lounge in bed with Inga after an afternoon of lovemaking, and having gone so long in not seeing her he further admitted to being "goddamned frustrated." But as a sign of how kindred in spirit Gunther and Inga were, he spoke of sex within the context of genuine love in a way that Inga had expressed, almost as eloquently, in her letters to Jack.* "Now about being in love," Gunther wrote, "it's like being alive, that is without it you aren't alive. . . . As to making love for the hell of it, listen, I have done quite a lot of that, but never unless there was either affection or a very strong aesthetic value attached."

Inga still had hopes for the relationship, but as Johnny's condition preoccupied Gunther more and more, his letters became less frequent, and it became clear fate had again deprived Inga of the chance of finding lasting happiness with a man who considered her an equal and a partner. As further evidence of how much Gunther and Inga were soul mates, he offered this thought that sounds very much like Inga:

> I had always thought that, essentially, life would come out all right; that there were painful things and unhappinesses [sic] and defeats and restrictions, but that nevertheless the final balance would be happy, that there was a kind of law of compensation for what you lost which gave you something in exchange, that, in a word, the world was okay, provided you faced it honestly. I still want terribly to feel all this, but, well, I am not so sure how. No, I'm not quite ready to resign from the human race, but I need help and sustenance.

---

*Gunther, sadly, did not preserve the letters he received from Inga.

Inga, too, craved sustenance. Personal or professional—either would suffice at this point in her life. She had left her job at MGM. She was discouraged that none of her ideas for scripts had been approved for production. The pay was good, but she did not feel useful, which was the measuring stick for self-worth that Olga had given her as a child and that remained her standard.

When her contract with MGM expired in the fall, legendary producer David O. Selznick hired Inga to help with publicity for Selznick's newest picture, *Duel in the Sun*, which he hoped would be the *Gone with the Wind* of Westerns. A violent tale of rape, incest, and miscegenation, *Duel in the Sun* was condemned by the Catholic Legion of Decency long before it was released, thereby guaranteeing that it would become a box office smash.

Selznick, however, took no chances. Enthralled with new marketing techniques that claimed public awareness of an upcoming film determined its success, Selznick devoted an "unprecedented" $2 million to a marketing campaign for *Duel in the Sun*. Some of the advertising was conventional and much was silly; tiny parachutes with pari-mutuel tickets and advertisements for *Duel in the Sun* were dropped on the Kentucky Derby, and a thousand balloons with free *Duel in the Sun* gifts were dropped on Times Square.

Inga was part of another stunt, only marginally more dignified. She was one of four stunningly attractive women, all former actresses or models, hired by Selznick to make promotional trips on behalf of *Duel in the Sun* to 130 cities where they would wine and dine editors, film critics, broadcasters—anyone who might plug the movie. One of the film's stars, Joseph Cotten, quipped, "Instead of sending four girls to 130 cities, Selznick should have sent 130 girls to four cities. That would be interesting."

According to *Life* magazine, the women were known as "the Four Urges." In addition to Inga, there was Anita Colby, whom Inga had declared the most photogenic woman on the globe and who was the daughter of the cartoonist who created Betty Boop; model Laura Wells; and the only brunette in the group, Florence Pritchett, fashion editor for the *New York Journal American* who shared with Inga the distinction of being one of Jack Kennedy's lovers. Pritchett was Kennedy's date at the Stork Club in 1944 when he met with John Hersey about writing an article on the *PT-109* episode. She and Jack continued to enjoy trysts through the 1950s, often in Havana, where Pritchett was the wife of Eisenhower's ambassador to Cuba. Whether Inga and Pritchett ever compared notes about Jack is unknown, but unlikely.

They probably did not have the chance, because each of the "Urges" traveled separately to different parts of the country. Inga was assigned to cover twenty Western cities, and all was well until trouble hit just before she arrived in Vancouver, British Columbia.

Even before she began her publicity tour, wary because of the episode with Boothby, Inga had asked John Wheeler at NANA to contact the Hearst papers with the request that they no longer run the INS photograph of her from 1936 that included the caption about being appointed chief of publicity for the Nazis in Denmark. At most of Inga's stops, the newspapers made no mention of her time in Nazi Germany.

But in what was now a wearisome routine, an enterprising editor at the *Vancouver Sun* dredged up the photo and stated as fact, "Hitler in 1936 made Miss Arvad chief of publicity for the Nazis in Denmark." The next day, the Canadian Labor-Progressive Party issued a statement, labeling Inga "a Nazi sympathizer," and suggested that Inga be barred from entering Canada.

Humiliated, Inga canceled her scheduled trips to Vancouver and Calgary, pretending she had strep throat in hopes this would nip the controversy in the bud. Wheeler sent a sympathetic telegram: "Sorry photograph with untrue caption is causing you trouble . . . before employing you we checked your record and know allegation untrue." Inga knew it was untrue, but wondered if this photograph that she had claimed to know nothing about would follow her to her grave.

Fortunately, this time the photograph cost her neither a prospective husband nor her job. Selznick kept Inga aboard, and she continued her tour with no further mention of the photograph or Nazi Germany. She still made headlines, but that was due to the remarkable attention the "Four Urges" were able to generate wherever they went.

In Houston, the film critic for the *Post*, Hubert Roussel, reported being overwhelmed when he met Inga at her hotel for an interview:

She came downstairs looking considerably like a movie actress herself. In one hand, she had a purse; in the other, she held demurely a half bottle of Scotch. "I don't drink," she explained, "but I thought maybe you'd like a highball." "Is this part of your routine?" I inquired. "Oh, no," she said, "But we try to think of the little things. This is very good Scotch. A man in Dallas drank the other half and it didn't hurt him at all." . . . I had met the New Order in press agents. The world seemed a little more fantastic than it had before dinner.

Many were scandalized by Selznick's ploy, and even he agreed that in promoting the film he had "broken all the rules of dignity." But it worked. Roussel gave Inga twenty column inches in the *Post*, while *Life* estimated that Inga and the other Urges, in interviews with some three hundred reporters and editors, generated more than four thousand column inches of newspaper coverage. When *Duel in the Sun* opened, there were "lines around the block" at theaters, even though ticket prices had been jacked up to $1.20. *Duel in the Sun* was the year's second-highest grossing film after *The Best Years of Our Lives*.

CHAPTER 67

"Man Who Knows Indians"

PERHAPS IT IS FITTING THAT AFTER PROMOTING A WESTERN MOVIE Inga would next fall for a cowboy—and not just a movie cowboy, but a real cowboy to boot. His name was Tim McCoy, and he was once voted "one of the ten greatest Western motion pictures stars of all time." When he died, the *Nogales Herald* noted that McCoy had not only been a star when "John Wayne, Ward Bond and Walter Brennan . . . were extras," McCoy had also known Buffalo Bill Cody, Wyatt Earp, and Bat Masterson in real life.

Cody was McCoy's life-long idol since age seven when he saw Cody and his famous Wild West show perform in 1898 in his hometown of Saginaw, Michigan. Because McCoy's father was the town's chief of police, he had the opportunity to meet the great showman in person and declared Cody to be "the most impressive man I had ever seen, unmatched either before or since."

In those days before the automobile defined the state, Michigan still had cowboys who broke and trained horses, and McCoy decided he, too, would make his living as a cowboy, but out West. At age eighteen, without telling his parents, he left the boarding school he was attending in Chicago and went as far west as the Chicago and North Western Railroad did, which was to Lander, Wyoming. Nestled in the beautiful Popo Agie (pronounced puh-po-shuh) River valley amid the foothills of the spectacular Wind River Mountains, Lander's motto, captured in the lyrics of "The Sons of the Pioneers" song about the place, was "Where the rails end, and the trails begin."*

---

* If the description sounds effusive (appropriately so), it is because Lander is the author's hometown.

Lander is also located just a few miles outside the Wind River Indian Reservation, home to both the Eastern Shoshone and Northern Arapaho tribes. With a mix of cowboys and Indians strolling the unpaved streets, and dance hall music and candlelight flickering into the night air from a host of saloons, Lander did not disappoint McCoy's vision of how a western town should look. McCoy worked on a variety of local spreads, scrupulously saving money so that he could buy his own ranch one day.

The local Native American population, particularly the Arapaho, fascinated him. A romantic who believed Native Americans could still see the world as it was before civilization, McCoy took the time to ingratiate himself with elder members of the Arapaho tribe, learning native sign language and many of their traditions. McCoy's friendly relations made him essentially an honorary member of the tribe, which bestowed upon him the name "High Eagle." This relationship would make him a Hollywood star.

When America entered World War I, McCoy joined several hundred other local cowboys in volunteering for a cavalry squadron, but when it became clear modern warfare made "rough riders" obsolete, McCoy transferred to the Officers Training Corp, and rose to the rank of lieutenant colonel. McCoy never saw combat, but when he returned to Wyoming he was appointed adjutant general of the state's National Guard, which made him a one-star general at age twenty-eight.

In 1923, a representative of the Famous Players-Lasky film company came to Cheyenne, Wyoming's state capital, to ask McCoy where the studio could find five hundred Native American extras for a $750,000 production of *The Covered Wagon*, the most lavish Western movie made to date. McCoy had become known as that important white character in the mythology of the Old West, what author Glenn Frankel termed the "Man Who Knows Indians." Given his friendly relations with Native Americans, McCoy said he was often asked, "What are Indians like?" To his credit, his usual response was, "What are *people* like?"

After explaining to the Hollywood executive that Native Americans would want to be treated well and paid a fair wage like any other group of actors, McCoy agreed to help negotiate a generous contract that ensured five hundred members of the Arapaho and Shoshone tribes would travel to Utah, where the movie was being filmed. The studio hired

McCoy to act as a consultant on the set, and so he resigned as adjutant general.

When McCoy, a handsome, broad-shouldered man, standing six-feet tall with blond hair and piercing blue eyes, arrived at the location shoot with his Native American retinue, he caught the eye of filmmakers. Fascinated by how McCoy occasionally communicated with the Indians through native sign language, they asked him to travel to Hollywood to star in a special prologue that would be tacked on to the beginning of the film that explained this method of communication. *The Covered Wagon* was a huge hit, grossing $3.5 million.

McCoy kept his ranch in Wyoming but stayed in Hollywood, where he eventually made nearly one hundred films, most of them Westerns. Some were "A-list" films, such as *The Law of the Range* (1928), which costarred Joan Crawford, but more were "B" pictures and serials intended to be half of a Saturday matinee double feature. Because he had been a real cowboy, there was an authenticity to his performance that made him more highly regarded than such peers as Tom Mix and Buck Jones.

If this brief sketch of McCoy makes him sound like a raw, uncouth cowpoke, nothing could be further from the truth. He was a sophisticate, dating to his time in Wyoming when many of the cattle barons were European, particularly British, aristocrats or New York swells, who mixed polo matches with roundups. McCoy's best friends in Hollywood were the quintessential English gentleman Ronald Coleman and the dapper William Powell. At home, McCoy preferred tweed to denim, and after a few cocktails it was said he lost his mild Western drawl and began to sound like Coleman. McCoy's first wife, Agnes, whom he divorced in 1931, was the daughter of British-born theatrical producer Henry Miller and the actress Bijou Heron.

Interested in politics, McCoy ran for the U.S. Senate in Wyoming in 1942 as a Republican but lost the primary to someone even more conservative, E. V. Robertson, who gained attention for claiming that Japanese Americans interred in a Wyoming camp were leading lives of luxury. Within forty-eight hours of losing the election, McCoy volunteered for service in World War II, despite being fifty-one years old. McCoy noted many aging Hollywood stars felt the same sense of duty, but in a jibe aimed at John Wayne, whom he considered a prima donna, McCoy said there were "a few who were younger who were content to do their bit on the back lot of a studio. Ironically, some of them would later become the most rabid of America's super-patriots."

McCoy served in France, engaged primarily in administrative duties for which he made "no apologies" being that he was fifty-two, and he struck up a friendship with an aging war correspondent whom McCoy called "Ernie" Hemingway. When the war was over, McCoy returned to Hollywood to find there was little market demand for a now fifty-four-year-old cowboy. McCoy retired and went east, purchasing a beautiful Georgian estate called Dolington Manor in Bucks County, Pennsylvania.

Inga was also heading east. Her work for *Duel in the Sun* complete, she concluded it was time to leave Hollywood, where she had become a fixture. She knew not only most of the movie's stars, she also knew all of the studio guards by name. There were temptations to stay. At one of her favorite restaurants, Seacomber's in Malibu, the gossip columns noted the handsome crooner David Street was seen "whispering lyrics" into her pretty ears.

The gossip columns were a key reason Inga wanted to leave. She was still livid with Parsons for helping revive the allegations that Inga had been a Nazi stooge. She sought Gunther's advice, and he was among those who encouraged Inga to return to New York City to pursue a more serious writing career.

Inga had always taken fashion very seriously. Always impeccably dressed, favoring classic lines over the latest fad, Inga paid a great deal of attention to how Hollywood dictated fashion trends:

> If Ingrid Bergman were to wear a flour sack for a dress . . . fifty million women all over the world would do exactly the same a month later. However, the striving of the individual after beauty and harmony, after some reconciliation between character and appearance, naturally shows in the style of dress, and there will always be a couple of million women who will individualize that flour sack.

Inga's take on fashion as the fulfillment of individual expression appealed to the legendary fashion editor at *Harper's Bazaar*, Diana Vreeland, who hired Inga to author beauty tips for the magazine. In June 1946, before she left for New York, Inga was invited to dinner at the home of her friend Brian Aherne, the English-born actor who had also invited along another old acquaintance visiting Hollywood: McCoy.

In his memoirs, McCoy recalled that the Ahernes insisted he come to dinner for he "simply must meet Inga, all the men are crazy about her." McCoy had enjoyed his time as a divorced bachelor in Hollywood and was skeptical that Inga offered any more delights than the many starlets he had known. "But I did meet her and she literally took my breath away," McCoy recalled. "She was the most beautiful woman I had ever seen, and unlike most who are similarly endowed, was down to earth and utterly devoid of vanity. I seldom left her side afterward."

Friends were amazed at the pairing. Hollywood columnist Harry Crocker quipped that "Inga must have wanted to learn Indian sign language." Inga was not head-over-heels in love with McCoy as she had been with men closer to her age, such as Nabi, Cahan, or Kennedy. Inga's feelings for McCoy were akin to those she had for Fejos; he was an interesting man she admired. But Inga still wanted children, and it was not clear the fifty-five-year-old McCoy, twenty-two years Inga's senior with three grown children from his previous marriage, wanted a second family.

Inga's feelings for McCoy were further muddied in November 1946 when Jack reappeared in Inga's life. Unlike those occasions during the previous four years when Jack and Inga had crossed paths and Inga had rebuffed Jack's advances, this time she succumbed and they were intimate. Roughly nine months later, Inga gave birth to a son.

CHAPTER 68

A final tryst

WE KNOW LITTLE ABOUT JACK AND INGA'S FINAL TRYST. THE ONLY source that it occurred is Inga's oldest son, Ronald McCoy, who said his mother told him about it more than twenty years after the fact. Ron, understandably, did not ask for details.

Jack had just won his first congressional race on November 5 and was traveling either to or from Washington when he met Inga in New York and they made love. After that, they never saw each other again.

Why did Inga relent and sleep with Jack when she had rebuffed his advances so many times the previous four years, ever since Jack told her on March 1, 1942, that they had to stop seeing each other? There is no single answer, of course, but when they met they were each in moods that ranged from euphoria to wistfulness to perhaps even fear. And so they held onto each other one last time.

Inga had predicted years before that the White House would be Jack's eventual destination. She believed she had played a small but key role in launching his political career. Now that Jack had climbed the first rung of the ladder on his way to the top, what better way for two old lovers to celebrate than in intimate embrace?

Inga was also uncertain where her relationship with McCoy was heading. As McCoy noted in his memoir, when he left Hollywood, he considered himself retired and intended to "enjoy what I perceived as my few remaining years . . . living them as a country gentleman." McCoy said of Inga, "Our spirits were akin," but McCoy was not sure he was financially or emotionally prepared to start a new family.

McCoy had lost the bulk of his savings in 1938 when, despite the lingering Great Depression, he decided to fulfill a lifelong dream and create a Wild West show just like Buffalo Bill's. It was awful timing. Business conditions were still bad. McCoy invested more than $100,000 of his own money and hired more than 150 performers, but the show closed after fewer than twenty performances. One matinee in Akron, Ohio, drew only sixty paying customers.

Inga had not given up on her dream of a home and children, but she felt time was running out. Still beautiful at thirty-three, she was beginning to feel older than her years. In addition to her rheumatoid arthritis, she now also suffered from gout. McCoy, twenty-two years her senior, may not have been the ideal man to save her from spinsterhood, but he was interesting and interested.

Inga certainly had no illusions that their brief rendezvous in New York had suddenly made marriage to Jack a possibility—just the opposite. Elected to Congress, Jack had begun his journey along "the unequalled highway to the White House," which meant that, for Jack, the case against marrying Inga was now stronger than ever. He would have been content with occasional assignations with Inga, for they would pose little political risk, but Inga had no interest in that type of relationship at all.

Love without commitment would have brought Inga no joy. Such an arrangement might work for a Florence Pritchett—she had a husband— but for Inga such an arrangement promised only pain and despair. Inga's earlier desire for the exhilaration of love and the excitement of the new was giving way to a simpler desire for peace and contentment. If marriage to Jack was not an option, then the only solution was separation. This final lovemaking was elegiac, except that shortly into the New Year, 1947, Inga discovered that she was pregnant—but by whom?

Inga told Ronald that she briefly considered getting an abortion, but decided against it because she was too far along in her pregnancy. But two other factors may have weighed more heavily. She must have thought how close her own mother came to aborting her and been grateful that she had not done so, but more importantly Inga had wanted to have a child for many years; now, she would have the opportunity to be a mother whether under ideal circumstances or not.

Inga probably did not tell Jack she was pregnant. If, by chance, the child was his, she knew that he, having just been elected to Congress, would likely counsel or pressure her to have an abortion to avoid scandal. When she had worried she was pregnant four years before, Jack had hardly reacted with enthusiasm, and the complications were greater now than they had been then.

Inga, believing the odds she was carrying Jack's child were small, did not confess to McCoy that she had had an encounter with Jack. McCoy, having no reason to believe he was not the father, was prepared to do the honorable thing and in a way that did not dishonor his prospective wife. He married Inga in a quiet ceremony with no guests on Valentine's Day 1947 in the village of North Castle, forty miles north of New York City.

When word got out the pair had married and reporters called for verification, McCoy and Inga were vague on the details and implied they had wed in November. When he spoke to a reporter ten days after the wedding, McCoy was quoted, "We've been married for quite a while." McCoy, the Associated Press report added, "declined to say where or when the marriage took place." When Inga spoke to reporters at roughly the same time, she said that she and McCoy had been married "for several months."

Virtually all the articles about Inga and McCoy's marriage noted that Inga had interviewed Hitler, and that Hitler had declared her "the perfect Nordic beauty." One typical headline read "Film Star Weds Dane Who Pleased Fuehrer." Inga's connection to Hitler was also included in all the news announcements when Ronald was born on August 12, 1947, seven months after their wedding and nine months after Inga's tryst with Kennedy. A few newspapers even republished the photo from 1936, the caption of which alleged Inga had been named chief of publicity for the Nazis in Denmark, which again proved Inga's dictum that "we pay for everything in life."

Ronald, meanwhile, grew up to be blonde and looked a great deal like McCoy, which no doubt greatly relieved any lingering anxiety Inga may have had.

Many of Inga's friends expressed surprise at learning that she had finally married, and while those who knew McCoy liked him, they were surprised Inga had married someone so much older, which in their mind may have precluded Inga from having children. Some were hurt they had not been invited to the ceremony. Sir Charles Mendl said he felt wounded to have learned of the wedding from "a comparative stranger," but added, "the main thing is that you are happy."

Inga was happy at the prospect of realizing her dream of motherhood, but her mother was not happy with her new son-in-law. Unlike most of Inga's previous suitors, McCoy had felt no obligation to woo Olga.* Older and more assured, McCoy also shared a headstrong personality with Olga, which prevented them from ever becoming close. Olga missed the more deferential Fejos to the point that when she came east from California to visit Inga and McCoy, she also sought to see Fejos—if he was willing to see her. Fejos replied to Olga's query: "I am sorry that you have written in your letter such awful lines that ' . . . but if you prefer to sever the old ties completely . . .' Mor ("Mother"), Darling, how could you? The affection I have had for Inga and you will stay with me always. It couldn't perish . . . I know that we had our misunderstandings— possibly all on account of jealousy over Inga, whom we both loved so dearly—but inside I have always had a special tender part of my heart reserved for you."

With a young family to support, McCoy unretired. He flirted with radio in New York City, but he knew where he was most likely to make a good living. In 1948, the family moved to California where Inga gave birth to another son, Terence. In 1950, McCoy was given a television show on KTLA in Los Angeles, where he told stories of the Old West with a special emphasis on stories about Native Americans. Many genuine Native Americans performed on the show, demonstrating native dances and other lost traditions. The show's costar was also a supposedly Native American actor who went by the name Iron Eyes Cody; it was later learned that Cody was an Italian immigrant from Louisiana.

In 1952, McCoy's show moved to the CBS affiliate in Los Angeles, KNXT, where McCoy won an Emmy for his work (without a costar this

---

*Jack had also had little interaction with Olga, but Kick made up for that oversight by being particularly attentive to Olga when she was in Washington.

time) "telling the audience about the real history of the West." Despite the critical acclaim, McCoy's show lost its sponsor the following season and the show was canceled. For McCoy personally, this was a blessing.

Faced with the need to make a living, he revived an act he had done back in the 1930s both for his short-lived Wild West show and a longer tenure he had enjoyed with Ringling Bros. and Barnum & Bailey circus. McCoy now worked for the Kelly, Miller Brothers Circus before later joining the Carson and Barnes Circus (although he found time to appear in two Westerns and have a cameo in *Around the World in Eighty Days*).

These years were "good ones," McCoy remembered. Each summer, Inga and their two sons would join the circus, with the boys working as clowns in costumes handmade by Inga. A *Los Angeles Times* profile said Ronald and Terence had "ideal summer jobs," but the boys admitted they looked forward to going back to school. They enjoyed payday but had few opportunities to spend their wages as they rose each day at 5 a.m. to help the circus move to the next town.

But while the McCoys were together during the summer, McCoy was on the road another seven months a year without his family. It was a familiar pattern for Inga. Once again, she was left behind while the man she loved pursued his dream. While still in California, amid old friends and with her mother nearby, McCoy's absence was bearable. But that would soon change when Inga moved to Arizona, especially since she was denied the ranch she had so often dreamed of having there.

The man who had been part of that dream, Jack Kennedy, was also about to get married, though Inga still so haunted his thoughts that he nearly called off the wedding.

CHAPTER 69

Jack and Jackie (and Inga)

IN AUGUST 1953, WHILE ON VACATION IN SOUTHERN FRANCE, THIRTY-six-year-old Jack Kennedy met a beautiful, blonde Swedish aristocrat named Gunilla von Post, who had just turned twenty-one. That evening, Jack and von Post dined and danced. An hour later, as they sat under the stars looking out over the Mediterranean, Jack announced to von Post, "I fell in love with you tonight." He confessed he was due to marry Jacqueline Bouvier the following month, but said, "If I had met you one month before, I would have canceled the whole thing."

When Inga had been ambivalent about her future with McCoy she had fallen into Jack's arms. Jack, decidedly unenthused about marrying Jackie, fell into the arms of an Inga surrogate. Given that Jack pursued many and all types of women, such an assertion may seem spurious, but there are several clues that suggest when Jack looked at von Post he saw Inga, and this went beyond the two women's shared Scandinavian heritage. The intensity of Jack's feelings for von Post were so out of proportion to the time they spent together that it suggests his emotions were drawing on a deep memory.

Von Post had refused to sleep with Jack the day they met, and when they parted that night she assumed she would never see him again. But in March, having been married for six months, Jack took the trouble to track down von Post and begged for another meeting. Complications, primarily around Jack's health, prevented him from reuniting with von Post until August 1955, a full two years after their initial meeting. They shared a week of passion and corresponded for another year or so after that, but another planned rendezvous never came to fruition.

While they were together, von Post noted that Jack was "always talking about Paris," which was Inga's favorite city; von Post had never been there. Jack once suggested that he and von Post rendezvous in Copenhagen, Inga's birthplace, though Stockholm in von Post's native Sweden was nearby. Jack's demeanor around von Post mirrored his behavior with Inga. Von Post picked up, as Inga had, on Jack's need for "unconditional love" and for "someone who would love him for his weaknesses as well as his strengths." When Jack and von Post finally made love, he told her, "I feel as though I've been set free."

But von Post was not Inga, and the difference in Jack's relationships with the two women also underscores the depth of his connection to Inga. His letters to von Post, unlike his letters to Inga, share no deep thoughts or emotions; they are primarily short notes of affection ("You are wonderful, and I miss you") or hastily scribbled expressions of hopes to meet again. There is also what those notes meant to von Post. Inga spoke to no one outside her family about her relationship with Jack and kept his letters until her death; they were too personal to share. Von Post wrote a 1997 book that stretched what was essentially a one-week affair into 150 pages, and in 2010, the year before her death, she auctioned off her letters from Jack for more than $115,000.

There is a key similarity—the excuse Jack used to end the relationship. Jack told von Post he had sincerely hoped to divorce Jackie and marry her, but his father forbade it. Then Jack told von Post that Jackie was pregnant, which he hoped would improve his marriage. Jack and von Post stopped corresponding. Von Post married a Swedish man in 1956, and Jack stayed married to Jackie.

For many years, Jack's marriage to Jackie was not a happy one. As biographer Geoffrey Perret aptly put it, "The romance of Jack and Jackie was about them, not between them." If Jack had lost his 1952 Senate race to Henry Cabot Lodge, friends speculated that he would have never married at all, but he did win, which kept him on his timetable to become president in 1960.

Jack understood that while it is one thing to be a bachelor congressman, if he wished to become president he needed a wife. Several widowers had been president (Woodrow Wilson being the last), but the only bachelor president had been James Buchanan, who faced insinuations about his sexuality throughout his term in office. Joseph Kennedy told his son a wife and family were now "political necessities."

Jack's rush to become president (at forty-three, he remains the youngest man elected president) was due to his long-held belief that he, suffering from so many ailments, did not have long to live. Physicians confirmed his premonition in 1947 when Jack became seriously ill during his first trip to Ireland. Specialists in Britain diagnosed Jack as suffering from Addison's disease, a rare disorder that prevents the adrenal glands from producing hormones, thereby damaging the body's immune system. Before 1930, Addison's disease had a 90 percent mortality rate, but fortunately for Jack a synthetic replacement hormone was available in 1947 that doctors told him could extend his life possibly another ten years.

As biographer Michael O'Brien noted, "The prospect that he would almost certainly be dead by 1957 must have haunted Kennedy." Worsening this sense of mortality was the death of his beloved sister, Kick, who was killed in a plane crash in France on May 13, 1948, along with her scandalous new fiancé, the Earl Fitzwilliam, who was still in the process of divorcing his first wife. Kick remained the only Kennedy independent enough to defy her parents' mores.

Inga, who had so enjoyed Kick's friendship, almost certainly sent condolences to Jack and the Kennedy family, but there is no record of an acknowledgment. Jack was too disconsolate. He did not attend Kick's funeral in England, but instead took part in a small memorial service among family and a very few friends in Hyannis Port.

Jack met Jackie the year before Kick's death while Jackie was still a student at Vassar. He flirted with her then and again four years later at a Washington dinner party hosted by a journalist friend named Charles Bartlett, but Jackie rebuffed Jack's advances both times, and he did not bother to call or contact her again. Jackie instead pursued her own life that has several odd intersections with Inga's story.

Through the assistance of family friend Arthur Krock, still the *Washington Times-Herald*'s "staff procurer," Jackie was hired by the newspaper for a job similar to that held by Inga, but which paid $2.50 a week more. Jackie was an "Inquiring Photographer" for the *Times-Herald* who took pictures and wrote short profiles of Washington's most interesting people. One of her subjects, as he had been for Inga, was Jack.

Jackie also had a mentor familiar to Inga: John White, the man who had been Kick's beau and Jack and Inga's "beard" when Kick and Inga worked at the *Times-Herald*. Jackie's relationship with the now forty-year-old White, however, was strictly platonic. White now worked at the State Department but clearly missed his halcyon days among pretty young reporters at the *Times-Herald*. He took Jackie under his wing, coaching her writing and building up her confidence.

When Jack and Jackie met again in early 1952, they viewed each other differently—this time through the lens of cold calculation. Planning to win his Senate race, Jack needed a wife who would enhance his presidential aspirations. Jackie checked all the boxes: she was beautiful, educated, sophisticated, socially prominent, and unencumbered by any previous marriage or scandal. There was another reason Jack found Jackie appealing; he intuited that she would tolerate his promiscuity.

Jackie's father, John Vernou "Black Jack" Bouvier III, was a dashing Wall Street stockbroker and a philanderer whom she nonetheless adored. Jackie, like Kick, assumed that all men were like their fathers. "I don't think there are any men who are faithful to their wives," Jackie once said. Jack knew Jackie had a "major father-crush."

Bouvier had accustomed his daughter to a life of privilege, but Black Jack had nearly gone bankrupt following the Crash in 1929. His wife divorced him, and Jackie's stepfather, Hugh Auchincloss, was ungenerous with his stepchildren. Jackie, who found Jack charming, made the decision that she needed a wealthy husband to finance the lifestyle she desired; Jack was a member of one of the wealthiest families in the world. "Essentially, she was motivated [to marry Jack] by a desire for money," said television correspondent and family friend Nancy Dickerson.

As those who marry for money usually discover, they earn it. Despite having been warned by Jack's friends, Jackie was still unprepared for just how humiliated she would be by Jack's constant need for other women and his coldness in their own relationship. Jack, who had rhapsodized about how well he and Inga knew each other, seemed uninterested in Jackie as a person. When *Look* magazine interviewed Jack for a profile on

Jackie, he struggled to describe his wife, providing such less-than-intimate insights as "she has a splendid memory and she speaks many languages" before giving up a moment later and urging the reporter, "Why not do a story on me [instead]?"

Unlike with Inga, Jack never wrote Jackie a letter beyond a rare postcard while on a senatorial fact-finding mission. He even proposed to Jackie by telegram. Jackie spent almost every weekend alone, and when Jack was home he was preoccupied with work or spent time with his male friends. "[I might] as well be in Alaska," Jackie lamented.

Even a pregnancy and an ensuing miscarriage did not rein Jack in. In 1956, while Jack was cruising the Mediterranean with a bevy of European beauties (none of them von Post), Jackie gave birth prematurely to a little girl she named Arabella. After receiving the news, Jack did not bother to contact his wife for two days. Only when he was convinced that not being at Jackie's side would damage him politically did he return to the United States. Joseph Kennedy, who saw in Jackie some of the same qualities he admired in Kick, begged, bribed, and harangued Jackie not to divorce Jack and ruin his career. Jackie gave in and sounded all too much like Inga when she told a friend, "You can't beat them [the Kennedy family]. They're just too strong."

This was the nadir of the Kennedy marriage. Happily, it improved marginally following the births of their children, Caroline and John Jr., and even more so as Jack realized that Jackie's popularity as first lady dramatically enhanced his own image. But the real turning point occurred in August 1963 when, sadly, Jackie again gave birth prematurely to a boy named Patrick who died two days later. Unlike in 1956, this time Jack was loving and attentive. In gratitude, following her recovery, Jackie said she would, for the first time as first lady, accompany Jack on an important political trip. They would travel to Texas together in November.

CHAPTER 70

"Inside the tent pissing out"

INGA FOLLOWED JACK'S POLITICAL CAREER WITH INTEREST. THE DEMO-
cratic National Convention in 1960 was held in Los Angeles, and Inga
briefly considered driving to Memorial Coliseum to watch Jack give his
acceptance speech before deciding that being part of a crowd of eighty
thousand had no great personal meaning. She missed Jack's declaration
that his planned administration would offer a "New Frontier" for the
American people, but she did send him a telegram of congratulations.
Lost in an avalanche of similar good wishes, Inga never received a
response.

Another who closely watched the rise of Jack's political career and
sent his own message after his nomination was J. Edgar Hoover. When
Jack emerged as a potential running mate for Adlai Stevenson in 1956,
Hoover asked aides what the FBI files held on Jack. As evidence of how
little thought Hoover had given Jack when he was just a navy ensign,
when told about the voluminous material on Inga, Hoover allegedly
replied, "You have misinterpreted the files. You're talking about the older
brother of John F. Kennedy."

Hoover thought so little of Jack that he apparently did not notice
when Jack, once elected to Congress, reportedly tried to retrieve his FBI
file (which was actually Inga's file). Jack knew the Bureau had kept a file
on his and Inga's affair; his father had told him so. Jack was less clear on
exactly what was in the file, and there is no solid evidence that he suspected Hoover had in his possession recordings of him and Inga making
love.

Tape or no tape, for quite obvious reasons Jack never wanted it to become public that he had had an affair with a suspected spy. It would have demonstrated exceptionally poor judgment by a young politician who was desperately trying to craft an image as a statesman thoughtful beyond his years. Further, if Inga's connection to Hitler and other leading Nazis had been made public, it would also have generated a new round of unflattering stories regarding his father's views about Germany in the 1930s. Whether it would have triggered stories about Jack's womanizing is unlikely; the press of that time still considered that topic off limits.

Finally, and what should not be discounted, Jack considered his relationship with Inga deeply personal. He had demonstrated a vulnerability to Inga that he usually kept hidden. Given that he was a bit of an exhibitionist and considered his machismo a political asset, having people listen to him engaging in vigorous sex might not have embarrassed him much at all, but he had expressed fears and insecurities to Inga that he would have wanted no one else to hear.

One of Jack's congressional aides, Langdon Marvin Jr., has claimed that Jack attempted several times to retrieve his file from the FBI. Marvin also claimed that Jack believed Hoover had tapes. When Jack was elected to Congress, "one of the things on his mind was the Inga Binga tape," Marvin said. "He wanted to get the tape from the FBI. I told him not to ask for it, he'd never get it." Rebuffed, Jack tried again when he was a senator despite Melvin's alleged warning: "I told him not to be stupid." He never retrieved the file, but when it appeared Jack might become president, Hoover left him in no doubt that such a file existed.

On July 13, 1960, the day Jack secured the Democratic presidential nomination and the day Inga sent him a congratulatory telegram, Hoover directed aides to prepare a summary of everything the FBI had in its files on Jack. Hoover received a nine-page memorandum by the end of the day that noted that the Kennedy family generally had a positive relationship with the FBI—Joseph Kennedy's incessant flattery had paid off—and that Jack was a staunch anticommunist. The memo noted that accusations of voter fraud had been made against the Kennedy campaign during some of the primary elections, and then under the heading "Miscellaneous," just before noting Jack had also been seen at parties with prostitutes while in the company of Frank Sinatra, the memo noted that Jack had "carried on an illicit relationship with another man's wife during World War II." The next day, Hoover ordered that Inga's file be moved to his private office where he could review it and have easy access to its contents going forward.

Shortly thereafter, Hoover had a conversation with Jack's brother and campaign manager, Robert F. Kennedy, to alert RFK that while the FBI had heard a great deal of gossip about his brother, including about Jack's relationship with Inga, he wanted to assure the Kennedys that whatever damaging information might be in his possession it would be secure in Hoover's private files. This conversation established a pattern Hoover repeated throughout the Kennedy presidency.

"I suppose every month or so he'd send somebody around to give information on somebody I knew or a member of my family or allegations in connection with myself," RFK later said. "So that it would be clear— whether it was right or wrong—that he was on top of all these things and received all of this information."

Hoover made no threats. He made no demands. He didn't need to. "If he had directly blackmailed any president, I'm sure the president would have cut his legs off," syndicated columnist Jack Anderson once explained. Rather, Hoover used "a friendly approach." Pretending to pro- tect the president, Anderson said, Hoover would say something like: 'There's some information that we've heard that your enemies might get, Mr. President. . . . And we would like you to know we're helping to guard this information so that it won't get out.'"

Jack understood this "friendly" message—to the dismay and amaze- ment of his friends and supporters. The day after Jack won the election over Richard Nixon, he hosted a dinner with friends at Hyannis Port and asked them what first actions he should take as president. The first idea tossed out during this "animated" discussion was that Jack should fire Hoover. Jack, "listening with apparent interest, egged his friends on," said one of the guests, historian and Kennedy aide Arthur Schlesinger Jr.

Unaware of Hoover's files on Jack and Inga, and certain that Jack shared their antipathy toward Hoover, Schlesinger said those who had suggested the director's removal were therefore "a little irritated" when

Jack announced the very next day that he had reappointed Hoover as FBI director for four more years. Even more perturbed was Jack's pal, Benjamin Bradlee, who at this time was still Washington bureau chief for *Newsweek*, who overheard Jack's call to Hoover, "telling J. Edgar Hoover how much he wanted him, was counting on him, to stay on during the Kennedy administration. Laid it on a bit thick, I thought."

Of course, while Bradlee knew about Jack's womanizing, including with Bradlee's sister-in-law Mary Pinchot Meyer, he was unaware of how large a file Hoover had, and how that file would grow throughout Jack's presidency as his sexual escapades continued, including some very dangerous affairs that, had they been known at the time, might have forced him out of office.

By keeping Hoover "inside the tent pissing out, than outside the tent pissing in," to borrow Lyndon Johnson's phrase about the FBI director, Jack believed he could keep these stories buried, though he never doubted Hoover's willingness to use the information he had to his advantage. Therefore, when Hoover confronted Jack about two of his more egregiously risky affairs while president, one with Judith Campbell Exner, who was also mistress to two mob bosses, and another with Ellen Rometsch, who was suspected of being an East German spy, Jack immediately ended the relationships.

Fear of Hoover and his files also help explain the appointment of Jack's younger brother, Robert, as attorney general. The traditional narrative is that Joseph Kennedy pressured a reluctant Jack to appoint Bobby as a reward for his service to Jack's campaign. But knowing how Hoover threatened to expose Jack's affairs with Inga and many others, it is also possible that Jack thought placing Bobby as head of the Department of Justice was one more check to ensure the story of his and Inga's romance (and his other dalliances) never saw the light of day—at least while he was alive.

Chapter 71

She cried for hours

In 1959, while Jack was touring the country gearing up for his run for the presidency, Inga traveled to Europe and reconnected not only with two old loves but also with her love for adventure as she concocted a crazy plan to interview Soviet leader Nikita Khrushchev.

In 1958, television was good to Tim McCoy. He won several thousand dollars on the game show *The $64,000 Challenge* (a spin-off of *The $64,000 Question*) by correctly answering questions on Western lore. Then he was lauded on *This Is Your Life* where one of his gifts was a set of airline tickets to Europe.

McCoy felt an obligation to maintain his performance schedule with the Carson and Barnes Circus, and so he encouraged Inga and oldest son, Ron, now eleven, to use the prizes to travel to Europe in 1959. The younger boy, Terry, ten, opted to stay with his father that summer and travel with the circus.

It was Inga's first trip overseas since arriving in America in 1940, and she and Ron first traveled to Copenhagen to see family and old friends. Through mutual acquaintances, Inga's first husband, Kamal Abdel Nabi, heard Inga was on the continent and asked if they could meet in Paris. Nabi had served as Egypt's ambassador to France under President Gamal Abdel Nasser from September 1955 until 1958 when Egypt and Syria joined to form the short-lived United Arab Republic. Nabi had played a key role in world diplomacy during the Suez Crisis of 1956. Now he was a successful businessman.

Still tall, dignified, elegantly dressed, and familiarly addressed as

"Monsieur l'Ambassadeur" when he took Inga and Ronald to some of the finest restaurants in Paris, Inga was surprised to see that Nabi had lost his luxurious head of hair and was now bald with a closely trimmed moustache. She was also surprised that Nabi had become religious and happily taught Ron the rituals of Islamic prayer.

Nabi again teased Inga that, in his view, they were still married because he had not divorced her in accordance with Islamic custom. While Nabi laughed when he said it, Inga was concerned enough that he might be serious that she scotched Nabi's offer to take Ron for a quick trip down the Nile River, worried Nabi might not bring him back until she agreed to return to him.

Over dinner one night, Nabi told Inga that he would have become prime minister of Egypt had they remained married. A few weeks later, while visiting London, Robert Boothby told Inga that if she had married him he was in no doubt he would have become Britain's prime minister.

"They were quite serious about it; they weren't kidding around," Ronald recalled. Exactly why these men believed Inga would have made their destiny they did not say, but it was one of Inga's gifts to make men feel they could do anything—even reach their full potential. Inga was flattered and amused. She was used to men saying extravagant things to her, only to learn that words did not always translate to action.

Boothby had been made a peer the year before on Harold Macmillan's recommendation, despite Boothby's ongoing affair with Lady Dorothy. Boothby, now Baron of Buchan and Rattray Head, told Inga he received the honor only because Macmillan wanted the self-described "rebel" out of the House of Commons; Boothby caused a stir in Britain in the 1950s by being an outspoken proponent of civil rights for homosexuals.

Boothby, still tall, his now white hair combed straight back, wearing his expensive but rumpled three-piece suit and a polka-dot bow tie, invited Inga and Ron to the House of Lords to dine and to watch him give a speech on July 20, solely for their benefit. Over lunch, Boothby proved, as the Queen Mother had said, that he was still "a bounder" when he guffawed to Inga that when he knelt before Queen Elizabeth II to receive his peerage the first thought that came into his head was that the thirty-two-year-old monarch had "pretty attractive ankles."

These affectionate reunions stirred something in Inga. She felt young and liberated. She remembered how Olga had groomed her to "be something." Back in Copenhagen, with their summer abroad winding down, she hatched a plan to travel to the Soviet Union with the intention of interviewing Khrushchev. The Cold War was at its height, and the USSR was where the biggest story in the world was, just as Nazi Germany had been in the 1930s.

Inga went to the Soviet embassy in Copenhagen and secured a travel visa, but her friends and family—perhaps some of the same ones who fretted when she entered the Miss Denmark contest in 1931—told her once again that she was nuts. How would you even get in to see Khrushchev, they asked. Inga had a simple answer: the same way she had interviewed Hitler—"you just do it."

Inga was serious enough about her scheme that she had arranged to send Ron back to the States first, but in the end she relented and canceled her travel to Moscow. For the rest of her life, she regretted not having at least tried to see Khrushchev. Inga had once said she was pushed into adventure because of her mother, but after a lifetime of exploits it was clear that she also loved the excitement of new experiences.

Life was less adventurous back home in La Cañada, California, where she and McCoy had lived since 1954 and where she was active in the PTA and various civic organizations. She was also a short drive from the beach where she loved to walk and think. Still on a spiritual quest, each Sunday, while McCoy breakfasted at the Brown Derby if he was in town, Inga took the boys to church, usually a different one each week. McCoy was on the road ten months a year, but in familiar surroundings and with many friends and her mother nearby, she did not resent his long absences.

Then in 1962, McCoy announced that the family was moving to Nogales, Arizona, a border town of fewer than eight thousand people in the mountains south of Tucson. It was also located less than seventy miles from Benson, where Jack Kennedy had spent the summer of 1936. Though close, Inga was not going to realize her dream of a ranch in Arizona, even though she was married to a cowboy.

It was the age of drive-ins—drive-in restaurants, drive-in liquor stores, drive-in cleaners, and, of course, drive-in theaters. McCoy's idea was to develop a drive-in rodeo that would feature cowboys and appeal to fans on both sides of the border. The idea did not take off, and the drive-in rodeo closed after a single show.

McCoy was hosting a local Tucson television show on the Old West similar to the show he had in Los Angeles, but the pay was meager, and to make a living McCoy returned to the road, working in Tommy Scott's Country Caravan and Wild West Show, by McCoy's estimation, "three hundred and thirty days a year."

Had Inga been left behind *in* Nogales, raising two boys basically alone would have been hard enough. But McCoy built a home for the family on a very small acreage that did not even qualify as a "ranchette" six miles north of Nogales—and a most unusual home it was. McCoy designed it himself with no input from Inga: "The house is strictly my husband's baby," she told a local newspaper.

Built in the "Spanish territorial" style around an interior courtyard, McCoy named the house "Los Arcos" ("The Arches"). But he built it without central heat, and the only way to go from the bedrooms to the kitchen or living room was to go outside. Even though McCoy was a father of two, there were no bedrooms for the boys. Ron was given a bed in a walk-in closet in his mother's suite, while Terry's bed was in a sitting area in his father's suite.

Inga and McCoy had separate bedrooms, a not-so-subtle sign that they were no longer intimate and had not been for several years. Inga had never been passionate about McCoy, but she had a deep affection for her husband. She admired his honesty, something she felt the other men in her life often lacked, and she thought he was interesting and amusing, for McCoy was a wonderful storyteller.

But more than anything she admired his gumption and his work ethic. McCoy was not a brilliant man, in the manner of most of her previous husbands and lovers, but Inga had never met a man who worked harder or who drew on every talent and brain cell he had to succeed. McCoy understood that Inga worried about money, and he was determined to ensure his family's finances were always sound.

Inga marveled that McCoy continued to maintain the pace he did to support his family into his old age (he was eighty-two and still working when Inga died). When McCoy was on tour at age seventy-six, he fell down twelve marble steps, a mishap that left his arm in a sling and him unable to lift his bullwhips. But he still performed that night and got up at 5 a.m. the next day and drove 250 miles to the next stop for the next show. "How he does it is way beyond me," Inga told her sons. "He is a miracle by himself in his own little category. I do admire his 'guts.'"

Inga insisted that she learned to enjoy living in Nogales. Always interested in people, Inga found the community a fascinating combination of businessmen, ranchers, and artists. She particularly enjoyed volunteering at the public library, partly so she could get first dibs on new books as they arrived. A sign, however, that Inga never felt fully at home there is that, despite being ten minutes from the Mexican border, this woman who had previously mastered four languages never bothered to learn Spanish.

Inga had been living in Los Arcos less than a year when an event happened that further tinged the house with sadness. Jack and Jackie Kennedy had traveled to Texas to raise money for the upcoming 1964 presidential campaign and to help heal a rift in the Texas Democratic Party. While riding in an open limousine in Dallas, Jack was shot by a lone sniper who claimed to be a Marxist. Sitting next to Jack in the car was Jackie, in a spot that under different circumstances might have been occupied by Inga.

Inga heard a bulletin on the radio as she drove to pick up Ron from school for lunch. Ron said he told his mother there was a bad joke going around school that the president had been shot. "Be quiet," Inga said. "It's no joke." They drove home in silence and once there, Inga, like tens of millions of Americans, tuned into the television news as the story unfolded. When it was confirmed that Jack was dead, Inga silently rose up from her chair, went into her bedroom, and shut the door. She stayed there and cried for hours.

CHAPTER 72

"A butterfly who still has the dust on the wings"

INGA RARELY SPOKE ABOUT JACK WHEN HE WAS ALIVE; FOLLOWING HIS murder, she could not speak about him even to her family. She kept a copy of the local newspaper's coverage of the assassination, and saved a thirty-two-page campaign booklet from Kennedy's 1960 race that was filled with photos, including two of him shirtless from his navy days that made her smile.

She had a few mementos from their time together: his letters, the pair of hurricane lamps he had given her as a gift, and the plaque of her "Did You Happen to See?" column on Jack that he had given her to keep. One day, the son of some close friends who were visiting at Los Arcos saw the column displayed on the wall. "Mrs. McCoy, I didn't know you knew John Kennedy!" the boy enthused. "He was president of the United States, dahling [sic]," Inga replied, "lots of people knew him."

She seldom said more than that. In 1965, the Arizona chapter of Theta Sigma Chi, the national journalism fraternity for women, honored Inga. In an interview with the *Tucson Daily Citizen*, Inga noted that when she worked at the *Washington Times-Herald*, "I talked with nearly every dollar-a-year man in Washington." She omitted any mention that she had also interviewed the just martyred president.

Inga's silence was remarkable given that the country was in the midst of what could only be described as a mania for all things Kennedy. Jackie Kennedy had deliberately and ingeniously planted the idea with journalists that her late husband's presidency was a modern-day Camelot—"a magic moment in American history when gallant men danced with beautiful women, when great deeds were done and when the White House became the center of the universe," as journalist Theodore White put Jackie's vision into words.

Jack and Inga would have snickered at such a conceit, but many did not. For years after Jack's death, it was a rare issue of any women's magazine that did not feature Jackie on the cover. Books about Kennedy quickly began rolling off the presses. Eventually, their number exceeded two thousand; fifty years after the fact, there were more than one thousand on the assassination alone. Anyone with a Kennedy story to tell told it, and the stories kept coming, good or bad. As late as 2012, a woman who had been a nineteen-year-old White House intern revealed that Jack had taken her virginity fifty years before. Yet Inga, who had one of the most fascinating Kennedy stories of all, kept mum.

She gave a clue why as she came to terms with another part of her past and began to speak openly about her interviews with Hitler and her association with other leading Nazis. She gave a lengthy interview to the *Arizona Republic* in 1969 in which she said, "The reason I talk about it [Hitler] at all is because I think it's history. I found out it's history not so much because I've gotten older and it's long ago but because when I talk to my children . . . I've learned that when they ask me questions about old times and what I did and things like that, it's like history. You could be talking about Napoleon. Napoleon isn't any further away than Hitler was, not to this particular generation because it's all history."

But for Inga, Jack was not history. A death ends a life, not a relationship, and Jack remained in her heart, as much a figure of the present as the past.

While Inga was alive, only one journalist mentioned her relationship with Jack in print. Drew Pearson, who gave the tip about Inga and Jack to Walter Winchell, devoted a portion of one of his "Washington Merry-Go-Round" columns in 1966 to the influence Joseph Kennedy wielded over his children. Pearson wrote, "When the late President Kennedy was a young naval officer in Washington, he fell madly in love with Inga Arvad, a *Washington Times-Herald* newsgal, older than he. Whereupon, old Joe pulled some strings to get his son transferred to the Pacific. It broke up the relationship and almost killed his son. In the Kennedy family, there could be no doubt about who was boss."

Big Joe's power was no revelation to Inga. Fortunately for Inga, the column by Pearson, whose influence had waned considerably by 1966, did not generate other media interest. Prying into Kennedy's love life was not a national preoccupation—yet.

Inga, then, was not distracted from being what she had always wanted to be: a mother. "I think children are very like herring—they should be let loose from their parents at an early age," she said. When Terry was sixteen and announced he wished to move back to California by himself, Inga did not object; she had been married at seventeen, after all, and loved the ocean as much as Terry did. Experience, she believed, was life's best and most reliable teacher.

While Terry loved surfing and cars, Ron became immersed in politics. Twice he won a national oratory contest sponsored by the American Legion, and was also elected president of Boys Nation, another civics program sponsored by the American Legion that has produced a remarkable number of politicians, including President Bill Clinton, who as a teenager famously was filmed shaking hands with then-President Jack Kennedy. Later, Ron would become student body president at Arizona State University.

With his oratory and political interests, Ron reminded Inga of Jack, which may be why she made the astonishing decision to tell Ron that she "had always loved Kennedy," adding the jaw-dropping bombshell that Kennedy might be his father. Ron, who was in college at the time, said this revelation "blew my head right off," although he discounted the possibility it was true, given that he bore a clear physical resemblance to McCoy and virtually none to Kennedy.

Ron did not believe that his mother thought it true either. He later speculated that Inga had been in a particularly wistful mood that day, just a few years after Jack's death. She had told Jack so many times that she wished to have his children that perhaps it remained a recurring daydream and her disclosure to Ron a form of "wish fulfillment," he said. Also, Ron mused, by connecting him with Kennedy, perhaps Inga hoped to inspire him to pursue what seemed a budding political career. Ron staggered

Terry with this astonishing disclosure, which infuriated Inga. She wished to keep this between her and Ron, but no more was said and the matter was forgotten—for the time being.

Ron did work on Richard Nixon's 1968 campaign but did not pursue a career in politics. Inga had long marveled at how her two sons "couldn't be more different," and hoped as they grew up that they would each appreciate the other's finer points. Interestingly, even though Ron and Terry were "different as night and day," each ended up in careers in education. Ron became a college professor specializing in Native American history, while Terry taught auto mechanics and shop at both the high school and community college levels.

After Terry graduated from high school and went into the air force (he served in Vietnam), Inga was left alone at Los Arcos. She had developed a friendship via mail with the mother of one of Ron's college girlfriends, and they exchanged thoughts on parenting and the passage of time. "Somehow I can't quite get used to the idea that I am starting to live in memories and treasuring them," Inga wrote. "Mother of course did that, but then she seemed so much, much older, and she was. I was born when she was pushing 40 [Olga had actually been thirty-five], but she never seemed old till the last few years."

Inga had been at Olga's side when she died in Los Angeles in November 1965 at the age of eighty-seven. Before she died, Olga wrote to tell Inga that she had "given me all that Life has been worth living for. How much I could never explain." Then she had a message for Ron: "Your Darling Mother has suffered very much which you yet do not understand. I love her with all my heart. She is an angel to me."

Olga did not spell out which sufferings she was talking about. Perhaps she was lamenting Inga's blind spot when it came to men, and how she could never be content if she was not in the company of a man. But Inga also suffered physically. Despite her active life, Inga was fragile. She often wondered if the wandering she and Olga had done while she was a child had worn her out before her time. She was only in her fifties, but was beginning to have the health problems of a much older woman.

Inga took 10 milligrams of prednisone every day for her rheumatoid arthritis, suffered from migraines, and her doctors noted that she "bruised easily." She had hypertension and had suffered a mild stroke in early 1964, just a few months after Kennedy's murder. She suffered from both macular degeneration and cataracts that led to her wearing thick-lens glasses that still could not fully correct her vision. Despite all these ailments, following a thorough examination in 1972 when she was fifty-eight, her doctors declared her to be in "fair health," although they did recommend she stop smoking, which she did not. Still the "odd bird" she had been to classmates in Denmark, Inga used often-exotic cigarette holders, partly because she incorrectly thought they made cigarettes safer to inhale.

With her children grown and her husband on the road most of the year (Tim McCoy had appeared in his last film, *Requiem for a Gunfighter*, in 1965), Inga spent a great deal of time reading. She now also began to contemplate long-form writing. She noted people had urged her to write her autobiography for the past twenty years, and now Inga believed she was ready to do so. "My own life before my marriage and before the children, that's sort of something I sit and look at it like a movie," she said. "I think I could write about it because it would be completely dispassionately [*sic*]."

Inga began making notes for a possible autobiography and wrote letters to old friends to confirm recollections and dates. Her recent visits with Kamal Abdel Nabi and Robert Boothby had stirred old memories. She made inquiries about Paul Fejos, and learned he had died in 1963, leaving his widow (and fifth wife) Lita Binns in charge of the Wenner-Gren Foundation for Anthropological Research.

"It pleased me no end to hear that you are going to write your life's story. And you have something to tell," Lothar Wolff wrote Inga. "I was somewhat disturbed by your statement that you will only say the 'nicest things' about Paul. If this will be the underlying tone of your book it will be neither truthful nor exciting. . . . Therefore, if you are really serious about it and want to make it mean something you should tell it the way it was and not the way you'd have wanted it to be." Sharing the judgment Sheilah Graham made in her critique of Inga as a gossip columnist, Wolff added, "You aren't the vicious type anyway."

Inga never got around to writing the book, and so she wondered what she ought to do with her letters from Jack. She wrote Arthur Krock, who comforted her by telling her that "Kennedy never forgot" about her. Krock suggested she donate Jack's letters to the John F. Kennedy Library that was under development in Boston (the current location opened in 1979), but following an exchange of letters, Inga told Jack's youngest brother, Senator Edward Kennedy, that she had thought it over and decided to leave the letters with her sons, a decision Kennedy said he understood.

With no book, Inga passed on her wisdom through letters to her sons with hope that some might sink in, for as she once noted, "A mother is always a mother, and at times that can be some kind of drawback. They have listened so long to her that I am not even sure they hear all what one says."

Inga hoped Ron and Terry would hear her when she offered advice on finding the right wife, and her advice might have served as her own epitaph. It was all well and good to find a woman who is pretty, Inga said, "but to me it is more important that she is a warm and vibrant person, like a butterfly who still has the dust on the wings, a thing which probably sounds silly to you, but when you grow older you will know what I mean.* Some keep that dust come hell or high water, some never have it, or it rubs off too soon."

Despite her doctors declaring her in "fair health" just the year before, death came quickly for Inga. In the fall of 1973, she could tell something was wrong. A colonoscopy revealed that she had colon cancer, but further tests revealed the cancer had already spread to her liver. She was in intense pain.

Terry came home to care for his mother, but Tim felt obligated to finish the season with Tommy Scott and His Country Caravan. He hoped that Inga would hold on until he could return. In November, he wrote her a final letter. The consummate showman, McCoy paid Inga the ultimate tribute from a performer—that she was a "trouper." He had had a tough show the night before, McCoy said, and it reminded him of a previous summer in the circus when the property boy had failed to show up and Inga had dashed across the back lot and came back carrying

---

* "Dust" on a butterfly's wings are actually the small scales that give their wings vibrant color and, when warmed in the sun, allow the butterfly to fly.

McCoy's lariat, rifle, and property box, "a hell of a load for anyone to carry." Inga had always been "a great trouper in every phase of our life together," McCoy wrote. "Whatever your man was trying to do you were right there with him."

Being "right there" with her man was what Inga had tried to do her entire life, usually to the detriment of her own dreams and aspirations. Nabi, Fejos, Kennedy, Cahan, Boothby, Gunther, and McCoy—she had loved them all in their time, but in varying degrees each of them let her down in some way. They all recognized that Inga was their ideal partner in their quest for greatness. Yet in different ways, they each left her behind when all she wanted to be was "right there."

Shortly after the cancer spread, Inga lost her appetite and stopped eating. She died on December 12, 1973, two months past her sixtieth birthday. McCoy had gotten home in time to be by her side. Despite all the thought Inga had given to what it meant to have religious faith, there was no funeral service. When McCoy died five years later, her ashes were interred with his in McCoy's hometown of Saginaw, Michigan.

As she lay dying, she talked to Terry about her regrets in life. To Terry's dismay, she was hard on herself—"she should have done this, she wished she'd done that." She wondered about her place in the afterlife. But most of all, she told Terry, while she had seen a great deal and done a great deal, she wondered what she had accomplished in life.

To the very end, Inga was haunted by her mother's great ambition that she "be something." She had been told all her life that she possessed "an embarrassment of riches," and had qualities that promised greatness. She might have been the "next Pavlova," a peer of Garbo, or another Dorothy Thompson. Perhaps she had too many choices, too many options. She had enjoyed a modicum of success in several fields, but she never seemed to have the desire or made the commitment to become truly outstanding in any single one. Rather than pursue greatness for herself, she was content to be muse and helpmate—or at least *try* to be a helpmate—to men she believed were destined for greatness.

Despite these deathbed second thoughts, Inga understood that success as measured by the world often requires less admirable qualities that she would not indulge. She had admired Jack for having the "sufficient meanness" and "tough hide" to be successful in politics. Inga realized that she was a terrible gossip columnist because she was unwilling to hurt others to further her career. "Heart never brought fame," she said.

But Inga had too great "a gift for happiness" to feel short-changed, and she achieved her primary ambition of a home and children. Along the way, she also helped make a president. Had her relationship with John Kennedy been widely known, Inga might have been famous in life, or at least infamous—and possibly wealthy—but she did not desire notoriety.

In the latter part of the twentieth century, the saying "well-behaved women seldom make history" began appearing on bumper stickers, T-shirts, and coffee mugs. Most do not know this feminist rallying cry was coined by historian Laurel Thatcher Ulrich in an obscure 1976 scholarly article which noted that Puritan women in colonial America received public recognition for their contributions to their family and community only once, during the eulogy read at their funerals. Denied a funeral, this book is Inga's eulogy.

Epilogue

J. Edgar Hoover died May 2, 1972, and Richard Nixon resigned as president on August 9, 1974. These two disparate events combined to foil Jack and Inga's hope that their romance would remain hidden from public view.

Without Hoover, there was no subsequent FBI director with the prestige or inclination to protect Hoover's "Personal and Confidential" files—at least those not destroyed by Helen Gandy. In 1973, Attorney General Elliott Richardson issued a directive that all "inactive" FBI files should be made available to professional historians.

Nixon's Watergate scandal, coupled with disillusionment over how the American government had handled the war in Vietnam, led many to question the veracity and integrity of our nation's leaders. There was a demand for greater transparency in government and greater access to public records. Congress significantly strengthened the Freedom of Information Act in 1974, which led to a burst of new scholarship.

As Watergate unfolded in late 1972 and early 1973, Clay Blair Jr., who had been editor in chief of the *Saturday Evening Post* during the Kennedy administration, said Nixon's scandal made him reconsider the truth behind another presidency and the role he had played in helping develop "the Kennedy mystique." Blair, assisted by his wife, Joan, began to wonder: "Behind the image, what was Jack really like?"

There had been other "exposés" of Kennedy's presidency, such as Victor Lasky's *JFK: The Man and the Myth*, but these tended to focus on Kennedy's supposed political sins. The Blairs, who insisted they went into their project without any preconceived bias, were among the first to focus on Kennedy's personal life, and particularly his youth.

The resulting book, *The Search for JFK*, published in 1976, contained several "earth-shaking" revelations, according to journalist John Judis, including that Kennedy did suffer from Addison's disease, that his behavior during the *PT-109* debacle was more ambiguous than the heroic narrative created by the Kennedy public relations machine, that Arthur Krock was the driving force behind making *Why England Slept* a success, and that Kennedy's philandering was on a far greater scale than previously understood. Also included was his relationship with Inga.

The Blairs were the first to write about Jack and Inga's relationship. As a dozen sources added bits and pieces to the story, in late 1973, ten years after Jack's assassination, the Blairs tried to track down Inga herself, only to learn that she had just recently died. The Blairs reached out to Tim McCoy for an interview, but McCoy demurred because he was too grief stricken and referred the Blairs to their oldest son, Ronald.

Ronald told the Blairs that if Inga were still alive, she would have refused to be interviewed as would he, but still grieving for his mother, Ronald now thought talking about Inga, dead barely a month, would be "like therapy in a sense." Ronald believed he had an agreement with the Blairs that not all of their January 19, 1974, interview would be taped and that he would be allowed to edit that portion of the book manuscript related to his interview. The Blairs later vigorously denied they had agreed to any such conditions.

Ronald was dismayed to learn that the Blairs intended to include in their book his disclosure that Inga had told him of her final tryst with Jack in November 1946, and of the possibility, raised by Inga, that Kennedy was his father. Those revelations caused a stir in the media, but more so within the McCoy household. Ronald's father was "devastated" to learn that Inga hid this intimate encounter with Jack, that she shared with Ronald her anxiety (or possibly hope) that he might have been Jack's son, and that Ronald shared this information with the Blairs. "I am just amazed our relationship survived," Ronald said, but he and his father resumed collaborating on Tim's autobiography and, with Terry's strong encouragement, the relationship healed. It is notable that Ronald, as a college professor, specialized in the history of the Plains Indians, the subject dearest to his father's heart.

Ron threatened the Blairs with litigation, which never occurred, but the damage was done. The tabloids particularly had a field day with the revelation that Ronald might be JFK's "Love Child," as the publication *Midnight* phrased it. The Blairs' decision to include the story of Inga possibly being pregnant by Kennedy is curious because they state in their book that they doubted it was true. "Inga Arvad had a tendency to romanticize her background and associations with the great and near-great," the Blairs wrote, indicating that they had not learned much about Inga, "perhaps Ronald had inherited this trait." Yet when promoting the book, Clay Blair was quoted in one tabloid as stating unequivocally that he believed Ronald was Kennedy's son, adding, "He looks like Jack"—even though Ron did not.*

There were condemnations of the Blairs' book. An editorial in the *Arizona Republic*, coming to the defense of a local resident, labeled the stories about Jack and Inga "dirt on a grave," and added, "to describe [Inga] as a Nazi spy at this late date is absurd . . . [and] is to fly in the face of well-known facts. To tie her alleged espionage to John Fitzgerald Kennedy is disgraceful."

Kennedy is still fondly remembered by the American public, which continues to rate him as a great president even if historians do not. But it is also true that in popular memory he is as often remembered today for his sexual peccadilloes as for establishing the Peace Corp or initiating the moon program.

The idea of the Kennedy presidency as "Camelot" was one extreme, but since the 1970s the pendulum has swung to another extreme so that there has been, in the words of historian Garry Wills, "a good deal of indiscriminate beating up on all things Kennedy." While many of the revelations regarding Kennedy's life and presidency are true and many of the criticisms valid, this revisionism has made Inga an innocent victim, just as she was while being persecuted—not too strong a word, I think—by the FBI.

Inga was no saint. She was a married woman when she began her affair with Jack. Jack was a philanderer—but not with Inga. Between the two of them, there was genuine love.

---

* Clay Blair Jr. died in 1998 and so could not confirm whether he was accurately quoted.

As this book has tried to do, Clay Blair Jr. once laid out the reasons he believed the story of Jack and Inga is "of overriding national interest and historical importance." Had Jack's relationship with Inga become known, Blair noted, he would probably not have become president. As it was, Jack was nearly cashiered out of the navy, the affair led to his transfer to the South Pacific, and the existence of the FBI file on the affair made Jack susceptible to "blackmail" by J. Edgar Hoover and others aware of its contents.

But there is one more reason why the tale of Jack and Inga's romance is both interesting and important. Through his relationship with Inga we see as clearly as we ever may the qualities that made Jack Kennedy such an appealing figure to so many—"the charm that makes birds come out of their trees," the bemusement at human folly, and the sincere desire to create a better world. Historical revisionism can make us forget those qualities when the supposed search for what Jack or any public figure is "really like" is measured only by uncovering negative information. Foibles alone do not define a life any more than a mythology created by a bereaved widow does.

With Inga, Jack was tender, vulnerable, and sentimental. Theirs was a very special relationship that he treasured. Decades after his assassination, as researchers combed through Jack's papers, they discovered a cache of letters he had bundled together from a handful of people who had meant the most to him. These were letters from his parents, Kick, Joe Junior—and Inga. That Jack placed Inga's letters with those of his closest family members is a great testament to the place she held in his heart. Nor is it any wonder that he saved and cherished Inga's letters, for they are full of love and wisdom gleaned from living one of the most extraordinary lives imaginable.*

---

*Inga's letters can be viewed on the John F. Kennedy Library website, while Inga is also slowly popping up in popular culture. In addition to being a character in the Dan Simmons novel *The Crook Factory*, her relationship with Jack is the subject of the Julian Wiles play *Inga Binga*, and the chamber musical *Too Close to the Sun* composed by Scottish rock musician B. A. Robertson, formerly of Mike + the Mechanics.

ACKNOWLEDGMENTS

CREDIT FOR THIS BOOK MUST BEGIN WITH ITS SUBJECT, INGA ARVAD, who so scrupulously saved her correspondence, kept a large file of clippings and photographs, and wrote reminiscences—some in the moment, others years later—of key events in her life. These materials, plus her extensive FBI file, are the stuff biographers' dreams are made of.

Heartfelt thanks go to Inga's two sons, Ronald McCoy and Terence McCoy, who simply could not have been more generous with their time, their candor, and access to the materials in their control. They have long realized what an exceptional woman their mother was and that her story demanded a truthful telling. Never did either suggest censoring any aspect of Inga's life. I hope they find this book worthy of her.

This book relies on the work of many outstanding scholars (all appropriately cited, I hope), but three should be singled out for special appreciation. The first is Nigel Hamilton, one of our finest biographers, who was one of the first to write extensively about Inga and John Kennedy's relationship. Not only was the work done for his *JFK: Reckless Youth* invaluable, I was overwhelmed by his personal kindness in offering suggestions and encouragement. The second is Ilja Luciak, who helped separate myth and reality regarding Axel Wenner-Gren; I look forward to his upcoming biography on "The Electrolux King." Third is the Danish journalist Ann Mariager, author of the only other full biography of Inga, *Inga Arvad: Den Skandaløse Skandinav* ("The Scandalous Scandinavian"). Mariager was able to access a variety of Danish publications and former acquaintances of Inga that I would have missed without her work.

Hopefully, Mariager's book will someday be available in English, but since it is not yet, I am very thankful that Christine Beaulieu did such an outstanding job of translating Mariager's book for me. Christine, and also her mother, Aase Beaulieu, provided valuable insights into Danish character and history, as well as descriptions of Danish sites important to Inga's story. This would be an inferior book without their help.

Special gratitude goes to Page Huidekoper Wilson, Inga's colleague at the *Washington Times-Herald* and as elegant a woman today as she was described seventy-five years ago, who was very kind to invite me into her home and share such vivid recollections of those days. Nogales's resident historian, Axel Holm, who knew Inga while still a lad, shared some very rich memories of his exotic family friend.

Many archivists deserve recognition. This profession attracts unusually dedicated and helpful people, such as Martha Wagner Murphy, Mark Murphy, and their colleagues at the National Archives and Records Administration; and Rick Ewig, Ginny Kilander, Rachael Dreyer, and others at the University of Wyoming's American Heritage Center—I am so proud that my alma mater has such a wonderful archival facility.

Other thanks go to Roslyn Pachoca and her colleagues at the Library of Congress, Mark Mahoney at the Wenner-Gren Foundation, and Rachael Guadagni at the John F. Kennedy Presidential Library. Inga's letters to Kennedy can be viewed on the library's website. A snafu prevented me from accessing some of the papers held at the Massachusetts Historical Society, but I want Brenda Lawson, Dan Hinchen, and Kittle Evenson to know their efforts were still appreciated.

Everywhere I turned, people were happy to help me track down even the smallest thread in Inga's story, including Tonia Britton, deputy clerk of Nevada's Second Judicial District Court; Melissa Hilgendorf, who reviewed David O. Selznick's papers at the University of Texas's Ransom Center; and Katherine Hamilton-Smith, a dear friend and reader of an early draft of the manuscript who sought access to John Gunther's papers at the University of Chicago.

Other dear friends who provided extraordinarily helpful feedback and suggestions that made this a better book include Hank Stern, M. P. Mueller, Rick Thamer, Kristen Lummis, Julia Wallace, Karen Deike, and Gary Conkling. You are wonderful friends!

Of course, there would be no book without my brilliant, hardworking agent, Laura Dail, and my equally superb editor, Keith Wallman.

This is our third book together for Lyons Press, where I continually receive outstanding support. Every author should get to work with such a dedicated team. Added to the "team" for this book is my enthusiastic publicist, Kim Dower, better known as "Kim from LA." With her help, may this book reach a wide audience!

Finally, I wish to acknowledge my family, particularly my children, William and Grace, who no doubt got tired of Dad being behind a close door for so many hours, but they motivate me to do my best. And then there is my wife, Patti. This book is dedicated to her, but I cannot begin to detail what a help she has been with this book as editor, researcher, sounding board, wordsmith, and much more. She deserves a coauthor credit, which she refused. No spouse could provide more loving support than Patti, and she is why I am the luckiest man on Earth.

NOTES

COLLECTIONS CITED

FBI = Records of the Federal Bureau of Investigation; Office of the Director, J. Edgar Hoover; Official and Confidential Files, 1924–1972, Inga Arvad/Mrs. Paul Fejos, Boxes 4–7 (Record entry 435011), National Archives and Records Administration II, College Park, MD

JCBP – Joan and Clay Blair Jr., Papers, Series I, Research Files, 1975–1993, "The Search for JFK," Boxes 37–56, University of Wyoming American Heritage Center, Laramie, WY

JFKL = Papers of John F. Kennedy, Personal Papers, Correspondence, 1933–1960, Friends, Arvad, Inga, John F. Kennedy Library, Boston, MA

RMP = Ronald McCoy Papers

TMP = Tim McCoy Papers, Boxes 1–6, University of Wyoming American Heritage Center, Laramie, WY

TeMP = Terence McCoy Papers

PREFACE

7. "she took it as something to be expected": Peter Kihss, "Finding of Lost Incan Cities Only One of Many Thrills to Wife of Dr. Fejos," *New York World-Telegram*, February 11, 1941, RMP.

7. the "perfect Nordic beauty": Report by C. A. Hardison, January 6, 1942, FBI.

8. "Some people live those lives": Peter Kihss, "Finding of Lost Incan Cities Only One of Many Thrills to Wife of Dr. Fejos," *New York World-Telegram*, February 11, 1941, RMP.

8. the audacity to make up such a character: Nigel Hamilton, *JFK: Reckless Youth*, p. 684.

8. "to have done all that was attributed to her here": Dan Simmons, *The Crook Factory* (Avon Books: New York, 1999), pp. 127–28.

8. "I sort of close the door behind me": Burke Johnson, "Hitler Is History," *Arizona Republic*, January 5, 1969, pp. 42–46.

9. "*the* love of John F. Kennedy's life": Frank Waldrop, "JFK and the Nazi Spy," *Washingtonian Magazine*, April 1975, p. 90.

9. Krock wrote, mimicking Kennedy's famous Boston accent: Arthur Krock to Inga Arvad McCoy, July 12, 1965, RMP.

9. "that makes birds come out of their trees": "Did You Happen to See?" by Inga Arvad, *Washington Times-Herald*, November 27, 1941, p. 2.

10. "the unequalled highway to the White House": Letter from Inga Arvad to John F. Kennedy, February 23, 1942, JFKL.

10. "I'm a firm believer in the power of the woman behind the man": Grace Grether, "Blonde Dynamo Here to Tell about New Selznick Movie," *Salt Lake Tribune*, February 8, 1946, p. 14.

10. "the freest most exhilarating of all feelings": Inga Arvad to John F. Kennedy, undated but believed to be approximately February 9, 1942, JFKL.

10. "ALWAYS [her emphasis] to be attached to some male": Inga Arvad McCoy to Ronald McCoy, March 10, 1969, RMP.

10. Inga was his equal in charisma: Joan Blair and Clay Blair Jr., *The Search for JFK*, p. 160.

10. would have made a remarkable first lady, but . . . : Peter Kihss, "Finding of Lost Incan Cities Only One of Many Thrills to Wife of Dr. Fejos," *New York World-Telegram*, February 11, 1941, RMP.

11. "made every other relationship seem small and artificial": Nigel Hamilton, *JFK: Reckless Youth*, p. 447.

11. "love love more than he loves politics": Richard Norton Smith, *On His Own Terms*, p. 365.

12. "success is merely a great deal of fortuitous accidents": Nigel Hamilton, *JFK: Reckless Youth*, p. 683.

13. "We pay for everything in life": Inga Arvad to John F. Kennedy, January 26, 1942, JFKL.

PROLOGUE

14. "were days of intense physical pain": Doris Kearns Goodwin, *The Fitzgeralds and the Kennedys*, p. 735.

14. "deep abrasions and lacerations of the entire body": Edward J. Renehan Jr., *The Kennedys at War*, p. 270.

14. walking with a pronounced limp: Nigel Hamilton, *JFK: Reckless Youth*, p. 606.

15. scolded Joseph P. Kennedy Jr.: Nigel Hamilton, *JFK: Reckless Youth*, p. 659.

15. "was only a kid" of nineteen: Joan Blair and Clay Blair Jr., *The Search for JFK*, p. 320.

15. "might have been able to save those other two": Nigel Hamilton, *JFK: Reckless Youth*, p. 606.

15. since his arrival in the South Pacific: Joan Blair and Clay Blair Jr., *The Search for JFK*, pp. 319–21.

15. "and have got another boat": David Pitts, *Jack and Lem*, p. 99.

16. "when Inga walked out of my life": Nigel Hamilton, *JFK: Reckless Youth*, p. 614.

16. "a fungus that grows in your ears": John F. Kennedy to Inga Arvad, undated but April 1943, RMP.

17. "I know mine would": John F. Kennedy to Inga Arvad, undated but ca April 1943, RMP.

17. "but you're one I still have": John F. Kennedy to Inga Arvad, undated but ca April 1943, RMP.

17. "be there with blood in my eye": John F. Kennedy to Inga Arvad, undated but ca April 1943, RMP.

18. "Hoover had put a microphone under the mattress!": Nigel Hamilton, *JFK: Reckless Youth*, p. 489.

18. "over the break-fast table": John F. Kennedy to Inga Arvad, undated but ca September 1943, RMP.

19. "rather spoils the whole thing for me": David Pitts, *Jack and Lem*, p. 99.

20. "an extremely bright twenty-six years": John F. Kennedy to Inga Arvad, undated but ca September 1943, RMP.

CHAPTER 1

22. "before, or after, ever did her justice": Doris Kearns Goodwin, *The Fitzgeralds and the Kennedys*, p. 630.

22. "graceful as those of a dancer": Muriel Lewis, "The Dragon Hunters of Komod [*sic*]: A Sea King's Daughter from Over the Sea," contained in Report by W. H. Welch, April 8, 1942, FBI.

23. Graduate School of Journalism at Columbia University: Ann Mariager, *Inga Arvad*, pp. 134–35.

23. "Like a lot of icing on the cake": Nigel Hamilton, *JFK: Reckless Youth*, p. 434.

23. "the most beautiful & luscious blonde ever known": John Gunther to Inga Arvad, April 18, 1947, RMP.

23. "glowed with health and joy," Waldrop said: Frank Waldrop, "JFK and the Nazi Spy," *Washingtonian Magazine*, April 1975, p. 90.

23. "down to earth and utterly devoid of vanity": "State Balls" from undated and untitled news article, by Muriel Lewis, included in Report by W. H. Welch, April 8, 1942; "down to earth" from Tim McCoy and Ronald McCoy, *Tim McCoy Remembers the West*, p. 260.

23. "warm laugh, she was vivid, lively, quick": Ann Mariager, *Inga Arvad*, p. 151.

24. "an internal gift for happiness," Huidekoper said: Page Huidekoper Wilson interview, JCBP.

24. "that living is a great and glorious experience": Inga Arvad to Ronald McCoy, August 12, 1959, RMP.

24. "she'd *done* so much, been *involved* in so much": Nigel Hamilton, *JFK: Reckless Youth*, p. 685.

25. "as only countesses in Oscar Wilde's plays do": Steve Hauck, "The Beauty Queen Who Interviewed Hitler," Carmel-by-the-Sea *Pine Cone*, October 7, 1971, p. 21.

25. two individuals entwined in one conversation: Malcolm Gladwell, *The Tipping Point*, pp. 83–84.

25. "I'm very fond of human beings": Report by W. H. Welch, April 8, 1942, FBI.

25. "being in her presence increased their own worth": Terrence McCoy interview with author, June 19, 2015.

25. was full of fascinating tales and insights: Report by W. H. Welch, April 8, 1942, FBI.

25. "She could understand different points of view": Joan Blair and Clay Blair Jr., *The Search for JFK*, p. 157.

CHAPTER 2

27. as her husband was a naturalized American citizen: Report by M. M. Cummins, June 7, 1941, FBI.

28. Fejos intended to find them: John W. Dodds, *The Several Lives of Paul Fejos*, p. 70.

28. she told a reporter, "and so do I": Peter Kihss, "Finding of Lost Incan Cities Only One of Many Thrills to Wife of Dr. Fejos," *New York World-Telegram*, February 11, 1941, RMP.

28. "it is not popular to speak German in public": Inga Arvad diary, March 18, 1941, RMP. Inga kept a very short-lived diary, perhaps as a class assignment while at Columbia. Sadly, it covers only a few days.

29. than any other American except President Roosevelt: Gioia Diliberto, *Debutante: The Story of Brenda Frazier*, p. 101.

29. "walk around naked in the sunshine!": Ann Mariager, *Inga Arvad*, p. 124.

29. "she has bewitching evening clothes": Ann Mariager, *Inga Arvad*, p. 125.

29. "but [a] talented business woman": Ann Mariager, *Inga Arvad*, p. 128.

30. an informant for the Bureau: Percy Foxworth to J. Edgar Hoover, December 23, 1941, FBI.

31. "five Negro servants": Ann Mariager, *Inga Arvad*, pp. 129–30.

31. "but as a method of expression": Hamilton Sanger to Inga Arvad, undated, ca 1930, RMP.

31. "fancy to display itself in the form of sauciness": Hamilton Sanger to Inga Arvad, undated, ca 1930, RMP.

31. "Fejos in the middle of the jungle receiving such news": Statement attached to Lothar Wolff letter to L. B. Nichols, July 5, 1944, FBI.

CHAPTER 3

32. she could fly to Peru and be with her husband: Percy Foxworth to J. Edgar Hoover, October 29, 1942, FBI.

32. which she attended briefly at age sixteen: "Graduate School of Journalism at Columbia University, Class of 1940–41" brochure, RMP.

33. "one of the best families in Copenhagen": Report by E. J. Zack, February 14, 1942, FBI.

33. "'She doesn't need to'": Ann Mariager, *Inga Arvad*, pp. 135–36.

33. "[her] energy and will power" into her schoolwork: Ann Mariager, *Inga Arvad*, p. 135.

34. an inscribed photo set in an expensive silver frame: Ann Mariager, *Inga Arvad*, p. 132.

34. "and maybe we fantasized our way to the rest": Ann Mariager, *Inga Arvad*, p. 137.

34. "obviously pro-Nazi": "John F. Kennedy and the Nazi Spy," MPI Home Video (1991).

35. "gave me the brush off," he acknowledged: Ann Mariager, *Inga Arvad*, p. 135.

36. "However, she feels no bitterness about the seizure of Denmark": Helen Woolsey to the Federal Bureau of Investigation, November 16, 1940, FBI.

36. "feeling that we had been somehow threatened": Helen Woolsey to the Federal Bureau of Investigation, November 16, 1940, FBI.

36. "suspicious of her though without reasonable evidence": Helen Woolsey to the Federal Bureau of Investigation, November 16, 1940, FBI.

37. "if I put myself in their position I would have resented that": Burke Johnson, "Hitler Is History," *Arizona Republic*, January 5, 1969, pp. 42–46.

37. "said much on the subject": Report by M. M. Cummins, June 7, 1941, FBI.

CHAPTER 4

39. she still felt "terribly married": Peter Kihss, "Finding of Lost Incan Cities Only One of Many Thrills to Wife of Dr. Fejos," *New York World-Telegram*, February 11, 1941, RMP.

39. such a "mismatched pair": Ann Mariager, *Inga Arvad*, p. 137.

40. "isn't necessary to squeeze the lemon to the last drop," Olga said: "Olga Arvad's Diary for 1941," FBI.

40. "She must have a blind spot where men are concerned": "Olga Arvad's Diary for 1941," FBI.

40. "It is a sorrowful reward": "Olga Arvad's Diary for 1941," FBI.

40. "stunned with grief and sorrow": "Olga Arvad's Diary for 1941," FBI.

41. proof that the befriended was no bigot: Jordan A. Schwarz, *The Speculator*, p. 9.

41. "jewels . . . and sables mentioned again": Jordan A. Schwarz, *The Speculator*, pp. 172–73.

41. Baruch had given Brokaw a yacht as a gift: Jordan A. Schwarz, *The Speculator*, p. 172.

41. "was as vigorously flirtatious as a man half his age": Sylvia Jukes Morris, *Rage for Fame*, p. 192.

42. "Women were forever finagling introductions to him": Jordan A. Schwarz, *The Speculator*, p. 171.

42. "we could wish to see his profile on a silver dollar": Inga Arvad, "Did You Happen to See?," *Washington Times-Herald*, July 17, 1941, p. 2.

42. assured Inga that she had the talent to "really be somebody": Inga Arvad to Olga Arvad, July 19, 1941, in a report by W. H. Welch, May 6, 1942, FBI.

42. "it won't do any good for him to be so much in love": Inga Arvad to Olga Arvad, July 19, 1941, in a report by W. H. Welch, May 6, 1942, FBI.

43. I was so stupefied by the beauty of this creature that I said I would: Arthur Krock interview, JCBP.

CHAPTER 5

44. "her unforgettable panther-like grace": Amanda Smith, *Newspaper Titan*, p. 5.

44. "the most hated" woman in America, too: Amanda Smith, *Newspaper Titan*, p. 4.

45. "while you were talking to the survivors": John R. White interview, JCBP.

45. "everyone knows everyone else's business": Amanda Smith, *Newspaper Titan*, p. 238.

CHAPTER 6

47. WENNER-GREN DENIES PEACE PARLEYS HERE: "Wenner-Gren Denies Peace Parleys Here," Inga Arvad, *Washington Times-Herald*, June 14, 1941, p. 1.

49. if only there was greater international cooperation: Axel Wenner-Gren, *Call to Reason*, p. 3.

49. Swedish steel that was vital to the German war effort: Stanley Ross, *Axel Wenner-Gren: The Sphinx of Sweden*, News Background, Report No. 27, 1947.

50. implicated either man in the crime: Thom Burnett, Ed., *Conspiracy Encyclopedia: The Encyclopedia of Conspiracy Theories*, p. 271. This volume offers a simple summary of the Oakes murder, which has inspired more than a dozen books, novels, and films.

CHAPTER 7

51. there is no evidence they were ever lovers: Joan Blair and Clay Blair Jr., *The Search for JFK*, pp. 144–45.

52. "troubled with the world conflict?": Report by Agent E. J. Zack, February 14, 1942.

52. no political ambitions or plans to negotiate any peace: Inga Arvad, "Wenner-Gren Denies Peace Parleys Here," *Washington Times-Herald*, June 14, 1941, pp. 1–2.

52. 13,000 ARRESTED, "PLOT" CHARGED: *Washington Times-Herald*, June 14, 1941, p. 1.

53. "none so tore apart families and friendships as this fight": Lynne Olson, *Those Angry Days*, p. xviii.

53. turn Hollywood into a prowar propaganda tool: *Washington Times-Herald*, September 10, 1941, p. 1.

53. "We can't risk our whole freedom, our country, listening to them": *Washington Times-Herald*, September 14, 1941, p. 1.

54. secret bases located all across South America: "Argentina Bares Huge Nazi Army in S. America," *Washington Times-Herald*, September 7, 1941, p. 2-A.

54. within bombing range of the Panama Canal: "Columbia Hunts Nazi Airfields," *Washington Times-Herald*, September 13, 1941, p. 1.

55. doubled since the beginning of 1940: David Brinkley, *Washington Goes to War*, p. 106.

CHAPTER 8

57. "She had just the right tone": Frank Waldrop interview, JCBP.

58. "Inga earned her pay every day": Frank Waldrop, "JFK and the Nazi Spy," *Washingtonian Magazine*, April 1975, p. 90.

58. "like a hen mother guarding her chicks": Inga Arvad, "Did You Happen to See?" *Washington Times-Herald*, July 2, 1941, p. 2.

58. a pretty, globe-trotting "air-hostess": Inga Arvad, "Did You Happen to See?" *Washington Times-Herald*, July 4, 1941, p. 2.

58. "after all, a woman's logical place": Inga Arvad, "Did You Happen to See?" *Washington Times-Herald*, August 21, 1941, p. 2.

59. "like a little boy trying to be awfully good": Inga Arvad, "Did You Happen to See?" *Washington Times-Herald*, July 9, 1941, p. 2.

59. "or like a Great Dane puppy": Inga Arvad, "Did You Happen to See?" *Washington Times-Herald*, September 12, 1941, p. 2.

59. "it is so—oh, so Spanish": Inga Arvad, "Did You Happen to See?" *Washington Times-Herald*, August 9, 1941, p. 2.

59. "Or is that too flippant?": Inga Arvad, "Did You Happen to See?" *Washington Times-Herald*, August 9, 1941, p. 2.

60. in the history of the University of Tennessee: Inga Arvad, "Did You Happen to See?" *Washington Times-Herald*, December 24, 1941, p. 2.

60. "man who paddles around in a pot of honey": Inga Arvad, "Did You Happen to See?" *Washington Times-Herald*, April 14, 1942, p. 2.

60. as "a Stevenson with balls": Dallek, *An Unfinished Life*, p. 259.

60. "walks into the hearts of people with wooden shoes on": Ann Mariager, *Inga Arvad*, p. 151.

60. "She was adorable, just adorable": Nigel Hamilton, *JFK: Reckless Youth*, p. 434.

61. "your article was perfectly fine": Clyde Tolson to Inga Arvad, January 31, 1942, RMP.

61. "fine aide to his famous boss, J. Edgar Hoover": Inga Arvad, "Did You Happen to See?" *Washington Times-Herald*, October 30, 1941, p. 2.

61. "every man here would go out and fight for her": Inga Arvad, "Did You Happen to See?" *Washington Times-Herald*, September 18, 1941, p. 2.

61. "in an improper light": Memorandum L. B. Nichols to Mr. Tolson, December 13, 1941, FBI.

63. "a lot of pull at the *Times-Herald*": Memorandum L. B. Nichols to Mr. Tolson, December 13, 1941, FBI.

63. or else they, too, were "working under orders": Memorandum L. B. Nichols to Mr. Tolson, November 14, 1941, FBI.

CHAPTER 9

64. "What are you, our staff procurer?": Frank Waldrop interview, JCBP.

65. in a city getting less elderly and less staid by the day: Nigel Hamilton, *JFK: Reckless Youth*, p. 421.

65. "if you tried to get someone off by yourself": Page Huidekoper Wilson interview, JCBP.

66. fifteen thousand more VD cases in the district than that: David Brinkley, *Washington Goes to War*, p. 75.

66. would not say the word *sex* out loud: Laurence Leamer, *The Kennedy Women*, p. 318.

67. prohibited two girls from ever being alone together: Lynne McTaggart, *Kathleen Kennedy*, p. 17.

67. "Dukie Wookie": Lynne McTaggart, *Kathleen Kennedy*, p. 33.

67. "'A roll in bed with strawberry jaaahm'": Lynne McTaggart, *Kathleen Kennedy*, p. 34.

68. her exuberance brought him out of his shell: Lynne McTaggart, *Kathleen Kennedy*, p. 45.

69. "carefully wrapped up inside a paper sack": Frank Waldrop interview, JCBP.

69. "Stoppa the bus! Stoppa the bus!": Lynne McTaggart, *Kathleen Kennedy*, p. 62.

CHAPTER 10

70. "I always knew she loved me": Barbara Leaming, *Jack Kennedy: The Education of a Statesman*, p. 18.

70. "so close at times I thought of them as twins": Doris Kearns Goodwin, *The Fitzgeralds and the Kennedys*, p. 482.

70. "furnish most of her laughs in the Convent": Laurence Leamer, *The Kennedy Women*, p. 200.

71. "a good impression on Kick": Lynne McTaggart, *Kathleen Kennedy*, p. 11.

71. "Super, super": Inga Arvad memoir, "Kennedy 1941–42," RMP.

72. "exuding animal magnetism": Inga Arvad memoir, "Kennedy 1941–42," RMP.

72. "If I don't, it will look quite bad": Robert Dallek, *An Unfinished Life*, p. 81.

CHAPTER 11

74. "She was totally woman": Nigel Hamilton, *JFK: Reckless Youth*, p. 434.

74. "Join at end": Doris Kearns Goodwin, *The Fitzgeralds and the Kennedys*, p. 630.

75. "some older, marvelous practitioner": Doris Kearns Goodwin, *The Fitzgeralds and the Kennedys*, p. 630.

75. "I'll be happy to teach him," she said: Nigel Hamilton, *JFK: Reckless Youth*, p. 423.

75. "the old mistress for the young boy": Nigel Hamilton, *JFK: Reckless Youth*, p. 435.

75. on two hands, with fingers left over: Ron McCoy interview with the author, April 9, 2015.

76. "You know that women can never trust them": Lynne McTaggart, *Kathleen Kennedy*, p. 62.

77. "But I wouldn't trust him as a long-term companion, obviously": Nigel Hamilton, *JFK: Reckless Youth*, p. 423.

77. "with a naïve, spirited person like this": Joan Blair and Clay Blair Jr., *The Search for JFK*, 151.

77. Inga enthusiastically followed orders: Inga Arvad Memoir, "Kennedy 1941–42," RMP.

79. astonishingly objective for so young a man: Inga Arvad, "Did You Happen to See?" *Washington Times-Herald*, November 27, 1941, p. 2.

CHAPTER 12

81. in the Far East with her husband, Paul Fejos: Muriel Lewis, "The Dragon Hunters of Komod [*sic*], A Sea Daughter from Over the Sea," contained in Report by W. H. Welch, April 8, 1942, FBI.

81. "that as an *embarrass de richesse*": Muriel Lewis, "The Dragon Hunters of Komod [*sic*], A Sea Daughter from Over the Sea," contained in Report by W. H. Welch, April 8, 1942, FBI.

81. "I never look back," she said: Muriel Lewis, "The Dragon Hunters of Komod [*sic*], A Sea Daughter from Over the Sea," contained in Report by W. H. Welch, April 8, 1942, FBI.

82. "I was taken aback": Inga Arvad to John Kennedy, January 20, 1942, JFKL.

82. an odd distinction: Muriel Lewis, "The Dragon Hunters of Komod [*sic*], A Sea Daughter from Over the Sea," contained in Report by W. H. Welch, April 8, 1942, FBI.

82. "get me the corner seat": Muriel Lewis, "The Dragon Hunters of Komod [*sic*], A Sea Daughter from Over the Sea," contained in Report by W. H. Welch, April 8, 1942, FBI.

83. "she was so in love with Dad": Inga Arvad to John Kennedy, January 20, 1942, JFKL.

83. "in the happy life of the moors of Denmark": Inga Arvad to John Kennedy, January 20, 1942, JFKL.

84. "to change, to rise, has been left out": Judith Thurman, *Isak Dinesen*, p. 48.

84. "love at first sight": Inga Arvad to John Kennedy, January 20, 1942, JFKL.

84. other ambitions for Olga and refused: Inga Arvad to John Kennedy, January 20, 1942, JFKL.

85. equally shared by men and women: Judith Thurman, *Isak Dinesen*, p. 62.

86. being stuck with a dirty diaper pin: Ann Mariager, *Inga Arvad*, p. 25.

86. Arvad was a Petersen family name: Ann Mariager, *Inga Arvad*, p. 26.

86. "threw mother's new fountain pen on the floor": Inga Arvad to John Kennedy, January 20, 1942, JFKL.

86. "not much, but it's something": Inga Arvad McCoy to Ronald McCoy, March 10, 1969, RMP.

87. dressed "all in black," and crying: Inga Arvad to John Kennedy, January 20, 1942, JFKL.

87. "I told her, 'Don't cry, you have got me'": Inga Arvad McCoy to Ronald McCoy, March 10, 1969, RMP.

CHAPTER 13

88. GATWICK RACING—LATE WIRE: Paul Fussell, *The Great War and Modern Memory*, p. 86.

90. feature of every ensuing summer vacation: Ann Mariager, *Inga Arvad*, p. 28.

90. "at least that's how the talk went": Ann Mariager, *Inga Arvad*, p. 30.

92. the legendary Russian ballerina: Inga Arvad to John Kennedy, January 20, 1942, JFKL.

CHAPTER 14

94. "they will just lie down and die of shame": Inga Arvad memoir, "Beauty Queen 1931," RMP.

94. between the ages of sixteen and twenty-five: Ann Mariager, *Inga Arvad*, p. 12.

94. as she glances over her shoulder: Ann Mariager, *Inga Arvad*, p. 12.

94. "to the point of departure," Inga recalled: Inga Arvad memoir, "Beauty Queen 1931," RMP.

94. only to appear "lovely": Ann Mariager, *Inga Arvad*, p. 13.

96. "into the promised riches of filmdom": Ann Mariager, *Inga Arvad*, p. 15.

96. "bewitching and fine": Ann Mariager, *Inga Arvad*, p. 17.

96. farm girl than of a worldly sophisticate: Ann Mariager, *Inga Arvad*, p. 19.

96. opportunities she declined: Inga Arvad memoir, "Beauty Queen 1931," RMP

97. "all this luxury and constant festivity . . . boring": Ann Mariager, *Inga Arvad*, p. 34.

CHAPTER 15

98. and ignored the rule: Inga Arvad memoir, "Kamal, 1931," RMP.

99. "more bohemian," Inga recalled: Inga Arvad memoir, "Kamal, 1931," RMP.

100. "I was ill at ease": Inga Arvad memoir, "Kamal, 1931," RMP.

101. "and married life started": Inga Arvad memoir, "Kamal, 1931," RMP.

101. "I hated it": Inga Arvad, biographical notes in own hand, untitled and undated, RMP.

101. "we can always put it in the bathroom": Inga Arvad, biographical notes in own hand, untitled and undated, RMP.

101. "from one extravaganza to the other": Inga Arvad memoir, "Kamal, 1931," RMP.

102. postcoital snack in the kitchen: Inga Arvad, biographical notes in own hand, untitled and undated, RMP.

102. "we hadn't gone off the gold standard yet": Inga Arvad memoir, "Kamal, 1931," RMP.

102. "It was too different, too foreign," she said: Inga Arvad memoir, "Kamal, 1931," RMP.

103. "cash to pay for the resoling of a pair of shoes": Inga Arvad memoir, "Kamal, 1931," RMP.

CHAPTER 16

104. "by committing such a blunder": Ann Mariager, *Inga Arvad*, p. 36.

104. "an empty life [that] simply isn't bearable": Ann Mariager, *Inga Arvad*, pp. 36 and 38.

105. better and often worse than animals: Ann Mariager, *Inga Arvad*, p. 36.

105. "Southern Negro of our cotton plantations": Alfred Pearce Dennis, "The Land of Egypt: A Narrow Green Strip of Fertility Stretching for a Thousand Miles through Walls of Desert," *National Geographic*, March 1926, Vol. 49, No. 3, p. 289.

105. "and West is West": Ann Mariager, *Inga Arvad*, p. 38.

106. "they will obtain a far better result": Kamal Abdel-Nabi to Inga Arvad, dated only "the 7th," ca 1932, RMP.

106. "regular criticism of the social order in Egypt": Kamal Abdel-Nabi to Inga Arvad, dated only "the 7th," ca 1932, RMP.

106. she never mailed the card: Ann Mariager, *Inga Arvad*, p. 36.

106. to get out of Egypt: Inga Arvad memoir, "Kamal, 1931," RMP.

107. "had I to give up everything": Kamal Abdel-Nabi to Inga Arvad, undated, ca 1933, RMP.

107. ambassadors, had another wife: Inga Arvad memoir, "Kamal, 1931," RMP.

107. "be capable of fitting in everywhere": Ann Mariager, *Inga Arvad*, p. 38.

CHAPTER 17

109. Bauder believed would be easier to market globally: Ann Mariager, *Inga Arvad*, p. 39.

109. Chaplin had declared a "genius": John W. Dodds, *The Several Lives of Paul Fejos*, p. 35.

109. "anything so prosaic as facts": John Wakeman, ed., *World Film Directors*, p. 315.

110. "to be more interesting than accurate": John Wakeman, ed., *World Film Directors*, p. 315.

110. innovative productions of Shakespeare: John Wakeman, ed., *World Film Directors*, p. 316.

111. Molnar's play *The Glass Slipper*: John Wakeman, ed., *World Film Directors*, p. 316.

111. "closer to painting than the theater": John Wakeman, ed., *World Film Directors*, p. 315.

111. "'You are either crazy or you're a genius!'": John W. Dodds, *The Several Lives of Paul Fejos*, p. 28.

112. Hale's usual salary was $5,000 per week: John Wakeman, ed., *World Film Directors*, p. 316.

112. "the most difficult thing is to live alone": *Lonesome: A Film by Paul Fejos*, The Criterion Collection, 2012.

113. "I had fallen out of love with Hollywood": John W. Dodds, *The Several Lives of Paul Fejos*, pp. 48 and 46.

113. "his favorite girls were always young": John W. Dodds, *The Several Lives of Paul Fejos*, p. 50.

113. "showered it with roses": John Wakeman, ed., *World Film Directors*, p. 317.

CHAPTER 18

114. "who auditioned me that same day": Ann Mariager, *Inga Arvad*, p. 41.

115. "phases of the moon as well as the time of day": John W. Dodds, *The Several Lives of Paul Fejos*, p. 52.

115. "young, immature, and too frivolous": Report by Joseph M. Kelly, March 16, 1945, FBI.

115. "we tore out each other's hair" during filming: Peter Kihss, "Finding of Lost Incan Cities Only One of Many Thrills to Wife of Dr. Fejos," *New York World-Telegram*, February 11, 1941, RMP.

115. "spent a great deal of his time in the Arvad home": Statement attached to letter from Lothar Wolff to L. B. Nichols, July 5, 1944, FBI.

116. "the one I've played in my private life": Ann Mariager, *Inga Arvad*, p. 42.

116. "But the artist does also come from nature": Ann Mariager, *Inga Arvad*, p. 43.

116. "headstrong" prima donna: Statement attached to letter from Lothar Wolff to L. B. Nichols, July 5, 1944, FBI.

116. natural charm came through in the film: Ann Mariager, *Inga Arvad*, p. 46.

117. according to one critic: Ann Mariager, *Inga Arvad*, p. 44.

117. gushed that Fejos "can do everything": Ann Mariager, *Inga Arvad*, p. 48.

117. travel to Paris to make films: Ann Mariager, *Inga Arvad*, p. 47.

CHAPTER 19

120. "There was no question but that she had a hold on him": Nigel Hamilton, *JFK: Reckless Youth*, p. 456.

121. "She liked being with Jack; he amused her": Nigel Hamilton, *JFK: Reckless Youth*, pp. 684–85.

121. *Times-Herald* editor Frank Waldrop said: Nigel Hamilton, *JFK: Reckless Youth*, p. 434.

121. "You're just the sweetest thing in the world": Memorandum G. C. Burton to Mr. Ladd, February 3, 1942, FBI.

122. "Absence does not make the heart grow fonder": ARV Summary, February 2, 1942, FBI.

122. it was "his idea of manliness": Robert Dallek, *An Unfinished Life*, p. 24.

122. "sharing in the excitement she generated": Rose Fitzgerald Kennedy, *Times to Remember*, p. 187.

122. "Or just a better actress than I was?": Garry Wills, *The Kennedy Imprisonment*, p. 41.

123. Joe was sixty at the time: David Nasaw, *The Patriarch*, p. 611.

123. "and they were absolutely serious": Doris Kearns Goodwin, *The Fitzgeralds and the Kennedys*, p. 724.

123. "leave your children alone": Doris Kearns Goodwin, *The Fitzgeralds and the Kennedys*, p. 353.

124. never told him that she loved him: Geoffrey Perret, *Jack*, p. 19.

124. blamed her religious piety for being that way: Robert Dallek, *An Unfinished Life*, p. 70.

124. "He wasn't in it for the cuddling": Robert Dallek, *An Unfinished Life*, p. 151.

124. Truman or Eisenhower: Michael O'Brien, *John F. Kennedy: A Biography*, p. 577.

124. "little empathy for the trained intelligent woman": Michael O'Brien, *John F. Kennedy: A Biography*, p. 703.

125. "You see, I haven't any time": Margaret L. Coit oral history, June 1, 1966, JFKL.

125. seventeen-year-old Jack reported to his roommate: Robert Dallek, *An Unfinished Life*, pp. 74–75.

125. "I'm not that kind of boy": David Pitts, *Jack and Lem*, p. 22.

126. "pro football quarterback than president": Joan Blair and Clay Blair Jr., *The Search for JFK*, p. 589.

126. request a photograph of him: Doris Kearns Goodwin, *The Fitzgeralds and the Kennedys*, p. 311.

126. "It must be my personality": Robert Dallek, *An Unfinished Life*, p. 45.

127. "a step in the right direction": Robert Dallek, *An Unfinished Life*, p. 46.

127. "I get terrible headaches": Richard Reeves, *President Kennedy: Profile of Power*, p. 290.

127. "It was a lovely time": Nigel Hamilton, *JFK: Reckless Youth*, p. 434.

CHAPTER 20

129. "an incomprehensible game to a Dane": Inga Arvad memoir, "Kennedy 1941–42," RMP.

130. "you can be my manager": Inga Arvad memoir, "Kennedy 1941–42," RMP.

130. "take all the scholastic honors": Doris Kearns Goodwin, *The Fitzgeralds and the Kennedys*, p. 262.

130. "would break into radiant smiles": Doris Kearns Goodwin, *The Fitzgeralds and the Kennedys*, pp. 351–52.

131. better than Joe at anything: Barbara Leaming, *Jack Kennedy: The Education of a Statesman*, p. 18.

131. "tied up with young Joe": Robert Dallek, *An Unfinished Life*, p. 107.

131. "Why don't you get a live one?": Robert Dallek, *An Unfinished Life*, p. 37.

131. "but it was a problem in my boyhood": Robert Dallek, *An Unfinished Life*, p. 28.

131. "I'm not bright like my brother Joe": Herbert S. Parmet, *Jack: The Struggles of John F. Kennedy*, p. 44.

132. Rose Kennedy acknowledged "distressed me": Rose Fitzgerald Kennedy, *Times to Remember*, p. 94.

133. "part of their normal work in their final year": Robert Dallek, *An Unfinished Life*, p. 64.

134. for he did not believe in "fidelity": Nigel Hamilton, *JFK: Reckless Youth*, p. 404.

134. "but maybe a tiny hope was gleaming": Inga Arvad memoir, "Kennedy 1941–42," RMP.

135. "sprinkled with good-natured gossip": Inga Arvad, "The Story," undated ca 1945/ 46, RMP.

137. "checking off names in a book": Interview with John R. White, JCBP.

137. "will divorce her present husband": Memorandum from C. H. Carson to Mr. Ladd, January 1, 1942, FBI.

CHAPTER 21

139. "American government made no effort to deny it": Institute for Historical Review, retrieved July 23, 2015, from http://www.ihr.org/jhr/v08/v08p389_Hitler.html.

140. in prosecuting anyone for the leak: Amanda Smith, *Newspaper Titan*, p. 395.

140. "personally responsible for Pearl Harbor": Frank Waldrop interview, JCBP.

141. "flashed as never before," Waldrop recalled: Frank C. Waldrop, "JFK and the Nazi Spy," *Washingtonian Magazine*, April 1975, p. 90.

141. government prosecution (though no one ever did): Amanda Smith, *Newspaper Titan*, p. 400.

141. 'treasonableness,' Waldrop said: Frank Waldrop interview, JCBP.

141. flak towers in the trees of Potomac Park: Frank C. Waldrop, "JFK and the Nazi Spy," *Washingtonian Magazine*, April 1975, p. 90.

142. private box during the 1936 Berlin Olympics: Page Huidekoper Wilson interview by author, February 22, 2015, Washington, D.C.

142. to senior Nazi officials in Germany: Page Huidekoper Wilson interview by author, February 22, 2015, Washington, D.C.

142. "that Arvad was a spy": Memorandum L. B. Nichols to Mr. Tolson, December 13, 1941, FBI.

142. "do you think it is possible Inga could be a spy?": Page Huidekoper Wilson interview by author, February 22, 2015, Washington, D.C.

143. "I was with Hitler in his box": Inga Arvad memoir, "Consequences," undated, RMP.

143. "I hear this all the time": Doris Kearns Goodwin, *The Fitzgeralds and the Kennedys*, p. 632.

143. an officer assigned to Naval Intelligence: Inga Arvad memoir, "Consequences," undated, RMP.

143. "as long as Mr. Baruch asked her for dinner": Frank Waldrop, "JFK and the Nazi Spy," *Washingtonian Magazine*, April 1975, p. 91.

144. Ladenburg's conversations with Baruch: Joseph Alsop, "Eleanor and Franklin Roosevelt Go Their Own Ways," *Pittsburgh Press*, January 26, 1982, p. B1.

144. could not be resolved internally at the *Times-Herald*: Inga Arvad memoir, "Consequences," undated, RMP.

144. and leave the matter in their hands: Amanda Smith, *Newspaper Titan*, p. 403.

145. "That's where I made my first mistake": Inga Arvad memoir, "Consequences," undated, RMP.

145. "this young lady is a Nazi spy. Good afternoon!": Ann Mariager, *Inga Arvad*, p. 169.

CHAPTER 22

146. "in the act of stealing a Gorgonzola cheese": Inga Arvad memoir, "Consequences," undated, RMP.

146. that the truth was that Inga was innocent: Memorandum S. K. McKee to the Director, December 12, 1941, FBI.

146. turn it over to the FBI: Memorandum S. K. McKee to the Director, December 12, 1941, FBI.

147. who wrote it in his report as "Wintergreen": Memorandum S. K. McKee to the Director, December 12, 1941, FBI.

147. "harassed her until her career was ruined": Memorandum S. K. McKee to the Director, December 12, 1941, FBI.

147. "with prominent persons in the United States": Memorandum S. K. McKee to the Director, December 12, 1941, FBI.

148. "they were cunning and clever in many respects": Memorandum S. K. McKee to the Director, December 12, 1941, FBI.

148. "you are not arrested that will prove that you are all right": Memorandum S. K. McKee to the Director, December 12, 1941, FBI.

148. "I had all of the FBI trailing me," Inga said: Inga Arvad memoir, "Consequences," undated, RMP.

149. "[her friend in the morgue] had in mind": Report by C. A. Hardison, January 6, 1942, FBI.

149. "perfect Nordic beauty": Report by C. A. Hardison, January 6, 1942, FBI.

CHAPTER 23

152. cinematic geniuses such as Fritz Lang and F. W. Murnau: Rory MacLean, *Berlin: Portrait of a City through the Centuries*, p. 203.

153. "arguably the most popular head of state in the world": Ian Kershaw, *Hitler: Hubris*, p. xxix.

153. unemployment rate was less than 5 percent: William Shirer, *The Rise and Fall of the Third Reich*, p. 231.

155. "that is always nice," Inga wrote to Olga: Ann Mariager, *Inga Arvad*, p. 53.

155. renowned female sculptor Renée Sintenis: Ann Mariager, *Inga Arvad*, p. 52.

155. the kind of interview" that she wanted to do: Ann Mariager, *Inga Arvad*, p. 52.

CHAPTER 24

156. helped facilitate a lively discussion: Inga Arvad memoir, "Sonnemann-Goering," RMP.

156. "it naturally turned to the latter": Inga Arvad memoir "Truth," undated, RMP.

156. mercy of the minister of propaganda: Inga Arvad memoir "Truth," undated, RMP.

156. discovered the affair and threatened divorce: Peter Longerich, *Goebbels: A Biography*, p. 302.

156. "ears stood on edge," Inga recalled: Inga Arvad memoir "Truth," undated, RMP.

157. "the First Lady of the Reich," as Hitler himself noted: Emmy Goering, *My Life with Goering*, p. 60.

157. "You have no credentials": Inga Arvad memoir "Truth," undated, RMP.

158. "I wish that I could be just as wonderful": Inga Arvad memoir "Truth," undated, RMP.

158. "my esteem for him grew with every word": Emmy Goering, *My Life with Goering*, p. 11.

159. "scooped the rest of Europe": Inga Arvad memoir "Truth," undated, RMP.

159. "I wonder if I now, by detours, have ended up on the right shelf?": Ann Mariager, *Inga Arvad*, p. 60.

160. "as a halo that frames her Gretchen-face [*sic*]": Ann Mariager, *Inga Arvad*, p. 63.

161. decorating Berlin's spring: Ann Mariager, *Inga Arvad*, pp. 62–63.

161. "I must have real love": Ann Mariager, *Inga Arvad*, p. 65.

162. "it gives me an inner satisfaction": Ann Mariager, *Inga Arvad*, p. 59.

162. "an interview with Adolf Hitler": Inga Arvad memoir "Truth," undated, RMP.

CHAPTER 25

163. "he is also a big personality": Ann Mariager, *Inga Arvad*, pp. 72–73.

163. "every day I kill off a couple of Jews": Ann Mariager, *Inga Arvad*, pp. 72–73.

163. "enthusiastic about the new Germany": Elke Fröhlich, General Editor, *Die Tagebücher von Joseph Goebbels, Teil I Aufzeichmungen 1923–1941, Band 3/I April 1934–February 1936* (K. G. Saur, München, 2005), p. 250 (translated by the author).

164. more sadistic interrogation methods: Inga Arvad memoir, "1935 Von Levetzow-Himmler," RMP.

164. "sounded like a pumpkin, you know": Burke Johnson, "Hitler Is History," *Arizona Republic*, January 5, 1969, pp. 42–46.

164. other signs of Nazi brutishness: Inga Arvad memoir, "1935 Von Levetzow-Himmler," RMP.

165. 'don't talk about it': Burke Johnson, "Hitler Is History," *Arizona Republic*, January 5, 1969, pp. 42–46.

165. "He isn't here anymore": Burke Johnson, "Hitler Is History," *Arizona Republic*, January 5, 1969, pp. 42–46.

165. "not inspire great sorrow": Otto Friedrich, *Before the Deluge*, p. 389.

166. "with all its frustrations and disappointments": William Shirer, *The Rise and Fall of the Third Reich*, p. 231.

167. "race question in marriage," he said: Ann Mariager, *Inga Arvad*, p. 69.

167. "haven't suffered under this as we have": Ann Mariager, *Inga Arvad*, p. 70.

167. gloom were the greatest hardships: Ann Mariager, *Inga Arvad*, p. 70.

168. "bitter, close-minded people": Erik Larson, *In the Garden of Beasts*, p. 106.

168. "bright faced and hopeful": Erik Larson, *In the Garden of Beasts*, p. 106.

168. "isn't life wonderful!": Ann Mariager, *Inga Arvad*, p. 68.

168. "three or six thumbs under the knee": Ann Mariager, *Inga Arvad*, p. 68.

169. "just as well run around the world on one leg": Ann Mariager, *Inga Arvad*, p. 68.

CHAPTER 26

170. "Ask him a question and he makes a speech": Andrew Nagorski, *Hitlerland*, p. 87.

170. "as if he were addressing a large audience": Andrew Nagorski, *Hitlerland*, p. 80.

170. "He couldn't stand anyone who wanted to talk," she said: Andrew Nagorski, *Hitlerland*, p. 37.

171. "as it did his entire political 'world-view'": Ian Kershaw, *Hitler: Hubris*, p. 448.

171. "on more observations about his personality": Andrew Nagorski, *Hitlerland*, p. 26.

172. I bet he crooks his little finger when he drinks his tea: Peter Kurth, *American Cassandra: The Life of Dorothy Thompson*, p. 161.

172. totally subsumed in his public role of "the Führer": Ian Kershaw, *Hitler: Hubris*, p. xxv.

173. "impossible without a feeling of moral outrage": Ian Kershaw, *Hitler: Hubris*, p. 601n.

173. "I just want little things about the Führer": Inga Arvad memoir, "1935 Hitler," RMP.

174. "impossible to sell outside the country—unfortunately": Ann Mariager, *Inga Arvad*, p. 85.

175. "The Führer says you may come over at once": Inga Arvad memoir, "Truth," RMP.

CHAPTER 27

176. statesmen and landscapes of the German countryside: Ann Mariager, *Inga Arvad*, p. 77.

177. Hitler and Inga were alone for the next hour and a half: Nigel Hamilton, *JFK: Reckless Youth*, p. 431.

177. "National Socialism lay the salvation of the world": Nigel Hamilton, *JFK: Reckless Youth*, p. 431.

178. "I also asked him why he wasn't married": Inga Arvad memoir, "Truth," RMP.

178. sentimental man of the people "with his dogs and tea": Despina Stratigakos, *Hitler at Home*, p. 3.

178. "They radiate power": Ann Mariager, *Inga Arvad*, p. 78.

178. "People would stand still [and] turn around": Ann Mariager, *Inga Arvad*, p. 78.

179. "become a speaker people listen to with pleasure": Ann Mariager, *Inga Arvad*, p. 79.

179. "couldn't possibly ask for more as a woman, could you?": Ann Mariager, *Inga Arvad*, p. 80.

179. "Please let me know the next time you come to Berlin": Inga Arvad memoir, "Truth," RMP.

179. "The Führer was thrilled with her," he added: Elke Fröhlich, General Editor, *Die Tagebücher von Joseph Goebbels, Teil I Aufzeichmungen 1923–1941, Band 3/I April 1934– February 1936* (K. G. Saur, München, 2005), p. 313 (translated by the author). The exact phrasing used by Goebbels was *ganz begeistert*, which can have several meanings, including "loved," but in the context presented by Goebbels "thrilled" seems the appropriate meaning.

179. "[Hitler] was even the least bit interested in me as a woman": Inga Arvad memoir, "Truth," RMP.

180. gain access to senior Nazi officials: Ann Mariager, *Inga Arvad*, p. 81.

180. while the Nazis were using Inga for propaganda purposes: Ann Mariager, *Inga Arvad*, p. 81.

181. "a matter of affectation, not emotion," as Ian Kershaw said: Ian Kershaw, *Hitler: Hubris*, p. 352.

181. "neither fish . . . nor fowl, neither fully homosexual nor fully heterosexual": Andrew Nagorski, *Hitlerland*, p. 82.

181. Hitler never did more than kiss her hand: Andrew Nagorski, *Hitlerland*, p. 44.

181. (particularly fond of and good with children): Andrew Nagorski, *Hitlerland*, p. 37.

181. "loved the opportunity to talk in private to Hitler": Charlotte Mosley, Ed., *The Mitfords: Letters Between Six Sisters*, p. 801.

182. "it didn't become anything serious": Ann Mariager, *Inga Arvad*, p. 82.

182. "regards to Miss Arvad's usefulness": Ann Mariager, *Inga Arvad*, p. 81.

CHAPTER 28

184. evenings with Olga, playing cards: Ann Mariager, *Inga Arvad*, p. 47.

184. She begged Olga to "console him well": Ann Mariager, *Inga Arvad*, p. 65.

186. "you'll make it there": John W. Dodds, *The Several Lives of Paul Fejos*, p. 54.

186. "like to work with native people," Fejos responded: John W. Dodds, *The Several Lives of Paul Fejos*, p. 54.

187. where they would live when Fejos returned: John W. Dodds, *The Several Lives of Paul Fejos*, p. 52.

188. "honored her for her 'perfect Nordic beauty'": Report by C. A. Hardison, January 6, 1942, FBI.

188. he could recall nothing about the photo: Report by C. A. Hardison, January 6, 1942, FBI.

189. "busy being just a wife," she said: Inga Arvad memoir, "Truth," RMP.

189. "IRRESPONSIBLE LIES," [her emphasis] she later wrote: Inga Arvad memoir, "Consequences," RMP.

CHAPTER 29

191. "an invention of the Jews and Freemasons": Guy Walters, *Berlin Games*, p. 14.

192. "before it had the satisfactory strength": Inga Arvad memoir, "Truth," RMP.

193. accompany him and join Hitler at the Olympics: Inga Arvad memoir, "Truth," RMP.

193. return to Europe until four months later: John Wakeman, Ed., *World Film Directors*, p. 318.

194. "two Jews stand on the winning podium": Guy Walters, *Berlin Games*, p. 265.

194. "a car stuffed with flowers" as consolation: Guy Walters, *Berlin Games*, p. 269.

194. many of the papers that chose to run it: Inga Arvad memoir, "Truth," RMP.

194. "a great personal friend" of Hermann Göring's wife": Inga Arvad, "Hitler Dreams of a Super-Nation," *Sunday Telegraph*, September 27, 1936, p. 15.

195. (a sentiment shared by few of her fellow reporters): Ann Mariager, *Inga Arvad*, p. 88.

195. "people who deserve the best the world can give them": Guy Walters, *Berlin Games*, p. 296.

195. "married life and the care of their children": Inga Arvad, "Hitler Dreams of a Super-Nation," *Sunday Telegraph*, September 27, 1936, p. 15.

196. "I shall do all I can": Inga Arvad, "Hitler Dreams of a Super-Nation," *Sunday Telegraph*, September 27, 1936, p. 15.

196. "Unfortunately, it doesn't look like I'll ever have the time": Ann Mariager, *Inga Arvad*, p. 90.

CHAPTER 30

197. double agent working *for* the Polish underground: Herlinde Pauer-Studer and J. David Velleman, *Konrad Morgen: The Conscience of a Nazi Judge* (New York: Palgrave MacMillan, 2015), pp. 23–24.

197. "Life is but a stage on which to play": Elizabeth P. McIntosh, *Sisterhood of Spies*, p. 23.

198. "Careless talk costs lives": Elizabeth P. McIntosh, *Sisterhood of Spies*. The poster is reproduced in the book in the photo section between pp. 188 and 189.

198. (leading salon in early nineteenth-century Paris): Inga Arvad memoir, "Spy offer," RMP.

199. "when I heard his voice amble on," Inga said: Inga Arvad memoir, "Spy offer," RMP.

199. "didn't divulge what was going on in my mind": Inga Arvad memoir, "Spy offer," RMP:

199. "anything against your own country," the man assured Inga: Inga Arvad memoir, "Spy offer," RMP.

200. she would soon receive a visit from the Gestapo: Inga Arvad memoir, "Spy offer," RMP.

200. noted the troubled look in his eyes: Inga Arvad memoir, "Spy offer," RMP.

200. "And that was my swan song" in Germany, Inga said: Inga Arvad memoir, "Spy offer," RMP.

CHAPTER 31

205. "my dear child" or "my darling baby of mine": Paul Fejos to Inga Arvad, June 26, 1937, and July 3, 1937, RMP.

205. go away into the jungle for two years: Ann Mariager, *Inga Arvad*, p. 95.

206. then have her return to Denmark: Paul Fejos to Olga Arvad, March 22, 1937, RMP.

206. Fejos happily reported to Olga: Paul Fejos to Olga Arvad, March 22, 1937 (undated handwritten addendum), RMP.

206. "[she] can hit a penny with it like anything": Paul Fejos to Olga Arvad, April 2, 1937, RMP.

206. humiliating exchange with his wife's mother: Paul Fejos to Olga Arvad, April 2, 1937, RMP.

CHAPTER 32

208. Chinese were forced to do: Ann Mariager, *Inga Arvad*, p. 99.

208. made up to supposedly look Chinese: Ann Mariager, *Inga Arvad*, p. 99.

208. "worthwhile somehow": Muriel Lewis, "The Dragon Hunters of Komod [*sic*]: A Sea King's Daughter from over the Sea," undated, contained in a Report Made by W. H. Welch, April 8, 1942, FBI.

208. (now the Indonesian capital of Jakarta): Paul Fejos to Inga Arvad, May 30, 1938, RMP.

209. "He doesn't dare!": Helen Harrison, "Jungle Preferred," *Salt Lake Tribune Sunday Magazine*, April 13, 1941, p. 8.

209. "Bad manners": Tim and Ronald McCoy, *Tim McCoy Remembers the West*, p. 258.

210. "a swiftness to make an elevator envious!": Helen Harrison, "Jungle Preferred," *Salt Lake Tribune Sunday Magazine*, April 13, 1941, p. 8.

210. "a Bond Street tailor might be envious!": Helen Harrison, "Jungle Preferred," *Salt Lake Tribune Sunday Magazine*, April 13, 1941, p. 8.

211. took a lick of the candy and smiled: Inga Fejos memoir, "Peipepteoman," May 6, 1941, RMP.

211. using straw for her blonde hair: Inga Fejos memoir, "Peipepteoman," May 6, 1941, RMP.

212. "sweet on the little stick and liked it": Inga Fejos memoir, "Peipepteoman," May 6, 1941, RMP.

CHAPTER 33

213. plump partridges, adorn the landscape: W. Douglas Burden, "Stalking the Dragon Lizard on the Island of Komodo," *National Geographic Magazine*, August 1927, Vol. 52, No. 2, p. 230.

214. "That is closer to the point," Fejos agreed: Inga Arvad memoir "Ngenakan," undated, RMP.

214. adorning her round arms: Inga Arvad memoir "Ngenakan," undated, RMP.

214. "any Hollywood darling," Inga wrote: Inga Arvad memoir "Ngenakan," undated, RMP.

215. filming was completed and Inga and Fejos left: Inga Arvad memoir "Ngenakan," undated, RMP.

215. "smile to herself and cheer up considerably": Inga Arvad memoir "Ngenakan," undated, RMP.

215. most precious possession, the Chanel No. 5: Inga Arvad memoir "Ngenakan," undated, RMP.

215. "she thought might please the beautiful child": Inga Fejos memoir, "Peipepteoman," May 6, 1941, RMP.

216. "he murmured, 'Darling'": Inga Fejos memoir, "Peipepteoman," May 6, 1941, RMP.

CHAPTER 34

217. "checked by the fear of seeming cheaply fulsome": Muriel Lewis, "The Dragon Hunters of Komod [*sic*]: A Sea King's Daughter from over the Sea," undated, contained in a Report Made by W. H. Welch, April 8, 1942, FBI.

217. but said Fejos had her safety in mind: Muriel Lewis, "The Dragon Hunters of Komod [*sic*]: A Sea King's Daughter from over the Sea," undated, contained in a Report Made by W. H. Welch, April 8, 1942, FBI.

218. "is unimaginable," Fejos wrote Inga: Paul Fejos to Inga Fejos, July 3, 1937, RMP.

218. currents of up to ten knots: Paul Fejos to Inga Fejos, July 9, 1937, RMP.

218. supply of drinking water, were lost: Paul Fejos to Inga Fejos, July 9, 1937, RMP.

218. unpleasant death from dehydration: John W. Dodds, *The Several Lifes of Paul Fejos*, p. 60.

218. lifeboats to pick up Fejos and his men: John W. Dodds, *The Several Lifes of Paul Fejos*, pp. 60–62.

218. Fejos said with his usual understatement: Paul Fejos to Inga Fejos, July 9, 1937, RMP.

218. badminton and cards with a glass of sherry: Ann Mariager, *Inga Arvad*, p. 105.

219. "INCLUDING NEW GUINEA!": Paul Fejos to Inga Fejos, July 9, 1937, RMP.

219. "I have something to say about it": Ann Mariager, *Inga Arvad*, p. 107.

219. "People [here] look just like people in Bangkok": Ann Mariager, *Inga Arvad*, p. 106.

220. "against human dignity to deny or thwart this": Graham Petrie, "The Travels of Paul Fejos," booklet of essays included with the Criterion Collection's DVD of *Lonesome: A Film by Paul Fejos* (2012).

CHAPTER 35

222. "touch the throne of God": Inga Arvad to Jack Kennedy, February 14, 1942, JFKL.

222. "Why do you believe in me?": Inga Arvad to Jack Kennedy, February 14, 1942, JFKL.

222. "That is faith," she said: Inga Arvad to Jack Kennedy, February 14, 1942, JFKL.

222. "a doomsday somewhere, sometime": Inga Arvad to Jack Kennedy, February 14, 1942, JFKL.

223. according to *Time* magazine: "Man of Peace," *Time*, June 29, 1942, p. 30.

223. producing Hollywood films: Peter Harry Brown and Pat H. Broeske, *Howard Hughes: The Untold Story*, pp. 110–11 (For photographs that demonstrate how opulent the boat was, see Robert Maguglin, *Howard Hughes: His Achievements and Legacy: The Authorized Pictorial Biography* (Long Beach, CA: Wrather Port Properties, 1984), p. 60.

224. "Come as you are!": John W. Dodds, *The Several Lifes of Paul Fejos*, p. 63.

224. new frontiers and lost civilizations: Ilja Luciak, from an as-yet-unpublished essay, "The Origins of the Wenner Gren Foundation for Anthropological Research: An Essay on the Complex Friendship Between Paul Fejos and Axel Wenner-Gren," prepared for *Current Anthropology*, 2015.

224. Wenner-Gren would never follow up on: Report by Joseph M. Kelly, March 16, 1945, FBI.

225. "just as it was ready to leap": John W. Dodds, *The Several Lifes of Paul Fejos*, p. 63.

225. "Mr. Wenner-Gren's castle in Sweden": Peter Kihss, "Finding of Lost Incan Cities Only One of Many Thrills to Wife of Dr. Fejos," *New York World-Telegram*, February 11, 1941, RMP.

226. "close to escape had to be shot": Ilja Luciak, from an as-yet-unpublished essay, "The Origins of the Wenner Gren Foundation for Anthropological Research: An Essay on the Complex Friendship Between Paul Fejos and Axel Wenner-Gren," prepared for *Current Anthropology*, 2015.

226. recall the event as it truly happened: Ilja Luciak, from an as-yet-unpublished essay, "The Origins of the Wenner Gren Foundation for Anthropological Research: An Essay

on the Complex Friendship between Paul Fejos and Axel Wenner-Gren," prepared for *Current Anthropology*, 2015.

226. "Hollywood teaches . . . personal sincerity": Muriel Lewis, "The Dragon Hunters of Komod [*sic*]: A Sea King's Daughter from over the Sea," undated, contained in a Report Made by W. H. Welch, April 8, 1942, FBI.

CHAPTER 36

228. continue his discussions with Wenner-Gren: Paul Fejos to Inga Arvad, May 30, 1938, RMP.

229. "but still back to civilization": Paul Fejos to Olga Arvad, October 30, 1940, RMP.

229. "but I miss her unspeakably": Paul Fejos to Olga Arvad, October 30, 1940, RMP.

229. from the war, which it did: Paul Fejos to Olga Arvad, October 30, 1940, RMP.

229. "Peru was not bona fide": FBI report, no author listed, March 1, 1945, FBI.

230. "tempting loot in all the world": Tim Wiener, *Enemies: A History of the FBI*, pp. 98–99.

230. supporting the Allied cause: Tim Wiener, *Enemies: A History of the FBI*, pp. 103 and 108.

230. Wenner-Gren-sponsored expedition was operating: "Argentina Bares Huge Nazi Army in S. America; Probe Claims 500,000 Troops Are Based at Strategic Points," no byline, *Washington Times-Herald*, September 7, 1941, p. 2-A.

230. Fejos, Wenner-Gren, or Inga: John W. Dodds, *The Several Lifes of Paul Fejos*, pp. 70–71.

231. "current or potential, in Latin America": Tim Wiener, *Enemies: A History of the FBI*, p. 98.

231. "was plausible enough as far as it went": "Man of Peace," *Time*, June 29, 1942, p. 31.

CHAPTER 37

232. "my husband works for Wenner-Gren": ARV Summary, Washington, D.C., March 7, 1942, FBI.

232. "as a private intelligence agent": Memorandum from Herbert Wechsler to J. Edgar Hoover, February 26, 1945, FBI.

233. party hosted by Cissy Patterson: Report by Kirby Vosburgh, March 15, 1945, FBI.

233. "never boring in her company": Namn Eftermann, "The Life of Axel Wenner-Gren—An Introduction," Wenner-Gren Internatioanl Symposium, The Wenner-Gren Center, Stockholm, May 30–31, 2012, Official Conference Booklet, p. 16 (Retrieved via http://blog.wennergren.org/wp-content/uploads/2012/08/AW-G-Conference-Book -2012.pdf).

233. "her drinking champagne, my listening": Inga Arvad, biographical notes in own hand, untitled and undated, RMP.

234. Washington to clear his name: Inga Arvad, "MGM," undated screenplay, ca 1945, RMP.

234. common in the 1940s: Author interview with Ronald McCoy, April 9, 2015, and author interview with Terence McCoy, June 19, 2015.

234. Wenner-Gren rejected the idea: Namn Eftermann, "The Life of Axel Wenner-Gren—An Introduction," Wenner-Gren International Symposium, The Wenner-Gren Center, Stockholm, May 30–31, 2012, Official Conference Booklet, p. 14 (Retrieved via http://blog.wennergren.org/wp-content/uploads/2012/08/AW-G-Confer ence-Book -201 2.pdf).

235. "two parents, NOT just one": Inga Arvad to Ronald McCoy, March 10, 1969, RMP.

CHAPTER 38

237. "toilet paper [arc] on a roll," Waldrop said: Amanda Smith, *Newspaper Titan*, p. 401.

237. "harassment, what have you": Nigel Hamilton, *JFK: Reckless Youth*, p. 429.

238. other "law and order" issues: Amanda Smith, *Newspaper Titan*, p. 401.

238. "they did not keep us fully informed": Report by Floyd L. Jones, December 12, 1942, FBI.

238. once she left the *Times-Herald*: Report by Floyd L. Jones, December 12, 1942, FBI.

238. "a Nazi sympathizer": Memorandum (no author) to Clyde Tolson and D. W. Ladd, March 10, 1942, FBI.

239. information she provided: Memorandum G. W. Hymers to D. M. Ladd, February 24, 1945, FBI.

239. "Mr. Hoover would know what she means": Phone message taken by L. B. Nichols for J. Edgar Hoover, December 17, 1941, FBI.

239. "while receiving treatment," Foxworth said: Percy Foxworth to J. Edgar Hoover, December 23, 1941, FBI.

CHAPTER 39

241. "any man in American history": Ovid Demaris, "The Private Life of J. Edgar Hoover," *Esquire*, September 1974, p. 21.

242. "no record of suspected illegal conduct": Athan Theoharis, ed., *From the Secret Files of J. Edgar Hoover*, p. 4.

242. Hoover told Attorney General Francis Biddle: Memorandum J. Edgar Hoover to the Attorney General, January 21, 1942, FBI.

243. "not less frequently than weekly": John Edgar Hoover to S. K. McKee, January 30, 1942, FBI.

244. "utterly unwarranted action": Jean Edward Smith, *FDR*, p. 549.

244. "greatly bothered any wartime President": Jean Edward Smith, *FDR*, pp. 552–53.

245. forwarded by local law enforcement agencies: Tim Weiner, *Enemies: A History of the FBI*, p. 73.

245. and approved his wiretapping plans: Tim Weiner, *Enemies: A History of the FBI*, p. 77.

245. gain entry into the United States: Jay Winik, *1944: FDR and the Year That Changed History*, pp. 218–21.

246. "spying which goes on in our country": Tim Weiner, *Enemies: A History of the FBI*, p. 80.

246. better at generating headlines than results: Raymond J. Batvinis, *Hoover's Secret War Against Axis Spies*, pp. 1–2.

246. an isolationist candidate in 1940: Tim Weiner, *Enemies: A History of the FBI*, p. 87.

247. source of America First's funding: Lynne Olson, *Those Angry Days*, p. 112.

247. that lasted until Hoover's death: Lynne Olson, *Those Angry Days*, p. 112.

CHAPTER 40

249. "nymphomaniac with a good sense of humor": Peter Duffy, *Double Agent*, p. 151.

250. "occupied with cataloging her love life": Peter Duffy, *Double Agent*, p. 151.

250. information on American military secrets: Tim Weiner, *Enemies: A History of the FBI*, p. 92.

250. experience in such matters: Tim Weiner, *Enemies: A History of the FBI*, p. 97.

251. tall as five-foot-eight: Memorandum S. K. McKee to the Director, December 12, 1941, FBI.

251. another said she was slender: Report by E. J. Zack, February 14, 1942, FBI.

251. "figured out between the two of them": Report by W. H. Welch, February 12, 1942, FBI.

252. "of continental, if not German, strain": Report by E. J. Zack, February 14, 1942, FBI.

252. obfuscating her true intentions: Memorandum J. Edgar Hoover to the Attorney General, January 21, 1942, FBI.

253. "colloquialisms and phraseologies": J. Edgar Hoover to S. K. McKee, February 10, 1942, FBI.

253. they were seeking to avoid exposure: War Department, MID 201, Inga Arvad, February 2, 1942, FBI.

253. "some country sausage for her": ARV Summary, July 17, 1942, Washington, D.C., FBI.

CHAPTER 41

254. "he is engaged to marry her": Memorandum J. Edgar Hoover to the Attorney General, January 21, 1942, FBI.

254. included a photograph of the young ensign: Report by C. A. Hardison, January 22, 1942, FBI.

254. "*Why England Slipped* [*sic*].": S. K. McKee to J. Edgar Hoover, February 3, 1942, FBI.

255. "and her friend Kennedy": Memorandum D. M. Ladd to Mr. E. A. Tamm, February 9, 1942, FBI.

255. "I have seen in a long time": Memorandum D. M. Ladd to Mr. E. A. Tamm, January 29, 1942, FBI.

CHAPTER 41

256. "convinced must be an FBI agent": Inga Arvad memoir, "Consequences," undated but ca 1945, RMP.

256. under investigation by the FBI?: Inga Arvad memoir, "Consequences," undated but ca 1945, RMP.

257. "being truthful," said she was: Inga Arvad memoir, "The Story," undated but ca 1945, RMP.

257. "and maybe bully her into returning to him": Inga Arvad memoir, "The Story," undated but ca 1945, RMP.

258. "now it [their marriage] is off again": Paul Fejos to Olga Arvad, December 23, 1941, RMP.

258. "enveloped her in his adoration": Inga Arvad memoir, "The Story," undated but ca 1945, RMP.

258. "be interested in political matters": Report by Joseph M. Kelly, March 16, 1946, FBI.

259. "love her way too much for that": Paul Fejos to Olga Arvad, December 23, 1941, RMP.

260. "when the lights are turned off": Olga Arvad to Inga Arvad, January 17, 1942, in report by C. A. Hardison, January 22, 1942, FBI.

260. avoid any shamus found on the premises: Memorandum R. P. Kramer to Mr. D. M. Ladd, January 28, 1942, FBI.

261. "without Paul's yet returning it": Olga Arvad to Inga Arvad, January 17, 1942, in report by C. A. Hardison, January 22, 1942, FBI.

261. "for the best for her children": Olga Arvad to Inga Arvad, January 17, 1942, in report by C. A. Hardison, January 22, 1942, FBI.

261. "gone wrong with yours or Jack's love?": Report by W. H. Welch, April 8, 1942, FBI.

261. "family might not like the idea?": Report by W. H. Welch, April 8, 1942, FBI.

CHAPTER 42

262. two thousand newspapers nationwide: Neal Gabler, *Winchell: Gossip, Power and the Culture of Celebrity*, pp. xi–xii.

262. "Walter Winchell's column?": Inga Arvad memoir, "Consequences," undated but ca 1945, RMP.

263. "Pa Kennedy no like": The *North Adams* (MA) Transcript, January 12, 1942, p. 9.

263. "small rat hole when it comes to gossip": Inga Arvad memoir, "Consequences," undated but ca 1945, RMP.

263. "out hunting again—but what?": Inga Arvad, "Did You Happen to See?" *Washington Times-Herald*, October 12, 1941, p. 2.

263. John White wrote in his diary: Doris Kearns Goodwin, *The Fitzgeralds and the Kennedys*, p. 633.

263. "the Beautiful Blonde Spy": Lynne McTaggart, *Kathleen Kennedy*, p. 108.

263. determined to wreck the paper: Doris Kearns Goodwin, *The Fitzgeralds and the Kennedys*, p. 633.

264. the most celebrated men of the day: Amanda Smith, *Newspaper Titan*, p. 406.

265. "expose any investigation of the FBI": S. K. McKee to J. Edgar Hoover, February 5, 1942, FBI.

265. "strong feeling for this Arvad woman": Neal Gabler, *Winchell: Gossip, Power and the Culture of Celebrity*, p. 306.

265. "You made Winchell's column": Nigel Hamilton, *JFK: Reckless Youth*, p. 438.

265. "I feel like hell about it": Nigel Hamilton, *JFK: Reckless Youth*, p. 438.

266. being caught in such a tempest: Doris Kearns Goodwin, *The Fitzgeralds and the Kennedys*, p. 633.

266. "do just as he wished": Lynne McTaggart, *Kathleen Kennedy*, p. 108.

267. "hot and bothered about it": David Nasaw, *The Patriarch*, p. 540.

268. "frivolous, but harmless," she replied: Doris Kearns Goodwin, *The Fitzgeralds and the Kennedys*, p. 631.

268. ". . . misguided relationship with a woman.": Doris Kearns Goodwin, *The Fitzgeralds and the Kennedys*, p. 633.

268. did not plan on seeking a third term: David Nasaw, *The Patriarch*, p. 368.

269. ". . . friend of the director's": Richard Gid Powers, *Secrecy and Power*, p. 357.

269. ". . . contribution you would get from anybody": David Nasaw, *The Patriarch*, pp. 559 and 675.

269. though not all of it: David Nasaw, *The Patriarch*, pp. 559 and 675.

CHAPTER 43

270. ". . . thought she was a spy!": Nigel Hamilton, *JFK: Reckless Youth*, p. 439.

270. Washington to avoid a scandal: Memorandum G. C. Burton to Mr. Ladd, January 17, 1942, FBI.

270. America entered its second month of war: Nigel Hamilton, *JFK: Reckless Youth*, p. 436.

271. ever have been elected president: Joan Blair and Clay Blair Jr., *The Search for JFK*, p. 153.

271. prevent Inga from traveling to Charleston: Memorandum Edward A. Tamm to the Director, February 3, 1942, FBI.

272. ". . . 'How was *he*—what did *he* say etc etc.'": Nigel Hamilton, *JFK: Reckless Youth*, p. 445.

272. ". . . didn't quit talking to her about Jack": ARV Summary, Washington, D.C., February 19, 1942, FBI.

273. ". . . she is a great girl'": Nigel Hamilton, *JFK: Reckless Youth*, p. 440.

273. "stated she is engaged to marry" Jack: S. K. McKee to Director, February 3, 1942, FBI.

273. visited his father in Florida: Nigel Hamilton, *JFK: Reckless Youth*, p. 440.

274. ". . . born to sunshine and happiness": Inga Arvad to Jack Kennedy, January 19, 1942, JFKL.

274. ". . . looking forward to seeing her," Inga said: Inga Arvad to Jack Kennedy, January 19, 1942, JFKL.

275. ". . . why she is so fond of you," Inga wrote: Inga Arvad to Jack Kennedy, January 19, 1942, JFKL.

275. ". . . love America more and more," she said: Inga Arvad to Jack Kennedy, January 19, 1942, JFKL.

CHAPTER 44

276. ". . . isn't it, young Kennedy?": Inga Arvad to Jack Kennedy, January 20, 1942, JFKL.

276. ". . . I saw the world crumbling": Inga Arvad to Jack Kennedy, January 20, 1942, JFKL.

277. ". . . carrots—and ice cream": Inga Arvad to Jack Kennedy, January 20, 1942, JFKL.

277. ". . . what makes Inga tick": Inga Arvad to Jack Kennedy, January 20, 1942, JFKL.

278. candidate for president: Robert Dallek, *An Unfinished Life*, p. 117.

278. ". . . We were sure he'd be a teacher or a writer": Robert Dallek, *An Unfinished Life*, p. 119.

279. ". . . Bobby—he's the lawyer": Herbert S. Parmet, *Jack: The Struggles of John F. Kennedy*, p. 56.

279. ". . . their careers rather than my own": David Nasaw, *The Patriarch*, p. 542.

279. John "Honey Fitz" Fitzgerald: Michael O'Brien, *John F. Kennedy: A Biography*, pp. 189–90.

CHAPTER 45

282. ". . . than pay [the] $2 admission": Inga Arvad to Jack Kennedy, January 26, 1942, JFKL.

282. ". . . anything that a woman should have": Inga Arvad to Jack Kennedy, January 26, 1942, JFKL.

283. but now Jack was the wary one: Inga Arvad to Jack Kennedy, January 26, 1942, JFKL.

283. ". . . 'We pay for everything in life'": Inga Arvad to Jack Kennedy, January 26, 1942, JFKL.

283. ". . . just in love—remember?": Inga Arvad to Jack Kennedy, January 26, 1942, JFKL.

283. ". . . His own and his father's": Inga Arvad to Jack Kennedy, January 26, 1942, JFKL.

284. ". . . too great a distance is put between us": Inga Arvad to Jack Kennedy, January 26, 1942, JFKL.

284. "Have you started making the baby yet?": Inga Arvad to Jack Kennedy, January 26, 1942, JFKL.

284. ". . . actions I might take someday": Inga Arvad to Jack Kennedy, January 27, 1942, JFKL.

285. ". . . why actually care?": Inga Arvad to Jack Kennedy, January 27, 1942, JFKL.

285. "The problems are unsolvable to me," she said: Inga Arvad to Jack Kennedy, January 27, 1942, JFKL.

285. ". . . That is the one I have": Inga Arvad to Jack Kennedy, January 27, 1942, JFKL.

285. ". . . afraid I shall never run out of it": Inga Arvad to Jack Kennedy, undated but believed to be January 28, 1942, JFKL.

286. "and by God you won't read it": Jack Kennedy to Inga Arvad, contained in Report by W. H. Welch, April 8, 1942, FBI.

286. ". . . even if we hadn't gone into the gardens": Jack Kennedy to Inga Arvad, contained in Report by W. H. Welch, April 8, 1942, FBI.

286. ". . . But I miss you": Jack Kennedy to Inga Arvad, contained in Report by W. H. Welch, April 8, 1942, FBI.

287. Inga left Jack's question unanswered: ARV Summary, Washington, D.C., January 31, 1942, FBI.

287. "Darling, you look best without anything": ARV Summary, Washington, D.C., January 31, 1942, FBI.

287. with her relationship with Jack: ARV Summary, Washington, D.C., February 2, 1942, FBI.

CHAPTER 46

288. when he was not in Washington: Inga Arvad to Jack Kennedy, dated "Friday 10:30 p.m." believed to be January 30, 1942, JFKL.

288. question of where she was from: Inga Arvad to Jack Kennedy, dated "Friday 10:30 p.m." believed to be January 30, 1942, JFKL.

288. ". . . a perfect copy of": Inga Arvad to Jack Kennedy, dated "Friday 10:30 p.m." believed to be January 30, 1942, JFKL.

289. "if he had to croak doing it": ARV Translations, Washington, D.C., February 2, 1942, FBI.

289. she had said to try to hurt Fejos: ARV Translations, Washington, D.C., February 2, 1942, FBI.

290. ". . . spies out all over the place": ARV Summary, Washington, D.C., February 2, 1942, FBI.

290. ". . . It amused me very much": ARV Summary, Washington, D.C., February 2, 1942, FBI.

290. ". . . when you are you going away?": ARV Summary, Washington, D.C., February 2, 1942, FBI.

291. "What all did your husband say?": ARV Summary, Washington, D.C., February 2, 1942, FBI.

291. ". . . what he could do by suing you": ARV Summary, Washington, D.C., February 2, 1942, FBI.

291. "I didn't intend to make you mad": ARV Summary, Washington, D.C., February 2, 1942, FBI.

291. think it over and let him know: ARV Summary, Washington, D.C., February 2, 1942, FBI.

292. ". . . she would overlook it. Maybe": Nigel Hamilton, *JFK: Reckless Youth*, p. 449.

293. ". . . and be able to afford it": Arthur Krock interview, JCBP.

CHAPTER 47

295. ". . . when I see an ensign": Inga Arvad to Jack Kennedy, dated "Tuesday," but apparently February 3, 1942, JFKL.

295. ". . . my subtle charm to illustrate": Inga Arvad to Jack Kennedy, dated "Tuesday," but apparently February 3, 1942, JFKL.

296. and the various filing fees: S. K. McKee to J. Edgar Hoover, February 10, 1942, FBI.

296. ". . . Warrant of Apprehension should be issued": Memorandum Edward J. Ennis to J. Edgar Hoover, February 4, 1942, FBI.

296. a warrant for Inga's arrest: Memorandum J. Edgar Hoover to Edward J. Ennis, February 20, 1942, FBI.

297. Inga was "a German spy": William J. Donovan to J. Edgar Hoover, January 24, 1942, FBI.

297. ". . . to the rumor you mention": J. Edgar Hoover to William J. Donovan, February 6, 1942, FBI.

298. ". . . intercourse on numerous occasions": Report by E. H. Adkins, February 9, 1942, FBI.

299. divorce Fejos: Report by E. H. Adkins, February 9, 1942, FBI.

299. "deemed worth preserving": Curt Gentry, *J. Edgar Hoover: The Man and the Secrets*, p. 376.

299. ". . . feared were among the items stored here": Curt Gentry, *J. Edgar Hoover: The Man and the Secrets*, p. 376n.

299. valuable information worth preserving: J. R. Ruggles to J. Edgar Hoover, February 9, 1942, FBI.

300. that FDR was snubbing him: Memorandum D. M. Ladd to Mr. E. A. Tamm, February 10, 1942, FBI.

301. "an official nature": Curt Gentry, *J. Edgar Hoover: The Man and the Secrets*, p. 729.

302. "You son of a bitch!": Arthur Krock interview, JCBP.

CHAPTER 48

303. ". . . I took it as such": Inga Arvad to Jack Kennedy, the date on letter is misprinted as December 4, but clearly was written February 4, 1942, JFKL.

303. "There is more truth than poetry to that": ARV Summary, Washington, D.C., February 10, 1942, FBI.

304. ". . . American women intelligentsia": Inga Arvad to Jack Kennedy, undated but written on February 9, 1942, JFKL.

304. "not to get mixed up in it at all": ARV Summary, Washington, D.C., February 10, 1942, FBI.

304. ". . . mother, father and love": Inga Arvad to Jack Kennedy, undated but written on February 9, 1942, JFKL.

305. home than the place she lived: Inga Arvad to Jack Kennedy, undated but written on February 9, 1942, JFKL.

305. ". . . don't even understand me now": Inga Arvad to Jack Kennedy, undated but written on February 9, 1942, JFKL.

306. ". . . love love more than he loves politics": Richard Norton Smith, *On His Own Terms*, p. 365.

306. proper word was "circumspect": Inga Arvad to Jack Kennedy, undated but written on February 9, 1942, JFKL.

306. ". . . three quarts of Haig whiskey": Inga Arvad to Jack Kennedy, undated but written on February 9, 1942, JFKL.

307. her chances in Hollywood: Memorandum attached to letter from Frank Buckley to J. Edgar Hoover, February 2, 1942, FBI.

307. "but I have forgotten that now": Nils Block to Inga Arvad, January 28, 1942, contained in report by W. H. Welch, February 2, 1942, FBI.

308. "go to bed with her": ARV Translations, February 9, 1942, FBI.

308. flew to Washington that very night: ARV Translations, February 9, 1942, FBI.

308. attaché at the British embassy: ARV Translations, February 10, 1942, FBI.

309. so little sleep the night before: Inga Arvad to Jack Kennedy, dated "Tuesday," though written February 11, 1942, JFKL.

CHAPTER 49

310. was copying all of his mail: S. K. McKee to J. Edgar Hoover, February 17, 1942, FBI.

311. ". . . Ever, Jack": Jack Kennedy to Inga Arvad, Febraury 13, 1942, included in a report by W. H. Welch, April 8, 1942, FBI.

311. ". . . man can be glad to be alive": Nils Blok to Inga Arvad, February 11, 1942, FBI.

311. ". . . the antithesis of more than I": Nils Blok to Inga Arvad, February 11, 1942, FBI.

312. around her apartment: ARV Translations, February 14, 1942, FBI.

312. love letters from a person's garbage: Memorandum J. K. Mumford to Mr. D. M. Ladd, February 27, 1942 (the envelope is within the same folder), FBI.

312. "It sounds so nice": ARV Translations, February 14, 1942, FBI.

312. "I guess so, sweet," she replied: ARV Translations, February 9, 1942, FBI.

312. to run a pregnancy test: S. K. McKee to J. Edgar Hoover, February 17, 1942, FBI.

313. ". . . It is a matter of finding the right place": Inga Arvad to Jack Kennedy, February 14, 1942, JFKL.

313. ". . . somewhere out West": Inga Arvad to Jack Kennedy, February 14, 1942, JFKL.

314. ". . . that is worth something": Inga Arvad to Jack Kennedy, February 14, 1942, JFKL.

314. "I would still be a spinster": Inga Arvad to Jack Kennedy, February 14, 1942, JFKL.

CHAPTER 50

315. but that it was also healthy: ARV Summary, February 16, 1942, FBI.

315. she had brought the subject up: ARV Summary, February 16, 1942, FBI.

316. promised to arrive on Friday: ARV Summary, February 16, 1942, FBI.

316. ". . . there is eternal sunshine": Report by W. H. Welch, March 4, 1942, FBI.

316. Ryan, was also taken with Inga: Doris Kearns Goodwin, *The Fitzgeralds and the Kennedys*, pp. 246–49.

317. ". . . who doesn't know a thing": ARV Summary, Washington, D.C., February 19, 1942, FBI.

317. ". . . difficult for her to marry him": Nigel Hamilton, *JFK: Reckless Youth*, p. 474.

317. Billings had poor eyesight: David Pitts, *Jack and Lem*, p. 87.

318. "He wanted active duty," Billings recalled: Nigel Hamilton, *JFK: Reckless Youth*, p. 457.

318. ". . . mother than in daughter": Sylvia Jukes Morris, *Rage for Fame: The Ascent of Clare Boothe Luce*, p. 436.

318. ". . . too mad, and too vain": Nigel Hamilton, *JFK: Reckless Youth*, p. 464.

318. ". . . unless I tell you what I think": Nigel Hamilton, *JFK: Reckless Youth*, p. 465.

319. "big silence on your part": Inga Arvad to Jack Kennedy, dated "Wednesday," believed to be February 25, 1942, JFKL.

319. ". . . pleasure of youth but not the responsibility": J. R. Ruggles to J. Edgar Hoover, February 23, 1942, FBI.

319. for the girl to get an abortion: Geoffrey Perret, *Jack: A Life Like No Other*, p. 50.

320. ". . . for discovering it so quickly": Inga Arvad to Jack Kennedy, February 23, 1942, JFKL.

320. "no damn good": J. R. Ruggles to J. Edgar Hoover, February 23, 1942, FBI.

320. Joe Junior's political careers: J. R. Ruggles to J. Edgar Hoover, February 23, 1942, FBI.

320. ". . . number of occasions," the FBI noted: J. R. Ruggles to J. Edgar Hoover, February 23, 1942, FBI.

321. ". . . you would tell me when you left": J. R. Ruggles to J. Edgar Hoover, February 23, 1942, FBI.

CHAPTER 51

322. ". . . sailor-boy throws me into raptures": Inga Arvad to Jack Kennedy, February 23, 1942, JFKL.

322. ". . . actually crosses their lips": Inga Arvad to Jack Kennedy, dated "Wednesday," which is believed to have been February 25, 1942, JFKL.

322. ". . . can't be quite like a white dove": Inga Arvad to Jack Kennedy, February 23, 1942, JFKL.

323. ". . . biggest fish in the ocean": Inga Arvad to Jack Kennedy, February 23, 1942, JFKL.

323. ". . . Charleston and Norfolk are so dull": ARV Summary, Washington, D.C., February 25, 1942, FBI.

323. "things will be easier": ARV Translations, February 24, 1942, FBI.

323. "I feel like hell," she told Fejos: ARV Summary, Washington, D.C., February 25, 1942, FBI.

324. "Of course I will go to bed with you," Inga replied: Confidential Danish Items, ARV Translations, WFO, February 27, 1942, FBI.

324. ". . . world ought to swarm with": Inga Arvad to Jack Kennedy, dated "Wednesday," believed to be February 25, 1942, JFKL.

324. ". . . that must be hard earned": Inga Arvad to Jack Kennedy, dated "Wednesday," believed to be February 25, 1942, JFKL.

324. ". . . diamonds cut by the unskilled hand": Inga Arvad to Jack Kennedy, dated "Wednesday," believed to be February 25, 1942, JFKL.

325. God destroyed Sodom: Inga Arvad to Jack Kennedy, dated "Wednesday," believed to be February 25, 1942, JFKL.

CHAPTER 52

326. decided not to meet Jack's plane: S. K. McKee to J. Edgar Hoover, March 5, 1942, FBI.

327. ". . . very long, which is unusual": Memorandum D. M. Ladd to Mr. E. A. Tamm, March 2, 1942, FBI.

327. ". . . these relations with Inga": S. K. McKee to J. Edgar Hoover, March 5, 1942, FBI.

328. it is almost certain that she did: Inga Arvad to Jack Kennedy, dated "Wednesday," believed to be February 25, 1942, JFKL.

329. ". . . divorce Fejos so she could marry him": S. K. McKee to J. Edgar Hoover, March 5, 1942, FBI.

329. "even though she feels lousy about it": ARV Summary, March 4, 1942, FBI.

329. ". . . but I certainly would like to": Nigel Hamilton, *JFK: Reckless Youth*, p. 480.

330. they themselves had overheard: Memorandum Edward A. Tamm to the Director, March 10, 1942, FBI.

330. "this treatment will shut her up": Memorandum Edward A. Tamm to the Director, March 10, 1942, FBI.

330. belonging to "Inga Fejos": Memorandum L. B. Nichols to Mr. Tolson, December 10, 1942, FBI.

331. "I had high hopes," said Jack: ARV Summary, Washington, D.C., March 7, 1942, FBI.

332. ". . . You're not holding out on me, are you?": ARV Summary, Washington, D.C., March 7, 1942, FBI.

332. ". . . What's illegal about being in love?": ARV Summary, Washington, D.C., March 7, 1942, FBI.

332. ". . . the chief actress in the play": ARV Summary, Washington, D.C., March 7, 1942, FBI.

333. Jack could only reply, "O.K.": ARV Summary, Washington, D.C., March 7, 1942, FBI.

333. ". . . Maybe it is the maternal instinct": Inga Arvad to Jack Kennedy, March 11, 1942, JFKL.

333. ". . . before the bird stopped [singing]": Inga Arvad to Jack Kennedy, March 11, 1942, JFKL.

333. ". . . I have been totally dead inside": Inga Arvad to Jack Kennedy, March 11, 1942, JFKL.

CHAPTER 53

335. about his continued longing for Inga: Michael O'Brien, *John F. Kennedy: A Biography*, p. 140.

335. ". . . in some position," Kennedy told Roosevelt: David Nasaw, *The Patriarch*, p. 543.

336. that Kennedy was being so hardheaded: David Nasaw, *The Patriarch*, p. 543.

336. ". . . deemed for older men," Macdonald wrote: Nigel Hamilton, *JFK: Reckless Youth*, p. 479.

336. ". . . whatever personal power is": Nigel Hamilton, *JFK: Reckless Youth*, p. 487.

337. ". . . wouldn't say yes, wouldn't say no": Nigel Hamilton, *JFK: Reckless Youth*, p. 489.

337. ". . . but he really wasn't": Nigel Hamilton, *JFK: Reckless Youth*, p. 509.

338. ". . . very uncomfortable for the time being": Inga Arvad to Jack Kennedy, April 6, 1942, JFKL.

338. but that was not possible: Report by W. H. Welch, June 17, 1942, FBI.

339. ". . . thing which ought to be beautiful": Inga Arvad to Jack Kennedy, April 23, 1942, JFKL.

340. only if he wanted to hear from her: Inga Arvad to Jack Kennedy, April 23, 1942, JFKL.

340. ". . . make you believe anything different": Inga Arvad to Jack Kennedy, April 23, 1942, JFKL.

CHAPTER 54

341. ". . . news it would have been mild": Inga Arvad to Jack Kennedy, May 25, 1942, JFKL.

341. ". . . look like a million again": Inga Arvad to Jack Kennedy, May 25, 1942, JFKL.

342. ". . . to explain the whole matter": Inga Arvad to Jack Kennedy, May 25, 1942, JFKL.

342. ". . . thrilling murder-story" by comparison: Inga Arvad to Jack Kennedy, May 25, 1942, JFKL.

342. fall in love with the South: Inga Arvad to Jack Kennedy, May 25, 1942, JFKL.

343. ". . . 'Heaven on earth'": Inga Arvad to Jack Kennedy, May 25, 1942, JFKL.

343. ". . . will be drunk greedily by you": Inga Arvad to Jack Kennedy, May 25, 1942, JFKL.

343. ". . . Even lovers shouldn't and too often do": Inga Arvad to Jack Kennedy, May 25, 1942, JFKL.

343. ". . . sit and do nothing at all": Inga Arvad to Jack Kennedy, May 25, 1942, JFKL.

344. ". . . write the obituary of the British Empire": Nigel Hamilton, *JFK: Reckless Youth*, p. 482.

344. Peru for more than two years: Judgment and Decree of Divorce, *Inga Arvad Fejos*

vs. Paul Fejos, No. 70784, Second Judicial District Court of the State of Nevada, June 3, 1942.

344. ". . . made it possible by going to Reno": Walter Winchell, "On Broadway," *Tucson* (Ariz.) *Daily Citizen*, July 4, 1942, p. 4.

CHAPTER 55

346. "a closing report be submitted to the Bureau": Memorandum E. A. Tamm to J. Edgar Hoover, March 6, 1942, FBI.

346. agreed with Tamm's recommendation: J. Edgar Hoover to Special Agent in Charge, April 11, 1942, FBI.

347. ". . . didn't seem to know his business": Frank Waldrop interview, JCBP.

347. ". . . would be very difficult to dislodge": Nigel Hamilton, *JFK: Reckless Youth*, p. 492.

347. ". . . under the name of Inga Arvad": Nigel Hamilton, *JFK: Reckless Youth*, p. 492.

347. ". . . to have her specially watched": Memorandum President Franklin Roosevelt to J. Edgar Hoover, May 4, 1942, FBI.

348. ". . . president's personal political tool": William C. Sullivan with Bill Brown, *The Bureau*, p. 37.

349. ". . . to interview the President": Joseph E. Persico, *Roosevelt's Secret War*, p. 58.

349. ". . . from his nebulous sources," Persico said: Joseph E. Persico, *Roosevelt's Secret War*, p. 190.

350. learn about Inga from Hanfstaengl: Memorandum J. Edgar Hoover to Clyde Tolson, E. A. Tamm and D. M. Ladd, February 10, 1942, FBI.

350. ". . . similar to that previously in effect": John Edgar Hoover to Special Agent in Charge, May 6, 1942, FBI.

350. ". . . careful consideration in the future": John Edgar Hoover to Special Agent in Charge, June 19, 1942, FBI.

351. ". . . decide if she was a spy or not": ARV Summary, Washington, D.C., June 24, 1942, FBI.

351. be angry at her for leaving: ARV Summary, Washington, D.C., June 24, 1942, FBI.

351. sever an important connection to Jack: ARV Summary, Washington, D.C., June 24, 1942, FBI.

351. ". . . same as the nasty ones": ARV Summary, Washington, D.C., June 24, 1942, FBI.

352. recounted the conversation to him: ARV Summary, Washington, D.C., July 24, 1942, FBI.

353. Jack promised to stay in touch: ARV Summary, Washington, D.C., June 24, 1942, FBI.

354. ". . . sending him off to sea duty": Nigel Hamilton, *JFK: Reckless Youth*, p. 494.

354. ". . . to be carried home": Inga Arvad to Jack Kennedy, May 23, 1942, JFKL.

CHAPTER 56

355. ". . . wish to do this in your own way": J. Edgar Hoover to Marvin H. McIntyre, July 16, 1942, FBI.

356. ". . . I thought you were *ambitious*": Lynne McTaggart, *Kathleen Kennedy*, p. 122.

356. ". . . with a home in New York": ARV Summary, Washington, D.C., July 29, 1942, FBI.

357. ". . . would tell her when it was over": ARV Summary, Washington, D.C., August 6, 1942, FBI.

357. ". . . someone else who might never come": Doris Kearns Goodwin, *The Fitzgeralds and the Kennedys*, p. 635.

357. not last six months: Lynne McTaggart, *Kathleen Kennedy*, p. 117.

358. ". . . There is no point to be gained": ARV Summary, Washington, D.C., August 3, 1942, FBI.

358. ". . . You're too pretty": ARV Summary, Washington, D.C., August 7, 1942, FBI.

359. ". . . situation rather blank": Nigel Hamilton, *JFK: Reckless Youth*, pp. 497–98.

591. "I don't know what I'm going to do": ARV Summary, Washington, D.C., August 7, 1942, FBI.

CHAPTER 57

360. ". . . as a dangerous alien": Memorandum J. Edgar Hoover to Assistant Attorney General Oscar Cox, August 15, 1942, FBI.

360. horrified beachgoers: David M. Kennedy, *Freedom from Fear*, pp. 566–69.

361. Inga arrived in New York: Tim Weiner, *Enemies: A History of the FBI*, pp. 110–14.

361. ". . . only person who can help me": Inga Arvad to Clyde Tolson, January 27, 1943, FBI.

362. ". . . a person like Nils Blok": Olga Arvad diary entry, April 20, 1941, FBI.

362. ". . . I hope to God he never will": Inga Arvad to Kathleen Kennedy, undated but ca Fall 1942, JFKL.

362. finite number of eligible women: Hamilton, *Reckless Youth*, p. 509.

363. ". . . little Miss Moffett, I envy you.": Letter from Inga Arvad to Kathleen Kennedy, undated but Fall 1942, JFKL.

363. ". . . that I pray for": Letter from Inga Arvad to Kathleen Kennedy, undated but Fall 1942, JFKL.

364. leading Nazis: Inga Arvad, "Top Nazis Romantic, but Urge Youth Marry to Breed," *Berkshire Eagle* (Pittsfield, MA), December 11, 1942, p. 20.

364. what love "is all about": Inga Arvad, "Top Nazis Romantic, but Urge Youth Marry to Breed," *Berkshire Eagle* (Pittsfield, MA), December 11, 1942, p. 20.

364. women workers with children: Inga Arvad, "Manpower Commission Tackles Worker 'Absenteeism' Problem," *Lincoln* (Neb.) *Star*, January 24, 1943, p. 2.

365. ". . . in order to escape through Mexico": Carl Hennrich to J. Edgar Hoover, April 6, 1943, FBI.

365. ". . . They prefer hard liquor": Inga Arvad, "New York Cafes and Night Clubs Don't Bother about Rationing," *Lincoln* (Neb.) *Evening Journal*, January 1, 1943, p. 11.

365. about such Nazi atrocities: Inga Arvad, "Being a Woman No Fun in Occupied Countries of Hitler's Europe," *Lincoln* (Neb.) *Star*, June 27, 1943, p. 22.

366. ". . . with the dirt of a mechanic": Inga Arvad, "Spirit of Nation Manifested by 'Flying Tigress of China,'" *Nebraska State Journal* (Lincoln), February 16, 1943, p. 3.

366. ". . . railroad fare back to New York": John N. Wheeler to Inga Arvad, August 17, 1943, RMP.

CHAPTER 58

367. column in NANA newspapers: Samantha Barbas, *The First Lady of Hollywood*, p. 314.

367. writer F. Scott Fitzgerald: Robert Westbrook, *Intimate Lies*, p. 447.

367. I will never get over Scott Fitzgerald": Sheilah Graham, *The Rest of the Story*, p. 2.

368. "the Bitch of the World": Samantha Barbas, *The First Lady of Hollywood*, pp. 206 and 240.

368. ". . . there is no doubt about it": Inga Arvad to William Cahan, undated but 1944, RMP.

369. "I couldn't seem to work up enough bitchiness": Tim McCoy with Ronald McCoy, *Tim McCoy Remembers the West*, p. 260.

368. ". . . hardest to avoid an interview": Sheilah Graham, "Hollywood Columnist Advises Successor on Filmdom Pitfalls," *Nebraska State Journal*, September 12, 1943, p. 30.

368. was not looking to dish dirt: Sheilah Graham, *The Rest of the Story*, p. 58.

369. ". . . we get down to skinning the Japs": Inga Arvad, "Studios Avoid Films with War Themes," *Winnipeg Tribune*, September 16, 1943, p. 15.

369. win the lead in *National Velvet*: Steve Hauck, "The Beauty Queen Who Interviewed Hitler," *Carmel-by-the-Sea* (CA) *Pine Cone*, October 7, 1971, p. 21.

369. ". . . definitely a standing invitation!": Anne Baxter to Inga Arvad, March 27, 1944, RMP.

369. ". . . same girl to whom he came back": Inga Arvad, "Hollywood Today," *Kingsport* (TN) News, March 8, 1944, p. 5.

CHAPTER 59

371. Jack wrote Inga in April 1943: John F. Kennedy to Inga Arvad, undated but April 1943, RMP.

371. ". . . knitting a pair of socks": John F. Kennedy to Inga Arvad, undated but April 1943, RMP.

372. ". . . from neither for 3 months": Nigel Hamilton, *JFK: Reckless Youth*, p. 618.

372. ". . . husband will still be there": Nigel Hamilton, *JFK: Reckless Youth*, p. 525.

372. ". . . enough to make you cry": John F. Kennedy to Inga Arvad, undated but April 1943, RMP.

372. ". . . be extremely glad to get back": John F. Kennedy to Inga Arvad, undated but April 1943, RMP.

373. ". . . wasn't in pain," a fellow officer said: Robert Dallek, *An Unfinished Life*, p. 88.

373. *PT-109* was "fucked up": Herbert S. Parmet, *Jack: The Struggles of John F. Kennedy*, pp. 111–12.

375. to her in a more timely manner: John F. Kennedy to Inga Arvad, undated but September 12, 1943, RMP.

375. ". . . shattered my morale out here": John F. Kennedy to Inga Arvad, undated but September 12, 1943, RMP.

375. "small celebration" on the base: John F. Kennedy to Inga Arvad, undated but September 15, 1943, RMP.

376. ". . . the years to come after the war": John F. Kennedy to Inga Arvad, undated but September 15, 1943, RMP.

376. ". . . I don't feel badly about it": John F. Kennedy to Inga Arvad, undated but September 15, 1943, RMP.

376. ". . . I want to leave it far behind me when I go": John F. Kennedy to Inga Arvad, undated but September 15, 1943, RMP.

377. "Much love, Jack": John F. Kennedy to Inga Arvad, undated but September 15, 1943, RMP.

CHAPTER 60

378. come back "embittered": Inga Arvad memoir, "Consequences," undated but May/June 1945, RMP.

378. ". . . His sense of humor was gone": Joan Blair and Clay Blair Jr., *The Search for JFK*, p. 352.

379. "the romance was over": Ronald McCoy interview, JCBP.

380. ". . . through it again," said Inga's son, Ronald: Joan Blair and Clay Blair Jr., *The Search for JFK*, p. 352.

380. ". . . two of my men included": Inga Arvad, "Tells Story of PT Epic: Kennedy Lauds Men, Disdains Hero Stuff," *Boston Globe*, January 11, 1944, p. 1.

380. ". . . at the base admired him greatly'": Inga Arvad, "Tells Story of PT Epic: Kennedy Lauds Men, Disdains Hero Stuff," *Boston Globe*, January 11, 1944, p. 1.

381. ". . . we just had to get them back'": Inga Arvad, "Tells Story of PT Epic: Kennedy Lauds Men, Disdains Hero Stuff," *Boston Globe*, January 11, 1944, p. 1.

381. "were wildly devoted to him, all of them": John Hersey interview, JCBP.

382. ". . . book before picking up the saw": Robert Dallek, *An Unfinished Life*, p. 103.

382. ". . . Listen to old granny's advice": Kathleen Kennedy to Inga Arvad, November 28, 1943, RMP.

383. ". . . I'd be married to him now": Kathleen Kennedy to Inga Arvad, February 6, 1944, RMP.

383. ". . . blow to the family prestige," she said: Doris Kearns Goodwin, *The Fitzgeralds and the Kennedys*, p. 677.

384. ". . . Joe Kennedy's body was ever found": Doris Kearns Goodwin, *The Fitzgeralds and the Kennedys*, p. 688.

384. ". . . but I think you'd love him," Kick said: Kathleen Kennedy to Inga Arvad, July 6, 1944, RMP.

385. ". . . always been my favorite in the family": Kathleen Kennedy to Inga Arvad, July 6, 1944, RMP.

385. ". . . Billy and Kick. . . . Life is so cruel": Doris Kearns Goodwin, *The Fitzgeralds and the Kennedys*, p. 696.

CHAPTER 61

386. ". . . anywhere else in the world": Inga Arvad, "Hollywood Letter," undated but 1945, RMP.

387. "My body and soul is yours for the taking": Various inscribed photographs by Hollywood stars, RMP.

387. ". . . I loved was in acute distress": William Cahan, *No Stranger to Tears*, p. 5.

388. ". . . her high cheekbones": William Cahan, *No Stranger to Tears*, p. 72.

388. marriage was already "crumbling": William Cahan, *No Stranger to Tears*, p. 72.

389. ". . . though none [*sic*] of them know it yet": Inga Arvad story, untitled and undated but 1945, RMP.

389. did not even kiss on their first date: Inga Arvad story, untitled and undated but 1945, RMP.

389. standard treatment for arthritis: William Cahan, *No Stranger to Tears*, p. 74.

390. ". . . what can be done about it?": Inga Arvad to William Cahan, undated but late 1944, RMP.

390. "was on the edge of brilliance": Inga Arvad to William Cahan, November 24, 1944, RMP.

390. ". . . or maybe I am like a clam," Inga said: Inga Arvad to William Cahan, dated "Sunday evening" but late 1944, RMP.

390. ". . . it is all ready for a new coat": Inga Arvad to William Cahan, dated "Thursday evening" but late 1944, RMP.

390. ". . . relationship to the rest of mankind": Inga Arvad to William Cahan, undated but late 1944, RMP.

391. ". . . To my great relief, he did": William Cahan, *No Stranger to Tears*, p. 73.

CHAPTER 62

392. ". . . I would give a fig for today": Inga Arvad to William Cahan, undated but late 1944, RMP.

392. ". . . It makes for dull reading": Sheilah Graham, *The Rest of the Story*, p. 66.

392. ". . . she was all sugar," she said: Sheilah Graham, *The Rest of the Story*, p. 66.

393. ". . . and now I know you are": Sheilah Graham, *The Rest of the Story*, p. 65.

393. ". . . looking at a sunset": William Cahan to Inga Arvad, December 23, 1944, RMP.

393. ". . . I know that makes you laugh": Inga Arvad to William Cahan, dated "Tuesday" but November 1944, RMP.

394. ". . . stood on my head or my feet": Inga Arvad to William Cahan, dated "Tuesday" but November 1944, RMP.

394. ". . . happened in your life," she wrote: Inga Arvad to Jack Kennedy, undated but December 1944, RMP.

394. She begged Jack to call again soon: Inga Arvad to Jack Kennedy, undated but December 1944, RMP.

395. ". . . nor does he have any Nazi sympathies": Statement by Lothar Wolff attached to Lothar Wolff to L. B. Nichols, July 5, 1944, FBI.

395. working at the direction of Nazi Germany: Memorandum Herbert Wechsler to Mr. J. Edgar Hoover, February 26, 1945, FBI.

395. ". . . considerable detail," Wechsler told Hoover: Memorandum Herbert Wechsler to Mr. J. Edgar Hoover, February 26, 1945, FBI.

395. fifteen general lines of inquiry: Memorandum Herbert Wechsler to Mr. J. Edgar Hoover, February 26, 1945, FBI.

396. ". . . Wenner-Gren if he had any pro-Nazi views": Report by Kirby A. Vosburgh, March 15, 1945, FBI.

396. never do anything to harm the United States: Memorandum G. W. Hymers to D. M. Ladd, February 27, 1945, FBI.

397. ". . . theater at the present time": Report by Kirby A. Vosburgh, March 15, 1945, FBI.

397. ". . . write an article of a serious nature": Report by Joseph M. Kelly, March 16, 1945, FBI.

397. business interests, not national security: Namn Efternamn, "The Life of Axel Wenner-Gren: An Introduction," a paper presented at the Wenner-Gren International Symposium, Stockholm, The Wenner-Gren Center, May 30–31, 2012, retrieved from http://blog.wennergren.org/wp-content/uploads/2012/08/AW-G-Conference-Book-2012.pdf.

CHAPTER 63

400. red-haired Swedish actress Signe Hasso: Inga Arvad, Untitled and undated draft of magazine article, RMP.

400. Inga would soon be reminded: Inga Arvad, "Story of Signe Hasso," mailed to *Pageant* magazine on December 23, 1944, RMP.

401. unspecified confrontation: Inga Arvad to William Cahan, dated "Tuesday" but January 1945, RMP.

401. ". . . postwar Hollywood": Burke Johnson, "Hitler Is History," *Arizona Republic*, January 5, 1969, pp. 42–46.

401. coroner to cover up his crimes: Inga Arvad, Undated and untitled screen treatment, but April 1945, RMP.

401. "terribly exciting": Burke Johnson, "Hitler Is History," *Arizona Republic*, January 5, 1969, pp. 42–46.

402. ". . . to marry anyone," Inga told Cahan: Inga Arvad to William Cahan, undated but January 1945, RMP.

402. ". . . be a good husband for you?" he said: Inga Arvad to William Cahan, November 24, 1944, RMP.

402. ". . . love any of my husbands": Inga Arvad to William Cahan, undated but December 1944, RMP.

403. ". . . sensational bit of news I will close": Nigel Hamilton, *JFK: Reckless Youth*, p. 683.

403. "Do you think that's what really did it?": Michael O'Brien, *John F. Kennedy*, p. 180.

404. adoring fans when they left the restaurant?: Geoffrey Perret, *Jack: A Life Like No Other*, p. 128.

CHAPTER 64

405. "enormous appetite for life": Lynne Olson, *Troublesome Young Men*, p. 44.

406. one admirer termed "golden gravel": Robert Rhodes James, *Robert Boothby*, p. 454.

406. "From this conclusion, I cannot dissent": Matthew Parris and Kevin McGuire, *Great Parliamentary Scandals*, p. 104.

406. "All doors were open to me": Robert Boothby, *Recollections of a Rebel*, p. 44.

407. "consisted of aspirin and champagne": Robert Boothby, *Recollections of a Rebel*, pp. 203–4.

407. "Kennedy will not be filing tonight": Robert Dallek, *An Unfinished Life*, p. 115.

408. ". . . romance in an orange grove in California": Lynne Olson, *Troublesome Young Men*, p. 53 and Robert Boothby, *Recollections of a Rebel*, p. 206.

408. ". . . Winston Churchill ever had": Robert Boothby, *Recollections of a Rebel*, p. 89.

409. "a bounder, but not a cad": D. R. Thorpe, *Supermac: The Life of Harold Macmillan*, p. 93.

410. "... the more it smells," Inga said: Inga Arvad memoir, "Consequences," undated but May–June 1945, RMP.

411. knowing Boothby only three days: "Swedish [*sic*] Screen Writer to Wed," *Taylor* (Texas) *Daily Press*, May 22, 1945, p. 3.

CHAPTER 65

412. "might do me considerable political damage": Telegram Robert Boothby to Inga Arvad, May 23, 1945, RMP.

412. becoming involved with [a] public man": Telegram Robert Boothby to Inga Arvad, May 23, 1945, RMP.

412. "will almost certainly lose me [the] election": Telegram Robert Boothby to Inga Arvad, May 23, 1945, RMP.

413. "the scent of orange blossoms": Robert Boothby to Inga Arvad, June 3, 1945, RMP.

413. "... whole thing off until [the] election is over": Telegram Robert Boothby to Inga Arvad, May 23, 1945, RMP.

413. "I love him very much": Patricia Clary, "Nordic Beauty Loves Him Yet but Won't Wed Noted Briton," *Dunkirk* (NY) *Evening Observer*, May 24, 1945, p. 4.

414. "... ridiculous publicity to hamper his career": Patricia Clary, "Nordic Beauty Loves Him Yet But Won't Wed Noted Briton," *Dunkirk* (NY) *Evening Observer*, May 24, 1945, p. 4.

414. "... what will it shatter the next time?" she asked: Inga Arvad memoir, "Consequences," undated but May–June 1945, RMP.

414. "... he's a great friend of, cut him short": Inga Arvad memoir, "Consequences," undated but May–June 1945, RMP.

414. "... halo fell down and became a noose": Inga Arvad memoir, "Consequences," undated but May–June 1945, RMP.

415. "That's worth a thousand votes": Robert Boothby, *Recollections of a Rebel*, p. 206.

415. "... confidentially—how'm I doing?": Leonard Lyons, "The Lyons Den," *Amarillo* (TX) *Daily News*, August 24, 1945, p. 10.

416. "... should not be seen by others," he told his biographer: Robert Rhodes James, *Robert Boothby*, p. 457.

417. decades before, he did not say: D. R. Thorpe, *Supermac: The Life of Harold Macmillan*, p. 100.

417. "... I get a terrible headache": D. R. Thorpe, *Supermac: The Life of Harold Macmillan*, p. 102.

417. Macmillan's astonished silence: D. R. Thorpe, *Supermac: The Life of Harold Macmillan*, p. 102.

CHAPTER 66

418. "... face and arms from flaming paraffin": Harrison Carroll, "Hollywood," *Massillon* (OH) *Evening Independent*, June 13, 1945, p. 4.

418. ". . . how does your love swing around so fast?": William Cahan to Inga Arvad, May 26, 1945, and William Cahan to Inga Arvad, May 31, 1945, RMP.

419. ". . . sentimental wartime movie," Cahan remembered: William G. Cahan, *No Stranger to Tears*, p. 86.

419. ". . . hold your impatience in rein for just a bit longer": William Cahan to Inga Arvad, March 2, 1946, RMP.

419. "with a salary too small to support us": William G. Cahan, *No Stranger to Tears*, p. 87.

420. ". . . much sunshine in her hair and smile": John Gunther to Inga Arvad, February 4, 1946, RMP.

420. Inga as a "mild drizzly moon": John Gunther to Inga Arvad, October 20, 1945, RMP.

420. ever made was not marrying Gunther: Ronald McCoy interview, JCBP.

420. "an attractive youngster of twenty-nine.": John Gunther, *Inside U.S.A.*, p. 513n.

421. ". . . (I think flirtation is an admirable habit all in all)". John Gunther to Inga Arvad, February 11, 1946, RMP.

421. ". . . size of an orange. I got half of it": John Gunther, *Death Be Not Proud*, p. 33.

421. perk up his mood with "gay talks": John Gunther to Inga Arvad, May 21, 1946, RMP.

421. "When do we move to Arizona?": John Gunther to Inga Arvad, July 3, 1946, RMP.

421. ". . . honor to report I am not," Gunther wrote: John Gunther to Inga Arvad, July 3, 1946, RMP.

422. ". . . a very strong aesthetic value attached": John Gunther to Inga Arvad, June 3, 1946, RMP.

422. but I need help and sustenance: John Gunther to Inga Arvad, July 3, 1946, RMP.

423. marketing campaign for *Duel in the Sun*: Ronald Haver, *David O. Selznick's Hollywood*, p. 353.

424. ". . . That would be interesting": Erskine Johnson, "In Hollywood," *Frederick* (MD) *News*, February 5, 1946, p. 6.

425. suggested that Inga be barred from entering Canada: Clippings from the *Vancouver* (BC) *Sun*, dates February 1, 1946, p. 5, and February 2, 1946, p. 13, included in a scrapbook kept by Inga Arvad, RMP.

425. ". . . know allegation untrue": Telegram John Wheeler to Inga Arvad, February 2, 1946, RMP.

426. little more fantastic than it had before dinner: Clipping from the *Houston* (Tex.) *Post*, February 26, 1946, p. 5, included in a scrapbook kept by Inga Arvad, RMP.

426. "broken all the rules of dignity": Ronald Haver, *David O. Selznick's Hollywood*, p. 368.

426. four thousand column inches of newspaper coverage: "Love That Movie!: Publicity for 'Duel' Exploits Editors, Elephants, Texas, Tots and the Kentucky Derby," *Life*, February 10, 1947, p. 74.

426. second-highest grossing film after *The Best Years of Our Lives*: Ronald Haver, *David O. Selznick's Hollywood*, p. 368.

CHAPTER 67

427. "... Western motion pictures stars of all time": Script for "This Is Your Life," November 5, 1956, TMP.

427. Wyatt Earp, and Bat Masterson in real life: "Tim McCoy Succumbs at Huachuca," *Nogales* (AZ) *Herald*, January 30, 1978, p. 1, Special Edition, TMP.

427. "... unmatched either before or since": Tim McCoy with Ronald McCoy, *Tim McCoy Remembers the West*, p. 17.

429. "Man Who Knows Indians": Glenn Frankel, *The Searchers: The Making of an American Legend*, p. 19.

429. "What are *people* like?": Tim McCoy with Ronald McCoy, *Tim McCoy Remembers the West*, p. 160.

430. "... the most rabid of America's super-patriots": Tim McCoy with Ronald McCoy, *Tim McCoy Remembers the West*, p. 251.

431. "whispering lyrics" into her pretty ears: Dorothy Manners, "Keeping Up with Hollywood," *Cumberland* (MD) *News*, August 24, 1946, p. 13.

431. will individualize that flour sack: Inga Arvad, "Walter Plunkett," published in *Collier's* magazine, October 6, 1945, RMP.

432. "... I seldom left her side afterward": Tim McCoy with Ronald McCoy, *Tim McCoy Remembers the West*, p. 260.

432. "... wanted to learn Indian sign language": Tim McCoy with Ronald McCoy, *Tim McCoy Remembers the West*, p. 260.

CHAPTER 68

435. "... living them as a country gentleman": Tim McCoy with Ronald McCoy, *Tim McCoy Remembers the West*, p. 254.

435. emotionally prepared to start a new family: Tim McCoy with Ronald McCoy, *Tim McCoy Remembers the West*, p. 260.

435. sixty paying customers: Fred D. Pfening Jr., *Col. Tim McCoy's Real Wild West and Rough Riders of the World*, pp. 42–49.

436. weighed more heavily: Ronald McCoy interview, JCBP.

437. "... where or when the marriage took place": "Film Star Weds Dane Who Pleased Fuehrer," *Ogden* (Utah) *Standard Examiner*, February 25, 1947, p. 1.

437. had been married "for several months": "Surprise Nuptial," *Bradford* (Penn.) *Era*, March 1, 1947, p. 3.

437. "Film Star Weds Dane Who Pleased Fuehrer": "Film Star Weds Dane Who Pleased Fuehrer," *Ogden* (Utah) *Standard Examiner*, February 25, 1947, p. 1.

437. "the main thing is that you are happy": Charles Mendl to Inga Arvad McCoy, February 28, 1947, RMP.

438. ". . . tender part of my heart reserved for you": Paul Fejos to Olga Arvad, dated "Sept. 2," but 1947, RMP.

438. ". . . about the real history of the West": Tim McCoy with Ronald McCoy, *Tim McCoy Remembers the West*, p. 261.

439. to help the circus move to the next town: Bob Sherlock, "Boys Grow Blasé about Ideal Summer Jobs as Circus Clowns," *Los Angeles Times*, September 21, 1958, clipping in a scrapbook, RMP.

CHAPTER 69

440. ". . . I would have canceled the whole thing": Gunilla von Post with Carl Johnes, *Love, Jack*, pp. 31–32.

441. von Post's native Sweden was nearby: Gunilla von Post with Carl Johnes, *Love, Jack*, p. 43.

441. weaknesses as well as his strengths": Gunilla von Post with Carl Johnes, *Love, Jack*, p. 43.

441. "I feel as though I've been set free": Gunilla von Post with Carl Johnes, *Love, Jack*, p. 65.

441. letters from Jack for more than $115,000: Leonard Greene, "John F. Kennedy's Love Letters Written to Swedish Woman Sold at Manhattan Auction," *New York Daily News*, November 24, 2015, retrieved January 3, 2016, from: http://www.nydailynews.com/news/politics/john-f-kennedy-love-letters-sold-nyc-auction-article-1.2444872.

442. was about them, not between them: Geoffrey Perret, *Jack: A Life Like No Other*, p. 348.

442. were now "political necessities": Thomas C. Reeves, *A Question of Character*, p. 111.

442. ". . . dead by 1957 must have haunted Kennedy": Michael O'Brien, *Rethinking Kennedy*, p. 65.

442. and a very few friends in Hyannis Port: Lynne McTaggart, *Kathleen Kennedy*, p. 241.

444. that she would tolerate his promiscuity: Garry Wills, *The Kennedy Imprisonment*, p. 54.

444. ". . . faithful to their wives," Jackie once said: Robert Dallek, *An Unfinished Life*, pp. 194–95.

444. Jackie had a "major father-crush": Barbara Leaming, *Jacqueline Bouvier Kennedy Onassis: The Untold Story*, p. 8.

444. family friend Nancy Dickerson: Thomas C. Reeves, *A Question of Character*, p. 111.

445. "Why not do a story on me [instead]?": Thurston Clarke, *Ask Not*, p. 59.

445. "[I might] as well be in Alaska," Jackie lamented: Robert Dallek, *An Unfinished Life*, p. 194.

445. ". . . They're just too strong": Geoffrey Perret, *Jack: A Life Like No Other*, p. 226.

CHAPTER 70

447. the older brother of John F. Kennedy": Burton Hersh, *Bobby and J. Edgar*, p. 198.

448. "I told him not to be stupid": Joan and Clay Blair Jr., *The Search for JFK*, p. 160.

449. easy access to its contents going forward: Athan Theoharis, *From the Secret Files of J. Edgar Hoover*, pp. 31–32.

450. received all of this information": Edwin O. Guthman and Jeffrey Shulman, ed., *Robert Kennedy in His Own Words*, p. 128.

450. guard this information so that it won't get out'": Steve Dunleavy and Jake Weller, "Sinister Sex Files of J. Edgar Hoover," *San Antonio* (TX) *Star Sunday Magazine*, March 14, 1976, p. 4.

450. Kennedy aide Arthur Schlesinger Jr.: Arthur Schlesinger Jr., *A Thousand Days*, p. 125.

450. FBI director for four more years: Arthur Schlesinger Jr., *A Thousand Days*, p. 125.

450. ". . . on a bit thick, I thought": Benjamin C. Bradlee, *Conversations with Kennedy*, p. 34.

451. use the information he had to his advantage: Robert Dallek, *An Unfinished Life*, p. 301.

CHAPTER 71

453. ". . . they weren't kidding around," Ronald recalled: Ronald McCoy author interview, October 7, 2015.

454. old monarch had "pretty attractive ankles": Ronald McCoy author interview, October 7, 2015.

454. had interviewed Hitler—"you just do it": Ronald McCoy author interview, October 7, 2015.

455. "three hundred and thirty days a year": Tim McCoy with Ronald McCoy, *Tim McCoy Remembers the West*, p. 262.

456. ". . . my husband's baby," she told a local newspaper: Sue Giles, "Career Change Agreed with Mrs. McCoy," *Tucson* (AZ) *Daily Citizen*, March 1, 1965, p. 22.

456. "Los Arcos" ("The Arches"): Margaret Kuehlthau, "McCoy Home Is Reflection of Southwest," *Tucson* (AZ) *Daily Citizen*, March 2, 1963, pp. 62–66.

457. ". . . I do admire his 'guts'": Inga Arvad McCoy to Ronald McCoy, August 24, 1967, RMP.

457. never bothered to learn Spanish: Burke Johnson, "Hitler Is History," *Arizona Republic Arizona Sunday Magazine*, January 5, 1969, pp. 42–46.

458. She stayed there and cried for hours: Ronald McCoy interview, JCBP.

CHAPTER 72

459. "lots of people knew him": Axel Holm, "Nogales Woman Had Intimate Connection with Kennedy," *Nogales* (AZ) *International*, November 22, 2013, retrieved from http://

www.nogalesinternational.com/news/nogales-woman-had-intimate-connection-with
-kennedy/article_86af77a0-5388-11e3-bb7e-0019bb2963f4.html.

459. interviewed the just martyred president: Sue Giles, "Career Change Agreed with
Mrs. McCoy," *Tucson* (AZ) *Daily Citizen*, March 1, 1965, p. 22.

460. Theodore White put Jackie's vision into words: Sarah Bradford, *America's Queen*,
p. 286.

460. thousand on the assassination alone: Vincent Bugliosi, *Reclaiming History*, p. xiv.

460. ". . . not to this particular generation because it's all history": Burke Johnson, "Hitler
Is History," *Arizona Republic Arizona Sunday Magazine*, January 5, 1969, pp. 42–46.

461. no doubt about who was boss": Drew Pearson, "Washington Merry Go Round," *Los
Angeles* (CA) *Times*, August 12, 1966, Part II, p. 6.

461. ". . . parents at an early age," she said: Sue Giles, "Career Change Agreed with Mrs.
McCoy," *Tucson* (AZ) *Daily Citizen*, March 1, 1965, p. 22.

462. virtually none to Kennedy: Ron McCoy interview, JCBP.

462. seemed a budding political career: Ronald McCoy author interview, April 9, 2015.

462. appreciate the other's finer points: Mrs. Tim McCoy to Mrs. Charles (Ruth) Sharpe,
October 27, 1966, and February 16, 1967, RMP.

462. ended up in careers in education: Sue Giles, "Career Change Agreed with Mrs.
McCoy," *Tucson* (AZ) *Daily Citizen*, March 1, 1965, p. 22.

463. ". . . never seemed old till the last few years": Mrs. Tim McCoy to Mrs. Charles
(Ruth) Sharpe, October 27, 1966, and February 16, 1967, RMP.

463. She is an angel to me": Olga Arvad to Ron McCoy, December 1, 1964, RMP.

464. she stop smoking, which she did not: Reported dictated by Drs. Alan Jarrett and
David Paton, Baylor College of Medicine, February 9, 1972, RMP.

464. ". . . completely dispassionately [*sic*]": Burke Johnson, "Hitler Is History," *Arizona
Republic Arizona Sunday Magazine*, January 5, 1969, pp. 42–46.

465. "You aren't the vicious type anyway": Lothar Wolff to Inga Arvad McCoy, July 30,
1967, RMP.

465. "Kennedy never forgot" about her: Arthur Krock interview, JCBP.

465. ". . . even sure they hear all what one says": Mrs. Tim McCoy to Mrs. Charles
(Ruth) Sharpe, October 27, 1966, RMP.

465. ". . . or it rubs off too soon": Inga Arvad McCoy to Ron McCoy, August 21, 1966,
RMP.

466. ". . . you were right there with him": Tim McCoy to Inga Arvad McCoy, dated
"Friday or maybe Saturday," but postmarked November 1973, TeMP.

467. she wondered what she had accomplished in life: Terrence McCoy author interview,
June 19, 2015.

467. ". . . tough hide" to be successful in politics: Inga Arvad to Jack Kennedy, February
23, 1942, JFKL.

467. "Heart never brought fame," she said: Inga Arvad to Jack Kennedy, dated
"Wednesday" but February 25, 1942, JFKL.

EPILOGUE

471. "Behind the image, what was Jack really like?": Joan Blair and Clay Blair Jr., *The Search for JFK*, p. 9.

472. far greater scale than previously understood: John Judis, "This Book Was the First to Spill JFK's Secrets. So Why Has It Been Totally Forgotten?" *The New Republic*, October 28, 2013, retrieved January 15, 2016, via https://newrepublic.com/article/115383/very-good-jfk-biography-why-has-search-jfk-been-forgotten.

472. would be "like therapy in a sense": Ronald McCoy author interview, April 9, 2015.

473. the relationship healed: Ronald McCoy author interview, April 9, 2015.

473. as the publication *Midnight* phrased it: "Now Living in California: JFK's Secret Love Child . . . The Illegitimate Son He Had after Love Affair with Newspaper Columnist," *Midnight*, March 15, 1976, p. 1.

473. "perhaps Ronald had inherited this trait": Joan Blair and Clay Blair Jr., *The Search for JFK*, pp. 566–67.

473. even though Ron did not: "This Woman Was Mother of JFK's Child Say Researchers," *Midnight*, March 15, 1976, p. 10.

474. Blair John Fitzgerald Kennedy is disgraceful": "Dirt on a Grave," *Arizona Republic*, January 24, 1976, p. 6.

474. even if historians do not: Scott Farris, *Kennedy and Reagan: Why Their Legacies Endure*, pp. 1–13.

474. Blair beating up on all things Kennedy": Garry Wills, *The Kennedy Imprisonment*, p. xiii.

475. Hoover and others aware of its contents: Letter from Clay Blair Jr., to Les Steinau, January 28, 1976, JCBP.

475. Kick, Joe Junior—and Inga: Nigel Hamilton to Scott Farris, October 19, 2015.

BIBLIOGRAPHY

Alford, Mimi. *Once Upon a Secret: My Affair with President John F. Kennedy and Its Aftermath.* New York: Random House, 2012.

Barbas, Samantha. *The First Lady of Hollywood: A Biography of Louella Parsons.* Berkeley: University of California Press, 2005.

Batvinis, Raymond J. *Hoover's Secret War against Axis Spies: FBI Counterespionage During World War II.* Lawrence: University of Kansas Press, 2014.

Beauchamp, Cari. *Joseph P. Kennedy Presents: His Hollywood Years.* New York: Alfred A Knopf, 2009.

Blair, Joan, and Clay Blair Jr. *The Search for JFK.* New York: Berkley Publishing Corp., 1976.

Boothby, Robert. *Boothby: Recollections of a Rebel.* London: Hutchinson of London, 1978.

Bradford, Sarah. *America's Queen: The Life of Jacqueline Kennedy Onassis.* New York: Viking, 2000.

Bradlee, Benjamin C. *Conversations with Kennedy.* New York: W. W. Norton & Company, 1975.

Brinkley, David. *Washington Goes to War.* New York: Ballantine Books, 1988.

Brown, Peter Harry, and Broeske, Pat H. *Howard Hughes: The Untold Story.* New York: Signet, 1997.

Bugliosi, Vincent. *Reclaiming History: The Assassination of President John F. Kennedy.* New York: W. W. Norton & Company, 2007.

Burnett, Thom, Ed. *Conspiracy Encyclopedia: The Encyclopedia of Conspiracy Theories.* New York: Chamberlain Brothers, 2005.

Cahan, William, MD. *No Stranger to Tears: A Surgeon's Story.* New York: Random House, 1992.

Clarke, Thurston. *Ask Not: The Inauguration of John F. Kennedy and the Speech That Changed America.* New York: Henry Holt, 2004.

Dallek, Robert. *An Unfinished Life: John F. Kennedy, 1917–1963.* Boston and New York: Little, Brown and Company, 2003.

Davis, John H. *The Kennedys: Dynasty and Disaster, 1848–1984.* New York: McGraw-Hill Book Company, 1984.

Dilberto, Gioia. *Debutante: The Story of Brenda Frazier.* New York: Alfred A. Knopf, 1987.

Dodds, John W. *The Several Lives of Paul Fejos: A Hungarian-American Odyssey.* New York: The Wenner-Gren Foundation, 1973.

Duffy, Peter. *Double Agent: The First Hero of World War II and How the FBI Outwitted and Destroyed a Nazi Spy Ring.* New York: Scribner, 2014.

Farris, Scott. *Almost President: The Men Who Lost the Race but Changed the Nation.* Guilford, CT: Lyons Press, 2011.

———. *Kennedy and Reagan: Why Their Legacies Endure.* Guilford, CT: Lyons Press, 2013.

Fay, Paul. *The Pleasure of His Company.* New York: Harper and Row, 1966.

Friedrich, Otto. *Before the Deluge: A Portrait of Berlin in the 1920s.* New York: Fromm International Publishing Corporation, 1986.

Fröhlich, Elke, General Editor. *Die Tagebücher von Joseph Goebbels, Teil I Aufzeichmungen 1923–1941, Band 3/I April 1934–February 1936.* München: K. G. Saur, 2005. (Translated by the author).

Fussell, Paul. *The Great War and Modern Memory.* London and Oxford: Oxford University Press, 1975.

Gabler, Neal. *Winchell: Gossip, Power and the Culture of Celebrity.* New York: Vintage Books, 1995.

Gentry, Curt. *J. Edgar Hoover: The Man and the Secrets.* New York: W. W. Norton & Company, 1991.

Gibson, Barbara, with Ted Schwarz. *The Kennedys: The Third Generation.* New York: Thunder's Mouth Press, 1993.

Gladwell, Malcolm. *The Tipping Point: How Little Things Can Make a Big Difference.* Boston: Little, Brown and Company, 2000.

Goering, Emmy. *My Life with Goering.* London: David Bruce & Watson, 1972.

Goodwin, Doris Kearns. *The Fitzgeralds and the Kennedys: An American Saga.* New York: Simon and Schuster, 1987.

Graham, Sheilah, and Gerold Frank. *Beloved Infidel: The Education of a Woman.* New York: Henry Holt and Company, 1958.

Graham, Sheilah *Confessions of a Hollywood Gossip Columnist.* New York: Bantam Books, 1970.

———. *The Rest of the Story.* New York: Bantam Books, 1965.

Gunther, John. *Death Be Not Proud: A Memoir.* New York and London: Harper Perennial, 2007.

———. *Inside Europe.* New York: Harper & Brothers, 1938.

———. *Inside U.S.A.* New York: Harper & Brothers, 1947.

Guthman, Edwin O., and Jeffrey Shulman, ed. *Robert Kennedy in His Own Words: The Unpublished Recollections of the Kennedy Years.* New York: Bantam Books, 1989.

Hamilton, Nigel. *JFK: Reckless Youth.* New York: Random House, 1992.

Harris, Mark. *Five Came Back: A Story of Hollywood and the Second World War.* New York: Penguin Press, 2014.

Haver, Ronald. *David O. Selznick's Hollywood.* New York: Bonanza Books, 1980.

Hersch, Seymour M. *The Dark Side of Camelot.* Boston: Little, Brown and Company, 1997.

Hersh, Burton. *Bobby and J. Edgar: The Historic Face-Off between the Kennedys and J. Edgar Hoover That Transformed America.* New York: Carroll and Graf Publishers, 2007.

Higham, Charles. *American Swastika: The Shocking Story of Nazi Collaborators in Our Midst from 1933 to the Present Day.* Garden City, NY: Doubleday & Company, Inc., 1985.

James, Robert Rhodes. *Robert Boothby: A Portrait of Churchill's Ally.* New York: Viking, 1991.

Kennedy, David M. *Freedom from Fear: The American People in Depression and War, 1929–1945.* New York and Oxford: Oxford University Press, 1999.

Kennedy, John F. *Why England Slept.* Westport, CT: Greenwood Press, 1981.

Kennedy, Rose Fitzgerald. *Times to Remember.* Garden City, NY: Doubleday & Company, Inc., 1974.

Kershaw, Ian. *Hitler: 1889–1936 Hubris.* New York: W. W. Norton & Co., 1998.

Kershaw, Ian. *Hitler: 1936–1945 Nemesis.* New York: W. W. Norton & Co., 2000.

Kessler, Ronald. *The Sins of the Father: Joseph P. Kennedy and the Dynasty He Founded.* New York: Warner Books, 1996.

Knopp, Guido. *Hitler's Women.* New York: Routledge, 2003.

Krock, Arthur. *Memoirs: Sixty Years on the Firing Line.* New York: Funk & Wagnalls, 1968.

Kuhn, William. *Reading Jackie: Her Autobiography in Books.* New York: Nan A. Talese, 2010.

Kurth, Peter. *American Cassandra: The Life of Dorothy Thompson.* Boston: Little, Brown and Company, 1990.

Larson, Erik. *In the Garden of Beasts: Love, Terror, and an American Family in Hitler's Berlin.* New York: Crown, 2011.

Lasky, Victor. *J.F.K.: The Man and the Myth.* New York: Macmillan Co., 1963.

Leamer, Laurence. *The Kennedy Men: 1901–1963, The Laws of the Father.* New York: William Morrow, 2001.

———. *The Kennedy Women: The Saga of an American Family.* New York: Villard Books, 1994.

Leaming, Barbara. *Jack Kennedy: The Education of a Statesman.* New York: W. W. Norton & Company, 2006.

Leaming, Barbara. *Jacqueline Bouvier Kennedy Onassis: The Untold Story.* New York: Thomas Dunne Books, 2014.

Longerich, Peter. *Goebbels: A Biography.* New York: Random House, 2015.

MacLean, Rory. *Berlin: Portrait of a City through the Centuries.* New York: St. Martin's Press, 2014.

Maguglin, Robert. *Howard Hughes: His Achievements and Legacy: The Authorized Pictorial Biography.* Long Beach, CA: Wrather Port Properties, 1984.

Mariager, Ann. *Inga Arvad: Den Skandalose Skandinav.* Copenhagen: Gyldendal, 2008. (Translated for the author by Christine Beaulieu).

Martin, Ralph G. *Cissy: The Extraordinary Life of Eleanor Medill Patterson.* New York: Simon and Schuster, 1979.

Matthews, Chris. *Jack Kennedy: Elusive Hero.* New York: Simon and Schuster, 2011.

McCoy, Tim, and Ronald McCoy. *Tim McCoy Remembers the West: An Autobiography with Ronald McCoy.* Garden City, NY: Doubleday & Company, Inc., 1977.

McIntosh, Elizabeth P. *Sisterhood of Spies: The Women of the OSS.* Annapolis, MD: Naval Institute Press, 1998.

McTaggart, Lynne. *Kathleen Kennedy: Her Life and Times.* Garden City, NY: The Dial Press, 1983.

Morris, Sylvia Jukes. *Rage for Fame: The Ascent of Clare Boothe Luce.* New York: Random House, 1997.

Mosley, Charlotte, Ed. *The Mitfords: Letters between Six Sisters.* New York: Harper, 2007.

Nagorski, Andrew. *Hitlerland: American Eyewitnesses to the Nazi Rise to Power.* New York: Simon and Schuster, 2012.

Nasaw, David. *The Patriarch: The Remarkable Life and Turbulent Times of Joseph P. Kennedy*. New York: Penguin Press, 2012.

O'Brien, Michael. *John F. Kennedy: A Biography*. New York: Thomas Dunne Books, 2005.

———. *Rethinking Kennedy: An Interpretive Biography*. Chicago: Ivan R. Dee, 2009.

Olson, Lynne. *Those Angry Days: Roosevelt, Lindbergh, and America's Fight over World War II, 1939–1941*. New York: Random House, 2013.

———. *Troublesome Young Men: The Rebels Who Brought Churchill to Power and Helped Save England*. New York: Farrar, Straus and Giroux, 2007.

Parmet, Herbert S. *Jack: The Struggles of John F. Kennedy*. New York: Dial Press, 1980.

Parris, Matthew, and Kevin McGuire. *Great Parliamentary Scandals: Five Centuries of Calumny, Smear & Innuendo*. London: Robson Books, 2004.

Pauer-Studer, Herlinde and Vellman, J. David. *Konrad Morgen: The Conscience of a Nazi Judge*. New York: Palgrave MacMillan, 2015.

Perret, Geoffrey. *Jack: A Life Like No Other*. New York: Random House, 2001.

Persico, Joseph E. *Roosevelt's Secret War: FDR and World War II Espionage*. New York: Random House, 2001.

Pitts, David. *Jack and Lem: The Untold Story of an Extraordinary Friendship*. New York: Da Capo Press, 2007.

Powers, Richard Gid. *Secrecy and Power: The Life of J. Edgar Hoover*. New York: Free Press, 1987.

Reeves, Richard. *President Kennedy: Profile of Power*. New York: A Touchstone Book, 1993.

Reeves, Thomas C. *A Question of Character: A Life of John F. Kennedy*. New York: Free Press, 1991.

Renehan, Edward J., Jr. *The Kennedys at War: 1937–1945*. New York: Doubleday, 2002.

Rorabaugh, W. J. *The Real Making of the President: Kennedy, Nixon, and the 1960 Election*. Lawrence: University Press of Kansas, 2009.

Ross, Stanley. *Axel Wenner-Gren: The Sphinx of Sweden*. News Background, Report No. 27, 1947.

Schlesinger, Arthur, Jr. *Robert Kennedy and His Times*. Boston: First Mariner Books, 2002.

———. *A Thousand Days: John F. Kennedy in the White House*. Boston: Houghton Mifflin Company, 1965.

Schwarz, Jordan A. *The Speculator: Bernard M. Baruch in Washington, 1917–1965*. Chapel Hill, NC, 1981.

Shirer, William L. *The Rise and Fall of the Third Reich: A History of Nazi Germany*. New York: MJF Books, 1990.

Simmons, Dan. *The Crook Factory*. New York: Avon Books, 1999.

Smith, Amanda Smith. *Newspaper Titan: The Infamous Life and Monumental Times of Cissy Patterson*. New York: Alfred A. Knopf, 2011.

Smith, Jean Edward. *FDR*. New York: Random House, 2007.

Smith, Richard Norton. *On His Own Terms: A Life of Nelson Rockefeller*. New York: Random House, 2014.

Stratigakos, Despina. *Hitler at Home*. New Haven, CT: Yale University Press, 2015.

Sullivan, William C., with Bill Brown. *The Bureau: My Thirty Years in Hoover's FBI*. New York: W. W. Norton & Company, 1979.

Theoharis, Athan, ed. *From the Secret Files of J. Edgar Hoover*. Chicago: Ivan R. Dee, 1991.

Thomas, Evan. *Robert Kennedy: His Life*. New York: Touchstone, 2000.

Thorpe, D. R. *Supermac: The Life of Harold Macmillan*. London: Pimlico, London, 2010.

Thurman, Judith. *Isak Dinesen: The Life of a Storyteller*. New York: Picador USA, 1982.

Toland, John. *Adolf Hitler*. Garden City, NY: Doubleday & Company, 1976.

von Post, Gunilla, with Johnes, Carl. *Love, Jack*. New York: Crown Publishers, 1997.

Wakeman, John, ed. *World Film Directors, Vol. 1, 1890–1945*. New York: The H. W. Wilson Co., 1987.

Walters, Guy. *Berlin Games: How Hitler Stole the Olympic Dream*. London: John Murray, 2006.

Weinberg, Gerhard L. *A World at Arms: A Global History of World War II*. Cambridge and New York: Cambridge University Press, 1994.

Weiner, Tim. *Enemies: A History of the FBI*. New York: Random House, 2012.

Wenner-Gren, Axel. *Call to Reason: An Appeal to Common Sense*. New York: Farrar & Rinehart, 1938.

Westbrook, Robert. *Intimate Lies: F. Scott Fitzgerald and Sheilah Graham*. New York: HarperCollins, 1995.

Wiles, Julian. *Inga Binga*. Woodstock, IL: Dramatic Publishing Company, 2013.

Wills, Garry. *The Kennedy Imprisonment*. Boston: Little, Brown and Company, 1994.

Videos

Flugten fra Millionerne, Nordisk Tone-film (1934)
JFK: Reckless Youth, Echo Bridge Home Entertainment (2010)
John F. Kennedy and the Nazi Spy, MPI Home Video (1991)
Lonesome: A Film by Paul Fejos, The Criterion Collection (2012)

Index

photos are indicated by "P."

of, 190; flattery from, 32–33; as
informant, 189–90; support of, 109,
278
Walker, Robert, 216
Walker, Talbot, "Tot," 10
Wallenstrøm, Tove, 83
war: impact of, 304; Kennedy, J. F., on,
302–3; Kennedy, J. P., Sr., on, 44;
marriage during, 298; relationships
during, 216–17; as tedious, 299; U.S.
at, 28, 103
Ward, Barbara, 90
War Division, 183
war hero: Kennedy, J. F., as, xiii, xix; in
politics, xix
War Industries Board, 107
Washington, D.C.: freedom in, 38;
housing shortage in, 37; move to, 18;
paranoia in, 36; parties in, 38; restless
in, 258–59; transformation of, 30;
venereal disease in, 38
Washington Herald. See Times-Herald
Washington Post, 245
Wayne, John, 337, 346–47
Wechsler, Herbert, 317–19
Weimar National Theater, 120
Weimar Republic, 127
Wells, Laura, 341
Wenner-Gren, Axel, ix–x, p22; blacklist of,
181–82, 191; business with, 176;
commitment of, 175; dislike of, 183–85;
FBI on, 180; flattery of, 27–28; as international industrialist, 24; interview with,
27; introduction to, 173; as investor, 25;
in media, 26; in politics, 25–26; propo-
sition from, 182; recommendation from,
13; relationship with, 26–27; as sales
genius, 24–25; surveillance of, 27; suspicions of, 7, 23, 26, 180, 317–19
Wenner-Gren, Marguerite, 8–9;
commitment to, 175; dislike of, 183–85
Wenner-Gren Foundation. *See* The Viking
Fund
Westerby, Lou, 141

Wheeler, Burton, 42–43
Wheeler, John, 295, 342
White, Barbara. *See specific topics*
White, John, 4, 22, 41, 93; admiration
from, 211; as cover, 45; flattery from,
35; frustrations of, 46; as mentor, 357;
visit from, 288
White, Stanford, 22
White, Theodore, 368–69
White House, 350; Kennedy, J. F., in, xi
Why England Slept (Kennedy, J. F.), 42, 48,
275; popularity of, 97
Wicker, Tom, 192
Wiegand, Karl, 131
Wilder, Billy, 116
Wilder, Thornton, 129
Wills, Garry, 379
Wilson, Woodrow, 355
Wimbledon High School, 60
Winchell, Walter, xiii, 196, 277; gossip
from, 208–9
Winged Victory (Hart), 311
Wolff, Lothar, 10, 81, 372; as friend, 8; as
informant, 317; recommendation from,
13
women: admiration of, 33; celebration of,
62; in Egypt, 71; in feminism, 60, 62;
Hitler on, 138, 150–51; in journalism,
115–16; journalism on, 294–95;
Kennedy, J. F., on, 90; Kennedy, J. F.,
with, xvi, 88–89; in Nazi Germany,
129–30; respect for, 89; sexuality of, 64;
as spies, 152–53. *See also* specific
women
The Women (Luce), 272
Women's Army Corps, 294
Woolsey, Helen, 15
World War II: informants during, 191;
praise during, xv

York, Alvin, 29

Zahle, Britta, 117
Zimmerman Telegram, 194–95

About the Author

Scott Farris is the *New York Times* best-selling author of *Kennedy and Reagan: Why Their Legacies Endure* and *Almost President: The Men Who Lost the Race but Changed the Nation*. A former bureau chief for United Press International and political columnist, he has also worked for the governors of Wyoming and California, a U.S. senator, and the mayor of Portland, Oregon. He appeared on the 2011 C-SPAN television series *The Contenders*, and has been a guest on, among other programs, MSNBC's *Morning Joe* and *Melissa Harris-Perry*. His work has been published in the *New York Times*, *Washington Post*, and *Wall Street Journal*.